LITERATURE, THE *VOLK* AND THE REVOLUTION IN MID-NINETEENTH CENTURY GERMANY

Literature, the *Volk* and the Revolution in Mid-Nineteenth Century Germany

Michael Perraudin

Berghahn Books
New York • Oxford

First published in 2000 by **Berghahn Books**

www.berghahnbooks.com

© 2000 Michael Perraudin

Library of Congress Cataloging-in-Publication Data
Data available

British Library Cataloguing in Publication Data
A catalogue record for this book is available from the British Library.

Printed in the United Kingdom on acid-free paper

ISBN 1-57181-989-4 hardback

Contents

Introduction: The Folk Revival and Revolutionary Realities

This is a book concerned primarily with reflections in literature of what was called the 'Social Question' – the issue of the emergence in society of a class of the disaffected mass poor and the political implications of that emergence – in Germany in the era between the revolutions of 1830 and 1848, the *Vormärz*. Social revolution was widely expected, whether welcomed or feared, in these years, and it is an expectation which is deeply embedded in the literature of the time. The book's historical scope extends both back into the 1820s, when these anticipations were uncertain and not fully formed, and forward into the 1850s, when the 1848 Revolution had broken out and collapsed. But the *Vormärz* decades are its central preoccupation. Its focus is very much on literary texts and their intricacies: this is a work of literary criticism, not social history, except to the extent that the texts studied are themselves socio-historically significant. Moreover, these texts are more or less canonical ones. The intention is not so much to offer a survey of the theme as manifested in the generality of German literary writing in this period as to study its power and impact on celebrated and key works by authors who either were regarded at the time, or are seen now, as leading lights of the age: Heine, Büchner, Eichendorff, Mörike, Gotthelf, Grillparzer, Nestroy, Stifter and Storm. *Volk* and revolution are, we will see, not just an issue of literary marginalia, but a core preoccupation of very many of the pre-eminent writers and texts of this time, and represented a theme which found its way into, yet was far from exclusive to, the highest reaches of contemporary high culture. With some of the authors examined (Büchner, Heine), the fact that the Social Question had

1

a powerful effect on their writing is clear, and the aim of the discussion is to elicit how exactly it operated; with some of the others, the strength of such socio-political content is unexpected, while with yet others (in particular, Mörike) its presence at all is a surprise, and must be established and verified. Accordingly, the chapters of the book in which this less than uniform subject-matter is dealt with are themselves disparate, forming not so much a sequential account as a series of largely autonomous essays on specific writers and texts.[1] Finally, while the nine authors studied here are themselves diverse, geographically, socially, politically and aesthetically, what they all necessarily present are perspectives of the educated class. They were, either for the duration or at the outset of their careers, priests, journalists, lawyers, academics or middle-ranking bureaucrats, all more or less prosperous and all university-trained. Though a number of the works and writers discussed seek actively to recreate the voice and point of view of the people, factually the masses are object here rather than subject. Thus socially, too, this is not intended to be an all-embracing depiction. On the other hand, what it can be said to present is a composite of the attitudes towards the Volk which were conceivable within that educated portion of Vormärz society, from left to right, north to south and across the aesthetic and philosophical range. To that extent, a kind of comprehensiveness is achieved.

One decision which the book necessitated was terminological. The class about which the Social Question was posed had and has many names, in English and in German. 'Mass' and 'masses' are applicable in some, but not all contexts. 'Proletariat' and 'proletarian' are words which were often employed in a relevant sense at the time, though the Marxian narrowing of the concept and the subsequent general acceptance of this as its primary meaning are a difficulty. 'Plebeian' can be a useful adjective; but in its origins it suggests a specifically urban context and, in addition, its noun, at least in English, has degenerated into a mere term of abuse. 'The people' in English is inexplicit. The phrase 'the common people' has an archaic and faintly supercilious tone, though as a social designation it is often apposite. Most of these terms are used on occasion in the following chapters, where they are appropriate and effective. But I have preferred to take the word 'Volk' as the core term. It, too, is an imprecise and slightly elusive word: broader and less exclusively rural and pre-modern than English 'folk', though capable of being used in that sense; less socially aggressive than the French word 'peuple'; and needing in German to be differentiated –

2

yet hard to differentiate – from directly contemptuous terms for the lower orders such as 'Pöbel'. Above all, 'das Volk', unqualified, has and had connotations that are both social and national, and where the distinction between the two aspects is not absolute. The term's ambivalence is actually advantageous, precisely because it reflects and reproduces the ambivalence which is to be found in the writings of the time. The balance of connotations in the word when used by the authors themselves varies from individual to individual and text to text, and is a matter of ideology. When Büchner talks of the quest in which he is engaged, for 'ein . . . neue[s] geistige[s] Leben . . . im *Volk*' (see chapter two, below),[2] his meaning has no national component. Storm, by contrast, is arguably more interested in 'Volk' in its national than in its social aspect. Eichendorff, class-focussed but conservative, wishes 'Volk' to be a category for the dutiful, pious, orderly and essentially rural poor, distinct from an amoral urban rabble, and he struggles to sustain the distinction. Meanwhile, for Heine – an author who was socialist yet also nationally minded – national and class meanings coexist and fluctuate. But in all cases, whatever the sense, 'Volk' was what the authors themselves knew they were writing about. 'Unter Volk verstehen wir gewöhnlich eine ungebildete bildungsfähige *Menge*, ganze Nationen, insofern sie auf den ersten Stufen der Kultur stehen, oder Teile kultivierter Nationen, die untern Volksklassen, Kinder' – so Goethe wrote in 1808, in a celebratory definition which acknowledges all the word's aspects and pronounces itself at ease with their plurality.[3]

Writing about the Volk in Germany clearly did not begin with the Vormärz. A central strand of the writing with which this book is concerned is immediately traceable to a cultural tradition initiated in Germany in the middle of the preceding century, in the intellectual aftermath of Rousseau. Adelung's dictionary (volume 4, of 1780), in the midst of its own slightly untidy attempt to define 'Volk', observes:

> Einige neuere Schriftsteller haben dieses Wort in der Bedeutung des größten, aber untersten Theiles einer Nation oder bürgerlichen Gesellschaft wieder zu adeln gesucht, und es ist zu wünschen, daß solches allgemeinen Beyfall finde, indem es an einem Worte fehlet, den größten, aber unverdienter Weise verächtlichsten Theil des Staates mit einem edlen und unverfänglichen Worte zu bezeichnen.[4]

Whether this is etymologically accurate or not, Adelung signals awareness and approval of a new, dignifying way of writing about the masses which has emerged. His principal 'neuerer Schriftsteller' must be Herder. The *Sturm-und-Drang* Herder was not the only individual of his era in Germany, or even the first, to echo and to indicate admiration for folk culture, but he was the most influential figure, combining as he did philological researches, poetic composition of his own and an energetically expressed philosophy. Taking as his authorities and models above all English-language commentators and recent practical collectors of folk-songs, he composed the profoundly influential essay *Auszug aus einem Briefwechsel über Ossian und die Lieder alter Völker* (which was first printed in his anthology *Von deutscher Art und Kunst*, in 1773) and assembled the two-volume collection of German and translated foreign songs *Alte Volkslieder* of 1774 (formally published in 1778–79, with programmatic introductions added, as *Volkslieder*).[5] Herder's project is a post-rationalist, proto-Romantic cultural and epistemological critique, arguing that educated, civilised, rational modern man has lost a dimension of felt experience – of emotional immediacy and intensity, imaginative depth and concreteness – which primitive peoples and people possessed and possess. Such experience is inherent in folk culture, and specifically it is contained in folk-song; to regain it himself, modern man must collect and assimilate the ancient songs, and emulate them in his own poetic writing. Herder's project also has an incipient ingredient of cultural nationalism. His outlook is in many respects cosmopolitan: his song collection is assertively international, incorporating Slav and Hispanic items as well as British and Scandinavian ones, and the folk consciousness he extols is not on the whole nationally specific. But there is in his writing the idea of the 'Eigenheit eines Volks'[6] (a notion of the cultural difference between peoples which also directs his historical philosophy in the work *Ideen zur Philosophie der Geschichte der Menschheit*, of 1784–91, and elsewhere); and the *Alte Volkslieder* are impelled by a sense of German cultural (and more than cultural) lack and need for regeneration: 'Der Strom der Jahrhunderte floß dunkel und trübe für Deutschland . . .'.[7]

The mood in the 1770s, which Herder both shared and did most to promote, produced an upsurge of writing in emulation and adaptation of a folk manner, as well as of collecting of original folk-cultural texts, which had not significantly abated seventy years later. Within Herder's own time and context, it generated notably Bürger's ballad-writing, most famously his horror romance *Lenore* of 1773, and also Claudius's popularistic folk lyrics and short ballads through the 1770s and 1780s. Most significantly, it led to a good deal of work by Goethe. This included collected folk-songs (a handful of texts which were subsequently among the best-known of all German ballads were first collected by Goethe, at Herder's instigation, in Alsace in 1771[8]), numerous lyric ballads of his own (*Der König in Thule, Jägers Nachtlied, An den Mond, Der Fischer, Erlkönig* and others), his fragmentary *Fastnachtspiele* and farces of the 1770s, such as *Hanswursts Hochzeit*, and the *Faust* project itself, with its sources in popular theatre and the Volkslied.

In the decades which followed the early 1770s, literary writing based around folk models evolved and expanded. Collecting folk-song became an established activity, its results disseminated in periodicals and in a handful of anthologies which sought both to imitate and to outdo those of Herder. Members of the Romantic generation, as they began to write in the 1790s and early 1800s, found the practice thoroughly germane to their own outlook, largely sharing as they did Herder's critique of modernity and of the rational consciousness associated with it. Further anthologies appeared, the most important being Arnim's and Brentano's substantial collection of exclusively German, preponderantly lyrical and, in many cases, severely doctored songs, *Des Knaben Wunderhorn*, of 1806–8. *Wunderhorn* gave a substantial further boost to song-collecting, both by supporters and by critics of the two editors. Thereafter, collecting became increasingly philologically earnest and less creative, in line with the general emergence of *Germanistik* as a scientific discipline. It also tended to become provincial and dialectal, as many collectors focussed on corpuses of regional song and their linguistic specificity. Throughout the Vormärz, folk-song collecting continued to be a legitimate activity for the poetically inclined: Heine claimed, not necessarily truthfully, to have taken folk-songs from oral sources;[9] Büchner, as we shall observe, may genuinely have done so, and he certainly had some serious collectors among his close friends; Storm was, in the early 1840s, the co-editor of a folk anthology which included poetry; and many others were equivalently engaged.

From the beginning, as we have seen, the embracing of folk-song was a matter not only of collection but also of emulation. Goethe, Bürger and Claudius in their various ways established the Germanic folk manner of rhymed, four-line strophes of three- or four-stress lines, largely iambic/anapaestic rhythms, paratactical syntax, a heavily elided diction mixing archaism and colloquialism, and subject matter from rural popular life and German legend, as a powerful expressive resource for modern German poetry. The Romantics, especially the later Romantics (Brentano, Eichendorff, Uhland and others), reinforced the principle, developing this form – the so-called 'Volkston' – in its various nuances into the lingua franca of verse in German. Arnim, in his *Zweite Nachschrift* to *Wunderhorn* in 1818, suggests, not implausibly, that his and Brentano's anthology itself played a major role in this process.[10] In any event, by the time of the Vormärz the *Volkston* was indeed the dominant idiom of German poetry. For Heine it was entirely preponderant: in his considerable verse output, non-folk-song styles, where they do occur, are almost invariably ironic and designed to draw attention to themselves. It was similarly predominant for Storm in the late 1840s, for Geibel, for Hebbel, for the *Schwabendichter* Kerner, Pfizer, Schwab and Karl Mayer, for Lenau, for Keller, and for the political poets of the 1840s, such as Freiligrath, Herwegh, Dingelstedt and Hoffmann von Fallersleben. With other, more eclectic versifiers, such as Rückert and Mörike, the balance of styles is more even; but, even with them, the sense of the Volkston as a normal and natural idiom, from which other poetic idioms are self-conscious, formally reflective deviations, is very strong.

The cultural assets of the Volk, as rediscovered by the Sturm und Drang and its successors, were, of course, not confined to song, but reached much further, into the domains of folktale, saga and myth. By implication, the reawakening of pre-rational forms of consciousness and national identities also entailed self-discovery in and through myth. Already Herder's preoccupations had such a dimension, as seen in his interest in the ancient epics as a form of folk literature: in the Ossianic legends, and also, particularly, in the Danish *Kiämpe Viiser*, songs about elemental spirits and daemons from Germanic myth. Goethe's *Erlkönig* and *Der Fischer* are both direct developments of this last mythology. The vampirism of Bürger's *Lenore* and some others of his ballads is also a modern poetic attempt to enter the kind of mythic world signalled by Herder.[11] In subsequent decades this aspect of the folk revival likewise developed and expanded. Musäus's five-volume *Volksmärchen der Deutschen* of 1782–87 was an influential work, a collection of tales told in a modern voice with whimsical, often satirical, topical references, but which assembled for the contemporary world, in brilliant narrative detail, salient sagas – often myths of origin – of the different German regions and *Volksstämme*.[12] The Romantic movement again reinforced the trend, with its researches into and collecting of Märchen (culminating in Jacob and Wilhelm Grimm's *Kinder- und Hausmärchen* of 1812–15), of *Volksbuch* legends (published by Goerres and others), and of the mythology of the Germanic peoples (the Grimms' *Deutsche Sagen*, of 1816–18, and *Deutsche Mythologie*, of 1833).

Moreover, it made all this material the stuff of modern literature, identifying the Märchen as the form most apposite to the spirit of Romantic fiction, and producing fiction, verse and other art forms with powerful legendary and mythic ingredients. Friedrich Schlegel famously called for the creation of a *new* mythology;[13] indeed, various of the Romantics responded to the summons. But predominantly, the mythology which the movement addressed itself to and helped resurrect was that associated with the Germanic Volk.

The literati of the Vormärz were steeped in this tradition – in the mythology of the elemental spirits and other facets of pre-Christian myth, in German Märchen and saga. We see it in Heine with his *Elementargeister* (1835/37); and, indeed, imagery connected with this appears through most of his work, from *Die Harzreise* and the early ballads to *Der Doktor Faust. Ein Tanzpoem*, of 1847, and to some of his very last poetry. It is seen in Mörike, too, with his fairytales, and his poems concerning witches, elves, fire and water spirits and other daemons; in Storm, with his saga-collecting, the Märchen which he composed, and the mythic motifs that continue to appear in his stories even later on in his career; in Stifter, most strikingly with *Kazensilber*[14] from the *Bunte Steine*; and so on. Even Büchner, as the play *Woyzeck* and its Märchen allusions show (see chapter two, below), was fairly deeply versed in this lore. It was difficult even for comparatively cosmopolitan and rationalistic German authors of this time to exclude such material from their writing, such was its hold on their imagination.

Of course, the folk revival was always political, and in intricate, shifting ways – the expression of oppositions of a number of different kinds. For the Sturm und Drang it articulated antagonism towards the effete, rootless, Frenchified aristocratism which was considered to govern the fragmented German states of the time; for Bürger, in particular, it was part of an aggressively anti-aristocratic political stance. In Musäus, as we noted, a dimension of satire, directed against contemporary social and institutional corruption, is added to his legends; and in his version of the *Libussa* story, a regime is promoted which is based on 'Vernunft', 'Vaterlandsliebe' and a form of non-anarchic popular governance (in the hands of 'die biedern Bürger').[15] For most of the Romantics, writing after the upheavals of the French Revolution and its aftermath, and also, generally, from a different class position, the agenda had shifted somewhat. Arnim's essay accompanying and justifying *Wunderhorn*, entitled *Von Volksliedern* (and dated January 1805), is an elaborately regressive (patently Novalis-inspired) Romantic cultural-political critique, sharing a number of Herder's precepts, but adding to them a comprehensively anti-bourgeois slant: not only are rationalist academicism and the decadence and enervation of the current political regime in Germany attacked, but also cosmopolitanism, urbanisation, taxation, bureaucratisation, the cult of private property, liberal economics and its neglect of the lower classes, pernicious policies of universal education, the attempts to found a national theatre, mercenary soldiering, and a range of further issues. Against this is set an ideal of a re-spiritualised society, in touch with God, reconnected with the 'Boden des Vaterlandes', filled with 'Begeisterung', and living life according to ancient freedoms, after the fashion of the old *Handwerksburschen* and itinerant scholars.[16] The Volkslied and its producers are emphatically pre-modern, pre-capitalist and rural – thus different from the alienated poor of modern society: maybe, so the essay states at one point, it was actually the extinction of folk-song in France (i.e., by implication, the conversion of its Volk into a deracinated modern mass) which made the revolution of 1789 possible; and such a tendency must be – and, with *Wunderhorn*, will be – counteracted in Germany.[17]

However, the *Wunderhorn* songs themselves, appearing as they did in 1806 and 1808, took on a meaning somewhat different from the one to which Arnim's essay points; for the context of their publication was the battles of Austerlitz, Jena and Auerstädt, the humiliating Napoleonic occupation of Prussia and an intensifying nationalistic mood in many parts of Germany. The collection's purpose, as internal cultural critique, was superseded by its effect, which was as a proclamation of national greatness and renewal, in parallel, notably, with the contemporaneous *Reden an die deutsche Nation* of Fichte. Furthermore, this also became the principal agenda of the major folk-cultural publications which immediately followed. The most noteworthy example is Jacob and Wilhelm Grimm's *Kinder- und Hausmärchen*, which the brothers described as the product of 'altberühmte . . . Gegenden deutscher Freiheit' – while carefully suppressing the true French origins of several of their main stories.[18]

After the Restoration and on into the Vormärz, these ideologies, and others, too, are to be found associated with folk-cultural collections – from the Romantic conservatism of the later Goerres (*Altteutsche Volks- und Meisterlieder*, 1817), through the bourgeois-liberal nationalism which became the Grimms' standpoint and was that of many other academic ethnographers, the left-liberalism of Uhland (*Alte Hoch- und Niederdeutsche Volkslieder*, 1844–45), to the radicalism of Büchner's friend August Stöber (*Elsässisches Volksbüchlein*, 1842). A wide political spectrum is represented here. And the same ideological range, or an even greater one, is represented in the literary authors of the time who can be said discernibly to be creating a form of modern folk art. For Heine, both the German xenophobia and the repressive aristocratism of many of the Romantic folklorists were a continual problem, and his own adaptations of folk forms and contents involve a fairly self-conscious attempt to forge alternative, progressive-revolutionary political positions out of them. Büchner has quite similar purposes, though his approach is less self-conscious (and also entirely lacks Heine's attachment to the mythic and legendary aspects of folk culture). Eichendorff's motivation is an extension of Arnim's of 1805, so part of an implausible project to re-feudalise society. Gotthelf's aim is a different type of conservative regression. Storm's agenda is liberal-nationalist – but a Schleswig-Holsteinian rather than a pan-German nationalism. And other authors present yet more positions.

The folk revival was, indeed, the absolute precondition for the writing not only of these writers of the Vormärz, but even of others (for example, Grillparzer) who wrote about the Volk without as a rule seeking to emulate or recreate folk art,[19] for it had initiated habits and patterns for viewing and representing the masses which were new and enduring. At the same time, however, powerful political and social realities concerning the Volk also fed into these readings. As will be seen in greater detail in the chapters to come, the Volk were a very intrusive reality for the more elevated classes of society at the time. The demographic changes which accompanied incipient industrialisation, namely population expansion (the Prussian population, for instance, grew by well over 50 percent between 1815 and 1848[20]) and the beginnings of urban concentration, certainly meant increased visibility. Changes in the legal and economic status of the poor – the disintegration of the handicrafts system and of feudal structures of rural landholding, processes which were taking place throughout the Restoration period in different states and regions in a complex variety of ways, but basically steadily and inexorably – meant significantly wider population mobility than hitherto, an anonymisation, uprooting and apparent destabilisation of the poor, and manifest problems of vagrancy (illustrated in the coming chapters particularly by Gotthelf, Eichendorff and Nestroy). These structural shifts, combined with the deepening, and related, series of slumps which characterised the years from 1815 to 1848, brought a range of real or perceived symptoms of social breakdown: evident joblessness and hunger, begging, crime against property and the person, drunkenness, prostitution, epidemic and other disease[21] – all of them, in the minds of the wealthier classes, sources of social insecurity associated with the masses. The feared and, to some extent, realised consequence of such conditions was revolt. Food riots and other relatively minor forms of socio-political disorder, efficiently suppressed by the substantial garrisons which the German governments maintained for that purpose throughout their territories, were a feature of the Vormärz political landscape well before the famous weavers' uprising in Silesia in 1844, the harbinger of 1848.[22] From 1830 onwards, following the successful July Revolution in France and the political alarms and upheavals which it generated in Germany, the sense that a general revolution of the pauperised masses was a significant possibility set in; this expectation grew through the years up to 1848, as social conditions worsened further (and also as the activities of German revolutionaries in exile intensified and became known[23]). 1848 was the culmination of that development, and at the same time, in a certain sense, its exorcism: even for those members of the liberal middle class who saw their political hopes dashed by the bourgeois revolution's collapse (hopes of national unification, democratic constitutional reform and the like), the fear of the Volk had lost the visceral intensity it had possessed through the Vormärz years.

It would not be true to say, of course, that the Volk only became an object of social anxiety in German culture during the Vormärz. It can be asked, in fact, to what extent the folk revival in its earliest German beginnings was inspired as a counter-reaction to the spectacle of an unideal, more or less urban Volk – the kind of troubled social reality of which, for example, Goethe's Gretchen and other figures from Sturm-und-Drang drama are only mildly idealised representations. In the preface to the second volume of his *Volkslieder*, Herder observes: 'Volk heißt nicht, der Pöbel auf den Gassen, der singt und dichtet niemals, sondern schreyt und verstümmelt'.[24] One notes, too, how the contemporary British enthusiasts whom Herder adduces in *Volkslieder* as his authorities are themselves denizens of chaotic eighteenth century metropolises: Addison, editor of the London *Spectator*, and Thomas Percy, of Dublin.[25] However, it is very clear that a real turning point in writing about the Volk is the French Revolution of 1789. Of the pre-Vormärz texts alluded to so far, Arnim's essay of 1805 is the first in which the Volk actually have the potential to be threatening. But 1789 also brings some other very striking writing about the masses and the revolution which is only tangentially related to Herder's tradition.

We have, for example, Schiller's *Über die ästhetische Erziehung des Menschen* of 1795, which sees a world divided between the jadedness and depravity of the ancien régime and the 'Verwilderung' of the revolutionised masses. This text's whole purpose, seeking a Utopian 'third way' (reconciling spirit and body) towards a civilised, harmonious and truly free condition of humanity, is said by the author to be a public response to the 'Zeitumstände', specifically to the supposed disastrous release in recent historical events of the common people's animal impulses:

> In den niedern und zahlreichern Klassen stellen sich uns rohe gesetzlose Triebe dar, die sich nach aufgelöstem Band der bürgerlichen Ordnung entfesseln, und mit unlenksamer Wuth zu ihrer thierischen Befriedigung eilen . . . Die losgebundene Gesellschaft, anstatt aufwärts in das organische Leben zu eilen, fällt in das Elementarreich zurück.[26]

There are also Goethe's literary texts of the revolutionary aftermath, such as *Hermann und Dorothea* (1797), *Unterhaltungen deutscher Ausgewanderten* (1795) and *Novelle* (published in 1828, but conceived and begun in 1797[27]), none of which depict the revolutionary masses, but all of which allude to them with a type of elemental imagery – fire, flood, wild beast – which becomes common in the Vormärz.[28] In addition, we have the climax of Goethe's *Campagne in Frankreich 1792* (admittedly reconstructed in 1820–22 on the basis of memories and notes), where he quotes himself as proclaiming, after the Cannonade of Valmy, 'Von hier und heute geht eine neue Epoche der Weltgeschichte aus, und ihr könnt sagen, ihr seid dabei gewesen'.[29] The cannonade was not merely the turning point in the war: it was the moment when a republican army of plebeian volunteers, rushing out from revolutionary Paris, resisted and threw back the standing armies of the continental monarchies, a decisive moment of social shift and realisation of popular power. Goethe, in 1822, knew it had been so, and asserts in his text that he recognised its importance at the time. Significantly, Kant wrote in 1798 of this same episode at Valmy as the moment when a new form of political-moral legitimacy established itself in the world:

> Durch Geldbelohnungen konnten die Gegner der Revolutionierenden [the Coalition forces] zu dem Eifer und der Seelengröße nicht gespannt werden, den der bloße Rechtsbegriff ihnen vorbrachte, und selbst der Ehrbegriff des alten kriegerischen Adels . . . verschwand vor den Waffen derer, welche das Recht des Volkes, wozu sie gehören, ins Auge gefaßt hatten und sich als Beschützer dachten.[30]

In Hölderlin's early hymns we find echoes not only of the chaos of contemporary events ('der Vernichtungsstunde / Zügelloser Elemente Streit'), but also of the new role of the mass and the political importance of its physical needs ('Unentheiligt von der Sorge Flügel . . .').[31] Finally, we might mention Kleist and his earliest story, *Das Erdbeben in Chili*, of around 1805; whether or not Kleist's earthquake is to be read as a metaphor for the French Revolution itself, as some have argued,[32] it seems inescapable that the portrayal (and, in effect, analysis) of mob action at the story's climax reflects authorial knowledge of such phenomena in revolutionary Paris.[33]

The crucial ingredient in the new awareness to which all these texts bear witness is indeed the revolutionary crowd. Modern historiography has refined our understanding of the crowd and its functioning in the revolutionary years in Paris, revealing such elements as its shifting but frequently non-proletarian composition, its conservatism, defensiveness and basic fearfulness, its moralistic rather than nihilistic disposition, and the fact that it also held and was to some degree driven by ideological views.[34] Nineteenth-century writers were unable to register much of this, especially those who viewed the crowd as a bestial horde (from Edmund Burke and his talk of the 'swinish multitude' onwards[35]), but also even those who were less unsympathetic to the revolution in principle. Nevertheless, all were aware of the power of the crowd as revealed in revolutionary history – in accordance with St. Just's famous adage, 'Les malheureux sont les puissances de la terre'.[36]

In fact, the literature of the German Vormärz points to the availability of quite specific knowledge of the French revolutionary crowd's operation. Büchner's presentation of the Paris Volk in *Dantons Tod* has its questionable aspects, as we will see below; but his focus on the factor of hunger as the crowd's main motivation corresponds exactly to modern historiographic conclusions (which point to the causal importance of bread prices), and so, too, does his representation of the dependency of revolutionary leaders, particularly in the Jacobin phase of 1793–94, on the ideological sympathy of the crowd for their very survival. Eichendorff's *Das Schloß Dürande* (1836) has the revolutionary crowd entirely as a criminal rabble, manipulated by malign agitators, but here, too, there are signs of specific knowledge that reaches beyond cliché: the function of Paris inns and wine-shops as centres for negotiation and planning by the crowd, expeditions by organised segments of the crowd – sans-culotte armies – into the hostile countryside, and further details.[37]

Thus, a knowledge of the revolutionary crowd and a sense of the masses as a political force were the legacy of the French Revolution of 1789, in Germany and elsewhere. After the Restoration of 1815, with its apparently secure reestablishment of pre-French-Revolutionary power, and up until the end of the 1820s, this awareness was, it is true, in a degree of abeyance. For instance, an author such as the poet and critic Wilhelm Müller – liberal-democratic and anti-aristocratic in his politics and thoroughly immersed in folk-song and folklore – showed no signs of drawing such conclusions in the folk-cultural project he was evolving up to his death in 1827.[38] Eichendorff with his *Aus dem Leben eines Taugenichts*, of 1826, signals a similar state of consciousness, as we will see. Heine is less clear: the comparatively Herder-like appearance of his depiction of the Volk in works of the mid-1820s such as *Die Harzreise*, or his lyric poetry of the time, also generally suggests harmlessness. But, as chapter one will show, this portrayal contains a veiled message of future political emancipation. And the essays of 1828 and 1829 about London, which formed Heine's *Englische Fragmente*, clearly do perceive the prospect of revolution among the impoverished masses. Finally, we have Goethe's *Faust. Zweiter Teil*, Act 5 (probably written around 1825, even if not finalised till 1831), which reflects remarkably on the hubris of capitalist modernity and its potential demise at the hands of its wageslaves. With Faust the entrepreneur's grand industrial projects and the ghostly, drudge-like 'Lemuren' whom he musters to labour on them, while in reality they are digging his grave,[39] Goethe seems to display, as did Heine after his British visit, a perception related more to English than to German or French conditions of the time. And, generally speaking, their literary compatriots of the decade or so prior to 1830 do not show anything approaching such an intensity of awareness. However, the July Revolution of that year changed matters utterly. When the crowds took to the streets again in Paris and forced a new dethronement and change of power, and significant social and political disorder broke out in many areas of Germany, this told the German educated class as a whole in conclusive fashion that the force of popular revolution was still operative. Such a realisation, in conjunction with the real and manifest symptoms of social disintegration and conflict which they could see around them, did much to provoke the sharply altered general perceptions of the Volk which the Vormärz brought and which can be said to be among its defining characteristics.

The literature with which this book is concerned is thus the product and interaction of two main elements. The first is a long and substantial tradition of espousal of the art and culture of the Volk, as being a basis for a reform of consciousness and betterment of society. The second is various kinds of experience and historical knowledge of the modern masses in their social and political reality, specifically the unavoidable encounter with deprivation and symptoms of social disorder which all writers of the time underwent, and interpretations of these phenomena conditioned by awareness, above all, of recent revolutionary history. These factors come together and both blend and collide, to generate the new and intense forms of literary writing about the Volk which will be observed in the following chapters. They are, it is clear, part of a climate of obsession, an aesthetic and thematic struggle around the Volk, its identity and its social and political potential, which was taking place at this time. Surrounding our nine authors is a large body of work by further, nowadays less-celebrated writers reflecting on and in various senses interacting with the Volk. This could be said to include new perspectives contained in non-belletristic writing, from the proliferation of utterance by members of new proletarian-revolutionary groups after 1830,[40] to discussions of the Social Question by authors of conservative persuasion or origin, such as the 'socialphilosophisch' writings of the Bavarian aristocratic philosopher and theologian Franz von Baader in the early to mid 1830s,[41] or Bettina von Arnim's famous exposé of poverty, *Dies Buch gehört dem König* (Berlin, 1843). It certainly included rather more thoroughgoing efforts at direct popular communication through literature than most of our authors represent, bodies of writing (from Hebel's *Kalendergeschichten* of 1808–19 to Auerbach's and others' *Dorfgeschichten* of the 1840s, and beyond) which sought to capitalise on enhanced literacy levels and developing communications technologies to disseminate a literature of popular education and moral indoctrination.[42] Of the authors discussed here, Büchner, Gotthelf and Nestroy are the ones who (in extremely divergent ways) can be said to be closest to such endeavours. But, as was suggested earlier, it also included most of the field of literature by the educated for the educated, for which the idea of the Volk was ineluctable, connecting as it did with the authors' – and their audiences' – deep-rooted aesthetic conditioning, their political ideals and their social terrors.

Notes

1. Three chapters of the book are revised versions of previously published essays; details are given in the chapters in question, below. My particular thanks are due in the preparation of this introduction and some other sections of the book to my friends and former colleagues David Hill and Gert Vonhoff, who have provided essential comments and corrections.
2. Letter to Karl Gutzkow, June (?) 1836; in Büchner, *Werke und Briefe. Münchner Ausgabe*, eds Karl Pörnbacher, Gerhard Schaub, Hans-Joachim Simm and Edda Ziegler, Munich, 1988, p. 320.
3. From *Plan eines lyrischen Volksbuches*, 1808; in Goethe, *Werke. Hamburger Ausgabe*, ed. Erich Trunz, 12th edn, Munich, 1994, 12: 284–7, see p. 285 (edition subsequently referred to in this section as 'HA'). See also Egon Freitag, *Goethes Alltags-Entdeckungen. 'Das Volk interessiert mich unendlich'*, Leipzig, 1994, p. 13.
4. Johann Christoph Adelung, *Versuch eines vollständigen grammatisch-kritischen Wörterbuches Der Hochdeutschen Mundart*, 5 vols, Leipzig, 1774–86, vol. 4 (1780), cols 1612–14, see col. 1613.
5. Johann Gottfried Herder, *Sämmtliche Werke*, ed. Bernhard Suphan, Berlin, 1877–99, 5: 159–207; 25: 1–546 (edition subsequently in this section as 'SW'). See also Michael Perraudin, *Heinrich Heine: Poetry in Context. A Study of 'Buch der Lieder'*, Oxford, 1989, pp. 149–54.
6. Herder, SW 25: 314.
7. Herder, SW 25: 318.
8. See Herder, SW 25: 656f. (commentary); Goethe, *Dichtung und Wahrheit*, 2/10, HA 9: 408f., also 780 (commentary).
9. See Perraudin, *Heinrich Heine: Poetry in Context*, p. 147f.
10. *Des Knaben Wunderhorn. Alte deutsche Lieder*, eds Ludwig Achim von Arnim and Clemens Brentano, 3 vols, Heidelberg, 1806–8, 1: 479 (reproduced with original page numbers in Clemens Brentano, *Sämtliche Werke und Briefe*, eds Jürgen Behrens, Wolfgang Frühwald and Detlev Lüders, Stuttgart, 1975ff., see 8: 374).
11. 'Ich denke, Lenore soll Herders Lehre einiger Maßen entsprechen', wrote Bürger in 1773. Letter to Boie of 18 June, cited from Gottfried August Bürger, *Sämtliche Werke*, eds Günter and Hiltrud Häntzschel, Munich, 1987, p. 1211 (commentary).
12. See Johann Karl August Musäus, *Märchen und Sagen*, ed. Angela Müller, Cologne, 1997, for example, pp. 178, 195, 200–2, 406–10, 430.

13. *Rede über die Mythologie*, in Schlegel, *Schriften zur Literatur*, ed. Wolfdietrich Rasch, Munich, 1970, pp. 301–7, esp. p. 301.
14. On this spelling, see below, chapter 6, note 60.
15. Musäus, *Märchen und Sagen*, pp. 397, 428.
16. *Des Knaben Wunderhorn*, 1: 425–64, see 427f., 432–5, 439–48, 450f., 458–64 (in Brentano, *Sämtliche Werke und Briefe*, 6: 406–42).
17. *Des Knaben Wunderhorn*, 1: 428 (Brentano, *Sämtliche Werke und Briefe*, 6: 408).
18. See Brüder Grimm, *Kinder- und Hausmärchen*, ed. Heinz Rölleke, 3 vols, Stuttgart, 1980, 1: 18 (*Vorrede*), and John Ellis, *One Fairy Story too Many. The Brothers Grimm and Their Tales*, Chicago, 1983, pp. 32–6, 71, 92.
19. Even Grillparzer ventured in such directions occasionally, notably with his pseudo-*Volkskomödie*, *Weh dem, der lügt*, and with his *Libussa* drama, the historico-mythical depiction of the origin of the Czech nation.
20. See Hans-Ulrich Wehler, *Deutsche Gesellschaftgeschichte*, vol. 2, *Von der Reformära bis zur industriellen und politischen 'Deutschen Doppelrevolution' 1815–1848/49*, 2nd edn, Munich, 1989, pp. 7–24, esp. p. 10.
21. See inter alia Jürgen Kuczyinski, *Die Geschichte der Lage der Arbeiter in Deutschland von 1789 bis in die Gegenwart*, vol. 1/1, *1789 bis 1870*, Berlin, 1954, esp. pp. 9–156; Werner Conze, 'Vom "Pöbel" zum "Proletariat". Sozialgeschichtliche Voraussetzungen für den Sozialismus in Deutschland', *Vierteljahrsschrift für Sozial- und Wirtschaftsgeschichte*, 41 (1954), 333–64; Theodore Hamerow, *Restoration, Revolution, Reaction. Economics and Politics in Germany, 1815–1871*, Princeton, 1958; Eda Sagarra, *A Social History of Germany 1648–1914*, London, 1977, esp. pp. 389–401; Wolfgang Häusler, *Von der Massenarmut zur Arbeiterbewegung. Demokratie und soziale Frage in der Wiener Revolution von 1848*, Vienna, 1979, esp. pp. 80–123; Thomas Nipperdey, *Deutsche Geschichte 1800–1866. Bürgerwelt und starker Staat*, Munich, 1983, in English as *Germany from Napoleon to Bismarck, 1800–1866*, transl. Daniel Nolan, Dublin, 1996, esp. pp. 85–216; Wolfgang Hardtwig, *Vormärz. Der monarchische Staat und das Bürgertum*, Munich, 1985, esp. pp. 64–88; Wehler, *Deutsche Gesellschaftsgeschichte*, vol. 2, esp. pp. 281–96; Jürgen Kocka, *Arbeitsverhältnisse und Arbeiterexistenzen. Grundlagen der Klassenbildung im 19. Jahrhundert*, Bonn, 1990. The most famous contemporary factual account of social deprivation in Germany was that of Bettina von Arnim, *Dies Buch gehört dem König*, of 1843 (with its unpublished sequel, *Armenbuch*, compiled in 1844).
22. See, for example, Hardtwig, *Vormärz*, pp. 64, 240; Jürgen Kocka, *Lohnarbeit und Klassenbildung. Arbeiter und Arbeiterbewegung in Deutschland 1800–1875*, Berlin and Bonn, 1983, pp. 154–6.
23. See Wolfgang Schieder, *Anfänge der deutschen Arbeiterbewegung. Die Auslandsvereine im Jahrzehnt nach der Julirevolution von 1830*, Stuttgart, 1963.
24. Herder, SW 25: 323.
25. Herder, SW 25: 129f.
26. *Über die ästhetische Erziehung des Menschen in einer Reihe von Briefen*, 5th letter, in *Schillers Werke. Nationalausgabe*, eds Julius Petersen, Lieselotte Blumenthal and Benno von Wiese, Weimar, 1943ff., 20: 319; cf. also 2nd letter, 20: 311. Of a party with this, too, is Schiller's scathing review 'Über Bürgers Gedichte' of 1791, slating Bürger's apparent continuing aspiration to produce poetry that indulges the 'großer Haufen' and does not seek to elevate it. See

Schiller, *Nationalausgabe*, 22: 245–64, esp. 248–50. On this and other aspects of the present discussion, see also David Hill, 'Bürger and "das schwankende Wort *Volk*"', in *The Challenge of German Culture. Essays Presented to Wilfried van der Will*, eds Michael Butler and Robert Evans, London, 2000, pp. 25–36.

27. See *Goethe*, HA 6: 750–61 (commentary).

28. See HA 2: 444, 449f., 462, 498–501; 6: 160, 208, 491, 496–8, 500–3, etc.

29. HA 10: 235; see also 661–3, 685 (commentary). See also Nicholas Boyle, *Goethe: The Poet and the Age. Vol. 2. Revolution and Renunciation 1790–1803*, Oxford, 2000, esp. p. 128f.

30. Immanuel Kant, *Der Streit der Fakultäten* (1798); quoted from Jens Kulenkampff, 'Geschichtsphilosophie vor und nach der Französischen Revolution: Kant und Hegel', in *Revolutionsbilder – 1789 in der Literatur*, ed. Lothar Bornscheuer, Frankfurt/M., 1992, pp. 1–22, see p. 12.

31. Quotations from Hölderlin's second *Hymne an die Freiheit*, 1793. See Friedrich Hölderlin, *Sämtliche Werke und Briefe*, ed. Jochen Schmidt, 3 vols, Frankfurt/ M., 1992–94, 1: 134–8.

32. See, for example, Helmut Koopmann, 'Das Nachbeben der Revolution. Heinrich von Kleist: Das Erdbeben in Chili', in Koopmann, *Freiheitssonne und Revolutionsgewitter. Reflexe der Französischen Revolution im literarischen Deutschland zwischen 1789 und 1840*, Tübingen, 1989, pp. 93–122.

33. Related conclusions may also be drawn about his story *Die Verlobung in St. Domingo*. See Michael Perraudin, 'Babekan's "Brille", and the Rejuvenation of Congo Hoango. A Reinterpretation of Kleist's Story of the Haitian Revolution', *Oxford German Studies*, 20/21 (1991–92), 85–103.

34. See notably George Rudé, *The Crowd in the French Revolution*, Oxford, 1959, in particular pp. 179–89, 196f., 208f., 221–7.

35. See E.P. Thompson, *The Making of the English Working Class*, Harmondsworth, 1968, pp. 97f., and Rudé, *The Crowd in the French Revolution*, pp. 1–4.

36. Cited from Häusler, *Von der Massenarmut zur Arbeiterbewegung*, p. 100.

37. Cf. Rudé, *The Crowd in the French Revolution*, pp. 42–3, 127, 137–9, 206, 217.

38. See also below, the end of chapter 1, and Michael Perraudin, 'Wilhelm Müller und seine Zeitgenossen. Zum Charakter nachromantischer Poesie', in *Kunst kann die Zeit nicht formen: Dokumentation der 1. internationalen wissenschaftlichen Konferenz aus Anlaß des 200. Geburtstages von Wilhelm Müller (1794–1827)*, eds Ute Bredemeyer and Christiane Lange, Berlin, 1996, pp. 312–27.

39. Goethe, HA 3: 346–9, and cf. 711.

40. See *Frühproletarische Literatur. Die Flugschriften der deutschen Handwerksgesellenvereine in Paris 1832–1839*, ed. Hans-Joachim Ruckhaberle, Kronberg, 1977.

41. The sudden burst of essayistic *Schriften zur Societätsphilosophie* (this being the title of a segment of his collected works; see below) after 1830 from the conservative Romantic philosopher Baader is itself a symptom of the new mood. In texts such as 'Über die Revolutionirung des positiven Rechtsbestandes' (1831), 'Über den Evolutionismus und Revolutionismus oder die posit. und negat. Evolution des Lebens überhaupt und des socialen Lebens insbesondere' (1834), and the key work, 'Über das dermalige Missverhältniss der Vermögenslosen oder Proletairs zu den Vermögen besitzenden Classen der Societät in Betreff ihres Auskommens sowohl in materieller als intellectueller Hinsicht aus dem Standpunkte des Rechts betrachtet' (1835), he presented a fierce critique of

economic liberalism and the modern constitutional state for their un-Christian 'Geld-Servilismus', their willingness to cast 'die Proletairs' into a new 'Sclaventum', and the danger their policies contain of engendering disastrous social revolution. Baader's remedies are Romantic-aristocratic: a re-establishing of pre-capitalist community and God-given hierarchy, abolishing modern 'Entfremd[ung]' and re-integrating people of all classes within a 'Gesammt-Organismus'. But they are interestingly related, so others of his texts of the time specifically indicate, to a reading of recent French revolutionary writing, notably Lamennais. And their analysis of social ills has a great deal in common with the diagnoses presented by socialist thinkers of the Vormärz. See Franz von Baader, *Sämmtliche Werke*, ed. Franz Hoffmann, Leipzig, 1851–60, Part 1, vol. 6, pp. 55–72, 73–108, 125–44, esp. pp. 131f., 134, 142f. It seems also to have been Baader who first introduced the word 'proletarian' (as both 'Proletarier' and 'Proletair') into German.

42. See *Hansers Sozialgeschichte der deutschen Literatur vom 16. Jahrhundert bis zur Gegenwart*, vol. 5, *Zwischen Restauration und Revolution 1815–1848*, eds. Gert Sautermeister and Ulrich Schmidt, Munich, 1998, esp. Holger Böning, 'Volkserzählungen und Dorfgeschichten', pp. 281–312, Hainer Plaul and Ulrich Schmidt, 'Die populären Lesestoffe', pp. 313–38, and Ortwin Beisbart, 'Kinder- und Jugendliteratur', pp. 339–65; Friedrich Sengle, *Biedermeierzeit. Deutsche Literatur im Spannungsfeld zwischen Restauration und Revolution 1815-1848*, 3 vols, Stuttgart, 1971–80, esp. 2: 145–65 and 864–71; also Anita Bunyan, '"Volksliteratur" und nationale Identität. Zu kritischen Schriften Bertold Auerbachs', in *Deutschland und der europäische Zeitgeist. Kosmopolitische Dimensionen in der Literatur des Vormärz*, ed. Martina Lauster, Bielefeld, 1994, pp. 63–89.

1

Heine and the Revolutionary *Volk*

It is generally recognised that Heine's relationship to the *Volk*, in the range of senses the term had for him, was a complicated and difficult one. His tendency was to characterise his attitude (like that which he took to most of the world's important questions) as ambivalent and contradictory.[1] Perhaps characteristic, and certainly very striking, is the view expressed in his *Geständnisse* of 1854, where he speaks of his sense that the 'Gesamtinteresse des leidenden und unterdrückten Volkes' (B 6/1: 467)[2] takes moral precedence (and, indeed, 'die Emanzipation des Volkes war die große Aufgabe [meines] Lebens'; B 6/1: 468), but combines this with expressions of personal physical revulsion at their concrete reality, 'häßlich', 'schmutzig' and malodorous: 'die reinliche, sensitive Natur des Dichters sträubt sich gegen jede persönlich nahe Berührung mit dem Volke' (B 6/1: 468). Equivalent attitudes are struck in, among other places, *Ludwig Börne. Eine Denkschrift* of 1840, where we are told: 'Ich bin der Sohn der Revolution . . . Ich bin ganz Freude und Gesang, ganz Schwert und Flamme!' (B 4: 53), but also 'daß ich, wenn mir das Volk die Hand gedrückt, sie nachher waschen werde' ('. . . Man muß in wirklichen Revolutionszeiten das Volk mit eignen Augen gesehen, mit eigner Nase gerochen haben. . ., um zu begreifen, was Mirabeau andeuten will mit den Worten: "Man macht keine Revolution mit Lavendelöl"') (B 4: 75). The position implied is that expressed most clearly in the *Vorrede* to *Lutetia*, though in several other places, too (especially from the late 1830s onwards): the poet as political 'tribune' has been morally deeply committed to, and will even have been a significant intellectual agent of, popular revolution; but as an artist and aesthete he fears and dreads its

realisation. 'Sie gefiele . . . mir vielleicht,/Wenn ich andre Ohren
hätte!', as he says in the poem *Atta Troll* (B 4: 570).

The texts in which these pronouncements appear are works
intended to have a large element of self-depiction (unlike, for
example, the journalistic reports which make up the main body of
Lutetia). They are central instances of the 'beständiges Konstatieren
meiner Persönlichkeit' that Heine mentioned in *Ludwig Börne. Eine
Denkschrift*, and which is one of his deepest authorial impulses (B
4: 128). There is something faintly lacking in authenticity about a
dissonant self so repeatedly proclaimed. Self-characterisations are
always suspect, one feels, and all the more so such highly
schematic ones, many times repeated, by a generally narcissistic
personality. It is in a sense a pose, related as much to Heine's sense
of the intellectual-historical tensions of the age and his desire for a
paradigmatic role in relation to them, as to any fundamental senti-
ments he may have had. This is the poet who, so he told us on principle in 1830, reflected and communicated a basically 'zerrissen'
world through the 'Zerrissenheit' of his own heart (B 2: 405).
Occasionally, the pose slips – or is relativised – revealingly, as in his
report on a meeting of plebeian radicals in Paris in *Ludwig Börne*,
in which his voice shifts, as he speaks, into an ironic aristocratic
tone: 'Ein verwachsener, krummbeinigter Schustergeselle trat auf
und behauptete, alle Menschen seien gleich . . . Ich ärgerte mich
nicht wenig über diese Impertinenz' (B 4: 74).[3] Nevertheless, one
cannot say that Heine's proclaimed identity as an individual torn
between political radical and fastidious aesthete, or his asserted
relationship to the Volk as a struggle between commitment and
nausea, is simply false. In a sense, passages such as the one just
quoted merely refine the ambivalence. Behind all the problematical
self-characterising pronouncements lies, indeed, a relationship
which is intense, complex and subtly unfulfilled.

It is clear that Heine's picture of the Volk shifts over time. The
Volk he is concerned with in a range of works of the 1820s is
largely rural: silver-mining communities of the Harz in *Die
Harzreise*, the fisherfolk of the island of Norderney in *Die Nordsee.
Dritte Abteilung*, or the Jewish peasantry of Poland in *Über
Polen*. Only towards the end of the decade does his focus become
more urban: the poor of London in *Englische Fragmente* and the
Italians as witnessed in Austrian-occupied Milan in *Reise von
München nach Genua* (B 2: 542f., 371f.). And after 1830 his Volk is
almost never rural. In the 1820s, his depiction also has a strong
national component. The proposition from *Die Nordsee* III that

'Nationalerinnerungen liegen tiefer in der Menschen Brust, als man gewöhnlich glaubt', and the 'Schmerz über den Verlust der National-Besonderheiten die in der Allgemeinheit neuerer Kultur verloren gehen' (B 2: 236), are strong motivating elements in his view of the 1820s. A people possesses a distinctive cultural identity and deep common consciousness – effectively a race memory – based on generations of collective experience. The Italians with their submerged classical heritage, Christian traditions and recent history as victims of oppression, have such an identity. So too, differently and less admirably, do the English, with their culture and history of banal materialism (*Reise von München nach Genua*, B 2: 371). So also, significantly, do the Jews: Heine's involvement in Berlin in the early 1820s with the *Verein für Kultur und Wissenschaft der Juden* was concerned precisely with bringing to consciousness such cultural identity, and a number of his works of the time allude to it. And the Germans have such an identity, too. The Harz peasantry are in touch with it (as the educated classes are not), with their folk-songs, folktales and animistic nature mythology (B 2: 118–20). But it slumbers in every German breast.

The roots of these conceptions are, of course, primarily to be found in the thought of Herder. As was suggested in my introduction, that encompasses both Herder's anti-universalistic cosmopolitanism (articulated theoretically in the *Ideen zur Philosophie der Geschichte der Menschheit* and practically in his multinational collections of folk-songs), and the irrationalistic element in his account of popular consciousness, notably in the *Auszug aus einem Briefwechsel über Ossian und die Lieder alter Völker*. Heine's writings of the 1820s take active note of the more German-nationalistic output of the Romantic ethnographers, the Arnim and Brentano of *Des Knaben Wunderhorn* and the brothers Grimm with their *Kinder- und Hausmärchen*, but politically he makes a return – a conscious return – to Herder. At the same time, Heine's writings of this period emphasise repeatedly the harmony and intuitiveness of folk consciousness, its collective character, nature-proximity, pre-intellectual intensity and depth, in ways which are more or less contemporary common currency but are also ultimately traceable to Herder.

The new element which Heine, as compared with all his models, adds – as early as the 1820s – is that of social emancipation and revolt. The Volk he depicts in the 1820s, with the arguable exception of the poor of London in *Englische Fragmente* (B 2: 542, 598), is not overtly a revolutionary class. Generally, it is not only oppressed but also ignorant and superstitious. But the seeds of emancipation are present in its consciousness. In *Die Nordsee* III, the intuitiveness of the primitive fisherfolk of Norderney is akin to the 'synthetic understanding' – 'synthetische[r] . . . Verstand' (B 2: 234) – that the work extols in the Great Men of History, who by such consciousness advance historical progress – including Napoleon, the 'Mann der neuen Zeit' (B 2: 237) and incarnation of the French Revolution (B 2: 664; see also 4: 201). And the next historical hero, according to the text – or even the real hero whom Napoleon symbolised – is collective: 'Frankreichs Heldenjugend ist der schöne Heros, der früh dahinsinkt' (B 2: 239); or, as he writes a little later, 'Die Völker selbst sind die Helden der neuern Zeit' (B 2: 590; see also 3: 219). The poet himself, meanwhile, also has moments of such consciousness, in the flights of his Romantic-poetic imagination, but they are occasional, uncertain and ambivalent. In the poem *Bergidylle*, in *Die Harzreise*, the poet harangues a peasant girl bombastically about his role as an emancipator, a herald of the Third Age of Man. But beneath the surface and potentially, it is she and her fellows – in instinctual communion with nature and themselves, in a way which he again only patchily emulates – who have the power (B 2: 130–7). In *Reise von München nach Genua*, of 1828/29, finally, we have a Volk closer to consciousness, with an awareness of oppression and an esoteric 'Befreiungsgedanke' that find articulation in its characteristic cultural products, music and the commedia dell'arte (B 2: 353f.).

After 1830 Heine's world was different. In 1831 he moved to Paris and was exposed to day-to-day encounters with a modern, urban, mass *Volksleben*. Also, the July Revolution of 1830 had taken place. The revolution was not a turning point for Heine alone.[4] As was noted earlier, it was the moment which proved to conservatives and radicals what they had feared or hoped: that the spirit of the French Revolution was still abroad in Europe. And in literature it generated striking changes of political tone, particularly in depictions of the Volk. One thinks, among many other examples, of the deep change in the Romantic Eichendorff's view of the *Volk:* from the harmless and charming character of the Taugenichts, in 1826, to the daemonic revolutionary masses of *Das Schloß Dürande*, of 1837; or of the shift in the portrayal of artisanal poverty in Austrian folk comedy between Raimund's *Der Alpenkönig und der Menschenfeind* (1828) and Nestroy's *Lumpazivagabundus* (1833), from passivity to anarchic revolt (see below, chapters three and four). The common people had become empowered and dangerous. Before the July Revolution Heine's Volk had been ethereal and suffering (in *Reise von München nach Genua, Englische Fragmente*), or faintly comical (*Die Harzreise*), or smelly, very ugly, and even grotesque (*Die Nordsee* III, *Über Polen*), but never aggressive or actively threatening. For Heine after 1830, 'Volk' always carried, whether positively or negatively, immediate connotations of power.

In the main, therefore, the Volk which Heine witnessed in the early years of the July Monarchy was that of Paris. The journalistic reports in his *Französische Zustände* – which are not premeditated presentations of a shifting mind, as are most of his belletristic texts, but expressions of a mind genuinely shifting – reveal a range both of views and of terminology. Sometimes 'Volk' is those who had engendered the July Revolution and had supported Louis Philippe, directed by ideals of 'bürgerliche Gleichheit' (B 3: 156f.).[5] When Heine reports elegiacally on the uprising in the Rue Saint-Martin in June 1832, the rebels are, indeed, termed 'Volk', but are said explicitly not to include '[die] unteren Volksklassen . . . oder gar [den] Pöbel' (B 3: 220). At other times, notably in his description of the cholera epidemic of spring 1832, 'Volk' does include the poorest (B 3: 168ff.). The mind of its members also varies, from dangerous superstition and bloodlust ('der Volkszorn, [der] nach Blut lechzt'; B 3: 173, cf. 170f.), through ingenuousness and manipulability (for example, in their credulous Bonapartism; B 3: 161),[6] to instinctive percipience and dignified right-thinkingness ('Ich hatte tief hinabgeschaut in das Herz des Volkes; es kennt seine Leute'; 'Das Volk ließ sich nicht . . . täuschen'; B 3: 175, 178; cf. 160).

There is a 'deutsches Volk', too, in the *Französische Zustände* and other writings of the 1830s, a sorrowful giant, 'treu und unterwürfig' (B 3: 104), 'schlummersüchtig, träumend' (B 4: 120), but potentially violent and destructive, or like Gulliver, strapped down by Lilliputians but liable to burst his bonds (B 3: 105) – the same figure that we encounter in Heine's *Zeitgedichte* of the beginning of the 1840s about 'der deutsche Michel' (*Deutschland!*, *Erleuchtung, Verheißung* and others; B 4: 454, 430f., 424).

What is striking in Heine's writing at this time is the way the Volk is repeatedly invoked but relatively seldom actually described. The 'Börne-Buch' spoke of the touch of plebeian dirty hands and the smell of 'schlechtem Knasterqualm' (B 4: 75), but the originators of these sensory onslaughts on the poet are barely seen. In the *Französische Zustände*, a crowd protesting at the fall of Warsaw passes by, perceived as 'mißtönender Lärm. . . , sinnverwirrendes Getöse', and disturbs the poet's tranquillity (B 3: 69). Twice the glimpse of a starving man in the Paris street is briefly mentioned (B 3: 71, 151). The Bacchanal of the Paris carnival, with its potential for real social disorder, does draw the poet's attention (B 3: 151). But his only extended focus on the reality of popular life occurs during the cholera epidemic, when, significantly, he finds himself interrupted in the midst of a passage of theoretical reflections about revolution by the inescapable reality of the plague (B 3: 167f.).

This is all a complicated and shifting picture. In part, Heine's inconsistency and uncertainty reflect the generally experimental and provisional state of socialist thought in the 1830s. But the lack of clarity is also perhaps aggravated by our own presumptions. Our understanding of the revolutionary masses is conditioned by Marxian notions of proletarian revolution, and it requires an adjustment to see that, for Heine in the 1830s, revolution is above all a process after the image of 1789: its agents are not necessarily plebeian and may well be bourgeois; there is nothing strange, in fact, in the idea that its principal agents are political leaders, Great Men;[7] and the Volk in its consciousness may well lag behind, or even be in conflict with, revolutionary positions. It is instructive to note Heine's intense approval of a speech by Louis Philippe's prime minister, Guizot, in the early 1840s, on his, Guizot's, aim of consolidating the revolution (i.e. the July Revolution) by raising the common people to the level of education and culture represented by the existing laws and institutions of the state – that is, of the revolutionary July Monarchy.[8]

Around this time in the early 1840s, however, Heine's conception had indeed begun to take a direction more familiar to us, in response, one presumes, both to the developing political theory of the time[9] and to the reality of social conflict. In Heine's works of the 1840s the Volk of communism appears, the 'wilde[s] Heer des Proletariats, das alles Nationalitätenwesen vertilgen will, um einen gemeinschaftlichen Zweck in ganz Europa zu verfolgen, die Verwirklichung der wahren Demokratie' (B 5: 185). Their Utopia – of equality and bread – is not exactly the one which the poet himself desires – so, for example, the Cologne Cathedral episode in *Deutschland. Ein Wintermärchen* says (B 4: 593–5) (a work to which we will return in more specific detail in chapter five, below), or the 'Kommunistenkapitel' and the ending of *Atta Troll* (B 4: 517–19, 570), or many passages in *Lutetia* (e.g. B 5: 224, 232, 324f.,

336f., 394f., 406f., 497). But this is a class which has come to consciousness, to an acute awareness of the character and sources of its own oppression. The poem *Die schlesischen Weber*, in which the voice of the people curses systematically the myths used to keep it in subjection (B 4: 455), makes this clear, as, repeatedly, do the reports from Paris in *Lutetia*. This Volk of the 'unteren Klassen' is 'wütend' and 'zerstörend' (B 5: 324, 375, 395), but it is free of superstition and illusion, of the 'Skelette des Aberglaubens', as *Deutschland. Ein Wintermärchen* puts it (B 4: 595). Heine depicts the common people in these texts somewhat as he had done in such works of the 1820s as *Die Nordsee* III and *Über Polen*, in grim and grotesque little scenes of squalor – but with the difference of a realised emancipatory consciousness, embittered and threatening, as opposed to one which is merely a distant potential. Especially interesting is the description in *Lutetia* of his visit to metal workshops in a Paris suburb, where the labour of the 'ouvriers', amidst flames and the din of hammers, images the revolutionary mood which is expressed, too, in their political reading and their songs (B 5: 251).

Even at this time, however, aspects of Heine's attitude are variable or obscure. At one point in *Lutetia* we find apparent support by him for the communistic Volk's challenge to the idea of property (B 5: 421f.); but in reports of his from early phases of the 1848 revolution the Volk is euphorically praised for its respect for property (B 5: 208f.). Generally, the degree of Heine's sympathy or lack of it for the communists is quite hard to pin down (and is probably intended to be so). We are also told on occasion in *Lutetia* that communist rule will indeed come, but will only be temporary – by implication because some sort of latent popular monarchism will assert itself (B 5: 373f., 405). Heine's work in general offers a stream of divergent prophesies ('Bin voller schlechten Profezeihungen', as he once said[10] – even though this was, in fact, one of his more accurate predictions). But there is also a suspicion that this tone of his had to do with his journalism's German audience, which was not tolerant of untempered talk of proletarian revolution. Altogether, one may say that many factors contribute to making identification of a unified position on Heine's part – even synchronically – very difficult.

After the 1848 Revolution and Heine's own physical collapse the position changes again a little, though less than is often suggested.[11] The self-presentational prose of his 'Matratzengruft' years of the 1850s, namely *Geständnisse* and the *Vorrede* to *Lutetia*, speaks of the loss of the poet's own Utopianism. But the proletarian Volk as a revolutionary class, to whom moral right and the future belong, essentially remains. In *Geständnisse*, the Volk is said explicitly to be 'Pöbel' (B: 6/1: 467); and a measure of reversion to the benighted Volk of earlier years – not only 'häßlich', but also 'dumm' and ignorant (B: 6/1: 467f.) – is discernible. But in the *Lutetia Vorrede* of 1855, the poet's famous expression of prospective distress at how his *Buch der Lieder* will be turned into paper bags for old women's snuff is accompanied by as powerful an expression as he ever offers of both rational ('logical', he calls it) and emotional commitment to the cause of the proletarian-revolutionary Volk (B 5: 232f.).

Finally, there are also verse depictions from these years of the 1850s in which the same divergence is to be found. The poem *Die Wanderratten* is barely different ideologically from *Die schlesischen Weber*. *Das Sklavenschiff* internationalises the question of the oppressed victims of capitalism, and also depicts a *Volk*, as earlier in Heine's writing, with an inchoate, pre-conscious sense of its own potential for freedom. And the starving protagonists of *Jammertal* show a stoicism towards their own suffering which links the poem above all with Heine's contemporaneous, personal lyrics of the experience of the mattress grave (B 6/1: 194ff., 305ff.).

The problem with the Volk for Heine – always – was its unavoidability. That does not mean in the domain of practical experience: on this level, he was, with the striking exception of the cholera epidemic of 1832, quite successful at avoiding its members. But philosophically and aesthetically they are the absolute heart of his view. The *volkstümlich* focus of his verse poetics is very clear – the fact that he resorted so very nearly exclusively to folk-song patterns in his choice of forms and tones, and this despite the thoroughly contemporary character of his thematic interests. But the background to this predilection is itself philosophical. As noted earlier, Heine's view in the early and mid 1820s, influenced by Herder and his Romantic heirs, emphasised the limitations of rationality, and idealised – with a degree of ambivalence – intuitive, imaginative, even quasi-mystic forms of knowing, which afforded a sort of holistic grasp of the truths of the world. This was possessed by Great Men (Napoleon, Goethe et al.), by the Volk (with its 'tiefes Anschauungsleben', 'synthetischer Verstand'), and occasionally and equivocally by the poet himself in his phases of poetic enthusiasm, such as the 'dithyrambic' outpouring at the end of *Die Harzreise* (B 2: 164–6). Beyond such fairly Romantic-sounding conceptions, however, other elements are hinted at in his view of this time, which are then developed fully in his philosophy of the 1830s, in *Zur Geschichte der Religion und Philosophie in Deutschland*. There he advocates and predicts a millennium, to be brought about by a revolutionary reawakening in European culture of a sensualism which has been repressed for centuries (ever since the end of antiquity). But this sensualism, he argues, has continued to survive beneath the surface throughout the centuries dominated by the Christian spiritualistic tradition, namely in the pantheistic culture of the Volk, above all that of Germany, who have conserved its memory in their tales, songs and especially their mythologies of the elemental spirits. Now a gradual process of coming to consciousness is happening: the Renaissance, Luther's Reformation, Lessing and the Enlightenment, Kant and Hegel, Saint-Simonism, even aspects of German Romanticism, which Heine mischievously identifies as animistic and crypto-pantheist. But the final stage will be the coalescence of this intellectual strand with the revolutionised Volk itself. A revolution and emancipation will result in which joy and 'Genuß', gratification of the senses, are life's realised goals. Now leadership of the revolution will pass from the French to the Germans, who not only bring to it their philosophical tradition, but also in whose subliminally pantheistic Volk the sensualistic-emancipatory potential is strongest. To quote a number of passages from the end of *Zur Geschichte der Religion und Philosophie*: 'Durch diese Doktrinen haben sich revolutionäre Kräfte entwickelt, die nur des Tages harren, wo sie hervorbrechen . . . können'; 'die dämonischen Kräfte des altgermanischen Pantheismus [werden] beschwör[t]', 'jene . . . germanische Kampflust . . . rasselt wieder empor'; 'Es wird ein Stück aufgeführt werden in Deutschland, wogegen die französische Revolution nur wie eine harmlose Idylle erscheinen möchte' (B 3: 638–40).[12]

In these reflections by Heine on the breakthrough of sensualist pantheism there is one crucial linking image for him, namely the Bacchanal, to which dozens of references occur in his works. The sensualistic/pantheistic impulse is for him both metaphorically and concretely expressed in Bacchanalian festival.[13] His cultural-historical allegory *Die Göttin Diana*, of 1846, presents the final victory over spiritualism in the form of an explicit Bacchanal, with Tannhäuser resurrected by Bacchus and cavorting with him, Diana and Venus (B 6/1: 435f.). *Die Götter im Exil* of 1853, Heine's essay about Christianity's demonisation of the classical gods, uses scenes of secret Dionysia to express humanity's deep, enduring desire for emancipation of the senses. Bacchus is the central deity in Heine's cosmology, the 'Heiland der Sinnenlust' (B 6/1: 404–6). And there are many other expressions of the same idea. The aspect of the Volk which interested Heine most strongly and consistently was its festivals – of song, dance, intoxication, sensual libertinism and social disorder – and, with them, Bacchanalian association was always present in his mind. Already in *Briefe aus Berlin*, of 1822, he describes the 'allen Ständen gemeinsam' winter masked balls in Berlin, at which 'ein bacchantischer Geist . . . mein ganzes Wesen ergriffen [hat]' (B 2: 44–7). In Paris, equivalent – though more plebeian and more chaotic – festivals are regularly mentioned and described: in *Französische Zustände* the Mardi Gras of 1832 (B 3: 151–3); also the festival of Demi-Carême, which saw the start of the cholera epidemic (B 3: 170); and, in *Lutetia*, the carnival of 1840, with its frantic mass revelry: '. . . dämonische Lust', 'satanischer Spektakel', 'wütendes Heer', 'Tempeldienst der Heiden' etc. (B 5: 395, 391).

Moreover, this Bacchanalian impulse of the Volk, the deep expression of its urge for emancipation and gratification of the senses and its memory of a freer past, is manifested not only in its festivals and celebrations, but also (as I suggested earlier) in the other cultural domain of its myths – especially the myths of the 'pantheistic' German people. Hence Heine's repeated focus, in numerous works, both literary and theoretical, on quasi-Bacchanals of the German mythical calendar: Walpurgisnacht and the witches' sabbath (in *Die Harzreise*, *Der Doktor Faust. Ein Tanzpoem*, *Lutetia*), the midwinter solstice (*Deutschland. Ein Wintermärchen* – see chapter five, below), Johannisnacht and the Wild Hunt (*Atta Troll*). Walpurgisnacht and the others are further outbursts of repressed popular memory and yearning. Most explicit of all are the *Erläuterungen* to *Der Doktor Faust*, where Bacchanal, witches' sabbath and Paris folk-dance are expressly connected (B 6/1: 395).

The most concentrated social expression of this impulse is, indeed, in dance. This is a motif which occurs repeatedly throughout Heine's writings,[14] and almost always with a politically emancipatory undertone: Laurence's dance in *Florentinische Nächte*, that of the bear in *Atta Troll*, the dance of the slaves in *Das Sklavenschiff*, the cancan of the Paris masses in *Lutetia* (B 1: 592–4, 4: 499f., 6/1: 197f., 5: 394f.), and many others. The last-named of these is Heine's most explicit and, as it were, advanced presentation of the nexus, where this 'dämonisch', erotic, Walpurgis-like 'Tanz des Volks'[15] wordlessly mocks 'jede Art von Begeisterung, die Vaterlandsliebe, die Treue, die Familiengefühle, den Heroismus, die Gottheit' – in short, all the values of civil society – and aggressively articulates the will to revolution (B 5: 395). But it also illustrates the element of ambivalence which, characteristically, is in Heine's approach to the popular Bacchanal in its real social manifestations. Most of his response is fascination, attraction and ideological affinity. But the Bacchanalian Volk is also terrifying and horrible. His moralising against the cancan may, like other aspects of *Lutetia*, be a concession to his readership. It was Heinrich Laube who warned him in 1842 that, for his German public, the word 'cancanieren' was somewhat worse than 'onanieren' (HSA 26: 49). But the Bacchanalian mob of, for example, the cholera epidemic, killing in 'heidnisch' and 'dämonisch' fury those whom it superstitiously blames for the epidemic (B 3: 173), is not beautiful. At such moments, Heine tends indeed to share the perspective of his class (including that of the police of Paris, who correctly saw popular festivities – Mardi Gras and the others – as moments of high revolutionary danger; e.g. B 5: 246, 393).

Such ambivalence in Heine would perhaps be unproblematical, were it not for a further crucial dimension of his philosophy of the Volk, which is his own direct theoretical identification with them in their Bacchanalia. In Heine's complicated, imaginative, pseudo-mythical way of thinking, not only was Napoleon symbol, 'Inkarnation' and historical agent of the Revolution of the Volk (or, vice versa, the Volk was Emperor; B 2: 604), but in a certain sense so too was the poet himself. As 'Tribun und Apostel' (B 2: 468), his role, at whatever cost to himself, is to bring the people to revolutionary consciousness – so, for example, the Cologne Cathedral episode in *Deutschland. Ein Wintermärchen* says (B 4: 593–5). This is the purpose of his exposition of the theory described above. But the role as herald or mouthpiece transmutes into identity: 'Ich selber bin Volk', he says in *Zur Geschichte der Religion und Philosophie in Deutschland* (B 3: 515). And, particularly, he is one with the Bacchanalian Volk. We saw how, in the early works, the instinctual consciousness of the Volk – which later, in works of the 1830s, was explicitly identified as its Dionysian awareness – was something to which the poet had a kind of access himself, with moments – ambiguous moments – of 'mystic' knowledge, in *Die Nordsee* III, *Die Harzreise* and elsewhere. And these moments, bursts of poetic enthusiasm and imaginative expansion, are conceived as Bacchanalian. The word 'Dithyrambe' – Bacchanalian hymn – which is used to characterise the enthusiastic ending of *Die Harzreise* is precisely meant and not fortuitous. In *Geständnisse*, of 1854, he speaks of his earlier 'kühnsten Dithyramben zur

Verherrlichung des Kaisers [Napoleon]', which 'durch die ansteckende Gewalt der Begeistrung . . . einen heitrern Kultus [schufen] . . . Ich schwang davor das lachende Weihrauchfaß' (B 6/1: 511). Here Heine is referring particularly to his poetic travelogue of 1828/29, *Reise von München nach Genua*. And in that work, in just such a dithyrambic passage, the poet tells how he was lured to Italy, full of the 'Freiheitsgefühle' of 'ein neuer Frühling', by 'den jungen Frühlingsgott' Bacchus himself (B 2: 326). For Heine, interestingly, Bacchus here is the god of both poetry and freedom; and the poet, as he said, is 'Volk', at any rate in his Bacchanalian moments.

The difficulty with Heine's claim of identity with the *Volk* is the obvious discrepancy between such a claim and the literary and essayistic depictions of the Volk in his works, which actually seem to signal great remoteness. We find them, as it were, mediated through their cultural products, their folk-songs and folktales: for example, in *Die Harzreise*, where the Harz mountain people are characterised in images drawn in part from the Brothers Grimm, and are focused on in their own affinity with the tales; or in *Reise von München nach Genua*, where the portrayal of the Italians becomes a description of the *commedia dell'arte*. The use of the Volk in the arguments we have noted concerning the inadequacy of rational consciousness certainly has a large element of instrumentalisation about it (in *Die Nordsee* III, *Die Harzreise* etc.). Where they are indeed directly described, they are, on the one hand, reduced to subhuman primitiveness – as with the 'Eingeborenen' of Norderney, 'geistesniedrig . . . [in] ihren kleinen Hütten . . . herumkauern[d]' (B 2: 213) – and, on the other hand, elevated into poetry, like the Italians, 'diese blassen, elegischen Gesichter . . .' (B 2: 349).[16] They are envisioned mythically, sometimes through what are supposedly their own myths (Walpurgisnacht, Johannisnacht etc.), most often through Heine's recurrent Bacchanalian imagery. Above all in the basically non-poetic contexts of his Paris journalism one is struck by how habitually and inescapably the mythical identities intrude: how, for example, even his description of the most powerful reality of popular life that he ever faced, the cholera epidemic, swiftly acquires such mythical resonances (B 3: 170–3).

Finally, there are Heine's numerous other metaphorical representations, especially in his verse: the repeated personifications of the German Volk as Michel (in poems such as *Erleuchtung*, *Verheißung*, *Das Kind*, *Deutschland!*, *Michel nach dem März*;

B 4: 430f., 423f., 454; 6/1: 270); and, above all, his animal imagery, in which the Volk in various forms appears as dog (*Ludwig Börne, Der tugendhafte Hund*; B 4: 60, 6/1: 291–3), bear (*Atta Troll*; B 4: 509ff., 517ff.), wolf (*Deutschland. Ein Wintermärchen*; B 4: 603f.), horse (*Pferd und Esel*; B 6/1: 293–5) and, most frequently of all, as rat (*Ludwig Börne, Lutetia, Die Wanderratten*; B 4: 75, 100f.; 5: 413; 6/1: 306f.).[17] It is true that his famous poem *Die Wanderratten*, which depicts proletarian revolt through imagery of the Pied Piper, is mainly an ironic articulation of contemporary bourgeois anxieties. But the Volk is none the less emphatically animalised.

The reason for such modes of representation is partly aesthetic. Heine lived in an age of realism and shared its moral imperatives, namely the sense of an artist's obligation to write about the material – social and political – world and to reflect its central realities. His, as he said, was no 'weitabgelegenes Winkelherz' (B 2: 405). Nevertheless, his literary imagination was essentially or primarily not realistic but symbolic, in fact the kind of imagination which his book *Die Romantische Schule* explicitly viewed as characteristic of the Romantic-spiritualist tradition (B 3: 366–70). Perhaps most strikingly *Deutschland. Ein Wintermärchen* illustrates the principle, concerned as this text is with the most specific contemporary political phenomena, but always discerning, isolating and interpreting symbols: the River Rhine, Prussian eagle, Pickelhaube helmet, Kölner Dom, Kyffhäuserberg and others. Heine once boasted of himself, 'der [ich] die Signatur aller Erscheinungen so leicht begreife' (B 1: 593) (and elsewhere: 'Das Erscheinende überhaupt [ist] . . . nur Symbol . . . der Idee'; 'in der Kunst bin ich Supernaturalist'; B 3: 45f.). The fact is, that the quest for 'Signaturen' entails a kind of inability to stop short at the phenomena themselves, a disposition which characterises more than just his authorial relationship with the Volk.

Be that as it may, it is clear that Heine's attitude to the Volk is highly theoretical, non-empirical and above all lacking in empathy. This is even the case with his most apparently unmetaphorical, unmythical and thus atypical-seeming poetic depictions, such as the poems *Die schlesischen Weber* and *Jammertal* (B 4: 455; 6/1: 305). *Die schlesischen Weber* is an exception in that it gives the Volk a direct voice, without the intrusion (beyond the first strophe) of the poetic persona. But it is a very systematic, theoretical kind of speaking; the *Weber* themselves appear, after all, as faintly animal, as well as daemonic and spectral, and entirely non-individual. Only, perhaps, with *Jammertal*, the two 'arme Seelen' starving to death in

31

their garret, might it be said that an experience of popular deprivation is directly evoked – and even in this case there is a suspicion that the sufferers are addressing each other in phrases which are really echoes of Heine's early love lyrics.[18]

Heine's use of the Volk is, as we shall see, one among very many literary 'projects' involving such subject matter during the *Vormärz*, and indeed before and after that period. Approximately speaking, his approach is to adopt in detail the Romantic reactionary instrumentalisation of the Volk, but convert its notions to the modern world and a progressive, more or less revolutionary agenda. As Georg Lukács has said, and, indeed, Heine himself implied, the work of such writers as the *Wunderhorn* editors, the Romantics Arnim and Brentano, was itself crypto-revolutionary,[19] and Heine's endeavour was to bring these tendencies to the surface. But his was certainly not the only path to a post-Romantic literary realisation of the Volk. In the late 1820s, the poet Wilhelm Müller had already turned from sentimental imitations of the *Wunderhorn* lyric to detailed ethnological researches and a poetry based on this, in which folk communities supposedly articulate their own cultural character.[20] In the 1830s and 1840s, we have new conservatisms, such as Gotthelf's anti- revolutionary, anti-urban, xenophobic Swiss folk fiction (discussed in chapter three, below); or moderate-liberal undertakings such as Auerbach's literature of popular enlightenment;[21] and many others. And maybe most interestingly in connection with Heine, we have Büchner in the mid 1830s, producing, in the development from *Dantons Tod* to *Woyzeck*, a literature which both accords the Volk a central role in a grand intellectual-historical system (as Heine does), and also (as Heine really does not) works towards an utterance in which the deprived Volk of the modern world express themselves, both collectively (in their lifestyles, customs, attitudes and cultural products) and individually and subjectively, in tragic experience. Whatever the complexities and beauties of Heine's enterprise, it lacks the quality of empathy, a realistic ability to share the common people's seeing and feeling, which – as the next chapter will demonstrate – Büchner possesses, and without which, in a sense, such a project is incomplete.

Notes

1. And many commentators have echoed this judgement. See, for example, Walter Grab, *Heinrich Heine als politischer Dichter*, Heidelberg, 1982, p. 45: '. . . ambivalente Einstellung zu den Volksmassen'. An earlier version of the present

chapter was published in German as 'Heine und das revolutionäre Volk. Eine Frage der Identität', in *Vormärzliteratur in europäischer Perspektive II. Politische Revolution – Industrielle Revolution – Ästhetische Revolution*, eds Martina Lauster and Günter Oesterle, Bielefeld, 1998, pp. 41–55.

2. Volume and page numbers given in the text and notes of this chapter, preceded by the initial 'B', refer to Heinrich Heine, *Sämtliche Schriften*, ed. Klaus Briegleb, München, 1969–76. Briegleb's *Werkausgabe* is the most frequently used edition of Heine, even following the completion of the *Düsseldorfer Ausgabe* (Heine, *Historisch-kritische Gesamtausgabe der Werke*, ed. Manfred Windfuhr, Hamburg, 1973–97); I use the former as the basis for quotation here on account of its wide availability.

3. Comparable with this in their irony are passages such as the seventh Caput of *Atta Troll*, in which the bear also suddenly begins to speak in an aristocratic voice: 'Mich verletzte stets am meisten/Jenes sauersüße Zucken/Um das Maul – ganz unerträglich/Wirkt auf mich dies Menschenlächeln!/. . ./Weit impertinenter noch/Als durch Worte offenbart sich/Durch das Lächeln eines Menschen/Seiner Seele tiefste Frechheit' (B 4: 512) – or such as the poem *Die Wanderratten*, where the perspective through which the revolutionary rats are viewed is gradually transformed from one of initial neutrality into that of the ruling class ('. . . Die radikale Rotte/Weiß nichts von einem Gotte', etc.; B 6/1: 306).

4. See Fritz Mende, 'Heine und die Folgen der Julirevolution', in Mende, *Heinrich Heine. Studien zu seinem Leben und Werk*, Berlin, 1983, p. 44: 'Die Pariser Julirevolution ist das politische Ereignis, das Heines Leben am nachhaltigsten beeinflußt hat'. Cf. also Helmut Koopmann, 'Heines politische Metaphorik', in *Heinrich Heine. Dimensionen seines Wirkens*, ed. Raymond Immerwahr, Bonn, 1979, pp. 68–83.

5. According to Benno von Wiese, Heine '[hat] immer wieder klare Trennungsschranken errichtet . . . zwischen dem Volk als einem positiven Begriff und der Masse bzw. dem Pöbel als negativem'. See von Wiese, *Signaturen. Zu Heinrich Heine und seinem Werk*, Berlin, 1976, p. 143 (chap. 4, 'Zum Problem der politischen Dichtung Heinrich Heines'). This is an exaggeration and simplification. However, it is the case that 'Volk' occasionally appears in his writings in direct antithesis to the masses.

6. Cf. also Heine's famous exclamation in *Ludwig Börne. Eine Denkschrift*, 'Armes Volk! Armer Hund!' (B 4: 60).

7. Cf. also Büchner's contemporaneous drama *Dantons Tod* (1835), in which the role of the Great Individual is explicitly called into question, but in a way which seems to suggest that the author is conscious of challenging prevailing notions.

8. Quoted by Fritz Mende, 'Heine und die "Volkwerdung der Freiheit"', in Mende, *Heinrich Heine. Studien*, p. 64f. See B 5: 461, *Lutetia*.

9. See inter alia Leo Kreutzer, *Heine und der Kommunismus*, Göttingen, 1970; Jean Pierre Lefebvre, 'Marx und Heine', in *Heinrich Heine. Streitbarer Humanist und volksverbundener Dichter. Internationale wissenschaftliche Konferenz, Weimar 1972*, ed. Karl-Wolfgang Becker, Weimar, 1973, pp. 41–61.

10. Letter of 1 April 1831, in Heine, *Säkularausgabe. Werke, Briefwechsel, Lebenszeugnisse*. eds Nationale Forschungs- und Gedenkstätten der klassischen deutschen Literatur (Weimar) and Centre National de la Recherche Scientifique (Paris), Berlin and Paris, 1970ff., 20: 435. Edition subsequently referred to in this chapter as 'HSA'.

11. Many commentators see a transformation in Heine's attitude at this point. See, for example, Dolf Sternberger, *Heinrich Heine und die Abschaffung der Sünde*, Hamburg, 1972, p. 26f. That view is contradicted by Michel Espagne, 'Heine als Gesellschaftskritiker in Bezug auf Karl Marx', in *Rose und Kartoffel. Ein Heinrich Heine-Symposium*, ed. Antoon van den Braembussche, Amsterdam, 1988, pp. 55–68, see p. 60.

12. Heine's ideal revolution was, one might add, always a revolution of consciousness. His enthusiasm for Guizot in 1843 was a reaction to the latter's plea for a consolidation of the revolution through a humanisation of the masses: a 'Volkwerdung der Freiheit', as Heine called it, was to be brought about, the Volk must go through a process of education which would make it worthy of the (in origin middle-class) revolution (*Lutetia*, B 5: 461; see also Mende, 'Heine und die Folgen der Julirevolution'). And Heine's enthusiasm for the relatively unbloody July Revolution twelve years earlier was similar. He saw in it, at least for a time, a 'Volkwerdung . . . [der] Revolution' – 'die Revolution . . . als ganzes Volk . . . wiedergeboren' – in that the Volk had acted there no longer as a benighted rabble, but had shown itself for the first time as a humane, enlightened force (*Einleitung zu: 'Kahldorf über den Adel'*, B 2: 664).

13. See inter alia Lia Secci, 'Die Dionysische Sprache des Tanzes im Werk Heines', in *Zu Heinrich Heine*, eds Luciano Zagari and Paolo Chiarini, Stuttgart, 1981, pp. 89–101; Burghard Dedner, 'Politisches Theater und karnevalistische Revolution. Zu einem Metaphernkomplex bei Heinrich Heine', in *Signaturen – Heinrich Heine und das neunzehnte Jahrhundert*, ed. Rolf Hosfeld, Berlin, 1986, pp. 131–61 (pp. 149–55).

14. See, for example, Barker Fairley, *Heinrich Heine. An Interpretation*, Oxford, 1954, pp. 24–46; Benno von Wiese, *Signaturen*, pp. 67–133 (chap. 3, 'Das tanzende Universum').

15. Cf. also Heine's *Die Götter im Exil*, B 6/1: 406: 'Bacchuszug. . . , de[r] Cancan der antiken Welt'.

16. See also the poem 'Wir saßen am Fischerhause' of 1823/24, in which these two extremes are juxtaposed and thematised as contrary Utopias – the 'schmutzige Leute' of Lapland, 'plattköpfig, breitmäulig und klein', versus the 'schöne, stille Menschen' of the Ganges (*Buch der Lieder, Die Heimkehr*, no. 7, B 1: 111).

17. On Heine's 'Volk-Hund' metaphor, see Klaus Briegleb, *Opfer Heine? Versuche über Schriftzüge der Revolution*, Frankfurt/M., 1986, pp. 88–100. See also, among others, Barker Fairley, *Heinrich Heine*, pp. 112–34; Alfred Opitz, '"Adler" und "Ratte": schriftstellerisches Selbstverständnis und politisches Bewußtsein in der Tiermetaphorik Heines', *Heine-Jahrbuch* 20 (1981), 22–54.

18. See Michael Perraudin, 'Heinrich Heines Welt der Literatur. Realistisches und Antirealistisches in seinem Werk', *Vormärzliteratur in europäischer Perspektive III. Zwischen Daguerreotyp und Idee*, ed. Martina Lauster, Bielefeld, 2000, pp. 15–29 (p. 26f.).

19. Georg Lukacs, 'Heine und die ideologische Vorbereitung der 48er Revolution', in *Text und Kritik 18/19: Heinrich Heine*, ed. Heinz Ludwig Arnold, 1st edn, 2nd impression, Munich, 1971, pp. 31–47, see p. 38.

20. See Wilhelm Müller, *Werke. Tagebücher. Briefe*, ed. Maria Verena Leistner, Berlin, 1994, 2: 55–69; also Michael Perraudin, 'Wilhelm Müller und seine Zeitgenossen. Zum Charakter nachromantischer Poesie', in *Kunst kann die Zeit nicht formen: Dokumentation der 1. internationalen wissenschaftlichen Konferenz aus Anlaß des 200. Geburtstages von Wilhelm Müller (1794–1827)*,

eds Ute Bredemeyer and Christiane Lange, Berlin, 1996, pp. 312–27, esp. p. 324f.. On Müller, see, in addition, my introduction.

21. See Anita Bunyan, '"Volksliteratur" und nationale Identität. Zu kritischen Schriften Berthold Auerbachs', in *Deutschland und der europäische Zeitgeist. Kosmopolitische Dimensionen in der Literatur des Vormärz*, ed. Martina Lauster, Bielefeld, 1994, pp. 63–89.

2

Towards a New Cultural Life.
Büchner and the *Volk*

I am concerned politically and culturally at this moment with express-
ing what I consider to be positive and assertive and revolutionary in
working-class experience. I consider that the role of any artist seriously
committed to the working class is that of eliciting from the working
class in its many aspects those areas in which it triumphantly demon-
strates the potential for a true proletarian consciousness and culture
which sections of the working class are capable of creating . . . The
artist, then, is concerned with the translation of working-class experience into action on the stage in order to preserve and further the progressive, revolutionary, deeply humanist elements of working-class
awareness.[1]

These words, clearly, are not those of Georg Büchner, but were
spoken a good deal more recently. They come, in fact, from
a noted radical radio producer for the BBC in the 1950s and
1960s named Charles Parker, the co-creator of a genre of play-
cum-documentary termed the 'radio-ballad', in which the speech
of working-class individuals talking directly about their lives and
experience was interspersed with folk-songs, recorded sound
effects and other material. However, it may be said that, in some
detail and with minimal adjustments, Parker's words can stand as
a motto for the project which Büchner himself was evolving in the
1830s. Indeed, Parker's aim as a middle-class playwright to transcend, in some sense, his social origins, and create a drama in
which working-class culture can articulate itself, stands in a tradition of which Büchner was one of the very earliest exponents.
Büchner was less explicit on the subject, at any rate in writings
which have survived him. But he comes close to such a statement
in one well-known late letter, written a few months before he

began work on *Woyzeck* in 1836. In it he tells his correspondent, 'Ich glaube, man muß . . . die Bildung eines neuen geistigen Lebens im *Volk* suchen und die abgelebte moderne Gesellschaft zum Teufel gehen lassen':[2] moribund modern society should go to the devil and in the common people the creation of a new cultural life – thus one might render the difficult term 'geistig' here – is to be sought.[3]

However, if this was at a certain stage the goal Büchner envisaged, it is certainly not one which was realised as he began his literary works. Indeed, there is arguably an anomaly in the fact that an author with such powerful socialistic political convictions and consistent hostility to the class of the wealthy and educated should focus so clearly, in all but one of his main literary texts, on the mental sufferings of individuals from that class, with the common people being substantially marginalised.

In *Dantons Tod*, his first literary work, the Volk is, of course, an essential ingredient in the historical logic which is at the heart of the play. As noted in my introduction, the presentation of the crowd in the play indicates on Büchner's part a detailed assimilation of the new understanding of the role of the masses in history that the events of the early 1790s in Paris had impressed on thinkers in Germany and elsewhere.[4] However, he adds a further dimension of his own to the reasoning. For Büchner the academic neurologist, soon-to-be author of a treatise on animal nervous systems, it is the dictates of the nervous system which are the fount of human behaviour, of the 'nature' according to which each person acts: the pursuit of gratification on the one hand (sexual enjoyment and other pleasures, more or less obvious or subtle), and the avoidance of pain on the other (the pain of injury, of hunger, of thirst, of cold). The juggernaut of the Revolution rumbles on, crushing more and more of the revolutionaries themselves in its path, because of its or their incapacity to allay the hunger and cold of the poor: every scene in the play which depicts the Paris crowd explicitly mentions their physical deprivation. So their hunger has to be assuaged with a surrogate gratification, 'heads instead of bread' must be thrown to them (Act III/10, MA 121; cf. IV/7, MA 130f.). As Büchner says, both in the play and in a letter, physical deprivation is a fundamental 'lever' of the machine of the Revolution.[5]

Nevertheless, despite all this, the play's primary concern remains not the poor themselves, but the experiences, tragic experiences, of the middle-class revolutionaries, above all Danton, who are being carried along by such a logic.[6] And the often remarked-upon parallel structuring of the play, by which crowd scenes alternate with scenes of the revolutionary leaders, does not fundamentally mean a parallelism of equals: the crowd scenes reflect ironically on the deliberations and agitations of the leaders, not vice versa. In fact, compared with what Büchner does in *Woyzeck*, and measured against the realist aesthetic which he articulates in various places (in *Lenz*, in his letters, even in *Dantons Tod* itself), one could go so far as to say that the scenes of the Volk in *Dantons Tod* are deficient, that they do not convincingly show the author 'immersing himself in the life of the most humble individual and rendering that life in its finest nuances' (*Lenz*),[7] but are somewhat too close to the marionette-like artificiality which Büchner condemned.[8]

His crowd-characters' dialogue, as a first point to consider, is not on the whole based on first-hand observation. A good deal of it is culled from the punning clowns and crowd repartee of Shakespeare (indeed, various of the scenes can be shown to contain comparatively specific Shakespearean echoes).[9] And when this is not so, the characters from the Volk seem to speak in a paler version of the language of persiflage and metaphoric bravura which Danton and most of the other revolutionaries also use, sounding more like Jean Paul or Heine than like sansculottes. Behaviourally, too, the picture offered tends to the caricatural and standardised: often the Volk are used for a comedy of stupidity (as with the drunken Simon in the second scene of the play); and when they do not have a comic function (or even when they do), they are often merely cruel. Doubtless the Paris crowd was, indeed, not lacking in cruelty and stupidity, but both of these characteristics could be shown in ways more differentiated than most of Büchner's scenes attempt. His observation of the crowd in these scenes does not particularly display the empathy with and love for the common people which he later apparently announced,[10] and arguably demonstrated.

That, we might say, is one side of the story in *Dantons Tod*. There is another side, however, consisting in signs which seem indeed to be starting to emerge in the play of a focused interest in the common people and their culture, for their own sake. In the scenes of the crowd, there are just hints of an acknowledgement that the revolutionary crowd of Paris might indeed have had a distinctive collective culture of its own, in costume and forms of address at least, and possibly also with a suggestion of more substantial cultural patterns: its dialectical penchant (e.g. I/2, MA 73f.; III/10, MA 121), and its *Witzkultur* (as in the scene where the mob is sufficiently appreciative of a young bourgeois captive's joke to spare him from lynching; I/2, MA 74). Then there is the 'Marion Scene'. The prostitute Marion also does not speak in a voice which is socially distinctive. But she is a plebeian character who is shown engaged in complex inner experience. Martens, for one, sees her as a tragic sufferer, a prefiguration of Marie in *Woyzeck*.[11] That in some sense she prefigures Marie is clear, but her tragic suffering is equivocal: for, on the one hand, she is contented in her eroticism, and free of Danton's besetting consciousness ('Danton, deine Lippen haben Augen'; I/5, MA 82);[12] yet, on the other hand, she is fundamentally alone, without the identification with another or others which each of Büchner's works suggests to be the only possibility of human happiness, and, as a prostitute in syphilis-ridden eighteenth-century Paris, she is condemned to an early death. Marion is, in the end, an ambiguous character, resistant to unitary interpretations; but that basic ambiguity itself is a token of how seriously the character is taken in Büchner's play.[13]

Thirdly, there are the ingredients of German popular culture which Büchner builds into his play, in the form of eight folk-song extracts sung at various stages. It has been remarked that these songs are sung only by members of the Volk and by a *woman* of the wealthy class,[14] so implying a Herder-like association of both with an ideal of natural harmony and simplicity of consciousness. However, it has also been noted that the content of the songs tends to replicate Danton's own pessimistically clear-eyed insights into human behaviour, and into life and its purposes.[15] As Büchner employs them, they are songs about transience and the senselessness of human striving, about amorality, urge and the pursuit of momentary gratification, about loneliness, estrangement and death. In fact, Lucile's are the songs of loneliness, whilst the *carpe diem* songs are put in the mouths of the poor. Only one song, that of the ballad-singer in the 'Promenade' scene (II/2, MA 93), could be construed as *social* in its implication, possibly, although not conclusively, a song of the pain of toil. Sometimes Büchner uses a song extract to convey the same meaning as that which the complete poem had had; sometimes he changes the meaning by selection; and sometimes we cannot be sure what he has done, because the song's models are unknown. One extract is taken verbatim from the Romantic collection *Des Knaben Wunderhorn*,[16] another was probably written by the poet and novelist Wilhelm Hauff in the 1820s in a doctored collection which he published,[17] but many of the others point to folk-song variants, not published in full until later, if at all, to which Büchner had personal access.

Perhaps the most interesting usage concerns the Ophelia-like Lucile, into whose mind folk-song snatches come, as it were realistically. First there is 'Ach Scheiden, . . . / Wer hat sich das Scheiden erdacht' (II/3, MA 97), the song of parting which comes to her before Camille's arrest as an unexpected intuition, preceding conscious knowledge. Then there is the 'Night Visit' song which she sings, deranged, outside Camille's cell (IV/4, MA 126): the strophe suggests a reuniting, but extant songs in which versions of it occur are largely stories of unachieved or unhappy visits, with the couple in one way or another separated or estranged;[18] and Büchner causes the images of the song to carry beyond the bounds of the singing and permeate the character's consciousness and fantasy through the speech which follows ('Komm, komm, mein Freund! Leise die Treppe herauf, sie schlafen Alle. Der Mond hilft mir schon lange warten. Aber du kannst ja nicht zum Tor herein, das ist eine unleidliche Tracht'). Finally, her third song, the 'Reaper Death' folk-song on the guillotine steps, has likewise found its way into the singer's wider consciousness – with the images of roses and bells, and the stoical phrase, 'Wir müssen's wohl leiden', which is a quotation from the song (IV/8–9, MA 132f.);[19] and it also evidently helps supply the clarification of thought and the resolve to act for which the concluding two scenes show her struggling. Folksong, in short, invests the deranged Lucile's mind with a fantasy which contains an underlying intimation of truth, while for the lucid Lucile, perhaps, it encapsulates and clarifies bitter realities and her appropriate responses to them. We can see that, although in *Dantons Tod* the role of the Volk in the text may as yet be essentially only a functional one and their depiction still comparatively generalised, there are indications, nevertheless, of an incipient interest in the individual experience of the poor and deprived, and of an attention to and valuing of their cultural distinctiveness.

In *Lenz*, the semi-fictional prose narrative which Büchner composed late in 1835, a little less than a year after completing *Dantons Tod*, the Volk again appears as an important *secondary* focus of the text, although in ways somewhat different from its function in the play. This is the text in which we encounter what are usually thought to be Büchner's principal aesthetic statements about an art concerning itself with the poor and humble (MA 144–6). We find here the proposal that life and 'Möglichkeit des

Daseins' must be art's sole criterion; also the suggestion that the only literature truly to have displayed such a life-awareness is the New Testament, folk-song, Shakespeare and, now and again, Goethe; and then the notions mentioned previously about the need for the artist pursuing this goal to immerse himself in the being of the humblest person (also the *ugliest* person), and to possess a love which is the precondition of such empathy ('Man muß die Menschheit lieben, um in das eigentümliche Wesen jedes einzudringen; es darf einem keiner zu gering, keiner zu häßlich sein, erst dann kann man sie verstehen'). However, it is again difficult to claim that the text manifestly pursues these ideals. The work does, it is true, aim at and achieve an extraordinary empathetic access to the mind of its hero; but this hero is Lenz, the tormented middle-class artist-genius. For Büchner's Lenz himself, though, the Volk are an intense focus. Materially needy but apparently spiritually calm and secure (MA 140), they present a model of stability and clarity on to which he can fasten in his existential and/or psychological crisis.

There is a little uncertainty here. Does *Lenz* contain the uncomfortable implication, which is also not dispelled by *Dantons Tod*, that a certain kind of existential crisis is an experience primarily undergone by intelligent educated males? Are the Volk in the story indeed simple and harmonious? Is the view of Lenz the character, in whose perspective we are strongly caught up, also Büchner's, or is it relativised, as the view of a Herder-influenced member of the *Sturm und Drang*? At one point in the story we are shown a peasant household in the mountains, the members of which seem, indeed, to be undergoing spiritual and psychological suffering (MA 147f.) – perhaps an illustration of the principle of 'ugliness' to which Lenz's aesthetic demands attention; and the encounter is in the event a severe further disruption for Lenz, after which his despair greatly intensifies. We might coherently see the Lenz character as adhering to a falsely harmonious image of the Volk, which is effectively in conflict with his own stated aesthetic, and is an image which Büchner the author is purposely undermining. But the signs in the text are not quite conclusive that this is what is meant.

In Büchner's third literary text, the comedy *Leonce und Lena*, of 1836, the hungry poor are relegated to a single, if memorable, satirical episode, in a play concerned mainly with tracing the *Weltschmerz* of a prince. The play is conceived, at any rate in part, as a reverse image of the realist aesthetic announced in *Lenz* and elsewhere: it is assertively artificial, demonstratively theatrical, a work based (in contrast to Büchner's other texts) not on documentary recordings of empirical events but on a montage of play-ingredients not very far from plagiarism. One might say this suggests a logic by which the marginalisation of the Volk in the text implies their central importance in the real world. But, on the other hand, the work does not operate wholly in a domain of artificiality and the socially unreal. For at the same time, with the character Valerio, it keys directly into what is, in fact, a folk-play tradition.

At moments in the play, especially in the second act, Valerio is Hanswurst, the gross clown of German popular comedy since the seventeenth century, whose function was to present a cynical counterview of human nature to the idealised view articulated by his social betters. When the play juxtaposes Valerio's desire to eat and drink, and his thieving and his self-preserving cowardice,[20] with Prince Leonce's dreams and ennui, Büchner echoes the Hanswurst tradition, just as two of his direct sources, comedies by Tieck which actually had central clowns called Hanswurst,[21] had also done.

Büchner's interest in this tradition is itself interesting, but it is not very substantial. Büchner's pseudo-Hanswurst is not a sustained critic of the delusion, hypocrisy and self-indulgence of the prosperous classes, like the aggressive Hanswurst of Goethe's fragment *Hanswursts Hochzeit* in the 1770s, or like the Hanswurst derivatives in the sharper Austrian folk-theatre plays contemporary with Büchner, notably Nestroy's *Lumpazivagabundus* (discussed in chapter four, below). Often Valerio speaks with the same voice as Leonce, especially in the later stages of the play; they are never radical antagonists, but appear much more as another of the pairs of friends at the centre of each of Büchner's works. And the play's debunking of its princely protagonist is kept distinctly equivocal by Büchner.

Thus in each of Büchner's works before *Woyzeck* we are left with hints of the move towards the Volk and their culture to which his aesthetic utterances point. But undoubtedly it is the *Woyzeck* play, with its marginalising of the upper-class characters and its centralising of the poor and their experience, which represents the decisive further step and drawing of conclusions. *Woyzeck* is a play *of* the Volk in a range of ways, perhaps more and less evident. First, it is so in a number of respects on a representational level. The work is clearly notable for its presentation of its central, plebeian characters, Woyzeck and Marie, not in the patronising, distancing image of creatures of nature, simple and uncorrupted, but as (in one critic's phrase) 'der Erlösung bedürftig',[22] humanly in need of redemption. 'Die Geringsten' are made heroes of tragedy. Second, equally evidently, the work presents a tragedy in which, to a novel degree, central social factors which impinge on the life of the poor, deprivation and economic oppression, are ingredients in the pressures upon the protagonists. Third, in a wider framework, the play offers a kind of mimesis of the social life of the poor, a range of what have been disparagingly called 'volkstümliche Milieustudien'[23] which are themselves remarkable: scenes of street life (the children playing, the soldiers passing); scenes of labour and economic life (the 'Freies Feld', the Jew's shop); scenes of the institutions of popular diversion and consolation (the inn, the fair); and scenes of a deprived domesticity (Marie with her child, Woyzeck and Andres in their barracks).[24] Concerning the last of these: quite incidentally, it seems, a detailed picture is drawn of a kind of social matrifocality by default, with family life and upbringing being shown to be in the charge of the women of several generations (Marie, the grandmother, the young girl), the only male in residence being the halfwit and the other men occasional visitors and suppliers of money, their visits made occasional either by choice (as with the Drum Major), or by constraint (as with Woyzeck). Even though a systematic analysis of such things is not evidently being undertaken, the play none the less provides a close and highly plausible observation not just of social life but also of the social structure and organisation of the economically oppressed common people of Büchner's time.

There is a fourth aspect to the representation of the Volk in Büchner's play, however, which is perhaps the most interesting of all. This is the way, or ways, in which it seeks to depict their very mind – their distinctive language and the cognition which generates it or proceeds from it. In contrast to the comparative homogeneity of expression of *Dantons Tod*, the *Woyzeck* play shows a strong and ironic awareness of varying *codes* of utterance and understanding.[25] In the utterances of the Captain and the Doctor, Büchner pillories varieties of civilised discourse, symptoms of the 'Armseligkeit des menschlichen Geistes' which was his scornful judgement on post-Cartesian philosophy following a period of intensive reading in 1835.[26] We have come a long way (although the connection is there) from the intellectual exchanges in the Luxembourg prison in *Dantons Tod*, in which brilliant characters are shown elegantly demonstrating their appreciation of a philosophical aporia (III/1, MA 105-7), to the contemptuous depiction of the speech and thinking of the privileged in *Woyzeck*. This play shows a language of overt syllogism, equipped with all the appropriate substantive abstractions and logical connectors but ending in tautology ('Moral, das ist wenn man moralisch ist'; H4,5, MA 240), and systems of understanding which conflict with the reality of life, deny humanity, conflict with each other, and cancel each other out.[27]

In contrast to this we have the language and consciousness of the common people. Clearly we see in Woyzeck at certain stages a 'Volksmensch' entering the conceptual world of the privileged and breaking its bounds, beginning to sense the relativity of its assumptions, as in his discussion with the Captain: 'Ja Herr Hauptmann, die Tugend! ich hab's noch nicht so aus. Sehn Sie, wir gemeinen Leut, das hat keine Tugend, es kommt einem nur so die Natur, aber wenn ich ein Herr wär. . . , und könnt vornehm reden, ich wollt schon tugendhaft sein' (H4,5, MA 241). Here he also enters into the *language* of the privileged, and he struggles with it. It is, as Volker Klotz says, an 'uneigentliches Sprechen',[28] not his own, but he is *not* (*pace* Klotz) simply floundering, for behind the hesitancy as he broaches the code of his betters is an awareness which exceeds theirs.

So much is fairly evident. But the further question to be asked is what the play says about how and why he is able to make such a challenge, in the scenes in which we do witness the 'eigentliches Sprechen' – the true language – of the poor, when they speak among themselves. The following exchange, between Marie and Woyzeck, after she receives the Drum Major's gift, may be taken as an example:

Woyzeck: Was hast du?
Marie: Nix.
Woyzeck: Unter deinen Fingern glänzt's ja.
Marie: Ein Ohrringlein; hab's gefunden.
Woyzeck: Ich hab so noch nix gefunden. Zwei auf einmal.
Marie: Bin ich ein Mensch?
Woyzeck: s'ist gut, Marie. – Was der Bub schläft. Greif ihm unter's Ärmchen, der Stuhl drückt ihn. Die hellen Tropfen stehn ihm auf der Stirn; alles Arbeit unter der Sonn, sogar Schweiß im Schlaf. Wir arme Leut! Das is wieder Geld Marie, die Löhnung und was von mein'm Hauptmann.
Marie: Gott vergelt's Franz.
Woyzeck: Ich muß fort. Heut Abend, Marie. Adies.
Marie (allein, nach einer Pause): Ich bin doch ein schlecht Mensch. Ich könnt mich erstechen. – Ach! Was Welt? Geht doch Alles zum Teufel, Mann und Weib. (H4,4, MA 239)

The language, predictably, is very unhypotactical: it is extremely short of conjunctions, of prepositions other than positional ones, and of structures signalling logical relationships. At the same time it is – or the thought processes implicit in it are – highly associative. As Woyzeck speaks, looking at the child, the child's perspiration suggests to him toil, which then suggests poverty, which suggests money, the money he gives to Marie. The association is freely pursued. And there is also the extraordinary associative leap which Marie makes, from the discovery of her misdeed, Woyzeck's 'Ich hab so noch nix gefunden. Zwei auf einmal', to her cry of agony 'Bin ich ein Mensch?' – 'Am I human?'.[29]

As an adjunct of its associative quality, this language is also often intensely figurative – not so much in the passage quoted above, but frequently elsewhere. Such figurativeness takes a variety of forms. There are repeated simple similes (the Drum Major is 'wie ein Baum', 'wie ein Löw', 'wie ein Stier'; H4,2, H4,6, MA 235, 241), and elaborated ones (night insects hum 'wie gesprungne Glocke', the moon for Woyzeck gleams 'wie ein blutig Eisen'; H1,16, H1,15, MA 253). There are what are evidently standard extended metaphoric hyperboles from the *Volksmund*, such as Margreth's 'Sie, Sie guckt siebe Paar lederne Hose durch' (H4,2, MA 236),[30] or the Drum Major's 'Der Kerl soll dunkelblau pfeifen' (H4,14, MA 249).[31] Then there are other tropic expressions, which seem to be detaching themselves, either partially or wholly, from a received collective phraseology, as with Marie's phrase: 'Trag Sie Ihre Auge zum Jud und laß Sie sie putze, vielleicht glänze sie noch, daß man sie für zwei Knöpf verkaufe könnt' (H4,2, MA 235f.), or with the Drum Major's threat: 'Soll ich dir die Zung aus dem Hals ziehe und sie um den Leib herumwickle?' (H4,14, MA 248) – or with extraordinary 'as if' images such as the Drum Major's and the Sergeant's admiration of Marie: 'Wie sie den Kopf trägt, man meint, das schwarze Haar müßt ihn abwärts ziehn, wie ei Gewicht, und Auge, schwarz, . . . Als ob man in ein Ziehbrunn oder zu ein Schornstei hinunteguckt' (H2,5, MA 237f.). One is reminded strongly here of observations made by the writer quoted at the beginning, Charles Parker, who speaks of how his working-class interviewees, all of them 'capable of giving succinct expression to [the] range of experience that shapes their lives', sometimes 'come up with . . . merely a working-class commonplace like, "1929, when the grass was growing in the shipyards"', and at other times with a 'brilliant phrase', as in the case of the engine driver who told him: 'Railways, it was a tradition, it was part of your life.

Railways went through the back of your spine like "Blackpool" went through rock'.[32] Again, the implication is of a highly tropic language, part standard and established, but part spontaneous, original and startling.[33]

Finally, on the subject of this metaphoric-associative language and consciousness in *Woyzeck*: its ultimate manifestation, presumably, is the recourse to myth and other kinds of analogical story, seen notably in the intrusion of images from Genesis and Revelation into Woyzeck's speech and imagination and from the Gospels and the Song of Solomon into that of Marie, as well as in the various elements of fairytale and folk-song which permeate the text (and to which I shall return below).

These questions about the language of the Volk in *Woyzeck* have been addressed, in varying ways, by a series of commentators. In *Der Dialog bei Georg Büchner* (1958), Helmut Krapp argued influentially that the play illustrates in the speech of its characters from the Volk, Woyzeck above all, an essential 'isolation of the word', the sentence 'zerstückelt . . . zu einer Reihe von Wörtern', thereby diminishing the words' 'grammatische, logische, bedeutungsmäßige Beziehung'; then (increasingly extravagantly) that 'die Textur setzt sich aus Einzelwörtern, Wortmotiven, zusammen', which 'keine Gedankenfolge mehr aus sich entl[assen]', and 'indem die Sprache von einem Wort zu seiner Wiederholung und zum nächsten Wort und seiner Reprise springt, Wörter wie Dinge gebrauchend, die man aufbauen kann, prägt sie . . . jene hemmungslose Dynamik aus, die Woyzecks Getriebenheit ist. Der Text . . . wird zum Gestammel . . . Woyzeck redet konfus . . . Der Sinn der Welt verdunkelt sich'. Indeed, Woyzeck 'entmächtigt sich durch seine Sprache, die als gebrochene Gewalt gewinnt und noch über dem Sprecher als schicksalhafte Macht sich behauptet'.[34] Subsequently, Volker Klotz offers a clearly related, but less immoderate view. He sees a paratactic language, presenting 'eine Folge von Einzelaspekten' and no overview, as being appropriate to characters who are unable to see events and their own actions from a synthesising distance; and these, including Woyzeck, are the characters of what he calls the 'open drama'. In their utterance, logical interconnectedness loses out to 'the individual, autonomous element' ('der selbständige Einzelteil') and to sensual plasticity ('sinnliche Anschaulichkeit').[35] Later, in a conception indicating the influence of both Krapp and Klotz, Walter Hinck's short general essay on Büchner talks summarily and a little inconclusively of how, in this language, 'das Einzelwort verselbständigt sich aus syntaktischen oder logischen Bezügen und nimmt letzte Möglichkeiten des spontanen Ausdrucks wahr', a language which he sees as that of the 'ganz in die Kreatürlichkeit verstoßener Mensch'.[36] Finally, Bo Ullman, in what appears at first sight to be a significant amendment of Klotz's view, tells us that in the character of Woyzeck Büchner had to find a way of depicting *reflection* without the aids of an articulate language; but then Ullman gives examples, quoted from Klotz, which tend not so much to sustain this as to return him to Klotz's conclusion, seeing this language as 'ein isoliertes Nebeneinander' *rather* than as reflection.[37]

Rather than engage directly with this unresolved and slightly ill-founded discussion as it stands,[38] I shall attempt briefly, as an alternative way of clarifying the issue, to place it in a new and broader context. This is the context of modern-day, extra-literary investigations of the character of working-class language, in which, indeed, some important connections with Büchner's play suggest themselves. Through the 1950s and 1960s, the sociologist Basil Bernstein developed a distinction between two basic types of 'speech code' which he discerned as characterising language in modern Western industrial societies. These, the so-called 'elaborated' and 'restricted' codes, were functions not of the grammatical systems of individual languages but of divergent 'systems of social relationships'. As the latter were in turn primarily conditioned by different types of basic work relationship, the code distinction was likely generally to correspond to class. Substantially, the restricted code is the communicative mode of the working class and the elaborated code the (primary) communicative mode of the middle class.[39] The elaborated code is one based on a 'universalistic' approach to meaning, in which meanings are made accessible independent of context, and are 'in principle available to all because the principles and operations have been made explicit and so public'.[40] The elaborated code thus entails a language which is full of the 'syntactic markers of the logical distribution of meaning, ... hypotheticals, conditionals, disjunctives, etc.', a language which is hypotactical, overtly logical and substantially literal. Its antithesis, the restricted code, is 'particularistic'. Where 'speech is played out against a back-drop of common assumptions, common history, common interests', meanings can be given in ways which are inexplicit, unelaborated and condensed, able to dispense with specified logical connections. Often, says Bernstein, this speech 'cannot be understood apart from the context and the context cannot be read by those who do not share the history of the relationships'. Moreover, 'if the speaker wishes to individualise his communication' within this collectively orientated mode, 'he is likely to do this by varying the expressive associates of the speech. Under these conditions, the speech is likely to have a strong metaphoric element . . . Whereas elaborated codes draw upon rationality, . . . restricted codes draw upon metaphor'.[41]

By way of illustration, Bernstein describes an experiment in which both middle-class and working-class children were asked to reconstruct verbally some textless picture stories which were shown to them. Middle-class children described the scenes explicitly, 'tak[ing] very little for granted'; they also tended to introduce 'linguistic expressions of uncertainty', and to show a strong awareness of the 'form' or 'frame' of their narrative. The working-class children, meanwhile, showed much less such awareness, their narratives involved little 'consider[ation of] the possibilities of alternat[ive] meanings', and they were inexplicit, appealed to shared knowledge of context (where the middle-class child's description might say 'a man is going down a street', the working-class child might offer 'he's going down there'), and altogether '[took] a great deal for granted'.[42]

On the other hand, says Bernstein, there were various operations which the middle- class child performed less well or less readily. Working-class children proved much more willing to perform role-play with the same story-pictures; they were also more expansive and imaginative in inventing stories around picture characters presented to them; and with word-association exercises they were also more imaginative – apparently less inhibited, for example, by the grammatical class of the proffered word.[43]

It is an instructive token of the modernity of Büchner's social awareness, or perhaps of a substantial real equivalence of social structure between early-industrial Germany and industrial capitalist societies of today, that much of Bernstein's observations and conception is signalled in Büchner's play. The indications of a form of communication between the characters from the Volk which is context-dependent and hard for the outsider to reconstruct, lacks logical connectors, tends powerfully to the metaphoric, has a quality of associative and imaginative unconstrainedness, and has a strong collective or communal element to it, are all aspects of Büchner's view, and are illustrated with considerable precision. And the observations of the antithesis, the speech code of the 'gebildete Klasse' (logically demonstrative, explicit, non-metaphoric, imaginatively inhibited), are likewise in many ways akin. At the same time, some divergences can be noted. For Bernstein, one senses (and he has certainly been understood in this way), the restricted code is ultimately an inferior form of communication, albeit with compensatory elements, and a handicap to its speakers in a diminishingly parochial world. That is not Büchner's implication. For him, we infer, the communicative mode and consciousness of the Volk, precisely because they are as they are, promise a path beyond the circumscribed and specious thought-systems of the educated class to a new, clear-sighted knowledge of human realities. They may be an obstacle in the class competition of the present, but they point to a revolutionary reconstituting of human consciousness in the future. Certainly he would not endorse Bernstein's suggestion of the 'un-distanced' character of working-class communication, unable to relativise and set in a wider context the content and processes of communication.[44] This is precisely what Woyzeck's consciousness (as above all in his exchange with the Captain on the subject of 'Tugend'; H4,5, MA 240f.) makes him *better* able to do.

Bernstein's conception has itself been strongly criticised. Notably, the American William Labov, writing on 'The Logic of Nonstandard English', has argued that the communication of members of economically deprived groups, speaking forms of the language highly deviant from the middle-class standard, is in reality capable of perfect logical rigour and intelligent detachment, and this is not acknowledged simply because of the ignorance and non-comprehension of the sociological researcher and the rest of his, the researcher's, class.[45] The implication is that Bernstein's perception of working-class communication as imaginative rather than dispassionate, metaphoric rather than rational, is a patronising and at best romanticising, at worst merely derogatory misapprehension, which is pedagogically highly damaging. The Büchner of *Woyzeck* would share the unwillingness to deny the 'große Klasse' analytical acuity; but on the other, less negative elements in Bernstein's picture (metaphor, imagination, communality, and so forth), he would not dissent. Büchner's attitude on this question is strikingly close to one important and influential modern sociological view; but other views are possible.

There is one further point to be added on the language in *Woyzeck*. It is often suggested that the language of the characters from the Volk in the play is adequately accounted for by saying that it is recognisably a faithful representation of Hessian dialect,[46] not only phonetically and grammatically but also idiomatically, that

Hessian is particularly strong in picturesque idiom, and so on. This seems to me misguided. Doubtless the language which Büchner was echoing was indeed Hessian dialect, but his is not a systematic dialect representation, after the fashion of J.P. Hebel and others of the time, with concomitant local-patriotic implications. As the sociological parallels drawn above have indicated, Büchner's analysis of language in *Woyzeck* is not primarily dialectal – based on geographical difference – but social; that is to say, it is based on a distinction of class. That, indeed, is what is so notable about his view.

The foregoing section has been concerned with what I called the representational aspect of Büchner's treatment of the Volk in *Woyzeck*, the various ways in which its members are observed and depicted. There is a further side to Büchner's focus on the Volk, however, which rather takes him beyond the mimetic, namely his systematic incorporation into his play of ingredients of popular culture. It is true that, to an extent, the singing of folk-song, reciting or alluding to fairytale, and reading, quoting from and imagining episodes from the Bible can indeed be seen as aspects of the play's realistic observation, in as far as these are, or are held to be, the cultural material in which the common people find expression of their authentic sense of life. A letter of 1837 indicates that Büchner thought the Volk, if it had *life*, did indeed sing folk-song.[47] And *Der Hessische Landbote* and epistolary remarks show how powerful an element he thought the Bible was in real popular awareness.[48] However, it also seems evident that the singing and telling and imagining in the play often extend some way beyond the plausible behaviour of individual characters, as they become, rather, a part of the play's objective thematic organisation, articulations of meanings of Büchner's which are distinct from the speakers' subjective intentions and motivations.

We can examine, in turn, how the principal elements of this culture – Bible, folktale, folk-song – operate in Büchner's play. The Bible is *the* 'Volksbuch' (as Klotz puts it[49]), full of echoes of the Volk's own experience and knowledge: their guilts, as Marie reads of Mary Magdalene; their joys, as she recollects the Song of Solomon in admiration of her lover; their horrors and revulsions, as Woyzeck sees Sodom and the chaos of Revelation; and their humanity, as he quotes to the Captain 'Suffer the little children'. It can also be turned around, as in the sermon of the *Handwerksbursch*, where New Testament phrases of moral optimism and adages about the vanity of earthly things are ironically combined and recast as a doctrine of radical scepticism.[50] The Bible is indeed a *Volksbuch*, but not quite an inevitable repository of wisdom.

With this last passage, the sermon of the *Bursche*, there is already little sense that it has a realistic function, specific to the speaker's individual condition of mind. But the biblical ingredient can detach itself further; and it does so, paradoxically, precisely in the figures of Woyzeck and Marie. Marie associates herself with Mary Magdalene, but, aside from that, the identity is one which the play itself objectifies. That is the reason why she is called Marie:[51] the naming is parabolic, creating an echo for the audience of the *erlösungsbedürftig* Mary Magdalene, although of course with the clear difference that here no redemption comes. The force of the very faint associations with Christ attaching to Woyzeck (pointed to by various critics, although denied by others)[52] is, I think, equivalent. These are invocations of archetypes of human suffering, guilt and redemption – though, again, now in a world where there is no redeeming – from the Volksbuch which the Bible is.

The folktale elements are somewhat more straightforward. The play as we normally read it has references to or elements from six or seven *Märchen*. The Fool in the scene in Marie's Chamber (H4,16, MA 231) enumerates phrases from three, of which the two known ones, at least, are fantasies of fortuitous enrichment of the impoverished. Then there is the Grandmother's Tale (H1,14, MA 252). This is not obscure in its origins, but is an artfully composed amalgamation of images and phrases from three stories from the Grimms' *Kinder- und Hausmärchen* of 1812–14.[53] The three are tales with anxiety-ridden and existentially insecure middles and happy endings. Büchner's concoction, of course, retains the former element and discards the latter. His is indeed in a sense an 'Anti-Märchen', as various writers have observed, for the vindication of the hero is folktale's archetypal conclusion, not just in the Grimms.[54] Yet folktale resolutions are not representations of the life of the Volk, but compensations for it. Rather it is the tribulations, terrors and oppressions which folktale heroes have to undergo on their paths to the customary happy ending, not the ending itself, that express truly the sense that the Volk has of its condition of life. Thus Büchner's Grandmother's Tale, we may deduce (and the author would certainly agree), is a distortion which actually captures the genre's fundamental popular-cultural meaning.

Folk-*song*, of course, is the most manifest ingredient from popular culture in the play, with something like sixteen song-singing episodes in the version we normally read, so well in excess of the song-singing quotient of any likely community of the Volk. They are articulations of a character's momentary conscious feeling, as with the drunken Drum Major's aggressive brandy song, or Marie's 'Soldaten, das sind schöne Bursch' (H4,14, MA 249; H4,2, MA 235). They can express an awareness which has not yet fully reached consciousness, as when Marie, having first met the Drum Major, sings the 'Zigeunerbu' seduction song, or an awareness which consciousness finds painful to articulate directly, as when Woyzeck sings the song of female lust, 'Frau Wirtin hat 'ne brave Magd' (H4,4, MA 239; H1,17, MA 253). They can articulate an individual's wider sense of life and of his or her position in it, as with Marie's two long verses in the play's second scene, beginning 'Mädel, was fangst du jetzt an' (H4,2, MA 236): deprivation, necessary self-sufficiency, seizing the moment. They are seen as automatic reflexes of popular-cultural life, as when the children sing their dancing and counting verses, 'Auf der Welt ist kein Bestand', 'Ringle, ringel, Rosekranz' and 'Der is ins Wasser gefalle' (H2,3, MA 237; H1,14, MA 252; H3,2, MA 255); but they are reflexes whose actual content expresses a deep communal pessimism (all of them are almost certainly death songs).[55]

Then, of course, they begin to transcend their singers, as, for example, when the journeymen in the inn sing the song of faithlessness, 'Ein Jäger aus der Pfalz' (H4,11, MA 247), or, perhaps, when Andres sings 'Frau Wirtin hat 'ne brave Magd' (H4,10, MA 246). It has been proposed, incidentally and interestingly, that the extent to which Büchner's folk-songs cease to articulate the perspectives of their particular singers and become generally thematically expressive increases significantly from *Dantons Tod* to *Woyzeck*.[56] Certainly, the overt pointers to psychological specificity have now gone, as when Lucile in *Danton* sang the song of parting, 'Ach Scheiden, ach Scheiden', and then asked 'Why did I think of that?' (II/3, MA 97). It is true that we remain some way short of the anti-realistic song insertions familiar from German Romantic literature, in which the song is wholly emancipated from the individuality of its singer – a strategy Büchner could be expected to dislike; compared with that, the folk-song-singing in *Woyzeck* is fairly thoroughly realistically integrated. But the tendency to detachment is nevertheless there, both in the sheer number of songs and in the frequent direct and evident functional relation of their occurrence to the play's widest themes.

Büchner's approach to folk-song is highly selective. His folk-song extracts express the knowledge of deprivation, the sense of the nearness of death and a life without meaning, the wish for oblivion and gratification, sexual desire, betrayal and isolation, and so on. They express these awarenesses either directly or, on occasion, through snatches from longer songs widely known to contain these meanings.[57] But very many actual folk-songs do not obviously convey this general pessimism, including even one or two from which Büchner selectively quotes.[58] In part his choice represents a specific critical gesture against the folk-song collections of his and previous generations, which tended to harmonise, bowdlerise and censor songs the content of which seemed immoral or socially dangerous:[59] Büchner concentrates especially on this type of song.[60] None the less, rather as with his use of folktale, we have overall a selection which imposes a tendentious interpretation on the entire corpus of folk-song (and arguably one with less textual justification than could be claimed for his reading of folktale).

Where Büchner's folk-songs actually came from is an interesting question, which has not yet been clearly resolved. Of the extracts in *Woyzeck*, no more than two have phrasally very close prefigurations in previously published (and still known) contexts.[61] A number are variants of songs that had been published previously, but usually these variants themselves do not appear in anthologies until after Büchner's time (anthologies the compilers of which cannot have read *Woyzeck*).[62] Some are songs first published in full after Büchner's death, including a couple published in Alsatian dialect versions by his Strasbourg friend August Stöber in 1842.[63] And some have never convincingly been identified, despite claims to the contrary.[64] There are altogether quite strong indications that he had access to songs more or less directly from the oral tradition, songs to which he may have made some, but not many, adjustments. Hinderer and others propose that this acquaintance came from a Gießen coachmen's inn which he is supposed to have patronised. That may be so, although other reports suggest he did not like alehouses.[65] But it seems unlikely that he had precisely memorised the texts of these songs, some of which turn up in later years with phrasing very close to his, straight from their oral origins.[66] Certainly Büchner had a retentive memory, as various aspects of his career and work-method indicate.[67] But the signs are that, from whatever source he had his songs (be it his own collecting, or that of others, or both), he kept them in a written-down form. The letter to his fiancée of 20

January 1837, during the writing of *Woyzeck*, suggests this, as he asks her to memorise 'die Volkslieder' – that is, a fixed body of songs – for their next meeting (MA 325). Other evidence suggests that, in fact, Büchner kept and worked with a notebook: the way, for instance, in which identical pithy phrases crop up in his letters and his works at some distance from one another, and not necessarily in the works first.[68] His executors mentioned finding in his possessions 'eine Art Tagebuch, das . . . reiche Geistesschätze enthält'.[69] As regards his folk-song interests, and for many other reasons, this notebook would indeed be an instructive document.

There is one further stage to which the folk-song element of Büchner's play is taken, which has not so far been touched upon here. The use of folk-song in *Woyzeck* does not end with songs that are quoted, for the play's imagery and plot are themselves deeply rooted in folk-song (and to a lesser degree folktale). Certain central motifs, such as the redness and blood imagery – especially with images of Marie's red mouth, and the red band Woyzeck sees around the dead Marie's neck – are echoes of folk-songs about retribution and killing.[70] A number of the figures in the play, with their generic titles, are themselves folk-song regulars: above all, the Drum Major, though also the Jew, the Journeymen, and even the Captain.[71] Moreover, the resemblance is a matter of character as well as name: Büchner's Drum Major is behaviourally the Drum Major of folk-song, the epitome of the erotically attractive man and aggressive seducer.[72] Finally, even the plot episodes of *Woyzeck* are echoes of folk-song. This is not to say they are not also reality: the ability of the documentary reports which Büchner read to replicate folk-song scenes simply confirms the latter's veracity. But numerous of Büchner's selections from and additions to his documentary material seem to have been suggested by, and to be designed to suggest, folk-song. The 'Liebesmord', the stabbing, the red blood motif and the removal of the ring replicate the famous 'Der eifersüchtige Knabe', the archetypal song of murderous jealousy.[73] The murder in the wood, the victim's fear, the blood on the clothing and the excuses in the inn are episodes from the equally famous Bluebeard song 'Ulrich und Ännchen'.[74] Furthermore, these, and related scenes and moments, also appear in numerous other well-known folk-songs.[75]

What emerges from all of this is that *Woyzeck* is not only a play *about* the Volk, though it is certainly that, but to some degree a *folk play*, too.[76] It is a play realised, or seeking to be realised, from a perspective of the Volk (the perspective from which, for example, the Doctor, the Captain, the Jew and the Fool are envisaged), and incorporating cultural productions (folk-song, folktale, and so on) through which popular wisdom and understanding express themselves. The play is a strenuous attempt at realisation of the project of a 'new cultural life in the Volk' by going beyond the educated class's observation of the Volk to an intimation of it and its being, as it were, from within.

Elements of Büchner's project are by no means without their parallels even before his own time. As my introduction suggested, Herder's praise in the 1770s of the consciousness of the Volk as possessing a profundity and intuitiveness which has been lost by modern, civilised, rational man, and which they, the Volk, show particularly in their art, is certainly a background to Büchner's undertaking, as is Herder's advocacy of an endeavour to collect and imitate that art, as being a path towards regaining such lost harmony.[77] Various German Romantic writers at the turn of the nineteenth century adapted and extended Herder's conception in line with their own feudal-medievalistic nostalgias; and after the Restoration, versions of these notions also began to appear, anticipating Büchner, in conjunction with a liberal- or radical-democratic ideology, notably (as we saw in the previous chapter) in *Die Harzreise* and other works of the 1820s by Heine. However, what writers prior to 1830 were often seeking in an idealised, effectively pre-lapsarian image of the Volk, and what they tended to be preoccupied with, were pointers for the improving self-development of the educated class. There is certainly an idealisation in Büchner, too, although his Volk are emphatically lapsed. But for him, in *Woyzeck*, the educated class is no longer of concern, and his interest is the development of the Volk itself. He takes the tradition of Herder's folk revival conclusively – a good deal more conclusively even than the Heine of the 1830s – into the domain of plebeian revolution. For that, ultimately, is the implication of his play *Woyzeck*. In a letter of 1836, Büchner had explicitly denied that the agency of bourgeois intellectuals could induce revolutionary change.[78] What his play therefore intimates is how, with Woyzeck himself as a kind of symbolic pathfinder breaking through the oppressive ideological myths of the common people's superiors to a new clarity,[79] and on the basis of an authentic culture and consciousness which they possess, a revolutionary reconstituting of society can be generated from within the 'große Klasse' itself.[80]

Notes

1. Charles Parker, 'The Actuality of Working-Class Speech', in *Workers and Writers. Proceedings of the Conference on Present-Day Working-Class Literature in Britain and West Germany, held in Birmingham, October 1975*, ed. Wilfried van der Will, Birmingham, 1976, pp. 98–105, see pp. 102 and 104. The present chapter is a revised version of an article first published in *Modern Language Review* 86 (1991), 627–44.

2. Letter to Karl Gutzkow, June (?) 1836; in Büchner, *Werke und Briefe. Münchner Ausgabe*, ed. Karl Pörnbacher, Gerhard Schaub, Hans-Joachim Simm and Edda Ziegler, Munich, 1988, p. 320. All references to Büchner's writings in the text and notes of the present chapter, prefaced by 'MA', relate to that edition. What Büchner understands by 'Volk', needless to say, is not precisely the industrial proletariat which Parker has in mind. The 'große Klasse' of the poor is located somewhat differently, its deprivation by implication differently explained, by the post-Marxian Parker in the modern era than by the early socialist Büchner in his early-industrial, only incipiently urbanised world of 1830s Germany. But the affinities between the two authors' perceptions and ideals bridge this divide, such as it is, and indeed are the more striking in view of it. It is also noteworthy, as my introduction observed, that Büchner's use of 'Volk', unlike that of all the other authors discussed here, even Heine, is entirely devoid of a national component.

3. This, it seems to me, is primarily the force the word 'geistig' has as Büchner here uses it – which none of its more customary renderings into English ('intellectual', 'mental', 'spiritual') convey. I do not claim novelty for associating the phrase 'neues geistiges Leben' with Büchner's literary works, though I shall show an extent and complexity in the undertaking the phrase signals which has not elsewhere been demonstrated. One earlier writer who makes the connection is Hans-Jürgen Geerdts in his short, polemical article 'Georg Büchners Volksauffassung', *Weimarer Beiträge* 9 (1963), 642–9 (see 648). His prime point, asserted more than it is demonstrated, is that Büchner seeks to reveal the 'Unzerstörbarkeit und Integrität der Volksmassen' in his plays by (above all) displaying 'den reichen Schatz der Volkspoesie' and releasing 'die Quellen der Volksweisheit' which this contains (p. 648). This judgement is rather narrow and ingenuous in its tone, but points in the right direction. Even more fleeting but basically similar observations are also found in one or two subsequent commentaries. In addition, Büchner's use of folk-song, specifically, is the subject of two pieces, by Gonthier-Louis Fink ('Volkslied und Verseinlage in den Dramen Büchners', *Deutsche Vierteljahresschrift* 35 (1961), 558–93) and Dirk Mende (*Untersuchungen zu den Volksliedeinlagen in den Dramen Georg Büchners*, Diss., Stuttgart, 1972). These are discussed in the relevant sections below. Otherwise, Walter Hinck's general survey 'Georg Büchner', in *Deutsche Dichter des neunzehnten Jahrhunderts*, ed. Benno von Wiese, Berlin, 1969, pp. 200–22, though it does not mention Büchner's notion of the 'neues geistiges Leben' and altogether has little space for detail, foreshadows more aspects of my topic than anyone else: the fact of Büchner's aesthetic 'Hinwendung zu [den] Volksschichten', his desire to render the language and consciousness of the Volk (though various of Hinck's perceptions on this strike me as mistaken – see below), and the notion of a *Volkskunst* dimension to *Woyzeck*. See Hinck, pp. 212, 217f.

4. See above, introduction, and cf. George Rudé, *The Crowd in the French Revolution*, Oxford, 1959, for example, pp. 42–3, 137–9.
5. I/5, MA 84, and letter to Gutzkow, June (?) 1836, MA 319f.. By a central irony of the text, the Dantonists with their sensualist philosophy (and especially Danton, who has drawn some further conclusions which his comrades have not) are closer to a perception of this reality than the Christian moralist ascetic Robespierre and his party. But the Dantonists, in living according to their philosophy and indulging themselves physically, ensure their own defeat and destruction by the party of Robespierre, whose ascetic self-denial resembles much more closely the life of unwilling deprivation which the Volk lead, and thus tips the scales of the latter's allegiance. See the crucial final speech of the Second Citizen in the mob scene before the Palace of Justice, III/10, MA 121.
6. Pace Geerdts, 'Büchners Volksauffassung', who contends that the Volk are the 'eigentliche Helden des *Danton*' (p. 643).
7. *Lenz*, MA 144. This summary translation, like other translations in the essay, is my own.
8. *Lenz*, MA 144, *Dantons Tod*, II/3, MA 95f.; letter from Büchner to his family, 28 July 1835, MA 306.
9. There are echoes of (at the very least) *Hamlet* V/1, *Julius Caesar* III/3, *Coriolanus* I/1, *Henry VI, Part Two* IV/2, *As You Like It* III/2 (see Shakespeare, *Complete Works*, ed. W.J. Craig, Oxford, 1971, pp. 901, 836, 701, 553, 228 respectively). Cf. especially Josef Jansen, *Georg Büchner: 'Dantons Tod'. Erläuterungen und Dokumente*, Stuttgart, 1969, pp. 86–90; also Walter Hinderer, *Büchner-Kommentar*, Munich, 1977, pp. 106–8, 119–22.
10. *Lenz*, MA 145; *Leonce und Lena*, III/1, MA 181. Cf. also remarks by his friend Wilhelm Schulz, dating from 1851, on Büchner's deep 'Achtung vor dem Volke, . . . Liebe zum Volke', and so forth; quoted by Thomas Michael Mayer, 'Büchner und Weidig – Frühkommunismus und revolutionäre Demokratie', in *Georg Büchner, I/II: Text und Kritik, Sonderband*, ed. Heinz Ludwig Arnold, Munich, 1979, pp. 16–298 (see p. 137).
11. Wolfgang Martens, 'Zum Menschenbild Georg Büchners. *Woyzeck* und die Marionszene in *Dantons Tod*', *Wirkendes Wort* 8 (1957/58), 13–20 (see p. 14).
12. This essentially is the one-sided view offered by Reinhold Grimm, 'Coeur und Carreau. Über die Liebe bei Georg Büchner', in *Georg Büchner, I/II: Text und Kritik, Sonderband*, pp. 299–326 (see pp. 307–11).
13. Marion has a focal role in John Reddick's view of the play. His essay of 1980, 'Mosaic and Flux: Georg Büchner and the Marion Episode in *Dantons Tod*', *Oxford German Studies* 11 (1980), 40–67, offers a perspective of erotic idealisation not far from that of Reinhold Grimm. However, in Reddick's book *Georg Büchner. The Shattered Whole*, Oxford, 1994, this is significantly amended to acknowledge and make sense of the character's ambivalence and the radically antithetical sexual messages the play contains (see pp. 166–203, esp. pp. 181–3, 191f.).
14. See Gonthier-Louis Fink, 'Volkslied und Verseinlage in den Dramen Büchners', p. 576.
15. Fink, 'Volkslied und Verseinlage', p. 579.
16. Lucile's 'Es ist ein Schnitter', IV/9, MA 132f., and *Des Knaben Wunderhorn. Alte deutsche Lieder*, eds Ludwig Achim von Arnim and Clemens Brentano, 3 vols, Heidelberg, 1806–8, 1: 55. *Wunderhorn* is reproduced with original page numbers in Brentano, *Sämtliche Werke und Briefe*, ed. Jürgen Behrens, Wolfgang Frühwald and Detlev Lüders, Stuttgart, 1975ff., vols 6–9.

17. II/2, MA 93. See Wilhelm Hauff, *Werke*, ed. Max Drescher, 6 vols, Berlin, n.d., 6: 135f. Cf. Ludwig Erk and Franz Böhme, *Deutscher Liederhort*, 3 vols, Leipzig, 1893, 2: 521f. Sources for Büchner's folk-songs have been extensively proposed in commentaries on his works, particularly the older commentaries, if not always in a disciplined and unspeculative way. Most recently, they have been tabulated in Dirk Mende's unanalytical *Untersuchungen zu den Volksliedeinlagen in den Dramen Georg Büchners*, pp. 287–301. The present discussion, where it is concerned with Büchner's use of folk-song (in relation to *Dantons Tod* and particularly to *Woyzeck*), sifts the putative sources critically, adds some new proposals, and offers interpretive clarification of what it was he chose to use, how it was used, and why. Fink's article, 'Volkslied und Verseinlage', the one piece other than Mende's devoted specifically to Büchner's folk-song usage, also aims to be a full survey of Büchner's songs, but without Mende's philological exhaustiveness; instead it offers somewhat more analysis, as it pursues a general thesis of the songs' role as an anti-idealistic 'chorus of nihilism' running through Büchner's plays (Fink, p.588; cf. also p. 568). It is thus mainly occupied with viewing the folk-songs as reinforcers of the works' existential themes, rather than as part of a wider project of Büchner's concerning the Volk itself. Several of its judgements are nevertheless useful, and are referred to here in text and notes.

18. See Erk/Böhme, *Deutscher Liederhort*, 2: 523–5 ('Abschiedsklage'), 463 ('Rechte Liebe'). Cf. also *Wunderhorn*, 1: 282 ('Der eifersüchtige Knabe') and 2: 19 ('Lenore', the *Wunderhorn* version).

19. Cf. Mende, *Untersuchungen zu den Volksliedeinlagen*, pp. 174, 182, who notes this effect.

20. See Act II/1, MA 175; II/2, MA 177f.

21. *Der gestiefelte Kater, Prinz Zerbino.* Cf. Hinderer, *Büchner-Kommentar*, esp. pp. 131, 134.

22. Martens, 'Zum Menschenbild Georg Büchners', p. 20.

23. Ibid., p. 16.

24. Respectively H1,4; H4,2; H4,1; H4,15; H4,11 and H4,14; H2,3 and H1,2; H4,4; H4,13 and H4,17 (MA 252, 235, 249, 247–9, 237–9, 248, 250). I use Lehmann's now largely standard system of scene designations (Werner Lehmann, *Textkritische Noten. Prolegomena zur Hamburger Büchner-Ausgabe*, Hamburg, 1967, p. 41). In this I follow the *Münchner Ausgabe* of Büchner of 1988 (see earlier note), from which edition's 'gründlich revidiert' version of the play (see MA 622) all quotations are also drawn.

25. Cf. Volker Klotz, *Geschlossene und offene Form im Drama*, Munich, 1960, p. 166: 'verschiedenartige Sprachbereiche . . . prallen aufeinander'.

26. Letter to Karl Gutzkow, Strasbourg, 1835, MA 311.

27. These 'systems of understanding' are exemplified respectively by (inter alia): the Doctor's 'unwissenschaftlich' rage (H4,8, MA 243), the Captain's 'Liebe' which is sexual desire (H4,5, MA 241); the Doctor's non-comprehension of Woyzeck's gentleness, the Captain's of his pity (H3,1, MA 251; H4,5, MA 240); the Doctor's and the Captain's codes in conflict, idealism and scientific empiricism at odds within the Doctor himself (H4,9, MA 244; H4,8, MA 242f.; and cf. Silvio Vietta, 'Sprachkritik bei Büchner', *Georg-Büchner-Jahrbuch* 2 (1982), 144–56, esp. 147, 153).

28. Klotz, *Geschlossene und offene Form*, p. 223.

29. Or: 'I'm only human'. I understand 'Mensch' here in its obvious sense, as 'human being', and am not persuaded by the alternative interpretation of this

line, as meaning principally 'Am I a whore?' (see, for example, Hinderer, *Büchner-Kommentar*, p. 198; Lothar Bornscheuer, *Georg Büchner: 'Woyzeck'. Erläuterungen und Dokumente*, Stuttgart, 1972, p. 8). As examples given in the Grimms' dictionary show, 'Mensch' in its pejorative sense of 'loose woman' ('*das* Mensch') was simply not used in this way, with the indefinite article and unqualified. See Jacob and Wilhelm Grimm, *Deutsches Wörterbuch*, ed. Moritz Heyne, 16 vols, Leipzig, 1885–1954, 12: 2033–8.

30. Cf. Bornscheuer, *'Woyzeck'. Erläuterungen*, p. 6.

31. Bornscheuer (*'Woyzeck'. Erläuterungen*, p. 23) reports an earlier commentator's view that Büchner had either misunderstood this saying, or consciously changed its meaning.

32. Parker, 'Working-Class Speech', pp. 101f, 99. For the uninitiated, 'rock' is a confection sold in British seaside resorts, a stick of pink-coated white sugar, through the whole length of which the town's name runs in small red lettering.

33. One might add, incidentally, that there is corroboration that Büchner was indeed pursuing a linguistic representation of the kind I have described in the fact that it is distinctly less stringently achieved in the earlier manuscripts of the play than in the final one. It is in the early manuscripts that we find the over-abstract Woyzeck of phrases such as the famous 'Jeder Mensch ist ein Abgrund, es schwindelt einen, wenn man hinabsieht' (H2,8, MA 217 – a scene actually crossed out by Büchner). Comparison of the last manuscript (H4) with these indicates a fairly systematic attempt at excision of such lines (compare H2,7, MA 216, with H4,9, MA 227), a general paring down of utterance (compare H2,6, MA 214, with H4,8, MA 226: Woyzeck becomes less verbose; cf. Bo Ullman, *Die sozialkritische Thematik im Werk Georg Büchners*, Stockholm, 1972, p. 105f.), but an augmentation of its associative-metaphoric dimension (compare H1,2, MA 200, first with H2,2, MA 210, then with H4,2, MA 220).

34. Helmut Krapp, *Der Dialog bei Georg Büchner*, Darmstadt, 1958, pp. 79–84.

35. Klotz, *Geschlossene und offene Form*, pp. 174–6.

36. Hinck, 'Georg Büchner', p. 216f. This disposition to cast Woyzeck as a primitive is one shared by numerous other critics. See, for example, Mende, *Untersuchungen zu den Volksliedeinlagen*, p. 102.

37. Ullman, *Die sozialkritische Thematik*, pp. 108f.

38. An extended critique of several of these commentators (though not of their assertions about the language of the Volk) is undertaken by John Guthrie, *Lenz and Büchner: Studies in Dramatic Form*, Frankfurt/M., 1984, esp. pp. 137–57.

39. The latter also have a measure of access to the restricted code, however, whilst the former are limited to this alone. Note that this account is of Bernstein's mature theory; the theory had passed through various prior stages.

40. Basil Bernstein, 'Social Class, Language and Socialization', in *Language and Social Context*, ed. Pier Paolo Giglioli, Harmondsworth, 1972, pp. 157–78 (see p. 164).

41. See ibid., pp. 172, 164f.

42. Ibid., p. 167f.

43. Ibid., p. 169f.

44. Although this is, of course, quite close to Klotz's view of Woyzeck, quoted above.

45. William Labov, 'The Logic of Nonstandard English', in *Language and Social Context*, ed. Giglioli, pp. 179–215.

46. See, for example, Alfons Glück, 'Der *Woyzeck*. Tragödie eines Paupers', in *Georg*

Büchner: 1813–1837. Revolutionär, Dichter, Wissenschaftler, Basel, 1987, pp. 325–32: 'Volkssprache und Dialekt hat Büchner mit geradezu phonetischer Genauigkeit festgehalten' (p. 331); similarly Julian Hilton, *Georg Büchner*, London, 1982, p. 137. Against this, Lehmann, *Textkritische Noten*, p. 47: 'Der *Woyzeck* ist kein Mundartenstück . . .'. See also Thomas Michael Mayer, 'Zu einigen neuen Lesungen und zur Frage des "Dialekts" in den *Woyzeck*-Handschriften', *Georg-Büchner-Jahrbuch* 7 (1988/89), 172–218.

47. Letter to Minna Jaeglé, 20 January 1837, MA 325.

48. This is on the presumption that many of the biblical elements in the *Landbote* were indeed Büchner's, as Thomas Michael Mayer argues. See Mayer, 'Büchner und Weidig', chap.3, esp. pp. 186f., 229 (and MA 447f.). Cf. also Büchner, letter to Karl Gutzkow, June (?) 1836, MA 319f.

49. Klotz, *Geschlossene und offene Form*, p. 199, note 348.

50. See respectively H4,16, MA 249; H4,6, MA 241; H4,1 and H4,8, MA 235, 243; H4,5, MA 240; H4,11, MA 247f.

51. Notwithstanding the presence of a Marie in Lenz's *Die Soldaten*, one of the likely models for Büchner's play.

52. Signalled above all in the 'Testamentszene', H4,17, MA 250. See, for example, Franz Mautner, 'Wortgewebe, Sinngefüge und "Idee" in Büchners *Woyzeck*', *Deutsche Vierteljahresschrift* 35 (1961), 521–57 (p. 544 and note 31); Wolfgang Martens, 'Über Georg Büchners *Woyzeck*', *Jahrbuch des Wiener Goethe-Vereins* 84/85 (1980/81), 145–56 (p. 154). Cf. also Hinderer, *Büchner-Kommentar*, p. 219f.

53. 'Die Sterntaler', 'Die sieben Raben' and 'Das singende springende Löweneckerchen'; these titles are noted in various places, including, with some discussion, in Hinderer, *Büchner-Kommentar*, p. 234. See Brüder Grimm, *Kinder- und Hausmärchen*, ed. Heinz Rölleke, 3 vols, Stuttgart, 1980, 1: 154–6, 2: 17–24, 269f.

54. See, for example, Vladimir Propp's famous *Morphology of the Folktale*, Bloomington, Indiana, 1958.

55. 'Auf der Welt ist kein Bestand', manifestly; 'Der is ins Wasser gefalle' is a drowning song (see the longer version reproduced by Bornscheuer,'*Woyzeck*'. *Erläuterungen*, p. 35); 'Ringle, ringel, Rosekranz' (cf. *Wunderhorn*, 3: KL86(b), and Erk/Böhme, *Deutscher Liederhort*, 3: 601f. and 604) is a falling-down song, very close to the English 'Ring a Ring o' Roses' song of the Plague.

56. See Fink, 'Volkslied und Verseinlage', pp. 587–92.

57. For example, H4,11, MA 247, the seduction/faithlessness song 'Ein Jäger aus der Pfalz'; cf. Erk/Böhme, *Deutscher Liederhort*, 3: 315.

58. For example, H4,1, MA 235, 'Saßen dort zwei Hasen'; see Erk/Böhme, *Deutscher Liederhort*, 1: 527.

59. See Michael Perraudin, *Heinrich Heine: Poetry in Context. A Study of 'Buch der Lieder'*, Oxford, 1989, chap. 5, 'Heine and the Folk-song', esp. p. 153. Cf. also Mende, *Untersuchungen zu den Volksliedeinlagen*, p. 18.

60. Cf. Fink, 'Volkslied und Verseinlage', p. 560.

61. The 'Warum? Darum!' exchange, H1,14, MA 252, and *Wunderhorn*, 3: KL73(d), cf. Bornscheuer,'*Woyzeck*'. *Erläuterungen*, p. 26; 'Hansel spann deine sechs Schimmel an', H4,2, MA 236, cf. Erk/Böhme, *Deutscher Liederhort*, 3: 406.

62. For example, 'Das Wirtshaus an der Lahn', H4,10, H1,17, MA 246, 253; see Erk/Böhme, *Deutscher Liederhort*, 2: 653.

63. August Stöber, *Elsässisches Volksbüchlein*, Strasbourg, 1842: 'Mädel mach's

Ladel zu', H4,4, MA 239; 'Der is ins Wasser gefalle', H3,2, MA 255. See Mende, *Untersuchungen zu den Volksliedeinlagen*, p. 295; Hinderer, *Büchner-Kommentar*, p. 258.

64. Notably proposals by Bergemann, in his edition, *Georg Büchners Sämtliche Werke und Briefe*, Leipzig, 1922, and Hans Winkler, *Georg Büchners 'Woyzeck'*, Diss., Greifswald, 1925; reproduced particularly by Bornscheuer,*'Woyzeck'. Erläuterungen*, for example, p. 6.

65. See Hinderer, *Büchner-Kommentar*, p. 209; cf. also Bornscheuer,*'Woyzeck'. Erläuterungen*, p. 7. Against this: Thomas Michael Mayer, 'Georg Büchner. Eine kurze Chronik zu Leben und Werk', in *Georg Büchner, I/II: Text und Kritik, Sonderband*, pp. 357–425, see p. 421, quoting Büchner's friend Wilhelm Schulz and others.

66. Mende's reflection, 'Büchner wird sie seiner Umwelt abgelauscht haben', does not seem very helpful; Mende, *Untersuchungen zu den Volksliedeinlagen*, p. 49. Similarly Fink, 'Volkslied und Verseinlage', p. 559.

67. In particular, the technique of quotational montage which seems to underlie *Leonce und Lena*.

68. For example, letter of 9–12 March 1834 to Minna, MA 288, and *Dantons Tod* (1835), II/5, MA 100, on 'das Muß'; or letter of June (?) 1836 to Gutzkow, MA 319, and *Dantons Tod*, I/5, MA 84, on 'materielles Elend' as 'Hebel' of the Revolution.

69. Caroline Schulz; quoted by Bornscheuer,*'Woyzeck'. Erläuterungen*, p. 70.

70. H4,4, MA 239; H4,7, MA 242; H1,19, MA 207. See such folk-songs as 'Der eifersüchtige Knabe' (Erk/Böhme, *Deutscher Liederhort*, 1: 163–70; *Wunderhorn*, 1: 282), 'Der gerächte Bruder' (Erk/Böhme, *Deutscher Liederhort*, 1: 160), 'Ulrich und Ännchen' (ibid., 1: 135; *Wunderhorn*, 1: 274). On the 'rote Schnur' image, see also Heine, *Memoiren*, in *Sämtliche Schriften*, ed. Klaus Briegleb, Munich, 1969–76, 6/1: 601 (edition henceforth as 'B'). On the blood motif in general in *Woyzeck*, see Werner Lehmann, *Textkritische Noten*, p. 61, also Hinderer, *Büchner-Kommentar*, pp. 226, 240f.

71. See, among many others: Erk/Böhme, *Deutscher Liederhort*, 2: 649 ('Tambours Liebeswerbung'); 2: 653 ('Das Wirtshaus an der Lahn'); 3: 283 ('Mädchen, trau den Soldaten nicht!'); 3: 599 ('Die verwandelte Katze'); 3: 424–41; 3: 259 ('Der unerbittliche Hauptmann').

72. See especially Erk/Böhme, *Deutscher Liederhort*, 2: 649, 'Tambours Liebeswerbung'. Cf. also the 'Tambour' in Heine's *Ideen. Das Buch Le Grand* (1827); Heine, B 2: 264, 271.

73. See above, note 70.

74. See note 70; also chapter 5, below.

75. For example, 'Meuchelmord der Geliebten' (Erk/Böhme, *Deutscher Liederhort*, 1: 180), 'Der gerächte Bruder' (ibid., 1: 160), and, generally, see ibid., 1: 112–92. One further suggestion which has been made as to Büchner's play's *volkstümlich* character concerns its structure, supposedly on the episodic 'Sprünge und Würfe' principle of a folk ballad according to Herder's analysis of the 1770s (see below, note 77). See, for example, Hinck, 'Georg Büchner', p. 218, and Mende, *Untersuchungen zu den Volksliedeinlagen*, p. 19f. But, as Guthrie has argued (*Lenz and Büchner*, p. 157), this is really quite questionable as a description of the structure of Büchner's play. The notion is best disregarded.

76. Cf. Hinck's (over-)statement ('Georg Büchner', p. 218): '*Woyzeck* ist eines der reinsten Beispiele balladesker Dramatik'.

77. Johann Gottfried Herder, 'Auszug aus einem Briefwechsel über Ossian und die Lieder alter Völker', in *Sämmtliche Werke*, ed. Bernhard Suphan, Berlin, 1877–99, 5: 159–207, esp. pp. 181–3, 186, 190, 201.

78. Letter of June (?) 1836 to Gutzkow, MA 319.

79. Pace Thomas Michael Mayer, 'Büchner-Chronik', p. 415, who sees the character Woyzeck rather as a portrait of a *non*-revolutionary state of consciousness. Similarly Geerdts, 'Büchners Volksauffassung', p. 647.

80. This is an interestingly deterministic view of popular revolution. To that extent it is a continuation of the revolutionary determinism which preoccupied Büchner in *Dantons Tod* ('. . . gräßliche[r] Fatalismus der Geschichte'; MA 288), except that the logic is now made to point to a positive, non-'gräßlich' outcome of the revolutionary-historical process.

3

The Fear of the *Volk*.
Conservative Literature of the
Social Question: Eichendorff
and Gotthelf

The impact which political and social developments of the *Vormärz* had on conservative minds, including the minds of conservative literary authors, is one of the most interesting aspects of the cultural history of the period. The July Revolution of 1830, as has already been noted, was a turning point in political consciousness, signalling to both partisans and opponents of radical change that the spirit of 1789, or perhaps of 1792, was still abroad in Europe. Despite the continuing and intensifying pressure of censorship, there was a new specificity and acerbity to political utterance in German after 1830, as writers reflected the greatly increased public sense of the centrality of political matters. At the same time, as we said, the demographic and economic developments of the 1830s and 1840s – population expansion, pauperisation, migration, incipient urbanisation and industrialisation – created an awareness of social forces and processes which had previously not significantly impinged on the educated consciousness. In particular, of course, the presence of the class of the mass poor, alienated from the values of civil society and threatening its stability and order, became an increasing focus of attention and matter of concern in the years up to 1848. For radicals such as Büchner and Heine, the notion that these masses and their sufferings were in some way related to modern directions in economic governance was near to hand, and they drew conclusions about the inevitability and/or propriety of social revolution as the solution to such evils. For liberals, the solutions to a phenomenon which they, too, could not overlook were much more difficult, since they tended to assent to, and desire the promotion of, the very processes – freedom of trade, freedom of employment, freedom of production – which were at the root of that phenomenon. This is, roughly speaking, the liberal conundrum on which the 1848 Revolution in Germany collapsed. For conservatives of the Vormärz, meanwhile – those who in one way or another dissented from the spreading ideology of economic and political liberty, feared its destructive social and moral consequences and preferred the maintenance or restitution of systems of traditionally based authority and order – it was possible again to view the growing signs of disorder and incipient social revolution with comparative clarity. There is a notable congruence at the period between the analysis of the 'Social Question' – the current parlous condition of the common people, its causes and its likely consequences – which is offered by conservative German political thinkers, such as Adam Müller, Goerres, Eichendorff and (most powerfully and emphatically) Franz von Baader,[1] and those of the revolutionary left, notably Marx. Even if the alternative Utopias they proposed were diametrically opposed, they shared the sense that the values and practices of political and economic liberalism were the cause, not the cure, of the pending social chaos.

It is as a consequence of such an awareness that some of the most exciting literary reflections produced during the Vormärz on the revolutionary stirrings at the base of society are conservative ones. In particular, there are two notable novellas from the years between the 1830 and 1848 Revolutions which – whatever other thematic preoccupations they have – are classic commentaries on this issue. These are Eichendorff's *Das Schloß Dürande*, of 1836, and Gotthelf's *Die schwarze Spinne*, of 1842. They are works by writers of fairly widely varying generational, social, regional and intellectual experiences – Romantic and post-Romantic, aristocratic and bourgeois, Roman Catholic and Calvinistic Lutheran Protestant, Silesian-Prussian and Bernese Swiss – whose conservatism accordingly also takes interestingly diverse forms, as we will see. But the texts have significant common features, too. They particularly resemble each other stylistically, in the oblique, quasi-allegorical approach which they employ towards their social subject-matter. The reasons for this are partly aesthetic, partly commercial and probably partly temperamental: the authors are in one way or another party to a Romantic heritage of symbolic fictional writing; their readerships did not especially wish to be told in a specific and concrete way about the prospect of social disorder; and there was probably a degree of reluctance on the part of the authors themselves to address the topic of revolution in an absolutely unmediated fashion, at least in literature. The result is a shared intricacy and allusiveness which more realistic approaches would not achieve. In addition – on a more thematic level – the works relate external social with inner psychological order; they locate a kind of salvation in a kind of spirituality; and they present the masses in ways which are quasi-mythic and in the end more or less dehumanising. In their similarities, as in their differences, these texts are a literary exemplification of the response by the conservative mind of the Vormärz to the threat of social revolution which preoccupied and terrified the age.

Eichendorff and *Das Schloß Dürande*: the Psychosis of Revolution

Eichendorff, despite the unworldly reputation he had in his own time and often subsequently,[2] was a deeply political writer, not just personally interested in the public events and developments of his day but with a world view in which politics – in particular, the politics of class – were absolutely central. Even the aesthetic to which he adhered and which was the basis of that reputation – namely a rejection of realistic representation and a seeming avoidance of real-world subject matter – was to a significant degree motivated by political ideology: realist literalism and specificity were for him symptoms of the pernicious materialism of the increasingly bourgeois-philistine age in which he found himself, and creating a literature which was geographically and historically open and inexplicit, and which also required a significant measure of allegorical, non-literal reading, was an act of political resistance, counteracting the *Zeitgeist*.

Eichendorff's political philosophy, with which it is a little hard to empathise nowadays, is above all an affirmation of values residing in his own, aristocratic class. Workless, non-materialistic and irrational as they are, they have a dimension of spontaneous spirituality, an actual or potential link to God, which fits them uniquely for governance, as the only class capable of directing and unifying society in God's image. Eichendorff's ideal political form is a kind of enhanced Catholic feudalism, very like that of Novalis in *Die Christenheit oder Europa* (1799).[3] For Eichendorff, more or less as for Novalis, the civilised world has been degenerating and disintegrating since the Reformation, in a process which has led through the Enlightenment and its heedless, self-righteous individualism to the political and industrial Revolution, and will lead on further, either into 'allgemeine Barbarei'[4] ('Hinter diesen letzten Trümmern einer tausendjährigen Kultur lauert . . . die Anarchie, die Barbarei, und der Kommunismus; der Proletarier hat an der willkommenen Bresche, wie zur Probe, schon die Sturmleitern angelegt'[5]), or possibly to some kind of reactive 'Regeneration des Gesamtlebens',[6] a return to the values of Catholic aristocratism – which, since 'Gott . . . selbst die Weltgeschichte dichtet',[7] ought surely to be the aim of divine providence.

In Eichendorff's view, the real aristocracy has itself contributed to the decline. Especially from the Thirty Years War onwards, so he indicates in the late essay *Der Adel und die Revolution* (probably written in 1857), a large proportion of the European nobility grew increasingly detached from its rural, landed roots, losing its old freedom, piety and *Naturwüchsigkeit* and becoming instead a servile, money-focused and amoral aristocracy of the court ('Dienstadel').[8] Their abuses and bad example were one cause of political revolution. Such a critique of sections of the aristocracy appears regularly throughout Eichendorff's work, from the decadent Prinz and Residenz in his first novel *Ahnung und Gegenwart*, through the depictions of Louis XVI's Versailles, and of old Dürande and his rococo chateau, in *Das Schloß Dürande*, to *Der Adel und die Revolution* and other texts of the 1850s. However, the aristocracy are as a class, he suggests, capable of regeneration, of reawakening to their old values, re-energising, and reassuming their ancient role of moral leadership. The virtuous Junker Graf Friedrich in *Ahnung und Gegenwart* is exploring such a vocation. The previously dissolute and unfulfilled young Graf Dürande in *Das Schloß Dürande* is stimulated into such a role in reaction to the French Revolution.[9] And if poems such as 'Wer rettet?' and 'Will's Gott!' (ca. 1848) attempt to see the revolution as God's purpose, a divinely induced clearing-of-the-decks to be followed by some kind of counter-revolutionary social regeneration under the sign of the cross, then the 'freie Söhne' who will or would construct the 'neuer Bau' (W 1: 451) cannot but be 'Aristokraten . . . , d.h. eine bevorzugte Klasse, die sich über die Massen erhebt, um sie zu lenken. Denn der Adel . . . ist . . . das ideale Element der Gesellschaft; er hat die Aufgabe, alles Große, Edle und Schöne, wie und wo es auch im Volke auftauchen mag, ritterlich zu wahren . . .

und somit erst wirklich lebensfähig zu machen' (W 5: 414). On the other hand, Eichendorff's conviction of the plausibility of such an outcome is always uncertain and seems to diminish over time. Friedrich retires to a monastery, to await a phase of conflict and chaos out of which the future golden age will eventually emerge (W 2: 379– 81). Young Dürande's heroic battle against the forces of revolution ends in his death, albeit with redemption (W 3: 460). Finally, the long French-Revolutionary poem *Robert und Guiscard* of 1854, a partial return to the subject matter of *Das Schloß Dürande*, ends with its surviving French aristocratic protagonist withdrawing permanently from public life into rather *biedermeierlich* domestic privacy (and morganatic marriage) in an arcadian Heidelberg (W 1: 676). Here there is a sense that the die really is cast for a modern world which passes the aristocracy by.

The moral decline and hoped-for recovery of the aristocracy is significant in Eichendorff's political scheme of things; but essentially more important is its concomitant, the rise to dominance of the bourgeois principle. Especially in the Restoration period, when educated German society in general was able largely to forget about the exterior pressures that had agitated it during the Napoleonic phase and concentrate on internal antagonisms, a good deal of Eichendorff's writing is a vituperative critique of middle-class values and their consequences. As suggested above, Eichendorff saw a world in which the rationalism, individualism, secularism, materialism and cosmopolitanism of the bourgeois enlightenment had cut man loose from the ties that bound him in harmonious community – communities of unreflecting faith, trust, obligation and love – and replaced these with delusory notions of rights and freedoms, behind which lay mere godless egotism. He termed the cultural process which he witnessed, ironically, 'eine allgemeine Seligsprechung der Menschheit', 'der vor lauter Hochmut endlich tollgewordene Rationalismus', 'eine Religion des Egoismus' (W 5: 408). The extensive satire of philistine material-ism, industriousness and utilitarian banality in *Aus dem Leben eines Taugenichts* – presented in opposition to the Taugenichts's own work-shy spirituality – is a serious manifestation of this critique.[10] By contrast, in Eichendorff's one previous published novella, *Das Marmorbild* of 1818, this dimension was wholly absent: in it the hero is emphatically designated an aristocrat ('Florio, ein junger Edelmann . . .'; W 2: 385), but the obstacles fac-ing him have no element of class conflict. By the same token, Eichendorff's novel *Dichter und ihre Gesellen* of 1834 differs from the pre-Restoration *Ahnung und Gegenwart* most notably in the elaborateness of its anti-bourgeois polemic, by the much greater sense it gives of the power and perniciousness of the bourgeois outlook (e.g. W 3: 278–83). And it ends, echoing but also deviating from the earlier novel, with its main hero resolving to set out into the world as a Catholic priest to join the great battle against the diabolic spread of an ideology of personal liberty and material self-interest – of the principle, 'Seid frei, und alles ist euer!' (W 3: 352.)

Already in the early years after the Restoration Eichendorff expressed in non-literary writings an awareness of the practical consequences of such an ideology for society, above all for those lower down the social scale. In *Über die Folgen von der Aufhebung der Landeshoheit der Bischöfe und der Klöster in Deutschland* (1819), he talks of how the replacement of an ecclesiastical-communitarian organisation of society by a modern (bourgeois) type of state, which views itself fundamentally as a compact for the securing of private property, leads to punitive exclusion of the propertyless: 'Die sehr beträchtliche Klasse der Armen [wird . . .] ganz eigentlich vogelfrei und außer dem Staate'.[11] Society ceases to be a 'geistige Gemeinschaft', with an unquestioning role of support for its poorer members, and becomes instead a repressive mechanism, the 'Staatszweck' achieved by means of 'eine wohlbediente Artillerie, eine wohlberittene Gendarmerie, mehrere Justizstellen und einige Galgen' (W 5: 472). Thus the modern ideology of freedom leaves the common people pauperised, oppressed and alienated.

This analysis did not for the time being impinge discernibly on Eichendorff's literary work. However, from the very beginning his literature entails a kind of rootedness in the common people. The poetry which was his earliest output emulated the folk-song patterns of metre, syntax, imagery and subject matter which he knew from Herder's *Volkslieder* and Arnim's and Brentano's *Des Knaben Wunderhorn*, and by implication shared those collections' cultural precepts. Thematically, such important early-Restoration texts as the poem 'Die zwei Gesellen'[12] and the story *Aus dem Leben eines Taugenichts* contain the clear implication that the Volk has the positive spiritual potential which the aristocracy also possesses. The Taugenichts is an honorary aristocrat, so it has been said, and as the character himself suggests.[13] And from *Ahnung und Gegenwart* through *Dichter und ihre Gesellen* to *Der Adel und die Revolution*, the best aristocracy is that which 'verst[eht . . .] noch das Volk, und [wird] vom Volke wieder begriffen'.[14] Eichendorff's starting point is an idealisation of and (at any rate notionally) a sympathy with the Volk, especially the rural Volk.

Until 1830, his literary texts maintain their idealisation securely. But the July Revolution marks a striking break, after which various changes occur.[15] Firstly, an extension of the kind of analysis which the earlier political essays had offered finds its way into literature. *Viel Lärmen um nichts* of 1832, for instance, contains one of German literature's first industrial scenes, a factory town in a valley, with its workers 'armes, ausgehungertes Volk': the scene says very clearly that capitalist economic organisation – 'die ernste praktische Richtung unserer Zeit', the factory owner calls it – impoverishes the masses (W 3: 27f.). Secondly, after 1830 Eichendorff seems unable any longer to create idealised individual characters from the Volk, as the Taugenichts had been. The story *Die Glücksritter* (published in 1841) is an interesting example. It has a Taugenichts-like character, the wandering musician and ex-soldier Siglhupfer, who in the end thwarts a band of robbers to find love. But Siglhupfer himself is an ambiguous figure: unlike the Taugenichts, he steals and lies, and he also has (and is remarked upon as having) a suspiciously good command of *Gaunersprache*, the language of robbers (W 3: 513, 526–8, 538). This is the Taugenichts turned brigand. Moreover – thirdly – the story as a whole is set in a context of social chaos and lawlessness, in the aftermath of the Thirty Years War. After 1830, Eichendorff has a striking propensity to set his stories in turbulent times: not only *Die Glücksritter*, but also, for instance, *Die Entführung* (ca. 1837), which takes place in the reign of Louis XV in France, in what is again said to be a time of brigandage and social anarchy (W 3: 470), and *Eine Meerfahrt* (1835/36), set in the West Indies in the era of the conquistador invasions. Even *Dichter und ihre Gesellen* has an extended interpellated narrative set in the Peninsular War (W 3: 187ff.); and the novel's version of modern Italy is interestingly infested with the Carbonari (W 3: 258f.). The basic early-Biedermeier tranquillity of *Das Marmorbild* and *Aus dem Leben eines Taugenichts* seems to have given way in Eichendorff's mind to a sense of prevailing social disorder.

Finally, and connected with this, a significant extension and reapplication of Eichendorff's habitual experiential themes seems to take place after 1830. The perils which threaten all Eichendorff's main characters, and which they either succumb to, or escape from through faith, are before 1830 primarily psycho-sexual. The daemonic, Dionysiac lure – imaged through unredeemed nature and various forms of non-Christian myth – which is experienced and eventually overcome by Florio, Friedrich and the Taugenichts, is of that character. After 1830, the erotic charge is diminished; and the 'Verwilderung' by which characters are threatened acquires a new social correlative. The chaos which is in individual characters' hearts standardly mirrors and is mirrored in the chaotic social world around them: so it is in *Eine Meerfahrt, Die Glücksritter, Die Entführung*, and other works.

The epitome of these new dispositions in Eichendorff's writing is, indeed, his story of the French Revolution, *Das Schloß Dürande*, published in 1836. The Volk that this text shows is multifarious, though it is almost entirely without individuality: Parisian rabble ('. . . ein wilder Haufe . . .: abgedankte Soldaten, müßige Handwerksbursche und dergleichen Hornkäfer, wie sie in der Abendzeit um die großen Städte schwärmen'; W 3: 438f.); a peasant community in pre-revolutionary harmony and happiness under monastic protection, then made miserable by the revolution (W 3: 433f., 453); revolutionary mobs, roaming the countryside and attacking aristocratic property (W 3: 449, 454, 456f.). The text tries sometimes to suggest that the last-named are corrupt and aberrant elements of the rural common people (W 3: 448, 456f.). But, although it blames the city as the fount of revolution, it does not insist that only the urban masses revolt. The aristocratic hero proclaims, as he prepares to defend his castle against the mob: 'Ich hab' nichts mit dem Volk, ich tat ihnen nichts als Gutes, wollen sie noch Besseres, sie sollen's ehrlich fodern, ich gäb's ihnen gern, abschrecken aber laß ich mir keine Hand breit meines alten Grund und Bodens' (W 3: 454f.). Whatever else this says, it acknowledges that even the rural Volk may be disaffected, out of control and an element in the forces of revolution. Also, whereas the text implies elsewhere that revolution requires leadership by malign individuals (W 3: 439, 456), Dürande's proclamation effectively admits that their revolt is autonomous mass action. This is a very long way from the individual and peaceable *Volksmensch* who is the Taugenichts.

The principals of *Das Schloß Dürande*, meanwhile, are rather like those of Eichendorff's novels, a constellation of major characters of whom each is in a different way psychically imperilled (though the story is unusual among his works in the final demise of all of its heroes). Gabriele, the female protagonist, is subject to the call of the wild, as other women round about her are not (W 3:

430-2); but she tends to be rescued in the most endangering moments, Taugenichts-like, by intrinsic piety. Thus at the beginning of the story, as rapacious lover and ferocious brother both lurk, she obeys a deep instinct and flees from them, through symbolic landscapes, to the physical and spiritual safety of a monastery (W 3: 426f.). None the less, she is actually the only one of the main characters endangered – after the fashion of earlier heroes of Eichendorff's – by her own eroticism. Her lover himself, the young Graf Hippolyt Dürande, mutates in the course of the story from dangerous seducer ('Du hast eigentlich recht falsche Augen, sagte sie . . .', '. . . wie ein Falk'; W 3: 424, 436) to noble, self-sacrificing hero, to a degree which suggests that Eichendorff's conception shifted during the writing and he neglected fully to tidy up the loose ends. But young Dürande is, in any event, envisaged as a product of the moribund world of the rococo aristocracy, bored, decadent and without beliefs, living as if accursed amidst its artificial gardens and dreary neo-classical palaces (W 3: 437f., 446). He is rather like earlier characters in Eichendorff – Friedrich's melancholic brother Rudolf in *Ahnung und Gegenwart* in his bizarre, denatured 'Waldschloß' (W 2: 335ff.), or the Taugenichts 'wie ein verwunschener Prinz' in his Italian castle (W 2: 514). But Dürande's condition is specifically a socio-historical one, the condition of his class, and he is rescued from it not by the sound of the post-horn and a letter from his Angel (as is the Taugenichts; W 2: 515-17), but by the new political idealism which the need to fight the revolution brings (W 3: 441).

Finally, the third protagonist, the master-huntsman Renald, who is Gabriele's brother and Dürande's enemy, is psychically threatened – like Dürande and unlike Gabriele – by impulses which are not identified as erotic, and the roots of which, in Eichendorff's account, are basically social. Renald's 'Verwilderung' (cf. W 3: 448), a descent into ferocity culminating in his leadership of revolutionary mobs on the rampage, is an effect of bourgeois mentality: enraged by Dürande's supposed seduction and abduction of his sister, he embarks on a campaign at law in Paris for the restitution of 'sein *Recht*' (W 3: 444), his fundamental rights under natural law – what Eichendorff elsewhere (in *Halle und Heidelberg*, of 1857) sarcastically called 'sogenanntes Naturrecht', 'Urrechte und Menschenveredelungen' (W 5: 417f.). At this point Renald learns of Dürande's innocence (W 3: 463), part-realises and part-represses his own transgression and, 'seines Lebens müde', sets fire to the castle and finds death, unredeemed, in the flames (W 3: 464f.).

This is indeed 'der vor lauter Hochmut endlich tollgewordene Rationalismus' (*Der Adel und die Revolution*; W 5: 408) – bourgeois enlightenment man, who, in his hubristic egotism, acknowledges no authority over his own conscience, no God-given, traditional hierarchy of respect and fealty, and who, with his 'alles verwischende Gleichmacherei' (W 5: 418), releases forces, 'gärende Elemente' (W 5: 407), in himself and the world which bring general destruction. 'Du aber hüte dich, das wilde Tier zu wecken in der Brust, daß es nicht plötzlich ausbricht und dich selbst zerreißt' (W 3: 465), the story memorably ends. Renald is, in short, a product of the *Zeitgeist* – which is also the *Zeitgeist* that engenders the French Revolution.

Renald's personal campaign in the story is intermingled with events around the outbreak of the revolution, as he journeys from pre-revolutionary rural Provence to a Paris in a state of incipient insurrection, and then returns during the succeeding wars to a Provence disrupted by the revolution. The story shows him entering the apocalyptic city and there staying at a cousin's inn ('der rote Löwe') filled with the rebellious riffraff ('ein wilder Haufe . . .', etc.; W 3: 438). Among these is a revolutionary orator, a diabolical figure intended to suggest Robespierre ('Bettler-Advokat'; W 3: 442), who approaches Renald, perceiving the rage that drives him, and predicts, despite Renald's own distaste, his coming revolutionary engagement ('Ihr seht aus wie ein Scharfrichter, der, das Schwert unter'm Mantel, zu Gerichte geht; es kommt die Zeit, gedenkt an mich, Ihr werdet der Rüstigsten einer sein bei der blutigen Arbeit'; W 3: 439). Later, when Renald and the others, together with the focus of the story, return to Provence, we are shown ancient social concord destroyed by the revolution: the idyllic world of pious obligations and protections around the priory of which Renald's aunt is abbess (W 3: 433f.) has been dissolved by a Paris commissar, the lands secularised and the population left in terror, as vengeful rabble advances across the countryside (W 3: 451–3). Renald's campaign is, in fact, not merely caught up in revolutionary events, but exemplifies and effectively incarnates the social and psychological processes which the revolution entails. The allegorical impulse which is so strong in Eichendorff's writing is manifested once more here: to a substantial degree, Renald *is* the French Revolution.

The association is reinforced in various ways. Above all, it is cemented by an adjunct of allegory, namely the story's patterns of metaphor and simile. The Revolution is imaged, in this story and widely in Eichendorff's time,[16] as fire, as lightning and storm ('Wetterleuchten'), as wild animal, and as diabolic possession (W 3: 449, 457, 460f.). At the same time, these are exactly the images which attach to the enraged Renald: 'Auf seiner Stirn zuckte es zuweilen, wie wenn es von ferne blitzte' (W 3: 425); 'Renald schüttelte sich wie ein gefesselter Löwe' (W 3: 438); 'Ihr kennt den Renald nicht, er kann entsetzlich sein, wie fressend Feuer – läßt man denn reißende Tiere frei aufs Feld?' (W 3: 450); '. . . als äugelte der Teufel mit ihm' (W 3 461); and other examples. Eichendorff, as it were, secures Renald's embodiment of the revolution tropically.[17]

A second notable element in the story's revolutionary referentiality is its striking Kleistian ingredient. As commentators have noted, Renald is modelled on Kleist's Michael Kohlhaas, likewise a bourgeois pursuing his *Recht* through the institutions of an aristocratic state as far as the monarch himself, and beyond, into revolt and mayhem. *Das Schloß Dürande* contains echoes of Kleist's story, not only with scenes that are repeated – the humiliating encounters with lawyers, the failed attempt to gain audience with the monarch, the incineration of the enemy's castle (W 3: 444–7, 464f.[18]) – but also with fairly specific words and phrases: 'Er wollte jetzt nur sein *Recht*', 'So hol ich mir auch mein *Recht*' (W 3: 444, 448) (*Kohlhaas*: '. . . versicherte, daß er sich Recht zu verschaffen wissen würde', 'So zweifle ich nicht, ich verschaffe mir Recht', 'daß mir . . . Recht werden muß'); 'er solle keine unnützen Flausen machen' (W 3: 445) (*Kohlhaas*: 'er . . . solle . . . die Staatskanzlei . . . mit solchen Plackereien und Stänkereien verschonen'; '. . . eine völlig grundlose und nichtsnutzige Plackerei'), etc.[19] In addition, it has interesting reminiscences of other work of Kleist's, specifically of the story *Das Bettelweib von Locarno*. The description, 'Renald, seines Lebens müde, hatte eine brennende Fackel ergriffen und das Haus an allen vier Ecken angesteckt' (W 3: 464), echoes the Marchese in *Das Bettelweib* ('Der Marchese, von Entsetzen überreizt, hatte eine Kerze genommen, und das [Schloß . . .] an allen vier Ecken, müde seines Lebens, angesteckt');[20] 'Das sind die Trümmer des alten Schlosses Dürande' (W 3: 465) invokes the beginning of Kleist's story;[21] and there are other details. Further, the sentence with which *Das Schloß Dürande* ends, 'Hüte dich, das wilde Tier zu wecken in der Brust, daß es nicht plötzlich ausbricht und dich selbst zerreißt' (W 3: 465; quoted earlier), is a version of one which Eichendorff later uses in his *Über die ethische und religiöse Bedeutung der neueren romantischen Poesie in*

Deutschland (published in 1847) explicitly to characterise Kleist the author:

> Hüte Jeder das wilde Tier in seiner Brust, daß es nicht plötzlich ausbricht und ihn selbst zerreißt! Denn das war Kleists Unglück und schwergebüßte Schuld, daß er diese, keinem Dichter fremde, dämonische Gewalt nicht bändigen konnte oder wollte, die . . . fast durch alle seine Dichtungen geht. So steigert sich in seiner besten Erzählung *Michael Kohlhaas* mit melancholischer Virtuosität, ja mit einer eigensinnigen Konsequenz . . . , das gekränkte, tiefe Rechtsgefühl eines einfachen Roßkamms bis zum wahnsinnigen Fanatismus, der rachelustig sich und das Land in Mord und Brand stürzt. (W 6: 227)[22]

Such a biographical approach to Kleist's heroes – presumably not only Kohlhaas, but also the finally deranged Marchese in *Das Bettelweib von Locarno*, and others too – may be misguided (though one is not entirely sure that it is). But the implicit view of Kohlhaas and his author which emerges from *Das Schloß Dürande* and *Über die ethische und religiöse Bedeutung der neueren romantischen Poesie* together is certainly remarkable and intelligent: Kohlhaas as a representation of bourgeois hubris leading to revolution; the story *Michael Kohlhaas* ultimately as a reflection on the French Revolution; and Kleist himself as a psychic product of the revolutionary Zeitgeist. These are notions which academic criticism of Kleist has only arrived at comparatively recently, after well over 150 years of effort.

Revolution for Eichendorff was not only a social but also a cultural and a psychological process. Cultural tendencies of the modern world – rationalist individualism, materialism, the rejection of divine or divinely ordained authority – entailed on an individual level a perilous loss of control over destructive, chaotic urges in the subconscious, urges against which, in a sense, all individual human life is an enduring struggle. And on a social level, permitting such a system of beliefs or such a condition of mind to become predominant resulted in an equivalent loss of social cohesion and control. Society as a whole succumbed to these impulses and relapsed collectively into 'Barbarei' and 'Bestialität' (W 5: 363, 414). Eichendorff in effect saw revolution as a kind of psychosis, rather in the same way as some writers of the period after the Second World War in Germany saw fascism.[23] Clearly the warning: 'Du aber hüte dich, das wilde Tier zu wecken in der Brust, daß es nicht plötzlich ausbricht und dich selbst zerreißt' (W 3: 465) is simultaneously an injunction to individual-psychological and to socio-political restraint and self-control, elements which Eichendorff sees as not just analogous, but causally linked. In the context of the decade of the 1830s in particular, with its resurgent revolutionary politics and its economic changes, combined with an evident and frightening growth in symptoms of disintegration (population growth, migration, impoverishment, crime), the analysis thrust itself upon him. The Enlightenment has released the masses into a condition of anarchy: 'Die zärtliche Humanität fraternisierte mit der Bestialität des Freiheitspöbels' (W 5: 414); and the only conceivable rescue from this horror is a restoration of social and individual-psychological control on Christian spiritual principles.[24]

Jeremias Gotthelf: Poverty, Revolution and Myth. *Die schwarze Spinne* and *Die Armennot*

Like Eichendorff, Jeremias Gotthelf too was a Christian conservative, a critic of the liberal Zeitgeist who blamed liberalism for the degenerate, chaotic and potentially revolutionary condition of the world that he perceived, but who also hoped for and sought to predict – in fiction, journalistic and essayistic writing, and elsewhere – a moral rebirth of society and politics according to sacral values. This much and more the two authors shared; yet in other respects there was a world between them. Gotthelf – the name adopted for himself as public Conscience of the Nation by 'Pfarrer [Albert] Bitzius zu Lützelflüh im Kanton Bern'[25] – lived in an environment which may have been subject to the same economic pressures as that of Eichendorff, but was politically utterly different from that prevailing in Prussia, or indeed anywhere in the *Deutscher Bund*, during the *Vormärz*. In the aftermath of 1830, Canton Bern, a political entity possessing greater de facto autonomy than any small or medium-sized state of the German Confederation, had undergone (in parallel with some nine other cantons) what was in effect a bloodless social revolution, when the previously ruling hereditary patriciate or aristocracy relinquished power, a democratic republican constitution was promulgated (in 1831) and a liberal govenment elected on a property-based franchise.[26] Gotthelf was personally involved in this revolution and was an enthusiast for the change it signified.[27] It seems, indeed, to have been constitutive for his political self-awareness. Until his death in 1854 he remained consistently hostile to the pre-1831 'Patriziat',

'Aristokraten', 'Altadel', whom he saw as arrogant, amoral and heedless of popular need.[28] He regarded the liberties of free self-expression and debate which 1831 brought – a combative free press – as fundamental to progress and social good health[29] (and his political writing is strikingly predicated on the extremely active public sphere which the new political system brought). Eichendorff, whose curriculum vitae included a spell as a Prussian censor, had no such notions. Also in some contrast to Eichendorff, Gotthelf always saw his political outlook as democratic and republican: 'Republikanismus', however it may be defined, is for him invariably an ideal term, the designation of the political world he wished to see.[30] Moreover, in his view, the ideal government – the manifestation of a true 'republikanischer Sinn' – is a 'Volksregierung': in a democratic system, government which is not 'volksnah' and fails to pay heed to 'Volksglauben', so which becomes detached from the interests and values of the Volk, is liable to and deserves to collapse.[31] Finally and correspondingly, Gotthelf had no sympathy for the defeatist and cynical aristocratic regimes which ruled in Metternichian Germany.[32]

Such positions could certainly not have been part of a conservative standpoint in the German states at the time; but they could in Switzerland.[33] Already quite soon after 1831, Gotthelf began to find himself at odds with aspects of liberal change in Bern. The Bern regime then underwent successive radicalisations in subsequent years of the Vormärz, notably in 1838 and 1846; and his disaffection intensified accordingly. He tended to associate the social crises of the time with the policies of these governments, and he steadily assumed the role of a public scourge of the 'radicalism' which they represented.[34] In 1849, Gottfried Keller noted simply: '[Gotthelf] gehört der konservativen Partei des Kantons Bern an, welche schon seit mehreren Jahren gründlich in Ruhestand versetzt ist. Daher wimmeln seine Schriften von Invektiven gegen die jetzigen Regenten und alles, was von ihnen ausgeht. Alles Unheil . . . vindiziert er ihnen'.[35]

The key struggles of Swiss politics in the Vormärz were between particularism and centralism and between ecclesiasticism and secularism, identified with the political right and left respectively, and Gotthelf's position as regards both was on the conservative wing. As a priest in a country parish, who also had a strong interest in questions of popular education, he was hostile towards secularising impulses which had already begun to appear in Bern in the very early 1830s, and particularly towards moves by the cantonal authorities to exclude the priesthood from a role in the expanding system of public schooling (SW 13: 34f., 38–50). Over time, this antagonism developed into a comprehensive sense that pernicious secularism was a facet of the Zeitgeist. At the regular moments of crisis over religious issues in Vormärz Switzerland, his stance was consistently anti-secularist – over the *Berufung* of David Friedrich Strauß to a Chair of Theology in Zurich in 1839 and the resulting successful popular revolt (the 'Zürichputsch') against the government responsible;[36] the dissolution of the monasteries in Canton Aargau in 1841;[37] the failed invasions of Lucerne in 1844 and 1845 by liberal 'Freischaren' from other cantons seeking to overthrow the Jesuit-influenced Lucerne government;[38] the *Sonderbundkrieg* of 1847, when secessionist Catholic cantons were brought to heel;[39] and others. This entailed the Protestant Gotthelf's adoption of resolutely, in some ways unexpectedly, ecumenical positions[40] – sympathetic to Roman Catholicism and even to the Jesuits[41] – on the basis that godlessness was the common enemy.[42]

Many of these matters of religious politics in Vormärz Switzerland were simultaneously issues of particularism, of the rights of individual cantons to pursue policies independent of any kind of central authority. The *Sonderbund*, first established in 1845, was an assertion of particularist cantonal rights; and its defeat and dissolution were followed by the promulgation of a new Swiss *Bundesverfassung* in 1848, significantly increasing central powers. Gotthelf was thoroughly hostile to this, as he had been to previous encroachments upon cantonal autonomy. Moreover, his particularism did not stop short at the level of the canton. Within Bern itself, he was generally opposed to the developments of administrative centralisation which the post-1830 governments implemented, that is, the transference of power, not only in educational matters but also in such areas as poor relief and the administration of justice, away from the localities and into the hands of the state bureaucracy in Bern City (SW 13: 47–9, 171f., 203, 214–22). This was an important phase in the consolidation of modern Switzerland, with the establishment of state-directed schooling, a centralised judicial and police system, modern modes of taxation and coordinated development of the infrastructure (road- and later railway-building). Gotthelf, as his journalism shows, was thoroughly interested in all these matters and inclined to join in the detailed public debates on them, to propose highly specific amendments, and even to demand additional state interventions when he desired them (e.g. SW 13: 162–6, 176f., 184–6).

His natural position, however, was one of hostility, on the basis that the developments taking place involved the taking of power by an increasingly intolerant and autocratic, even quasi- aristocratic, city bureaucracy, also that they entailed great scope for corruption, and that the removal of local self-determination meant a loss of self-reliance and of personal, familial and communal responsibility (see e.g. SW 13: 218f.). His essential instinct was towards a kind of pious communitarian form of governance, as being the one most likely to keep the citizen in moral good health, heedful of his own duties and respectful of God. It is to be suspected that the little councils of village men which take place in the first inner narrative in his story *Die schwarze Spinne* are images of the way Gotthelf fundamentally wished political decision-making to be (even if, in these cases, the decisions reached are not actually judicious ones; SW XVII: 33, 42f.).

Gotthelf's judgements of the secular, centralised liberal state and the society that accompanied it amount to a comprehensive, one might say indiscriminate, cultural critique. He sees, as we have noted, a bureaucratisation of society which weakens individual commitment to the common weal, and thereby also undermines the role of love as a social force (SW 13: 218f., XV: 128, 175). He sees libertarian judicial policies – the 'Unsinn' of 'sogenannte Rechtsstaaten' (SW XV: 125) – which spuriously emphasise the 'Grundsätze persönlicher Freiheit' over the need for public duty and order and encourage a legalistic regulation of human relationships ('verdammte Juristerei'), but neglect practical law enforcement and allow serious crime to go unpunished (SW 13: 90, 131 (and cf. 411), 204; XV: 125, 135). Keller says ironically: 'Er ereifert sich heftig über den eingerissenen Humanismus im Rechtsleben und sehnt sich nach der Blütezeit des Galgens und der Rute zurück'.[43] At the same time, Gotthelf sees a world of laissez-faire economics, which encourages the destructive exploitation of resources (for example, capitalistic deforestation; SW 13: 157, 180–90), relaxes controls on socially deleterious forms of profit-making (the deregulation of the sale of alcohol, the 'Wirtshauspest'; SW 13: 110–16, 184), permits the free importation of foreign factory goods at the expense of local handicrafts, and allows factory-building but does not direct it according to need (SW 13: 162–6). As he says sardonically, 'Das ist halt radikale Freiheit' (SW 13: 182). It is an economic system dominated by 'Aktiengesellschaften', 'Börsenspiel', 'Spekulier[en]' and 'Falliten' (SW XV: 121f.), to the detriment of values of thrift, providence, moderation and hard work right through the social fabric. It is a world directed by 'Schwindelei' or 'Schwindelgeist' (SW XV: 120ff., XI: 14), a concept which blends a suggestion of the mendacity and ruthlessness of capitalism with the idea of vertiginous speed – at once the physical speed of the steam age and the impatience, desire for instant fulfilment and reward, lack of 'Genügsamkeit' and 'Beharrlichkeit' (SW XV: 120), which is the mood of the times. The age is, in Gotthelf's parlance, diseased, suffering from various forms of 'Zeitkrankheit', 'Zeitübel', 'die Seelen [sind] befleckt mit der Cholera des Geistes'; or, alternatively, it is mired in vice, in a range of 'Zeitlaster' which make up the (im)moral Zeitgeist (SW XV 116f., 120–2; IX: 479f.).

Gotthelf had some sense that there were historical roots for the condition he diagnosed. Writing in 1839, he offered an analysis of the historical process not unlike the one which we encounter in Eichendorff, or which Novalis's *Die Christenheit oder Europa* had provided in more substantial form. He suggests, or seems to suggest, that the Middle Ages, especially its phase of cathedral-building, was an exemplary epoch in which man was inspired by heavenly love; but that he then 'sich selbst mehr und mehr zu verweltlichen . . . schien' (SW XV: 156), in a process culminating in the vanities of the aristocratic eighteenth century. The French Revolution then both destroyed this decadent culture and extended its materialism and sensualistic corruption. Elsewhere in the same work he talks of the evolution by which the previously harmonious 'Stände . . . traten . . . auseinander', common land was abolished, the population expanded, the economy became cash-based, and people grew egotistic, vain, fashion-obsessed and alienated from one another (SW XV: 100). Elsewhere again, he talks of the perilously libertarian, egalitarian, godless and hubristic ideology of the Enlightenment, its realisation in the middle-class revolution of 1789 and its continuing pernicious influence on social values and expectations in the modern era (SW XV: 96, 118f.). These pronouncements are polemical, unsystematic and often obscure; but they indicate, contrary to what one critic has said, that a sense of history as process is very much part of Gotthelf's view.[44] Moreover, Gotthelf also shares with many other nineteenth century practitioners of such historicism the asserted belief in a final, Utopian outcome and purpose of history; and for him, much as for Eichendorff and Novalis, it lies in a respiritualisation of man, a divinely induced return to the selfless piety of the medieval cathedral-builders ('. . . des wieder dem Himmel zustrebenden

Zeitgeistes, der vor vielen hundert Jahren die Münster geboren, die Klöster aufgebaut hat'; SW XV: 244). Their modern equivalents, he claims, will help build symbolic cathedrals, edifices of Christian love and charity sheltering the moral victims of the modern age (SW XV: 166–8; see also 245, 268).

The empirical basis of Gotthelf's ferocious critique was the social conditions of his time. The text from which many of the pronouncements above are taken is an extraordinary treatise-cum-sermon that he published in 1840, entitled *Die Armennot*, which is a portrayal of these conditions, supposedly a proposal for how to alleviate them, and also in many respects a key to his outlook. *Die Armennot* gives an emphatic account of the deprivation and degradation prevalent among the contemporary poor: disease, drunkenness, cold, hunger and dirt, mass begging, theft and violence, promiscuity, child-neglect, -exploitation and -abuse, unemployment, vagrancy and migration (e.g. SW XV: 183f.). Gotthelf focuses primarily on his own rural area, but is aware of the phenomenon's urban manifestations and their causes: 'Die in den Städten so fürchterlich anwachsende Armut der vor der Not in die Städte geflüchteten Landbewohner . . .' (SW XV: 146). He is aware also of mass destitution as an adjunct of a capitalist economy in more advanced societies than Switzerland, notably England and France, where the 'Elend' is 'unermeßlich' (SW XV: 170).

To this extent, Gotthelf's analysis of the 'Armennot' is congruent with the kind of materialist view of contemporary conditions which was emerging at the left end of the political spectrum, most famously with Engels's *Die Lage der arbeitenden Klasse in England* of 1845 and the *Communist Manifesto* of 1848. So it is too, more or less, in respect of his critique of laissez-faire governmental economic policies. However, in major ways it differs. For Marx and Engels (as, earlier, for Büchner, and occasionally, too, for Heine), the contemporary poor in their destitution are experiencing a devaluation of values, as they realise that the moral system by which they are exhorted and coerced to live – values of private property, family, hard work, providence, continence, faith in God and respect for authority – is an imposed system, without objective sanction, which merely articulates the interests of the ruling class and secures their power. For Gotthelf, by contrast, this system of values is utterly true, legitimate and divinely ordained. What is afflicting the modern world is a Zeitgeist – caused by economic and social conditions, by the modern economic system, by political neglect and by long-term developments in ideology – which is generally destructive of those values. It is a Zeitgeist (a favourite word of his) that is manifested at all levels of society: for example, in the corrupt frivolities of fashion, arts and entertainments, material acquisitions and public sociability. A fire-and-brimstone passage of *Die Armennot* says:

> Man setzt das Leben an Schachern und Schinden, an Bauen und Essen, schnell Fahren und schöne Gartenstecklein, an hoffärtiges Wesen mit Kleidern und Manieren, mit Worten und Kühen, mit Möbeln und Misthaufen, an Regenteln und Agenteln, an Tändeln und Repräsentieren, an Visiten und Badekuren, ans Tanzen und Lesen, an die verschiedenartigsten Dinge, aber selten an das eine, das not tut; im Moder sucht man das Leben und findet den Tod. (SW XV: 161)

But the corruption is at its deepest and most pernicious among substantial sections of the poor, who are utterly morally degraded. At worst, the 'innerlich so verwahrloste Armenmasse' (SW XV: 117) is in a state of animality. 'Das Tier [ist] in ihnen ernährt [worden]' instead of the 'Trieb nach Vervollkommnung', they wallow 'im Kote der Trägheit, der Sünde' (SW XV: 102, 107), their 'verdorbener, versunkener Sinn' is an 'inwohnende Hölle' of 'Neid', 'Selbstsucht', 'Eitelkeit', 'Gier' and above all 'Lust' (SW XV: 149, 206, 209) – he places considerable emphasis on their uncontrolled sensuality, sexual and otherwise: 'Der Genuß ist ihnen alles, an ihm hängen ihre Gedanken, das Sehnen nach ihm füllt ihr inneres Leben' (SW XV: 108).[45] The implication of this is that abject poverty is less an economic condition than a moral-psychological one – and, by extension, it is not primarily to be counteracted by financial measures. This is, indeed, to a considerable degree Gotthelf's view. Bureaucratically organised poor-relief, he indicates, tends merely to stimulate the 'Frechheit', 'Ungebührnis' and 'Gelüste' of the poor, as they come to regard alms as their entitlement: 'Es ist meine feste Überzeugung, daß man . . . , je mehr Geld man auf die bisherige Weise in die Armennot hineinwirft, die Not nur um so mehr vergrößert, gefährlicher macht' (SW XV: 92, 131f., 150f.). It is not even that there is a lack of work: the problem is the incapacity of the degraded poor to engage in it (SW XV: 149). The solution to the 'ansteckende Krankheit der Armut' (SW XV: 137) is not to encourage the malady, but to cure it; and the means to achieve this is moral education.

Education – meaning practical training, but also and above all moral and spiritual betterment – was key to Gotthelf's outlook in numerous respects. Most of his literary texts are

Bildungsgeschichten, and not because he had read *Wilhelm Meister*,[46] but because he saw his authorial role as fundamentally didactic, an extension of his function as a priest. Frequently, his writings also assume a consciously sermonic quality; certainly *Die Armennot* itself does, being written, as the author says, in 'tönenden Worten' (SW XV: 151). He was personally engaged with education in various ways. From 1835 to 1845 he was an official 'Schulkommissär' – Inspector/Supervisor of Schools – for his area of the canton. He also taught Swiss history for a short while in further education courses for schoolmasters.[47] A major focus of his journalism is the schools policies of the Bern government and their local implementation.[48] This was at a time when liberal governments in many places were preoccupied with school expansion and compulsion, with the purpose of enlightening and civilising the masses: it was an important policy concern of Louis Philippe's governments in France in the 1830s; the English were engaged in it likewise; and it was an issue through much of Switzerland. Gotthelf's own philosophy of education was holistic and spiritual. Strongly influenced as he was by the ideas of the Swiss educational reformer Johann Heinrich Pestalozzi (1746–1827) – who is lauded in *Die Armennot* (SW XV: 163f., 166, 245; cf. also 13: 45) – he held that the prime aim of education is to light the 'Götterfunken' in children, free them from their infant subjection to crude instinct and make them 'freudig und vernünftig' (SW XV: 164). Man is 'als Tier geboren, [er] bedarf . . . Menschen, welche seine Seele wecken, nähren, entbinden, um Mensch werden zu können' (SW XV: 111). For him, as for Pestalozzi, such education is mainly supplied by familial or parental love; and to the extent that it is not, schooling must be based on a pseudo-parental model.

In this connection, the children of the dissolute poor are a prime object of attention. In very many poor families, says Gotthelf, and also under conventional poor-relief arrangements (orphanages; fostering or indenturing), the children are exposed to influences which stimulate 'das Tier' in them (SW XV: 150f.), infecting them with a moral contagion – 'ansteckende Krankheit . . .' (SW XV: 137). To give them the 'ehrenwerte, tüchtige Gesinnung, einen echten christlichen Sinn' which they need – the spirit they require in order to be mentally able to work, and so to earn, and thus to achieve the prosperity which naturally comes from virtuous industry (SW XV: 138f., 209f.) – they must be removed from such influences. To this end, special family-like orphanages must be set up, with a house-father and house-mother who act as 'Götti' and

'Gotte' – loving god-parents – to the children and inculcate virtue in them. He himself has been involved in setting up just such an establishment and the results have been highly promising (SW XV: 235ff.; cf. 150f.).

Gotthelf's solution to world poverty is parochial and somewhat wishful, as his addendum to the text ten years later, after the upheavals of the 1840s, acknowledges with a hint of embarrassment (SW XV: 255). Its basic principle, that the social problem of the poor is to be cured by indoctrinating them into becoming civilised, may also strike us as a little crass, although one way or another it underlies a good deal of thinking on social reform, both in Gotthelf's day and our own. In any event, the view which it entails underpins most of Gotthelf's writing of the time when *Die Armennot* was written. For example, his best-known novel, *Uli der Knecht* (that is, *Wie Uli, der Knecht, glücklich wird*), of 1841, is a parable of the redemption of impoverished youth: thanks to the efforts of his paternalistically sympathetic and responsible *Meister*, the young orphaned hero is cured of his impulses to vice (drunkenness, fornication, prodigality, vanity, envy), is taught to enjoy a respectable, pious, temperate working life, and can thereby progress to due prosperity.[49] The novel is basically intended to exemplify the moral prescription of *Die Armennot*. Gotthelf's novella *Kurt von Koppigen*, of 1844, despite its medieval setting and aristocratic protagonist, in fact has a similar fable: a youth of impoverished, villainous, though noble family drifts into a life of amorality and heedless vice until finally cured, in this case by direct divine intervention (SW XVII: 225–358). As we will see shortly, *Die schwarze Spinne* of 1842 is likewise, although more subtly, rooted in such a view of things.

It is true that Gotthelf did not always depict impoverishment with quite the lack of sympathy which these works betray; and even texts such as *Uli der Knecht* and *Kurt von Koppigen* convey an appreciation of the practical, physical reality of deprivation which few other authors of the Vormärz achieve. The acme of such depiction is his novel *Käthi die Großmutter* (*oder: Der wahre Weg durch jede Not*[50]), of 1846/47, a work which is a concerted and notable act of empathy with peasant poverty. Its aged cottager heroine is shown reacting with Job-like fortitude to a series of catastrophes (hail, flood and – topically – potato blight), maintaining decency, cleanliness, piety and parental love amidst tribulation. She is saved from complete destitution by the charity of her neighbours, who respond to her own graciousness; and in the end she is rescued entirely from poverty by the quasi-angelic appearance of a wealthy orphan girl, drawn to Käthi, her son and her grandson by the love Käthi dispenses (see especially SW X: 336). Käthi's character and fate are intended precisely to illustrate that poverty need not lead to turpitude. With each succeeding disaster, however, and above all with that ending, the implication is discernible that virtue lifts people out of impoverishment; and from here it is a small step to the message of *Die Armennot,* that destitution *is* close to immorality.

Ultimately, what *Die Armennot* itself is concerned with is, of course, social revolution. As the author says: 'Ich werde wohl nicht nötig haben, lange zu beweisen, daß die Armut gefährlich geworden sei, daß die Verhältnisse der sogenannten Proletarier zu den Besitzenden oder der Nichtshabenden zu den Habenden so gespannt seien, daß sie einen Bruch drohen, der ganz Europa mit Blut und Brand bedecken würde, daß die Armut das feindselige Wesen sei, welches dem alten Europa am drohendsten gegenüberstehe' (SW XV: 87). Just as Büchner's, Heine's and Marx's exposure of the disillusionment of the masses with the values of civil society entails a prediction, implicit or explicit, that this consciousness will lead to revolution, so, too, Gotthelf sees the culture and values of the animalistic poor – improvident, hedonistic, sensualistic, impiously envious and without humility – as revolutionary. He indicates fairly specifically that rationalism and liberalism have laid the ground for this culture with their implicit 'Unglaube', emphasis on human rights and man-made laws, irresponsible notions of brotherhood, personal liberty and equality, and neglect of man's spiritual needs (SW XV: 96f; cf. 118–20, 124f.). He says, moreover, that the previous European revolutions were not conducted on behalf of the poor, who saw no benefit. The latter were merely used like fierce animals, fed and let loose by the revolutionaries upon their opponents and then once more encaged. But the poor draw their own conclusions, and are evolving their own embittered ideology of radical equality, expropriation and licence, which now threatens the world (SW XV: 118–20).

For Gotthelf at this time, poverty and social revolution are indeed integrally related notions, even if he does not use the latter term very frequently. Above all, the association is made apparent through the pattern of metaphor which he creates around the issue. *Die Armennot* offers a series of graphic analogies for poverty and its social threat; these are repeated throughout the text in a clearly premeditated fashion, so that they become, in effect, part of its sermonic rhetoric. The Armennot is disease: 'Pest' and 'Aussatz' and 'Krebs' (SW XV: 88, 90, 116, 144, 198f.). Related to this, it is also a 'Wunde', and (even less attractively) an 'Eiterbeule' on the point of bursting (SW XV: 90, 247–53). It is also various forms of natural mishap: flood, morass, storm, fire and eclipse (SW XV: 90, 95–7, 189, 199, 251–3). It is a rampant weed – 'giftige Wucherpflanze' – and terrifying wild animal – 'Giftschlange', 'gierige, zähnefletschende Wölfe' (SW XV: 149, 249f.). It is also a mythical monster: 'Schwarmgeister', 'Tier des Abgrundes', dragon, hydra (SW XV: 90, 96f., 197f., 252f.). Furthermore, the metaphors can expand within themselves. If the poor are a morass, they must be 'entsumpft', moral 'Säulen eingerammelt', to reclaim the terrain (SW XV: 189, 199). Most strikingly, Gotthelf's post-1848 postscript tells us how the 'Eiterbeule', the pustule of poverty, has now indeed exploded, like a volcano, 'einem feuerspeienden Berge ähnlich, einen Lavastrom ergießen[d]' (SW XV: 251f.). Thus metaphor begets further, horrific metaphor – rather as the spider in *Die schwarze Spinne* erupts and brings forth new spiders. Gotthelf's metaphors merge and cumulate.

This is authorial purpose, not just stylistic gaucheness or lack of control, as the very interesting beginning of *Die Armennot* indicates. Here, Gotthelf talks of how all peoples at any given time have a basic prime source of fear – 'Kummer' – which besets them. At different stages in the (central European) past it has been the menace of Turkish invasion, or the Black Death. More recently: 'An die Stelle der Pestilenz ist die Cholera getreten, welche durch die Weltteile zieht wie ein grausenhaftes, todbringendes Geheimnis' (SW XV: 85). Also, 'an die Stelle des Türken möchten die Politiker den Russen setzen, sie irren sich' (SW XV: 85). In fact, 'd[er] neue Türk' – 'das feindselige Wesen. . . , welches dem alten Europa am drohendsten gegenübersteh[t]' – 'ist die Armut', poverty and its revolutionary consequences (SW XV: 86f.). What is meant here, though it is not quite stated, is that such terrors imprint themselves deeply and lastingly on the mind of a people; they express themselves in the collective metaphors which are myth and also, over time, blur with the other fears (illness, natural catastrophe, monsters and ghouls) with which people are preoccupied. The implicit intention of *Die Armennot* as a whole, terroristic sermon that it is, is somehow to key into this dimension of the popular mind (where – so we note – 'people' specifically does not embrace the rabble poor, the 'sogenannte Proletarier', themselves; SW XV: 87[51]), and impose its message on the suggestible audience.

Something akin to this obtains in another text of Gotthelf's from around this time, an essay in similarly sermonic tone on *Die Wassernot im Emmental am 13. August 1837* (published in 1838). The *Wassernot* in question was a violent storm and disastrous flooding of the Emmental, with a number of deaths and some destruction of property, in the summer which followed a particularly harsh and long-lasting winter. The apparent purpose of Gotthelf's text is to explain these inflictions in terms of divine purpose – which it does in a shifting sequence of ways: God 'schr[eibt] ins Gedächtnis' of the inhabitants with these disasters; they express not his rage but his love; the storm is a punishment for lasciviousness; its din evokes the trumpets of the apocalypse; consciences are stimulated, so the inhabitants are morally beautified, by the catastrophe; individuals perform deeds of heroic self-sacrifice; some victims are 'sühnend Opfer'; the flood also punishes the negligence of the modern secular state (as recent publicly erected buildings, constructed without foundations, collapse); the flood is egalitarian, sweeping away rich and poor and reminding people of the insignificance of 'irdische Größe'; it inspires awe, a 'feierliche Stimmung', 'die schönsten Gefühle'; it is God's test for man; its ferocity actually mirrors both divine power and the chaos in the human soul; it loosens 'versteinerte Herzen', love is restimulated in men's hearts; a moral rebirth occurs, an 'unsichtbare Himmelsleiter [senkt] ins Tal sich nieder'; in the end, the *Wassernot* is 'des Herrn Predigt'.[52] As can be seen, this is not at all an attempt at systematic theological hermeneutics.[53] Rather, it tries, as did *Die Armennot*, to overwhelm and intimidate its audience. Like *Die Armennot*, too, it seeks to key into popular reflections – puzzlements, anxieties and prejudices.[54] And, again like the later text, it adduces historical memories and mythical associations which may exist in the popular mind: the flood is (like) the 'Hunnenheer'; it is also (like) both the Napoleonic invasion (of 1798) and the menace of the *Heilige Allianz*; and it is the 'Emmenschlange', the legendary great serpent with its dwarfish helpers which last burst forth eighty years previously (SW XV: 18f., 21f.). On some level, of course, the flood in the Emmental *is* the pending social catastrophe of the Vormärz. Gotthelf's *Die Wassernot* does not specify the association, but it is there in the metaphors and myths of his text, identical as they are to those around which *Die Armennot* is organised. Gotthelf's intention with *Die Wassernot im Emmental* seems to be somehow to evoke the social catastrophe without naming it; and the fortuitous flood disaster is to be the basis of a kind of moral homeopathy, generating the moral renewal needed to ward off greater cataclysms.

Composed barely two years after *Die Wassernot im Emmental* and *Die Armennot*, Gotthelf's best-known story, *Die schwarze Spinne*, is the most concentrated manifestation in his literary writing of the reflections which also produced these treatises. His contemporaneous novel *Uli der Knecht* had been straightforwardly a parabolic realisation of the prescriptions contained in *Die Armennot* for the salvation of the degraded poor. But *Die schwarze Spinne* ranges much more widely, not only echoing the essays' notions of social propriety, but also venturing into the domains of popular consciousness – anxiety and suggestibility, myth and collective memory – with which the essays are so interestingly concerned.

The present-day social world which this story depicts, in its framework narrative, is emphatically idyllic: a community of patrician farmers, living in productive harmony with God's nature, amidst prosperity and plenty, in great, clean farmsteads, heedful of religious and other tradition, and also respecting the natural social hierarchies of generation, gender and wealth (SW XVII: 6–24). These images seem to be Gotthelf's notion of a model society, a rurally based social structure centred around virtuously prosperous farm-owning families, who exercise beneficent and pseudo-parental authority and control over the potentially disorderly servants and landless labourers who are their dependents. However, the representation is not an attempt to depict current reality. The framework story's idyllicism, with its 'behaglich blickende Kühe', 'stämmige Mägde', 'schönes Haus', 'stolze Hühner und schöne Tauben' (SW XVII: 6–8), may not be ironic, but it is certainly self-conscious. As those essays and even *Uli der Knecht* indicate, Gotthelf saw, rather, a modern-day reality in which social and other conflict, misery and moral turpitude, predominate. One is struck how even *Die Wassernot im Emmental*, a work primarily concerned with fortuitous natural disaster, begins – as it were unprovoked – with a very specific scene of social deprivation in the midst of prosperity (SW XV: 9). The initial scenes of *Die schwarze Spinne* are an exercise in a sort of Schillerian sentimentality, showing the world as it ought to be and as it perhaps has the potential to become. It is, as the text tells us, a world in which Jacob's ladder is securely in place: '. . . [ein] Zeugnis, daß die Leiter noch am Himmel stehe, auf welcher Engel auf- und niedersteigen und die Seele des Menschen, wenn sie dem Leibe sich entwindet, und ihr

Heil und Augenmerk beim Vater droben war und nicht hier auf Erden' (SW XVII: 6);[55] in *Die Wassernot*, we remember, God's purpose in inflicting the flood was the urgent need to restore 'die unsichtbare Himmelsleiter' (SW XV: 81), currently thoroughly absent.

Unideal reality in *Die schwarze Spinne* is consigned largely to the historical past. The text's second inner story, the tale of the spider's second appearance in the fifteenth century, in particular portrays a social world reminiscent of the way Gotthelf commonly perceived his own present day. Here, the patrician farmers have been corrupted by materialism and vanity – jewellery, fashionable dress and extravagant new building (SW XVII: 80–2). They have lost their impulse to hard work; and they both neglect and torment their 'Knechte und Mägde', who are 'behandel[t] . . . wie unvernünftiges Vieh' (SW XVII: 81). This spirit has been stimulated especially by 'fremde Weiber', marrying in from outside, who exercise unhealthy and unnatural dominion over their husbands. In one such household, the servants, free of any moral control from their masters and under the influence of a red-headed, squinting agitator, degenerate into 'tierische[r] Übermut' – larceny, lasciviousness, sacrilege and abuse – which culminates in the catastrophic release of the spider (SW XVII: 80–6; cf. 88f.). So much of this is recognisable from *Die Armennot* and Gotthelf's journalism – especially the focus on the liability of the poor to moral degradation (irreligiosity and animal sensuality) and the contributory responsibility for this of the wealthy class, but even such details as the author's attacks on the feminism of the 1830s, his disapproval of urban clothing fashions and their rural encroachment, and his dislike of modern building.[56]

There is less of this in the first inner story, where the spider first appears. The principal mortal villain here is another foreign, unmotherly and unnaturally assertive woman (SW XVII: 32, 35); the populace turns from God in its desire to find comfort and escape misery; and the brutal amorality of the feudal lords who are the source of that misery certainly corresponds to Gotthelf's general estimation of the aristocracy and its values.[57] But on the whole this first sub-narrative is not such an implicit catalogue of modern social turpitude.

However, one further aspect of it is indeed noteworthy in connection with the judgements of *Die Armennot*, and simultaneously corresponds to a preoccupation of the framework tale. The core of the first inner story and token of the peasants' sinfulness is their concession to the devil of the soul of an unbaptised baby, and much of the episode's plot concerns the saving of two such babies. The framework, meanwhile, takes place around a baptism (on Ascension Day) and focuses on the obligations and anxieties of the child's designated godmother ('Gotte'). In *Die Armennot*, the key solution to the moral plague of poverty is said to be the rescue of the children of the dissolute masses, and their placing in the charge of a 'Götti' and 'Gotte' – parents in God (SW XV: 150f.). In the second story, finally, a baby is also born, this time to a woman of that class, a 'wildes Weib', who curses and blasphemes as her child arrives. The hero seizes the child in order to rush it to baptism and save it from the diabolic spider; and, as he does so, the woman herself seems to turn into the spider: 'Das unschuldige Kindlein hielt Christen in den Armen; stechend und wild, giftig starrten aus des Weibes verzerrten Zügen dessen Augen ihn an, und es ward ihm immer mehr, als trete die Spinne aus ihnen heraus, als sei sie es selbst' (SW XVII: 90f.). Thus *Die schwarze Spinne* variously echoes Gotthelf's Pestalozzian prescriptions for the salvation of the children of the dissolute poor.

The implication of the story of the spider itself, recounted by the old patriarch to whom it has been passed down through the generations, and apparently corroborated by the bung in an ancient wooden beam behind which the spider was banished (SW XVII: 72–4, 76, 92), is that it is a kind of folk memory, the community's mythic amalgamation – for, as it were, autodidactic purpose – of a plurality of historical experiences. It is approximately organised, to begin with, around salient moments from Swiss history (of which Gotthelf himself had, as we noted, been a teacher; SW 13: 58). The first appearance of the spider, dated by the aged storyteller as 'mehr als sechshundert Jahre her' (SW XVII: 25), so in the mid-thirteenth century, involves the peasants of the valley entering into a diabolic pact in response to the impositions of their German Knights-Templar overlords. It is thus a mythicised rendering of a moment of challenge to external feudal power; that is, it represents a memory of the epoch which produced the *Bundesbrief* of 1291 and the ensuing war of the three founding cantons against the Habsburg emperor, the foundation of the Swiss nation. This is also, of course, the moment which generated the most powerful of all Swiss myths, William Tell: Gotthelf's mythical invocation of that period is in some sense, too, an allusion to the myth-making which is altogether constitutive of Swiss national consciousness. The spider is then defeated, to reappear two centuries later (SW XVII: 81), in an age when: '. . . selbst an die heiligen Zeichen wagte die Hoffart sich, und statt daß [die] Herzen [der Menschen] während dem Beten inbrünstig bei Gott gewesen wären, hingen ihre Augen hoffärtig an den goldenen Kugeln ihres Rosenkranzes. So ward ihr Gottesdienst Pracht und Hoffart' (SW XVII: 80). This is the decadence of late medieval Catholicism, the abuses of which provoked Protestantism. The spider's second coming is, by implication, a mythical memory of the upheavals of the Reformation.[58]

The story is also implied to have further sources of a more or less historical character, however. The consequences of the spider's bite – blackening of the body and pustules (SW XVII: 65) – are clearly plague symptoms. The text even says at one point: 'Nun war der schwarze Tod zu Ende' (SW XVII: 74). Thus the spider appears as a recollection of the Black Death – the bubonic plague epidemics of the mid and late fourteenth century (1348 and thereafter), and conceivably also of the epidemic in the seventeenth century.[59] This is a prime association. But other ravaging disease is implicit also: the mass deaths of livestock (SW XVII: 53) suggest, as Karl Fehr has noted, a 'Viehseuchengeschichte'.[60] And the text hints, further, at the plagues of real vermin which could strike agricultural communities – with the spider said to be like a 'giftige Wespe', or with words such as 'Ungeziefer' and 'Plage' (SW XVII: 49, 55, 64). These are collective memories. But the story keys into more personal terrors, too. The spider's growth, on Christine's face and elsewhere, is cancerous: '. . . denn der Schmerz wuchs immer noch, und der schwarze Punkt ward größer und schwärzer, einzelne dunkle Streifen liefen von ihm aus, und nach dem Munde hin schien sich auf dem runden Flecke ein Höcker zu pflanzen' (SW XVII: 50). And its final touch is the agony of a heart attack or seizure: 'Da fuhren Feuerströme von der [Spinne] aus, der treuen Mutter durch Hand und Arm bis ins Herz hinein . . .' (SW XVII: 74).

One is struck by the basic irrationalism both of the mythopoeic process to which Gotthelf is pointing – the community generating the tale of the spider out of its real experiences, and the way the legend comes to function as a reinforcer of the community's moral rules – and also of Gotthelf's own engagement with that process: for he, as author, is likewise exploiting these visceral terrors for moral reinforcement. There is in this an element of demagogy, a quality which Gottfried Keller (without using the term) observed and disliked in Gotthelf generally.[61] Particularly noticeable is the role, remarked on above, that is played by foreigners in *Die schwarze Spinne*, in which all the main agents of the spider's arrival are from outside – Christine the 'Lindauerin', the 'schlau und kräftig' women 'aus der Fremde' who are the mother and wife of Christen in the second inner story, and the daemonic, red-headed, cast-eyed servant ('man wußte nicht, woher er kam') who finally releases the spider (SW XVII: 32, 81, 84). One contemporary reviewer was especially offended by this aspect of the text,[62] and one is inclined to agree. It is not so much that Gotthelf himself believes foreigners to be wicked, as that he holds popular xeno-phobia to be an emotion which can be utilised productively. Some-thing similar applies to the servant's squint, which popular superstition can regard as the mark of the devil, and which is also implicitly accorded such a meaning by Gotthelf's fiction. And it applies also, finally, to the character's red hair, with its Jewish connotations. Gotthelf was not a systematic anti-semite.[63] But he must have known of the ready association in popular conscious-ness of plague with the Jews, in particular of the great pogroms prompted by the Black Death throughout the German lands, including in Bern, in the late 1340s. With the red-headed agent of the plague in his story he again both hints at this ingredient of pop-ular bigotry as a historical issue, and yet also directly exploits the sentiment involved.[64]

Such elements are, one way or another, what the beginning of *Die Armennot* called 'd[er] Türk' (SW XV: 86), besetting anxieties of the popular mind. We are left free to extrapolate that further fears, not specifically alluded to in the text, can contribute to the emblem of terror which the spider is: the other contagions which *Die Armennot* mentions, leprosy and – in modern times – cholera (SW XV: 85, 88); natural disasters such as the periodic Emmental floods (which, according to *Die Wassernot im Emmental*, gener-ated the myth of the *Emmenschlange*; SW XV: 22); the Turkish invasions themselves, those of the Huns (SW XV: 21), or – again in relatively modern times – the Napoleonic invasion of 1798 (for which Gotthelf elsewhere used imagery similar to that surrounding the spider);[65] and, most importantly, poverty and revolution. The closeness of *Die Armennot* to *Die schwarze Spinne* – not just the proximity of their composition, but also the way that the story clearly builds on the essay's premeditated pattern of associative metaphor-cum-myth – makes it evident that, on some level, the story concerns the bogey of revolution, 'd[er] neue Türk' (SW XV: 86). Just as *Die Armennot* used metaphor and mythical precedent to stimulate in the essay's addressees a salutary dread of the possibility of social revolution, so, too, does *Die schwarze Spinne*. The story aims to base its menace on an agglomeration of pre-established terrors, perhaps with certain of the most recent 'Turks' – the French invasion, various natural catastrophes and the cholera – foremost. The cholera epidemic, of course, is already strongly connected in the contemporary mind with the threatening masses, thanks to its link with the dirt of poverty, its tendency to arise first in the slums, the proximity of the 1831/32 epidemic to the uprisings of 1830, and so on. Associations of the masses with plagues of vermin are also well established, as a poem such as Heine's *Die Wanderratten* suggests. Images of revolution as storm and flood and volcano are also prevalent at the time, as other discussions in the present book show: Gotthelf does not invent them. But what his story represents is a premeditated, systematic, manipulative attempt to construct upon such associations, and (more widely) upon the processes of popular mythopoeia, an experience of horror which will focus itself on – sensitise people to – the 'neuer Türk' of revolution, and induce moral resistance to it.

Die schwarze Spinne is indeed a conservative text, for which revolution is the devil's work. Even in its allusions to the great moments of Swiss history, a conservative logic is implicit: the demise of feudal power may have been inevitable and desirable, but those who are the agents of this change (the peasants who effectively challenge the authority of the Tempelritter with their diabolic pact) transgress in enacting it. One is reminded of the words of Büchner's Danton: 'Es muß ja Ärgernis kommen, doch wehe dem, durch welchen Ärgernis kommt':[66] the agents of historical change, despite its deterministic inevitability, incur guilt. For Büchner, however, such guilt is apparently subjective, a personal agony, whereas, for Gotthelf, it is evidently an objective moral state. Revolt, so *Die schwarze Spinne* implies, can never be legitimate, but is always a 'Vermessenheit' (cf. SW XVII: 31) against divinely ordained order; challenging this is hubristic and ungodly. This is the final message of Gotthelf's text, which the author seeks to insinuate: the appropriate response even to political injustice is stoicism, for he who rebels loses his soul.[67] It also brings the text very close to Eichendorff's *Das Schloß Dürande* and its hubristic hero, the revolutionary Renald, likewise an illustration of the moral ruination which revolution represents (Renald, who, like Gotthelf's Christine, meets a devil of revolution – the Robespierre-like 'Bettler-Advokat' – and in the end has himself become quasi-diabolic).[68] The ending of *Dürande*, 'Hüte dich, das wilde Tier zu wecken in der Brust, daß es nicht plötzlich ausbricht und dich selbst zerreißt',[69] is very clearly also a motto for *Die schwarze Spinne*; the spider is likewise a symbol of a *Verwilderung* which is simultaneously psychological and moral, individual and social. 'Schwarmgeister brachen aus der Tiefe, entfesselten die bösen Geister in des Menschen Brust', said Gotthelf two years after *Die schwarze Spinne*, in a sermonising past tense, about the current revolutionary mood.[70] Despite all their differences of geography, confession, class and birthdate, these two devout and deeply anti-revolutionary authors are agitated by the same perception of threatening social forces that are mirrored in individual psychology, and by a similar notion of the directions in which salvation might lie; and the imagery with which they work is correspondingly akin. There are substantial differences between the two of them: notably, the endeavour of Gotthelf the *Volksschriftsteller* actively to mould the mind of an audience which can in some measure be called popular is entirely absent from Eichendorff, despite the folk-literary elements in the latter's style. But their greater affinities are a powerful symptom of the directions in which the reactionary mind moved in the Vormärz – psychologising, spiritualising, allegorising and mythicising – in the face of social disorder and incipient revolt.

Notes

1. See Franz von Baader, especially 'Über das dermalige Missverhältniss der Vermögenslosen oder Proletairs zu den Vermögen besitzenden Classen der Societät in Betreff ihres Auskommens sowohl in materieller als intellectueller Hinsicht aus dem Standpunckte des Rechts betrachtet' (1835) (in Baader, *Sämmtliche Werke*, ed. Franz Hoffmann, Leipzig, 1851–60, Part 1, vol. 6, pp. 125–44), and my introductory chapter, penultimate footnote. As was remarked there, 'Über das dermalige Verhältniss' is the most important of a series of 'socialphilosophisch' essays that the Bavarian Romantic-aristocratic philosopher Baader wrote after 1830, and which contain an extremely trenchant critique of the social consequences of liberalism. Cf. also Hans Kals, *Die soziale Frage in der Romantik*, Cologne, 1974, pp. 235–42.
2. See, for instance, Theodor Storm, letter of 24 February 1854, in Storm, *Briefe*, ed. Peter Goldammer, Berlin, 1972, 1: 229.
3. See Novalis, *Schriften. Die Werke Friedrich von Hardenbergs*, eds Paul Kluckhohn and Richard Samuel, Stuttgart, 1960, 3: 507–24, especially 509 and 519–24.
4. Joseph von Eichendorff, *Werke in sechs Bänden*, eds Wolfgang Frühwald, Brigitte Schillbach and Hartwig Schultz, Frankfurt/M., 1985–93, 5: 363 (*Unstern*). References to this edition will appear in the notes or text of the present chapter with the prefix 'W'.

5. W 6: 365; *Die geistliche Poesie in Deutschland* (1847). See Peter Krüger, 'Eichendorffs politisches Denken', *Aurora. Jahrbuch der Eichendorff-Gesellschaft*, 28 (1968), 7–32, and 29 (1969), 50–69 (p. 53). Other substantial discussions of Eichendorff's politics include: Alexander von Bormann, 'Philister und Taugenichts. Zur Tragweite des romantischen Antikapitalismus', *Aurora. Jahrbuch der Eichendorff-Gesellschaft*, 30/31 (1970/71), 94–112; Helmut Koopmann, 'Eichendorff, *Das Schloß Dürande* und die Revolution', *Zeitschrift für deutsche Philologie*, 89 (1970), 180–207 (see especially p. 197f.); Wolfgang Frühwald, 'Der Regierungsrat Joseph von Eichendorff. Zum Verhältnis von Beruf und Schriftstellerexistenz im Preußen der Restaurationszeit', *Internationales Archiv für Sozialgeschichte der deutschen Literatur* 4 (1979), 37–67; Klaus Lindemann, *Eichendorffs 'Schloß Dürande'. Zur konservativen Rezeption der Französischen Revolution*, Paderborn, 1980, especially pp. 17–37; Franz Xaver Ries, *Zeitkritik bei Joseph von Eichendorff*, Berlin, 1997. A number of these items are discussed further in subsequent footnotes.

6. The phrase in fact occurs in Eichendorff's autobiographical essay *Halle und Heidelberg*, describing the cultural project of Romanticism; W 5: 444.

7. From the poem 'Will's Gott!' (ca. 1848); W 1: 451.

8. W 5: 391–8.

9. W 3: 440f.

10. Cf. Alexander von Bormann, 'Philister und Taugenichts', especially pp. 94–103.

11. W 5: 472. This is also, more specifically, his view of the directions in which the Stein/Hardenberg reforms in Prussia pointed. See *Halle und Heidelberg*, W 5: 416–18. Wolfgang Frühwald's highly informative but sometimes speculative article 'Der Regierungsrat Joseph von Eichendorff' (esp. pp. 53–61) presents Eichendorff as part of a 'reformkonservativ' (i.e. comparatively non-reactionary), as well as anti-centralistic wing of the Prussian bureaucracy, a tendency that was heir to the Stein-Hardenberg tradition, and was supposedly finally defeated around 1840, when Eichendorff took early retirement. This is not quite convincing: Eichendorff's principal superior and protector (Theodor von Schön) may have been in origin a Stein/Hardenberg reformer; but *Halle und Heidelberg* certainly indicates Eichendorff's own scepticism. Also, Berlin centralism was itself in many ways a Stein/Hardenberg tendency. In addition, and perhaps more importantly, Frühwald's article generally locates Eichendorff's political preoccupations to an excessive degree within the internal quarrels of the aristocratic bureaucracy, whereas what his texts show, rather, is a strong concern with the wider class politics of his time, and specifically with the paths that point to social revolution.

12. Originally entitled 'Frühlingsfahrt'; W 1: 224.

13. W 2: 454.

14. W 5: 397. See also W 3: 186, 5: 393–6.

15. According to Peter Krüger, the 1830 Revolution '[hat] Eichendorff . . . kaum überrascht'. See Krüger, 'Eichendorffs politisches Denken', p. 10. In a theoretical sense, this may have been so; but the evidence of Eichendorff's texts is that the event nevertheless came to him as a significant shock.

16. See the (slightly indiscriminate) account of such imagery by Hans-Wolf Jäger, *Politische Metaphorik im Jakobinismus und im Vormärz*, Stuttgart, 1971, especially pp. 20–47 and 71–3 (the latter a short 'Exkurs' specifically concerned with *Das Schloß Dürande*). See also my introductory chapter, above.

17. According to Helmut Koopmann, these images are essentially not to be taken

metaphorically, but are Eichendorff's own realism. The 'Entfesselung von Naturkräften mit katastrophalem Ausgang' is for the author a real process. See Koopmann, 'Eichendorff, *Das Schloß Dürande* und die Revolution', p. 189f. The point is well made; and yet the 'Gewitter' and the 'gefesselter Löwe' *are* metaphor. Cf. also Lindemann, *Eichendorffs 'Schloß Dürande'*, pp. 69–81.

18. See Heinrich von Kleist, *Sämtliche Werke und Briefe in vier Bänden*, eds Ilse-Marie Barth, Klaus Müller-Salget, Stefan Ormanns and Hinrich Seeba, Frankfurt/M., 1987–97, 3: 39–47, 57–9, 65.

19. Ibid., 3: 27, 53, 55; 45–7, 83.

20. Ibid., 3: 263.

21. '. . . befand sich ein altes, einem Marchese gehöriges Schloß, das man jetzt, wenn man vom St. Gotthardt kommt, in Schutt und Trümmern liegen sieht'; ibid., 3: 261.

22. See Klaus Lindemann, *Eichendorffs 'Schloß Dürande'*, p. 179 (also p. 150). Lindemann devotes some time to the associations with Kleist in *Das Schloß Dürande*, in order then oddly to assert that 'Eichendorff die Kleistsche Novelle . . . keineswegs zum Vorbild für sein *Schloß Dürande* nahm'. Clearly he did, and in a fairly premeditated way. See also Klaus Köhnke, '"Der Mensch in der Welt": Untersuchungen zu Eichendorffs Versepen', *Aurora. Jahrbuch der Eichendorff-Gesellschaft*, 37 (1977), 7–20, esp. 16f., on Kleistian connections in Eichendorff's epic *Robert und Guiscard*, which is thematically related to *Dürande*.

23. Strikingly, for example, in early novels of Heinrich Böll, such as *Wo warst du, Adam?* (1951).

24. Eichendorff's last piece of prose fiction, the 'Märchen' *Libertas und ihre Freier* (probably written in 1849), contains a curious final reflection on Volk and revolution. Here the Volk is allegorised as the lumpish giant Rüpel, enlisted in quest of Libertas, the spirit of freedom, by the bourgeois revolutionary Dr Magog ('Demagoge' . . .). Dr Magog mistakes the vulgar 'Silberwäscherin' Marzebille ('früher . . . Marketenderin mit den Aufklärungstruppen'; W 3: 594) for Libertas, and absconds with her. Previously, Rüpel and Magog have encountered a 'schöne Dame', identified by Rüpel as 'Ihre Majestät die Elfenkönigin', riding a stag through an enchanted forest and into a mysterious 'Traumschloß'. Later she is revealed as having been the real Libertas, escaping from imprisonment by the capitalist Baron Pinkus. Magog is indifferent to her and scornful of stories of 'einfältiges Waldesrauschen, alberne Kobolde, Mondenschein und klingende Blumen, . . . nichts als Romantik und eitel Märchen, wie sie müßige Ammen sonst den Kindern erzählten'. But Rüpel is fascinated and captivated (W 3: 585f.). At the end, having been deserted by Magog, he is '[von den] dankbaren Vögel[n] . . . als Hüter des Urwalds angestellt' (W 3: 595), thus mustered in the service of nature and the spirits of nature. The story's implication seems to be that the Volk still have their pre-rational affinity with nature and ancient culture, and away from the influence of radical bourgeois leaders, may regain contact with this domain. The allegory is crass and very wishful. It is, though, interestingly close to Heine's politically rather different contemporaneous discovery of the Volk's latent cultural consciousness. And it is particularly notable as a belated attempt by Eichendorff to demonstrate a degree of respect for even the modern common people, despite all their ugliness and destructive collective power.

25. This is Gottfried Keller's faintly sardonic designation. See Keller, review in

Blätter für literarische Unterhaltung, 18–21 December 1849; in *Keller über Gotthelf*, eds Franz Carigelli and Heinz Weder, Bern, 1969, p. 10. This volume consists in all of four reviews of Gotthelf by Keller, published in the same journal between 1849 and 1855.

26. See Hanns Peter Holl, *Gotthelf im Zeitgeflecht. Bauernleben, industrielle Revolution und Liberalismus in seinen Romanen*, Tübingen, 1985, p. 162 ff.

27. See the petition which Gotthelf signed and probably composed in December 1830; in Gotthelf, *Sämtliche Werke in 24 Bänden* [plus 18 *Ergänzungsbände*], eds Rudolf Hunziker, Hans Bloesch, Kurt Guggisberg and Werner Juker, Munich and Bern, later Erlenbach-Zurich, 1911–1977, 13th *Ergänzungsband* (*Politische Schriften, Erster Teil*, 1956), pp. 19–25 (and cf. 260f.). This edition will be referred to in the present chapter as 'SW', with the principal volumes denoted by Roman and the *Ergänzungsbände* by Arabic numerals. See also letter by Gotthelf of 18 October 1830, in SW 4: 94f; quoted by Klaus Lindemann, *Johannes Gotthelf: 'Die schwarze Spinne'. Zur biedermeierlichen Deutung von Geschichte und Gesellschaft zwischen den Revolutionen*, Paderborn, 1983, p. 245. And see Karl Fehr, *Jeremias Gotthelf (Albert Bitzius)*, Stuttgart, 1985, pp. 27–30.

28. See SW 13: 82–4, 116–29 (*Politische Schriften I*); SW XV: 196 (*Die Armennot*).

29. See SW 13: 36f., 109, 220.

30. See SW XV: 71 (*Die Wassernot im Emmental*); 128, 189; 13: 44f., 86.

31. See SW 13: 86, 108f., 132–5, 143–50 (especially 144).

32. See, for example, SW XV: 158; 5: 154 (and 408f.); 13: 220.

33. In a recent article, Hellmut Thomke has tried to argue that the differentness of Gotthelf's political context from the norm of the German *Restaurationszeit* means he cannot be termed 'conservative' or 'reactionary' at all. It seems to me, on the contrary, that the terms are entirely legitimate, but that his distinctive political environment must be examined to see what it was he reacted against or sought to conserve. See Thomke, 'Gotthelfs "Konservativismus" im europäischen Kontext', in *Erzählkunst und Volkserziehung. Das literarische Werk des Jeremias Gotthelf. Mit einer Gotthelf-Bibliographie*, eds Walter Pape, Hellmut Thomke and Silvia Serena Tschopp, Tübingen, 1999, pp. 227–41, esp. p. 240f.

34. See, for example, SW XV: 158f., 13: 51, 193f.

35. *Keller über Gotthelf*, p. 21.

36. See SW 13: 108, 132–5 (and cf. 412).

37. See Holl, *Gotthelf im Zeitgeflecht*, p. 165.

38. See Fehr, *Jeremias Gotthelf*, p. 60; Holl, *Gotthelf im Zeitgeflecht*, p. 166.

39. See Fehr, *Jeremias Gotthelf*, p. 63f.

40. See, for example, SW XV: 72, 148.

41. See Gotthelf's *Kalender*-article *Die Jesuiten und ihre Mission im Kanton Luzern* of 1844; SW XXIV: 44–61 (and cf. 280–93).

42. One notes how, in his story *Die schwarze Spinne* itself, of 1842, Gotthelf insinuates a message of confessional tolerance, with the Catholic observance of the peasants in the pre-Reformation inner narrative – confession, absolution and infant baptism – normalised and even made part of the teleology of the tale.

43. *Keller über Gotthelf*, p. 37.

44. Lindemann, *Gotthelf: 'Die schwarze Spinne'*, p. 180.

45. For the *Volksdichter* that Gotthelf was and as which he certainly regarded himself, these notions contain a surprising degree of distaste. Keller remarks significantly how unsympathetic Gotthelf is in his works to the *culture* of the

common people: their folk-songs play no role in his works, he views their festivals and entertainments as pernicious, corrupting and to be discouraged. See *Keller über Gotthelf*, p. 25f.

46. Gotthelf himself remarked: 'Ich lebte außer allem literarischen Verkehr, und keine Hand zog mich auf und nach'; letter of 23 March 1839, SW 5: 38.
47. See SW 13: 58 (commentary); also Fehr, *Jeremias Gotthelf*, p. 34.
48. See, for example, SW 13: 41–5, 65–72, 74, 223–8.
49. See especially SW IV: 7–50.
50. This was the subtitle to the first edition. See SW X: 494.
51. Pace Holl, *Gotthelf im Zeitgeflecht*, p. 22f. In a number of Gotthelf's pieces of political journalism in the 1830s, the word 'Volk' seems to be coterminous with the electorate of Canton Bern. As was noted earlier, Canton Bern at the time had a property franchise. See SW 13: 132–5, 143ff., 167f.
52. SW XV: 8, 15, 20f., 27, 30, 32, 65–7, 69, 78f., 81.
53. Renate Böschenstein speaks interestingly of 'das umgangene Theodizeeproblem' as a feature of Gotthelf's writing. See Böschenstein, 'Mythos und Allegorie: Zur Eigenart von Gotthelfs Schreiben', in *Erzählkunst und Volkserziehung*, pp. 151–70, esp. p. 170.
54. On another plane, it is a reflection on ways of seeing, suggesting the incoherent plurality of ways in which a phenomenon such as the *Wassernot* may be interpreted or responded to: myth, political force, sin, apocalypse, divine punishment, divine mercy, etc. etc. There is about this an interesting hint of relativism.
55. *Genesis* 28, v. 12.
56. For example, SW XV: 32, 161, 181f.
57. Cf. *Kurt von Koppigen*, SW XVII: 226–358.
58. The claim in a recent article on Gotthelf's historical writing that 'das Historische . . . kaum eine Rolle spielt' in *Die schwarze Spinne* seems inattentive. See Daniel Fulda, 'Geburt der Geschichte aus dem Gedächtnis der Familie: Gotthelfs historische Erzählungen im Kontext vormärzlicher Geschichtsdarstellung', in *Erzählkunst und Volkserziehung*, pp. 83– 110, esp. p. 84. In the same volume, Renate Böschenstein's article 'Mythos und Allegorie: Zur Eigenart von Gotthelfs Schreiben' has an interesting discussion (see esp. pp. 164–9) of 'mythic moments' in Gotthelf's stories (of which the angelic apparition in *Käthi die Großmutter* would be an instance); but she does not speak of the kind of national and popular myth-making implicit in *Die schwarze Spinne*.
59. At the time it was written, the story was part of a plan by the author for a series of 'Schweizersagen und Bilder', to be gathered into successive historical 'Abteilungen', namely the Dark Ages, early Middle Ages and early modern period. See letter of 24 August 1841, SW 5: 151. The collection which was eventually published (in five volumes, 1842–4), was much more loosely organised. But the conception of a kind of history of Switzerland through its myths is very much corroborated by these details of *Die schwarze Spinne*.
60. Fehr, *Jeremias Gotthelf*, p. 55. Cf. also Gotthelf's article of 7 July 1839, *Über die Maul- und Klauenseuche im Emmental*, complaining of how the spread of an epidemic has been aided by the authorities' culpable neglect; SW 13: 130f.
61. See *Keller über Gotthelf*, p. 19f.
62. Ludwig Seeger, 'Schweizerische Belletristik. *Bilder und Sagen aus der Schweiz*, von Jeremias Gotthelf', in *Einundzwanzig Bogen aus der Schweiz*, ed. Georg Herwegh, Zurich, 1843; reprinted, ed. Ingrid Pepperle, Leipzig, 1989, pp.

453–5. Cf. letter by Gotthelf of July 1843, SW 5: 325 ('. . . Schlingel von Rezensent').

63. Although anti-semitic moments do occur in his writing. See, for example, SW XV: 171.

64. The figure of the red-headed interloper also implicitly alludes to, and joins in the demonisation of, the foreign revolutionary agitators who were a preoccupation and source of concern for the authorities and more prosperous sections of the populace in contemporary Switzerland. The epitome of such revolutionaries, the Communist German *Schneidergeselle* Wilhelm Weitling, a figure of some prominence, was finally expelled from Switzerland in 1843. See Holl, *Gotthelf im Zeitgeflecht*, p. 204.

65. See Lindemann, *Gotthelf: 'Die schwarze Spinne'*, pp. 102–6.

66. Georg Büchner, *Werke und Briefe. Münchner Ausgabe*, eds Karl Pörnbacher, Gerhard Schaub, Hans-Joachim Simm and Edda Ziegler, Munich, 1988, p. 99 (Act II, Sc.5).

67. Cf. the author-narrator's condemnation in *Käthi die Großmutter* of those who demand temporal justice in respect of their poverty: SW X: 320.

68. Eichendorff, W 3: 438–40, 442, 457, 461.

69. Eichendorff, W 3: 465.

70. In a draft postscript to *Die Armennot*, dated by the author as ca. 1844; SW XV: 252.

4

Nestroy, the Rabble and the Revolution

Johann Nestroy did not suffer the problem which in one way or another beset Büchner, Heine and many other contemporaries in their folk-literary concerns and endeavours, that the literature they produced had no practical access at all to the real common people. In contrast to them, Nestroy was authentically and comparatively unproblematically engaged in producing work which could indeed be termed – and on one recorded occasion in his sparse correspondence he did term – 'Volcksdichtung'.[1] He wrote his seven dozen plays for performance in Vienna in institutions publicly labelled 'Volkstheater', and knowingly positioned them within the long tradition of anti-establishment comic drama for the lower orders which these institutions represented. While there are many uncertainties regarding the exact social make-up of Nestroy's audiences, it is clear, under any circumstances, that he reached parts of the body politic with his work which others could not.

The uncertainties about his audiences concern both the breadth of the social spectrum that these encompassed and how their composition may have shifted over time. There is, for instance, a claim regularly articulated in Nestroy criticism, originating apparently with Otto Rommel, that sharp price rises were implemented in the Viennese *Volkstheater*, under Karl Carl's leadership, in the late 1830s (the dates quoted vary) which significantly raised the social level of the audiences by excluding their poorest section, and that this is reflected in a shift in the character of Nestroy's plays.[2] Where evidence is offered for this scenario, it turns out to be rather insubstantial.[3] Ultimately the scenario is neither verifiable nor refutable, but it certainly seems sociologically and economically a

101

little implausible. Price and audience shifts in the performing arts do not generally occur in such a revolutionary fashion. The suggestion that by the end of the 1840s the Volkstheater audience was basically plutocratic requires a good deal more evidence than has hitherto been supplied.[4] And it is essentially more likely that any developments which occur in the content of Nestroy's plays are caused, if not by simple changes in authorial disposition, then by shifts in the tastes of the given audience, rather than by great upheavals in the audience's social composition.

In a slightly different vein, some writers on Nestroy like to suggest that his audiences were in themselves socially and ideologically riven, between the prosperous bourgeoisie in the stalls and the proto-revolutionary plebeians in the upper tiers, that these groups reacted antithetically to the plays, and that Nestroy himself addressed them diversely (in particular, that he sought to placate or delude the former while really communing with the latter).[5] There is very occasional evidence of a sharp divergence within an audience in its reaction to a particular play (for instance, with *Judith und Holofernes* in 1849[6]), and isolated reference is to be found in specific plays to the 'Galleristen' as a discrete and influential group within the audience. A *Kupferschmiedlehrjunge* says to a playwright in *Weder Lorbeerbaum noch Bettelstab*: 'Und wann Sie wieder ein Stück schreiben, so verfeinden S' Ihnen ja mit die Lehrbub'n nit; die letzte Galerie gibt nicht selten den Ausschlag, und da geb'n wir den Ton an'.[7] It is probable that his audiences were relatively more socially heterogeneous and stratified than those to be found in most forms of the modern theatre. Contemporary descriptions suggest quite a wide range in both social status and level of income, from moneyed bourgeois and aristocratic youth to artisans and servants.[8] However, notions that Nestroy's audiences were habitually in deep schism, and readings of his work based on such notions, are not really credible. After all, if a sizeable section of an audience hates a production, it is disrupted and it flops. The contemporary commentator whose descriptions seem to provide the prime ammunition for such a view, Moritz Gottlieb Saphir,[9] had his own tendentious reasons for presenting Nestroy thus (that is, for suggesting that the 'better' part of Nestroy's audience was, deep down, disaffected with the playwright). In reality, there must have been in Nestroy's theatre a general and fairly powerful coming together of the disparate social groups which made up the audience. This is also what contemporary descriptions (other than Saphir's) suggest.[10] Nestroy's public, one judges, was indeed a public of the Viennese *Volk*, embracing an extensive social range of the city's working (non-destitute) population, and he produced work which was highly proficient at catering for, conditioning and reconciling – not alienating parts of – that public's evolving taste.

The term 'Volk' was, of course, problematical, in Nestroy's ambit as elsewhere. Even disregarding the further complication of its usage in national contexts, there are signs in contemporary commentaries on Viennese conditions of discomfort at its ambiguity as a social concept. 'Das Theater an der Wien . . . war damals . . . ein Volkstheater im eigentlichen Sinne des Wortes', said the playwright Friedrich Kaiser in 1870, looking back on the *Vormärz*, '. . . wenn man das Wort "Volk" nicht etwa für identisch mit dem Wort "Pöbel" hält, sondern unter jenem die Mittelklasse der Residenzbewohner, Bürger, Beamte und die nicht bloß an sinnlichen Genüssen hängende Arbeiterschaft versteht'.[11] Whether or not Kaiser's nostalgic description of his and Nestroy's audience is accurate, the troublesome and important question of how far down the social scale 'Volk' extends is clearly signalled. Nestroy himself, in his post-revolutionary play *Lady und Schneider*, of 1849, alludes mockingly to this dilemma – the middle-class desire for a Volk which excludes the irredeemable rabble – when his hero, the aspirant revolutionary Heugeign, proclaims fatuously at a moment of triumph and enthusiasm: 'Man zeige mich dem Volk in seiner nobelsten Bedeutung!' (HKA 26/II: 46). Furthermore, this implicit sneer by the playwright underlines precisely the problem that many observers of the time had with Nestroy himself.

The aim of most contemporary bourgeois practitioners of forms of pseudo-*Volksliteratur* – Auerbach, Gotthelf and others – was idealistic: to induce the moral beautification of the common people by presenting them with ideal images of themselves, or with didactic, admonitory fables. Even such more radical practitioners as Heine may, in the end, be called idealists in that sense. Of course, an approach of this kind presupposed that such beautification was needed, and that the common people's existing moral state represented a problem or a danger. What observers of Nestroy in the 1830s and 1840s saw, by contrast, was a highly successful and powerful popular art, reaching deeply down the social scale, with an almost complete lack of such ambitions and ideals. Nestroy, in this respect as in others, was a radical anti-idealist.[12]

Some observers were admiring. In particular, commentators

responding to his first major success, *Der böse Geist Lumpazivagabundus oder Das liederliche Kleeblatt*, in 1833, were excited and impressed. Gustav Pabst, writing in the journal *Der Sammler*, spoke of the 'Talent..., welches der Verfasser in diesem Stücke für Schilderungen aus dem Leben gegriffener Volksscenen verräth', and saw great promise in the 'volksdramatische Richtung' which this signalled.[13] The Burgtheater actor Carl Ludwig Costenoble wrote in April 1833 of the enthusiasm for *Lumpazivagabundus* which he and most of his colleagues felt, with one exception: 'La Roche war der Einzige, der die Nase rümpfte und meinte, so etwas gehöre in die Hanswurstbude. – Diese weimarische, schöngeistische Zimpferlichkeit wird La Roche in Wien bald ablegen'.[14] Soon, however, such unease seems to have been Costenoble's own feeling towards Nestroy and his theatre. In a much-quoted passage of 1838 he noted: 'Sein Wesen ... erinnert immer an diejenige Hefe des Pöbels, die in Revolutionsfällen zum Plündern und Todschlagen bereit ist. Wie komisch Nestroy auch zuweilen wird – er kann das Unheimliche nicht verdrängen, welches den Zuhörer beschleicht'.[15] And a string of other significant commentators, from both inside Vienna and beyond it, were to write of him with similar distaste. Karl Gutzkow observed in 1845:

In Verbindung mit dieser Wut nach exzentrischen Vergnügungen kann sich auch die Bühne einen großen Teil der Schuld beimessen, zur Verwilderung des Volkscharakters beigetragen zu haben. Die *Zweideutigkeit* und die *Selbstironisierung* haben besonders in den Nestroyschen Stücken einen Einfluß auf die untern Klassen ausgeübt, die ihnen zwei der kostbarsten Kleinode des Volkscharakters raubte: sittliche Grundanschauung der Dinge und gläubiges Vertrauen gegen Menschen. Das ist entsetzlich, wie Nestroy, dieser an sich ja höchst talentvolle Darsteller, in seinem Spiel fast noch mehr als in seinen Productionen dem sittlichen Grundgefühl und der gläubigen Naivität des Volkes Hohn spricht. Man denke sich die bis zum Giebel gefüllten Theater, besetzt von Handwerkern und ihren Frauen und Töchtern und sehe diese Gestikulationen, diese Mienen, höre diese Späße, dieses Anwitzeln jeder überlieferten edlen Empfindung, diese zweideutigen Randglossen zu den Motiven von Tugend und Edelmut – es überlief mich kalt, ein ganzes Volk so wiehern ... zu sehen, wenn die Equivoque gezündet hat oder Nestroy, die Achsel zuckend, die Liebesversicherungen einer Frau, die Zärtlichkeiten eines Gatten mit einem satanischen 'O je!' oder dergleichen begleitet. Da steht nichts mehr fest, keine Liebe, keine Freundschaft, keine großmütige Hingebung. Die schamlosen gesungenen Couplets (die rechten *Cancans*, die bei den Franzosen aus der errötenden Sprache in den

stummen Tanz verbannt wurden) sagen es ja deutlich, daß . . .
Eigennutz die Triebfeder jeder Handlung ist. Es ist das fürchterlich,
eine Bevölkerung solchen blasirten Anschauungen überliefert zu
sehen.[16]

In 1848, Berthold Auerbach complained, regarding *Freiheit in
Krähwinkel*: 'Die echte Volkskomödie, wie sie einst erstehen
soll, ist hier zu einem wahren Scheusal, zum ekelhaften Abguß
aller Niedrigkeit geworden. Es ist jammervoll, daß solches noch
[i.e. following the successful accomplishment of the Revolution]
bestehen kann'.[17] Friedrich Theodor Vischer commented in 1861:

> Wir wollen nicht die tierische Natur des Menschen, wie sie sich just auf
> dem letzten Schritte zum sinnlichsten Genuß gebärdet, in nackter
> Blöße vors Auge gerückt sehen, wir wollen es nicht hören, dies kotig
> gemeine 'Eh' und 'Oh' des Hohns, wo immer ein edleres Gefühl zu
> beschmutzen ist, wir wollen sie nicht vernehmen, diese stinkenden
> Witze, die zu erraten geben, daß das innerste Heiligtum der
> Menschheit einen Phallus verberge . . . Es bedurfte natürlich eines so
> bedeutenden und erfindungsreichen komischen Talents, wie es in
> Nestroy versumpft ist, um ein Publikum gegen das tiefer und tiefer
> gehende Versinken ins Gemeine abzustumpfen, den Übergang vom
> gesunden Lachen in das Meckern des Bockes ihm unvermerkt
> einzugeben.[18]

And the playwright Bauernfeld said in a late memoir (of 1873): 'Die
Skepsis, die Weltverachtung und der krasse Egoismus [traten] im
Bunde mit der gröbsten Sinnlichkeit gewissermaßen als handelnde
Personen auf, und das Publikum wie sein Lieblingsdichter waren
immer bereit, jede bessere Empfindung, jeden freien, edlen
Gedanken zu verspotten, zu verhöhnen, in den Staub zu ziehen'.[19]
These passages of liberal critique, with their imagery of plebeian Dionysia (Bauernfeld spoke also of 'bacchantische[r]
Volksjubel' and 'Korybanteneinzug'[20]) and demonisation of
Nestroy as its agent, are only the most memorable and celebrated
expressions of what was a widespread view of him.[21] It is important to understand the politics of such criticism. The imperial
authorities were, of course, concerned throughout Nestroy's career
at the social challenge that his comic Volkstheater represented,
believing that it was liable to undermine among its audience the
values of order, decency, piety, respect, obedience which were perceived ultimately to underpin society and the state itself, and the
enduring rigorous censorship of his plays was motivated by this

concern. It should be noted also that the Austrian state's repression of material likely to disturb and mislead the common people did not focus solely on expressions which might be called left-wing, as its measures against popularist Catholic obscurantism during the Vormärz show.[22] But the authorities' objections to Nestroy's Volkstheater were often shared by bourgeois liberal opinion, including that of liberal partisans of the 1848 revolution. They standardly concurred with, and even exceeded,[23] the authorities' perception of the lower orders as dangerously morally defective and in crucial need of moral education and uplift – which they certainly did not find in Nestroy's work.

This does not mean, however, that Nestroy personally was more politically radical than they were. There is no contradiction in the fact that, for example, the critic Moritz Gottlieb Saphir, a prominent antagonist of Nestroy's and agitator in the 1840s for a more moral Volkstheater,[24] was a more radical supporter of 1848 than Nestroy. The disposition of some modern commentators to caricature Saphir as the leftist Nestroy's reactionary opponent is quite wrong.[25] Nestroy said in 1849, in a draft 'open letter' to his enemy, that the sight of Saphir parading through Vienna as a revolutionary had cured him of his own revolutionary and republican leanings:

> Ich saß da vom Freyheitsschwall so gut ergriffen wie Hunderttausend Andere, da weckte mich ein Wagengeräusch aus republicanischen Träumen . . . Du dummes Saphirchen, du selbst warst es. Du als Nationalgardist einen großen Säbel angeschnallt, . . . mit allen möglichen Bändern der Freyheit geschmückt . . . Da bekam ich ein degout von der Freyheit, die Vernunft behauptete ihr Recht wider, und ich sage es mit Stolz, ich bin ein Schwarzgelber [the Habsburg colours] geworden, und zwar vom allerschwärzesten Gelb.[26]

Nestroy opted in the end not to publish the letter; and there is also an element of semi-ironic posing about it. Nevertheless, it is one of the author's relatively few direct political statements and must be given a degree of credence.

Nestroy's politics are indeed difficult to pinpoint. His plays, produced under intense commercial and contractual pressures as they were, do not provide straightforward evidence, and we do not have a wealth of programmatic statements by him in other contexts. His attitudes seem likely to have been variable and mood-dependent: what the open letter to Saphir acknowledges most clearly is an uncertainty and mutability of opinion. They also seem very likely to have shifted over time – that is, with advancing age and greater personal prosperity and security. By the time that he began to express himself politically in correspondence in the later stages of his life – largely because his letters only then became sufficiently expansive to include such expressions – he appears to have been a fairly secure Habsburg royalist, a 'legitimistischer Patriot', anti-clerical and also anti-nationalist (that is, hostile both to the separatist national movements in the Austrian empire and to pan-Germanism).[27] One might have called his politics Josephinist (and occasionally critics suggest this[28]), except that to do so implies a rationalistic optimism which is not really germane to Nestroy. A letter of 1861 suggests, interestingly, that at that stage he saw his (conservative pessimist) contemporary Grillparzer, who had recently been nominated to the Austrian House of Lords, as a particularly reliable political voice. In any event, it is hard to imagine – although one cannot be sure – that these had been exactly Nestroy's views in the early phases of his career: when, for example, in 1836, at the age of 34, he was, absurdly, locked up in an imperial prison for extemporising slanderously on stage.[29]

There have been numerous less than convincing attempts by critics at defining Nestroy's political position. A recent book by Eva Reichmann has argued, lengthily and unpersuasively, that Nestroy's plays are altogether designed to communicate a 'konservative Gesellschaftsidee', that they aim to present 'eine den konservativen Gesellschaftstheorien seiner Zeit entsprechende Gesellschaftsord-nung als Lösung der sozialen Unzulänglichkeiten seiner Zeit'.[30] More interestingly, although with some polemical exaggeration, Rio Preisner argued that Nestroy's anti-idealistic outlook constituted an 'aufgeklärte[r] Konservativismus', directed especially against contemporary bourgeois liberalism.[31] Much more frequent, however, have been approaches which depict Nestroy more or less explicitly as a revolutionary socialist – for whom, for example, the problem with the 1848 Revolution was the insufficient radicalism of its bourgeois supporters. Thus Horst Denkler explains how Nestroy pursued a careful, veiled but systematic strategy of 'Abbau des . . . Akkreditierten' through the Vormärz, in anticipation of the moment when 'die Zeit für die revolutionäre Tat gekommen [wäre]': he devoted himself to revolutionising the Viennese theatre politically, thereby seeking to revolutionise the Viennese citizenry themselves, until 'die von ihm angebahnte Revolution des Empfindens und Urteilens in die Wiener Revolutionsereignisse des Jahres 1848 einmündete'.[32] Günter Berghaus follows a slightly different, but clearly related line, according to which Nestroy moved from revolutionary optimism in the early 1830s, through pessimism and resignation in the late 1830s and early 1840s, fresh optimism in the second half of the 1840s, to renewed but somehow more hopeful resignation in the 1850s, in response to supposed rightward or leftward shifts in the political tastes of his audience – but always with a basic 'humanistische Grundposition' and revolutionary commitment.[33] According to Erich May, meanwhile, the Volkstheater in the 1830s and 1840s was an enduring battle between a 'bürgerlichdemokratisch' tendency (Nestroy and others), on the one hand, and, on the other, a 'rückschrittlich', 'demagogisch', pro-'feudalabsolutistisch' view, which wanted a more moral drama to predominate: the most radically progressive position was reached in the early 1840s, after which – circa 1845 – a 'Verfall der VormärzPosse' occurred, reluctantly conceded to by Nestroy himself, a 'krasse . . . Veränderung' in which the genre lapsed into 'kleinbürgerliche[s] Pathos' and was politically severely '[e]ntschärf[t]'. Moritz Saphir was the arch-spokesman of the reactionary position, Nestroy the most radical ('kleinbürgerlich-plebejisch') representative of the progressive standpoint.[34]

These last scenarios not only tend to contradict each other, but are also individually disfigured – May's very informative book in particular is disfigured – by the fallacious desire which underlies them to make Nestroy into a kind of programmatic communist. If there is a truth about Nestroy's personal politics, it is probably that there was a gradual rightward shift over the course of his career, from a position of generalised anti-establishment cynicism in the Vormärz. Most of the time, Nestroy did not, of course, need a defined political position. He was not called upon or inclined to write politically programmatic material; he was not a theoreticallyminded author seeking self-definition; there were no political parties for him to join, and he generally had no vote. It is interesting, though, that at the point in his life when political positions did emerge and have to be displayed relatively clearly, around 1848, the expectations of his contemporaries seem to have been that Nestroy was or would be comparatively conservative. The anonymous *Flugblatt* in praise of *Freiheit in Krähwinkel* in which the writer pronounced: 'Ich hätte nie geglaubt, daß Nestroy so ultra liberal sein kann', is a significant document of the way in which he was – not necessarily inaccurately – perceived.[35]

It would seem that the plebeian-Bacchanalian element in Nestroy's comedy was not equated by contemporaries, or by Nestroy himself, with political radicalism. For his contemporary critics, both in the governmental establishment and among its liberal (bourgeois-revolutionary) opponents, the spirit of Nestroy's plays was, above all, 'pöbelhaft', a cynical, amoral, exploitative pandering to – a (Saphir's nice phrase) 'bestialische Stimulanz'[36] of – lumpen instincts. 'Nestroy ist kein Volksdichter', said the Berlin popular satirist Adolf Glaßbrenner emphatically in 1836, 'sondern ein Pöbeldichter'.[37] This was Nestroy cast in the kind of role which left-liberal opinion nowadays accords to the right-wing tabloid press. It is striking that when the literati of Austria – Grillparzer, Bauernfeld, Grün, Stifter and others – assembled their famous *Schriftstellerpetition* of 11 March 1845 to the government against the intolerable burden of censorship, Nestroy, the author whom censorship affected most intensely, was not invited to join. The association of such a noble-minded plea for liberty and responsibility with Nestroy's rabble-rousing amorality was not to be contemplated.

At the same time, it is clearly also the case that Nestroy's plays, or at least some of them, have what strikes us now as significant and potentially radical social and political content. Nestroy's 'pöbelhaft' social cynicism produces a de facto challenge to established values and social verities which, in effect, corroborates the kind of analysis that other, more premeditated and also essentially more moralistic social critics of the time (Büchner, Marx) take as the basis of a revolutionary socialist ideology: the sense of a world directed by self-interest, systems of values created by the wealthy and powerful to sustain and justify their position and legitimate their venality, a spreading awareness, especially among the poor, of the spuriousness and mendacity of such values, and a compensatory popular resort to hedonism. With Nestroy, the difference is that he has no disposition to discover idealistic alternatives to current reality, to be realised after the present world collapses. Nestroy's absolute incapacity to believe in human improvability is the key.

As one examines the specific content of Nestroy's socially and politically most evidently challenging plays – those works in which the social conflicts of the age seem to resonate most strongly – it is difficult to keep such a position securely in mind: an author providing radically critical, potentially socialistic social analysis on the basis of a more or less indifferentist political outlook. But this is, indeed, Nestroy's situation.

Nestroy's essentially most socially aggressive plays date from the first half of the 1830s, having been produced in the climate of challenge to the established order which followed the July Revolution, and by Nestroy as a relatively unestablished young man. Attempts by such as Horst Denkler to view the mid to late 1840s as Nestroy's most critical phase do not bear textual scrutiny.[38] Two plays in particular, *Der böse Geist Lumpazivagabundus* and its sequel *Die Familien Zwirn, Knieriem und Leim* (1833 and 1834), represent a triumphant destructiveness of outlook which he never quite achieved again. *Lumpazivagabundus*, of course, is Nestroy's *Woyzeck*, or his *Schloß Dürande*, the work in which he reflected most directly on the spirit of social disorder abroad in the world. Many contemporaries were intrigued and, in a way, distracted by the cheerful and novel social realism of the play – in particular in the inn scenes: waltzing to zither music, drinking pints of beer and schnapps, eating bread and kidneys, sleeping on straw, buying from hawkers, playing the lottery, singing, yelling and breaking glass (HKA 5: 81–94, 130; 143–55, 184f.). The critic Pabst, as we have seen, identified in the play a new 'volksdramatische Richtung' – the beginnings of an escape from the dreary magic-play elements which had come to pervade the popular theatre (HKA 5: 356). Even the censors, when they gave the play its imprimatur in 1834, accepted the argument of Nestroy's publisher that the work's 'derbere Volkssprache und größere Deutlichkeit' were justified by its status and purpose as 'Volksstück' (HKA 5: 493f.). Doubts about its propriety seem to have grown stronger over time and with repetition, as the play's powerful hold over audiences manifested itself. The most vituperative comments date from a couple of years later: 'ein Drama für betrunkene Hetären', 'Sodom und Gomorrha der Gemeinheit', and 'dieser eckelhafte Fuselmensch [Knieriem]'.[39] But the work's substantial subversiveness must have been perceptible in some sense from the outset, for it was clearly part of the basis of its success.[40]

A spirit of disintegration runs through much of the play. As one critic has said, its real and omnipresent hero is the 'evil spirit' Lumpazivagabundus himself, an 'allegorische Reduktion [des] Zeitgeistes'[41] and Faustian 'Geist der Verneinung'.[42] The 'liederliche Gesellen', Knieriem and Zwirn, with their attachment to no other values than gratification, are his incarnation. However, he is also theirs: they are the impecunious *Lumpen* and *Vagabunden* whom travelling journeymen were actually becoming in Vormärz Germany, a manifestly socially disorderly effect of the modern economy.[43] It should not be thought that, for informed contemporaries, such processes were a mystery.

The play is fairly, although not completely, systematic in its demolition of the values of civil society. The 'liederliche Gesellen' are shown lying, cheating, stealing, fornicating (implicitly), gambling, intoxicating themselves and practising or threatening violence (e.g. HKA 5: 80–92, 109–14; 142–53, 165–71), all with perfect insouciance, both on their own and on the author's part. Nestroy clearly had a sense that their pursuit of immediate personal gratification, of beer and skittles, was a class pattern, as Zwirn's exchange with a serving girl in Meister Hobelmann's bourgeois household suggests: '"Nicht wahr, das ist ein fades Leben da?" – "Da thun s'" nix als, arbeiten, essen, trincken, und schlafen, is das eine Ordnung?"' (HKA 5: 125, 181). There is also a notable aphorism of Nestroy's, which reflects significantly on the central motif of *Lumpazi*, concerning the compensatory importance of lottery betting for the deprived: 'Man redet gegen die Lotterie, ohne zu bedenken, daß sie die einzige Spekulation der Armen ist. Die Lotterie verbieten: dem das Reich der Träume verwehren, dem die Wirklichkeit ohnedies nichts geboten' (GW 6: 562). However, the journeymen's venality is also replicated in the play (less attractively) at other social levels, notably with the violence, larceny, lasciviousness and mendacity which surrounds Zwirn when he joins high society in Prague. Meister Hobelmann's household in Vienna appears to offer a moral antithesis – industrious, thrifty, moderate and monogamous. It supplies the ideal which the authorities and, conceivably, a good deal of public opinion wished to see finally affirmed by the play – indeed, which *was* affirmed, at least sufficiently strongly for one critic of the time to discover and approve in it a 'rein moralische . . . Tendenz' (HKA 5: 358). For a while, the scenes of petty-bourgeois domestic comfort, normality and good sense around Hobelmann and Peppi constitute a kind of alternative ethical centre to the journeymen's hedonism. Even here, however, there are signs of difficulty: hints of monetary greed and violence, and then the final, ironic tableau, with its implication of familial oppression (HKA 5: 100, 102, 132; 158, 160, 186f.).[44]

Then there is the play's framework in fairyland. That Nestroy saw the pattern of the *Zauberstück*, in which supernatural beings endeavoured to direct human actions, as a metaphor for social power and control, is evident in particular from his play *Die beiden Nachtwandler*, of 1836, in which the structure is reversed: two rich Englishmen are mistaken for and able to masquerade as supernaturals through the power their infinite wealth confers. In *Lumpazivagabundus*, fairyland is still fairyland; but the chief fairies present an image of ineffectual and troubled authority. The spirit Lumpazi is dominant, his 'Grundsätze' prevail in the higher as in the nether world, the rulers are unable to restore moral order by exhortation in either domain, and their only – ineffective – solution is coercion and tyranny.

The play's culminating expression of these realities is Knieriem's celebrated 'Kometenlied', with its sneering refrain, 'Die Welt steht auf kein Fall mehr lang' (HKA 5: 123f., 179–81). The song is a virtuoso blend of perceived manifestations of social and other disorder and disruption in the world which preoccupied or had preoccupied the public mind in the years after the July Revolution: the comet of 1832, and the apocalyptic anxieties and nihilistic reflections it induced;[45] the social and political chaos threatened by people like Knieriem himself, by the emergence of dispossessed, rootless, disaffected and politically uncontrollable masses ('. . . reist ohne Unterlaß/Um am Firmament und hat kein Paß;/Und jetzt richt ein so ein Vagabund/Uns die Welt bey Butz und Stingel z' Grund'; HKA 5: 123, 179); and disease, in particular the cholera epidemic of 1831/32, which people connected causally with the new demography of migration, urbanisation and pauperisation ('Der Sonn ihr G'sundheit ist jetzt a schon weg,/Durch'n Tubus sieht man's klar, sie hat die Fleck'; HKA 5: 180).[46] To these, Nestroy's song also joins some other phenomena as symptoms of a world disintegrating: brightly lit and ruinously tempting department stores, extravagant clothing fashions, and a high-circulation popular press. The connections – and the song as a whole – are not systematic and analysed. A significantly comparable text of the time, the 'London' chapter of Heine's *Englische Fragmente* of 1827, is a much more premeditated attempt to interlink the phenomena of a modern capitalist society (and suggest how the seeds of revolution lie within it).[47] Nestroy's song does not, for instance, try to indicate quite *how* absurd fashions and the *Pfennigmagazin* might be signs of incipient social collapse. But it is remarkable enough in presuming and signalling, in a song in a popular comedy, that the connections exist.

We must be a little careful, however, of taking such a critique of capitalism and portrayal of the logic of social disorder in the Vormärz as the play's sole and absolute meaning. What makes the investigation of Nestroy's messages difficult and interesting is that, in a conscious sense, he barely had any: the meanings in his comedies are not so much purposes as thematic impulses, disparate perceptions of the way the world is, which are quite able to contradict each other within a play, as well as between plays. Self-evidently, the exigencies of Nestroy's writing did not prescribe complete thematic consistency. In *Lumpazivagabundus*, the affirmation of petty-bourgeois normality in Peppi's and Hobelmann's household is outweighed, but it is not wholly cancelled out, by the proletarian 'revaluation of all values' which the 'liederliche Gesellen' perform. There is also, equivalently, a notable moment in the play when Zwirn and Knieriem are expected by the logic of their behaviour hitherto to pocket and squander money which has been offered to them in order that they can visit the supposedly sick Leim in hospital in a distant city, but in fact they do the opposite: '"Da könnts euch einen frohen Tag drum machen". – "Ja, das wollen wier auch". – "Aber auf eine andere Art, als der Hr. Hobelmann glaubt" . . . – "Wier bringen ihm das Geld" . . . – "Und kein Kreutzer wollen wier anbringen unterwegs, eher Hungerleiden" – " . . . Und wann mir die Gurgel beym Ellbogen herausschaut, als so ganzer soll er seine Hundert Thaler kriegn"' (HKA 5: 120, cf. 176f.). Such emancipatory anti-determinism – the characters decline to obey their own natures – is an impulse seen at various levels in Nestroy: in characters with bizarre and unexpected attributes; roles which temporarily break down and the character becomes the actor, or becomes no-one in particular; and the frequent episodes in his comedies in which individuals seek freedom from the roles society and the world have accorded them (*Einen Jux, Der Zerrissene* etc.). It is part of what generated, especially in the 1960s, a kind of existentialist strand in Nestroy criticism (the books by Hannemann, Preisner, Brill, etc.[48]), disposed to see him altogether less as a social revolutionary than as a sort of ontological nihilist. It also represents an interesting phenomenon in the context of manifestations of and reflections on characterological determinism in other German-language drama of the period (Büchner, Grillparzer, Hebbel and onwards to Hauptmann). But in any event, it is an ingredient to be recognised in *Lumpazi*: at a moment when the play might have finally endorsed and ratified its theme of dissoluteness, it opts not to do so. The characters choose, so to speak, to be whom they want to be. Principally, *Lumpazi* is indeed a play about contemporary social disintegration and the devaluation of values; but this is a preponderant, not an exclusive meaning. Other meanings co-exist complicatedly and unresolvedly with it and they require acknowledgement.

Nestroy's sequel to *Lumpazivagabundus*, the play *Die Familien*

Zwirn, Knieriem und Leim, of 1834, appears to have aroused greater official disapproval when first performed than did *Lumpazi*. Emperor Franz himself apparently complained about it, and a prohibition was placed on it in 1835 (HKA 8/I: 215–18). One can see why. The work lacks the exhilarating, liberating *Volkstümlichkeit* of *Lumpazi*, being located predominantly in a context of bourgeois domesticity. Its basic plot is also more conventional, with routine love intrigues providing an essential framework. But where it outdoes *Lumpazi* is in the rigour of its cynicism. The three journeymen of *Lumpazi* are revisited twenty years later, and are found in various forms of unbecoming degradation. Above all, the domain of petty-bourgeois familiality, which received only very muted criticism in *Lumpazi*, and sometimes appeared as a place of soundness and good sense, is here thoroughly denigrated. Knieriem has settled down to a domestic life of drunken wife-beating. Zwirn, having deserted wife and daughter and returned to itinerancy, reappears and is keen to marry off his now grown-up daughter for money. And Leim and Peppi have become bickering, exploitative and snobbish, preoccupied with marrying their children to grasping aristocrats for social advantage. The play is very exhaustive in its sceptical revaluation of values and discrediting of ideal sentiment: 'Überzeugt von der Aufrichtigkeit Ihrer Gesinnung, reiche ich Ihnen mit Genehmigung meiner gnädigen Eltern Herz und Hand', says a prospective betrothed, having just acknowledged her father's injunction: 'Greif zu, denk an die fünfzigtausend Gulden' (HKA 8/I: 52). 'Auf diese Weise [habe ich] alle meine Pflichten als Gatte und Vater erfüllt', says Zwirn of his abandonment of his daughter to uncaring foster parents (HKA 8/I: 26). Discord and dislike are the norm within marital life: 'Ich hab nicht nötig, nach dem Weibe eines andren zu trachten, ich hab selber eine, und mir is die z'wider g'nug' (HKA 8/I: 40). A *Couplet* which Knieriem sings about marriages in the locality is a sequence of tales of conflict, rage, contumely, vanity, adultery and family bankruptcy (HKA 8/I: 38). Love, one episode of the play indicates, is a sentiment which serves primarily to permit its object to subjugate and humiliate the sufferer (HKA 8/I: 62–5). And in other spheres: a character's creditors are delighted when he ceases to be friendly towards them, as it signals a new ability to pay (HKA 8/I: 59); or a girl sits at her dressing table and sings, 'Auf mich die Blicke fallen,/Geh ich wo immer hin,/Denn das schmückt mich vor allen,/Daß ich nicht eitel bin' (HKA 8/I: 227). 'Es herrscht', as the play says, 'Beständigkeit im Reich des Lasters' (HKA 8/I: 12).

The only general exemptions from this social cynicism are those accorded the three journeymen's own children, High-German-speaking characters who are barely part of the social reality of the play at all. They and their true love for each other are vindicated at the end, in routine Italian Comedy style – 'die . . . Sprossen jenes Kleeblatts zeigten edlen, biedern Sinn', intones the supervisory spirit Stellaris (HKA 8/I: 88) – and their parents, too, are finally perfunctorily *gebessert*. 'Ich bin zur Einsicht gekommen und kehr in meinen vorigen bürgerlichen Kreis zurück', says Leim piously (HKA 8/I: 91). As a whole, however, what the play conveys is that the dissoluteness which in *Lumpazi* was seen primarily at the social margins, among the deprived underclass (or among the shiftless pseudo-aristocracy of Prague), is paralleled in a moral corruption or vacuity at the core of orderly society itself. This is how Nestroy has extended the conception of *Lumpazivagabundus* for the play's sequel; and the authorities' greater distaste and concern at *Die Familien Zwirn, Knieriem und Leim* is unsurprising.

At the same time, the play lacks the proto-revolutionary ingredients which we, and certainly some contemporaries, found appealing in *Lumpazi*: the element of a diagnosis of the modern economic and social world, and the sense of a liberating abrogation of established values by the protagonists. In *Die Familien Zwirn, Knieriem und Leim* the main characters' vices are fairly joyless and not really liberating at all. The play contains one curious and famous moment of explicit socio-political challenge, when Knieriem tells the vain and mendacious aristocrat Mathilde: 'Es wird bald eine Stunde schlagen, wo es keine Fräuleins und keine Schuster mehr gibt . . . Der Unterschied der Stände hat aufgehört; Herrschaft, Bedienter, gnädiger Herr, Bettelmann, Fräuln und Schuster, das is itzt alles eine Kategorie' (HKA 8/I: 74f.). On the other hand, what he is specifically foreseeing is the arrival of the comet that same day – which duly fails to happen. His forecast of cosmic catastrophe is proved embarrassingly wrong, and life goes banally on; his political prediction is, presumably, also suspect; and certainly the comet itself, by missing its appointed date, loses a good deal of the force it had in *Lumpazi* as an image of the political future. For all its social destructiveness, *Die Familien Zwirn, Knieriem und Leim* does *not* really say: '*Die* Welt steht auf kein Fall mehr lang'.

Zu ebner Erde und erster Stock, which Nestroy wrote in 1835, is another early play of considerable social acerbity but no straightforward radical message. With its split stage it presents an

extraordinary graphic image of social division, inequality and conflict. The extravagance of the wealthy – the *Lieferant* Herr von
Goldfuchs and family on the upper floor – is elaborately and ironically contrasted with the deprivation of the poor – as the *Tändler*
Schlucker and his family on the ground floor approach starvation
(GW 2: 463–6). Other aspects of the social divide are acutely
observed: for example, how the poor are always frightened – of
figures of authority, of creditors, and of the wealthy themselves –
whereas the rich are naturally at ease (GW 2: 468f., 480, 518f.,
521). As Goldfuchs remarks ('*wohlgefällig*'), 'Eine Million ist eine
schußfeste Brustwehr, über welche man stolz hinabblickt, wenn
die Truppen des Schicksals heranstürmen wollen' (GW 2: 480).
The clichés of moral censure, through which the rich habitually
regard the poor, are satirically laid bare: '"Mir scheint, ihr seid ein
liederliches Volk" – "Fünf Kinder und ein schlechter Verdienst is
eine Liederlichkeit, die manche Haushaltung derangiert"'; '"Wer
kein Geld hat, soll auch nix essen" – "Versteht sich! Kinder haben
nie ein Geld und essen alleweil"' (GW 2: 469, 430). The play does
indeed convey a considerable sense of social injustice. On the other
hand, there are clearly features which work against such a mood,
parallelisms across the social divide. Manias such as gross paternal
unreasonableness operate both upstairs and downstairs; impulses
to corruption – both monetary and sexual – are evident both above
and below; and there is incitement and resort to violence on both
levels (although it is more naked and threatening among the poor)
(e.g. GW 2: 453f., 523f., 535, 538). The women in the play are uni-
versally reasonable, with mania and vice male attributes (a pattern
which is *not* standardly found in Nestroy). We also have salient
pronouncements from one of these rational women, from below
stairs, which seem to advocate an acceptance of inequality: 'Man
muß die Welt nehmen, wie s' is, und nicht, wie s' sein könnt'; 's
Glück is kugelrund; es kann alles noch anders werd'n' (GW 2:
441f.). And the outcome of the play confirms the latter proposition,
as the poor family gains a legacy and the rich one is bankrupted.
Of course, Nestroy's endings not uncommonly take the audience
into a domain of the patently unreal, serving to signal that the
reverse is or may be the truth. But it is not absolutely clear that this
is the intention here.

The key figure in the play, in this as in other regards, is the servant Johann, whom Nestroy played. He is a manipulative, cruel
and deceitful villain, who is defeated at the play's end. With his
daemonic aura, Johann is highly reminiscent of the symbolic,

satanic provocateurs of revolution who occur in texts by conservative authors of the time – the Robespierre figure in Eichendorff's *Das Schloß Dürande*, Gotthelf's *Grüner Jäger* in *Die schwarze Spinne*. Indeed, the moment in the play when Johann (temporarily) triumphs is proclaimed with what is practically a slogan of revolution: '(*Sich stolz emporrichtend und mit festem Tone.*) Jetzt bin ich der Herr!' (GW 2: 492) – 'We are the masters now'. At the same time, he is also a catalytic figure who reveals through statement and action the real basis of society: that honour, respect and social order are founded merely on wealth and crude self-interest (GW 2: 515f., cf. 521); and he is made the mouthpiece of the play's most considered and rational passages of specific social observation: a song about the spread and destructive consequences of gambling, and a little disquisition on insurance – about its extraordinary prevalence and the inadvisability of uninsured commercial speculation (GW 2: 496–8, 515). This is a play which has not resolved on a unified social view. It sees the injustices and the moral illusions and deceptions on which society was founded. It also sees the instability of the modern social and economic system – like the department stores, fashion industry and penny-magazine in Knieriem's *Kometenlied*, and many other phenomena that Nestroy was to observe (railway boom, factory industry et al.). Goldfuchs's disastrous mercantile speculation is a symptom of a world in some disorder. But the play does not predict a specific outcome from this or even commit itself morally to one. Its social analysis is ultimately indeterminate.

Der Talisman, which Nestroy wrote in 1840 on the basis of a French original and staged with immense success (see HKA 17/I: 109–38), has much in common structurally with *Zu ebner Erde*, having another catalytic outsider as its central figure, although a less satanic one. With its semi-bucolic setting, slightly tiresome word-playing repartee and comfortably *biedermeierlich* conclusion, *Der Talisman* seems in a way a mild, relatively unaggressive play. In the figure of Titus, however, there are a range of resonances which contain a substantial element of veiled social and other challenge. Titus is a recognisable Hanswurst,[49] not only carnal and venal himself, but recognising and revealing the carnality and venality of others. In particular, his juxtapositions of high ideal and feeding are familiarly Hanswurstian: '"Ich muß trincken, mich druckt's in Mag'n" . . . – "Die druckt's im Magen! o könnt' ich dieses seelige Gefühl mit ihr theilen!"'; '"Wenn nur frohe Hoffnung glimmt,/Endigt alles gut bestimmt . . ." – "Mit ein'm orndlichen

Mag'n –/. . . Man kann alles ertrag'n'" (HKA 17/I: 13, 74).[50] Titus
with his red hair is diabolic, tempting the characters into corruption: he is called at one point a 'Teuxelsmensch' (HKA 17/I: 17).
He is also, again with his red(headed)ness, the figure of a revolutionary, once more like various characters in both Eichendorff's
Das Schloß Dürande and Gotthelf's *Die schwarze Spinne*: labelled
'Vagabund' and (implicitly) 'Lump' (HKA 17/I: 62f., 51), he evokes
the same principle of social chaos which Lumpazivagabundus represented. It is a connotation reinforced by his status as journeyman
artisan, a member of the class from which such danger primarily
came, and further emphasised by the artisan's language Nestroy
gives him (not just conventional snippets of trade vocabulary, but
a general way of speaking that is strikingly aggressive, energetic,
profane and socially disrespectful). The redheadedness of Titus
and Salome and the prejudice it arouses suggest, in addition, Jew-
ishness and anti-semitism. Salome herself also represents and
articulates a complaint against gender prejudice (HKA 17/I: 22).
Finally, Titus in a sense is, or has, no character at all: he is free,
able to assume identities by choice and reducible to none, existence without essence:

> FRAU v. CYPRESSENBURG . . . (*Zu* TITUS.) Ich sehe Sie bald wieder.
> TITUS (*wie vom Gefühl hingerissen*). O nur bald – ! (*Thut, als ob er
> über diese Worte vor sich selbst erschrocken wäre, faßt sich, verneigt sich
> tief und sagt in unterwürfigem Tone.*) nur bald ein Geschäft, wo ich
> meinen Diensteifer zeigen kann. (HKA 17/I: 55)

An extension of Zwirn's and Knieriem's existentialistic moment in
Lumpazivagabundus, Titus's being is an evasion of and challenge
to bourgeois determinism: 'Da hab ich alle Verhältnisse abg'streifft
wie man ein engen Kaput auszieht in der Hitz, und jetzt steh' ich
in den Hemdärmeln der Freiheit da' (HKA 17/I: 15).

These are a large number of challenges. Clearly, they are not all
a matter of class politics: a view of *Der Talisman* which sees the
play merely as Nestroy's prediction (and advocacy) of social revolution does not do it justice.[51] What is really involved – here as elsewhere in Nestroy – is a multiplicity of critical perspectives, which
do not resolve into a single ideological stance, although they are no
less acute or significant for that.

The comedy *Der Unbedeutende*, which Nestroy wrote and performed in 1846, is notable in having yet another catalytic, critical
central figure (the carpenter Peter Span), but in this case one who
is a Good Man, and who figures in a plot concerning besmirched

and vindicated virtue. It is suggested that the play was a conces-
sionary response by Nestroy to the campaign by Saphir and others
in the 1840s for a 'new', morally affirmative *Volksstück*.[52] Indeed,
this may be so: besides the novelty of an honourable hero, details
such as the play's elaborate recreation of a village *Kirchweihfest* (M
5: 39 ff.) suggest some such purpose. The play was welcomed by
critics at the time for this aspect, and has been criticised for it
more recently. For instance, Siegfried Brill, in his book *Die Komödie
der Sprache*, has designated a group of Nestroy's plays, identified
as Volksstücke in this sense and with *Der Unbedeutende* prominent
among them, as 'failures' on the grounds that the 'positive
Aussage' they contain cancels out the thoroughgoing critique of
language which is to be regarded as Nestroy's overarching achieve-
ment.[53] This is a very obscure argument, though the implication
that a lurch into sentimentality or out of cynicism disfigures plays
by Nestroy, on the relatively rare occasions that it occurs, strikes
one as correct. However, it is not quite accurate to see *Der Unbedeutende* in this way. Apart from its basic proposition of Peter
Span's honourableness and his slandered sister's virtue and inno-
cence, this is, in fact, a very cynical play.

To begin with, the play's depiction of the Volk in this Volksstück
– at the Kirchweihfest and before it – is thoroughly critical: they
show themselves by turns spiteful, hypocritical, self-righteous, las-
civious, greedy and ignorant. These vices are particularly stimulated by the situation of Peter's sister Klara, traduced by a
treacherous member of the upper classes; but the play exploits
every incidental opportunity for such portrayal:

> [KIND.] Wie ich im Bett lieg, kommen die Gspenster.
> [MUTTER.] Wennst mir mitn Fürchten nicht aufhörst, so schick ich den
> Schwarzen über dich, mitn großen Sack, da steckt er dich hinein, und
> tragt dich in Wald hinaus.
> [KIND] (*halbweinend*). Uh mein!
> [MUTTER.] Begreif nicht, wie der Bub so furchtsam worden is (HKA
> 23/II: 25).

Moreover, there are moments in the play when the saintly Klara
herself begins to seem comically weird (HKA 23/II: 46). Peter
Span's rectitude, too, has moments of comic absurdity: the play
does have occasional problems of tone, with signs in its (not very
numerous) mawkish moments that the author is having difficulty
preventing his adopted note of sentimentality from lapsing into
ridicule (e.g. HKA 23/II: 46–9). And in any event, it is very striking

that Peter Span, despite his noble rectitude, is himself a thorough-going cynic. His *Couplets* and monologues are among the classics of Nestroy's scepticism (HKA 23/II: 19–22, 24, 59–64).

The play's approach to its characters drawn from the common people is thus primarily and powerfully satirical, with little ideali-sation. It is noticeable that, even at the end, when Klara's inno-cence has been revealed, the benighted villagers who have shunned her are made to realise their misapprehension, but are not particularly shown being morally cured. At the same time, how-ever, the play sets up a sharp opposition between a world of privi-lege, wealth and power on the one hand, and powerless and impecunious ordinary people on the other, with the latter tri-umphant at the end: 'PETER . . . Wenn Sie wieder einmal mit unbedeutende Leut in Berührung kommen, dann vergessen Sie ja die Lektion nicht, daß auch am Unbedeutendsten die Ehre etwas sehr Bedeutendes ist. (*Der Vorhang fällt.*)' (HKA 23/II: 83).

In fact, if the play's portrayal of the world of privilege is con-sidered in isolation, it seems socially highly critical. This is the domain of Baron von Massengold, apparently feudal aristocrat (lord of the manor) and capitalist millionaire all in one: his name suggests a totality of power. In his household, the 'Schloß', those who surround him are directed in much of their behaviour by fear of his authority. In a pattern which recurs elsewhere in Nestroy (*Der Schützling, Höllenangst* . . .), he is not depicted overtly as a tyrant, and is even seen at the play's end resolving events in the interests of justice and virtue; but all around him is anxiety at his power. His minions are 'Sklaven', the play suggests (HKA 23/II: 9). He himself is, and is able to be, wholly heedless: one of his entourage remarks: 'Was Vorsicht, was Rücksicht, wer mitten in Millionen drinnen steht, der sieht vor sich und hinter sich nur Mil-lionen, und braucht weiter keine Vorsicht, und keine Rücksicht' (HKA 23/II: 14). Moreover, the climate of the household is a basi-cally amoral one. Massengold and his entourage are merely amused by the villain Puffmann's supposed seduction of Klara Span, his 'momentane Michhinwegwerfung an eine unbedeutende Person' (HKA 23/II: 33f.). Monetary or other personal advantage is the main motivation of the entourage and the servants of the household. In the end, Puffmann is only defeated because an enemy of his within the household allies himself expediently with Peter Span in Span's campaign for justice.

Even Peter Span's own behaviour on entering the Schloß acknowledges the latter's norms, as he controls his anger and adopts the tone of obsequiousness towards his social superiors which is required to advance his cause (HKA 23/II: 58). At the same time, however, his campaign does represent a degree of social challenge, which is variously expressed. He speaks to Puttmann baldly of 'die angeborne Feindschaft zwischen Arm und Reich' (HKA 23/II: 71). There is violence in his demeanour, partly suppressed but also partly evident to his antagonists (HKA 23/II: 70, cf. 58). And at a significant moment towards the end, when Massengold seeks to placate his indignant tenants with a personal assurance based on his given social authority – 'Meine lieben Anwesenden, ich hoffe, mein Wort wird Euch genügen. Herrn Puffmanns Erklärung ist vollkommen befriedigend, läßt sich jedoch, zarter Beziehungen wegen, nicht füglich veröffentlichen' – Span rejects this authority: 'Alle Achtung vor Hochdero Wort, aber wenn die Beziehungen noch zehnmal so zart wären, . . . für laute Beschimpfung gibt's keine stille Erklärung' (HKA 23/II: 80).

This is not actually the concluding message of *Der Unbedeutende*, which ends a little later with the central villain humiliated, Massengold resolving matters like a benevolent deity and he and Peter Span in happy concord. As so often in Nestroy, the play as a whole is socially irresolute, with elements of clear class critique mixed with other ingredients – satire of general human frailty, images of social reconciliation and harmony – which countervail it. But the critique of power that the play contains is at least substantial and significant (and cannot be said to be rendered ineffective by the unusual rectitude of Nestroy's hero).[54]

When, finally, the upheaval of society and politics which Nestroy, along with everyone else, had sensed was coming, indeed occurred in 1848, the response in his plays was characteristically and interestingly disparate. We have a group of plays from and reflecting on the 1848 Revolution and its aftermath which illustrate particularly acutely the intricacy and inconsistency of his view. *Freiheit in Krähwinkel*, the work Nestroy composed and performed within the revolutionary year proper (and free for the first time from official censorship), is clearly a tempered affirmation of the revolution. It is aggressively critical towards the forces of reaction, emphasising cruelty, indifference and, in particular, corruption, though it focuses to a great degree on what was for Nestroy in a way a personal issue: the pre-revolutionary regime's censorship mechanisms.[55] The play's portrayal of the citizen-revolutionaries is vastly more sympathetic. The work's hero is himself an agreeable and clever revolutionary, and the work is, as it were, structurally pro-revolution: its conventional plot of parentally thwarted, then victorious, young lovers also supplies the process of events which leads to successful accomplishment of the Krähwinkel uprising. As the Flugblatt which was quoted above said: 'Ich hätte nie geglaubt, daß Nestroy so ultra liberal sein kann' (HKA 26/I: 196). At the same time, however, the revolutionary characters in the play are laughed at for their vanities and petty self-interests, and several heroic moments of the real revolutionary year are travestied (HKA 26/I: 36–8, 51f., 64) – to an extent sufficient to offend some liberal commentators.[56] The play also points equivocally to some of the revolution's fundamental problems. The anonymous and terroristic figure of a proletarian, which is one of Ultra's, the *Nestroy-Rolle*'s, incarnations (HKA 26/I: 69), alludes teasingly to the central, unresolved dilemma and bugbear of the bourgeois revolution, namely the pauperised masses and how they should be resisted or accommodated. The play's inclusion of the impersonated figure of a Russian prince-general, supposedly ready to march in with his troops, alludes to a real threat (HKA 26/I: 42–5). The work's suspect final proclamation, 'Die Reaction ist ein Gespenst, aber Gespenster giebt es bekanntlich nur für den Furchtsamen; drum, sich nicht fürchten davor, dann giebt's gar keine Reaction' (HKA 26/I: 77), as well as elements of the hero Ultra's second song shortly before this (HKA 26/I: 71–5) and the Bürgermeister's third dream vision of a victory for reactionary forces at the end of the first act (apparently omitted in later performances; see HKA 26/I: 256), all signal the possibility of the revolution's collapse.[57] The appearance of *Freiheit in Krähwinkel* in early July 1848 immediately followed the June Days in Paris, which were the first major conservative victory of the revolutionary year, so the uncertainty which the play intimates about the revolution's outcome must have been widespread. Nevertheless, Nestroy's fellow-playwright Friedrich Kaiser, an enthusiast for the revolution whom the play also briefly mocks (HKA 26/I: 51f.), reportedly complained that the work 'male den Teufel an die Wand' in an unfortunate fashion.[58] Certainly the play was, and it was doubtless intended to be, close to the margins of tolerability for its pro-revolutionary audience.

As compared with *Freiheit in Krähwinkel*, however, Nestroy's first play to follow the defeat of the revolution, *Lady und Schneider*, of February 1849, represents a fairly clear step to the right. Its central figure, the tailor and aspiring revolutionary politician Heugeign, is admittedly not the hypocrite and villain he is often represented to be by critics,[59] but rather a sympathetic enthusiast and 'Fantast'

(HKA 26/II: 25). His much-quoted cry: 'Sie müssen mich noch wo an die Spitze stellen, . . . liberal, legitim, conservativ, radical, oligarchisch, anarchisch oder gar kanarchisch, das is mir Alles eins, nur Spitze!' (HKA 26/II: 23), is not cynicism but passion. However, the play is structured around his political delusions and stupidity, as he misinterprets a series of aristocratic amorous and financial intrigues optimistically as revolutionary plotting, 'Staatsumsturz- und Terrorismusentwicklungen' (HKA 26/II: 79). Also, the work contains some prominent anti-revolutionary aphorisms, generally pronounced by Heugeign but detached (in songs or dreams) from him as a character: 'Ah, wenn d'Freyheit Communismus wird, nein,/Da hört es auf ein Vergnügen zu seyn' (HKA 26/II: 67); 'Das Volk is ein Ries in der Wiegen, der erwacht, aufsteht, herumtargelt, Alles zusammtritt, und am End wo hineinfallt wo er noch viel schlechter liegt, als in der Wiegen' (HKA 26/II: 17); etc. When Heugeign speaks politically with his own voice, he is a fool: 'Man zeige mich dem Volk in seiner nobelsten Bedeutung!' (HKA 26/II: 46); 'Meiner Seel, ich werd Agitator, nacher schau ich mich um a Paar Millionen Stimmen um' (HKA 26/II: 56). Various episodes depict revolutionary activity as an excuse for idleness, drunkenness or profiteering (HKA 26/II: 16, 47). And the play ends, apparently without irony, with Heugeign seeing 'Raison', renouncing his former 'Narr[heit]' and resolving to confine himself henceforth to marital politics only ('Fahr ab, Öffentlichkeit! . . .'; HKA 26/II: 79f.).[60]

The work's portrayal of its aristocratic characters is interesting. It really is a new development in Nestroy's plays of the late 1840s and early 1850s that characters from the high aristocracy begin to appear who are actually sentient human beings – not mere figures of menace or other power perceived from afar, but individuals whose own fates are significantly at issue. The aristocrats in whose society a good deal of *Lady und Schneider* takes place are, it is true, often corrupt, idle, snobbish or stupid. 'Wenn der sich 's Brod verdienen müßt!', says a character early in the play, contemplating the feckless and distracted Paul von Hohenhausen, '– für manchen Menschen is es a wahres Glück, wenn er a Graf is' (HKA 26/II: 10). But Paul von Hohenhausen thereby becomes a figure with detailed idiosyncrasies, like very many others of Nestroy's second-string characters, not just an impersonal foil for the principals. There are certain signs in the Nestroy of this time of a diminution in social antagonisms, or a widening of social perspective.[61]

Nestroy's other full-length post-revolutionary play to be

performed at this time, *Höllenangst*, of November 1849, is partly based on a French original, a comic political melodrama from 1831 – a derivation which the *Theaterzettel* carefully emphasised (HKA 27/II: 102–20, 277). Nestroy's selection of such a model at this time nevertheless clearly constitutes a response to the revolution, and the stream of references to 1848 which his adaptation contains reinforces the fact. Nestroy's play is organised not dissimilarly to *Lady und Schneider*, with a dense artisanal hero of pro-revolutionary sympathies, embroiled in and misconstruing the intrigues of aristocrats. Now, however, not only the artisan but also one of the aristocrats is a persecuted revolutionary; and the artisan's persecution is said to be due to his having helped the aristocrat to flee (HKA 27/II: 18, cf. 7f.).

As this constellation of characters suggests, the work is written in a generally more liberal spirit than *Lady und Schneider*. Not only is virtue clearly on the side of these heroes, but the aristocratic hero's main persecutor, a senior minister whose eventual death leads to the former's rehabilitation, is indicated to be part of a network of corruption. On the other hand, such a plot clearly also serves to defuse revolutionary antagonisms, for it minimises the revolution's class basis and personalises its politics. In fact, there is much of this kind of ambiguity or indeterminacy in the play. The artisan Wendelin sings a long initial song imagining demands for 'Gleichberechtigung' among minerals, plants and animals and concluding (in allusion to 1848 in Vienna), 'Als Sturm-Petition käm' zum Himm'l ihr Begehr'n –/Meiner Seel', 's müßt dem Himmel höll'nangst dabey wer'n' (HKA 27/II: 16): it is entirely unclear whether the song's message is that equality is absurdly contrary to nature, or that it is a universal and irresistible aspiration. Elsewhere, Wendelin and his father, Pfrim, have a dialogue in which Pfrim announces, 'Bey einem Andern kann man sagen, es is Lumperey, bey mir is es Bestimmung, daß ich immer in eine schiefe Stellung komm'. Glaub mir, Sohn, wir sind alle Zwey zu edel für diese Welt', but Wendelin immediately afterwards convincingly describes how 'Die Vorsehung hat mit die Reichen, mit die Glücklichen zuviel zu thu'n, für die Armen bleibt ihr ka Zeit' (HKA 27/II: 20): thus the exchange contrives to indicate both that the deprived suffer unjustly and that their sufferings are due to their own fecklessness. Finally, there are two further long songs which make explicit mention of 1848. In one, doubt is cast, first, on the claims of the authorities across Europe that order has been restored, and then the phenomenon of 1848 radicals who have turned into furious reactionaries is joked about (HKA 27/II: 29f.). In the other, a verse of persuasive sorrow for 'unser Freiheitstraum' is followed by one which says that political opposition is really motivated by personal indebtedness and sexual dysfunction (HKA 27/II: 55). The refrain of the first of these songs, 'Na da müss'n eim bescheidne Zweifel aufsteig'n' (HKA 27/II: 28– 30), contriving to say all and nothing, rather epitomises the play's evasiveness.

Höllenangst gives clear evidence that the censorship regime to which Nestroy was subject in late 1849 was less repressive than the one which preceded the revolution. Elements such as Wendelin's identification as a 'Proletarier', the contention that the devil is a businessman, the notion that aristocrats interbreed, a joke about papal absolutions, and the political details about governments and monarchs in the songs, would not have been tolerable before 1848 (HKA 27/II: 31, 45; 21; 39; 32f.; 29f.). Yet, at the same time, the play seems cautious: subtly uncertain as to just how far its satire can be pressed and inclined to retreat at salient moments. In the end, one cannot be clear to what extent the work's indeterminacy is tactic or philosophy, although presumably both are involved. One does conclude, though, that part of its intention is a kind of conciliation, appropriate to the new *Nachmärz* climate in which the revolution has formally failed, but where aspects of what it represented – a new liberality and openness, a relative weakening of social barriers – have found their way (supposedly) into the body politic. *Höllenangst* is socially a rather *hopeful* play.

Nestroy's other major play of the revolutionary aftermath is *Der alte Mann mit der jungen Frau*, composed some time in 1849 (probably even before *Höllenangst*: see HKA 27/I: 94), but not performed during Nestroy's life. It is commonly presumed, though the evidence is circumstantial, that this was because the work could not have hoped to pass the censors.[62] In any event, it is another play which shows some signs of struggling for a response to political circumstances. Set 'in einem kleinen Fürstenthum' (HKA 27/I: 9, cf. 13) – and thus avoiding a specifically Austrian location – it combines comic-sentimental drama on the topic of the title with a substantial sub-plot concerning the persecution of ex-revolutionaries. Kern, the dignified and tolerant hero, has not been a revolutionary himself, but in his 'theilnehmende . . . Gemütlichkeit' (HKA 27/I: 13) aids one who has escaped from imprisonment. The latter, Anton, a clerk, is a man of honour and conscience. Indeed, the play altogether acknowledges, particularly through its central mouthpiece, Kern, that the revolutionaries were people who possessed these qualities but succumbed to a brief passion ('. . . einen kurzen Freyheitsrausch'; HKA 27/I: 15), and they should now be treated leniently. Policies of general amnesty should now be pursued (HKA 27/I: 15). This is especially the case because so many people were complicit in the revolution:

> Was Sie gethan haben, das haben Hunderttausende, das hat, – sey's durch That, oder Wort, oder Gesinnung, – fast Jeder gethan. Wer kann bey der jetzigen Krisis in Europa sagen, 'ich war nicht dabey' – ? Die Revolution war in der Luft, Jeder hat sie eingeathmet, und folglich, was er ausg'haucht hat, war wieder Revolution. Da muß sich keiner schön machen woll'n. (HKA 27/I: 23f.)

– and because there has been such inequity in the subsequent treatment of the participants:

> Nach Revolutionen kann's kein ganz richtiges Straf-Ausmaß geben. Dem Gesetz zufolge, verdienen so viele Hunderttausende den Tod – natürlich, das geht nicht; also wird halt Einer auf lebenslänglich erschossen, der Andere auf Fünfzehn Jahr eing'sperrt, der auf Sechs Wochen, noch ein Anderer kriegt a Medaille – und im Grund haben s' Alle das Nehmliche gethan. (HKA 27/I: 24)

One notes that this not exactly a liberal position. The latter speech, addressed by Kern to Anton, is prefaced by the phrase, 'Verdammen Sie . . . Ihre Richter nicht' (HKA 27/I: 24). The perspective the play adopts, through Kern, is essentially that of a moderate supporter of authority, disposed to bend the rules and protect an honourable fugitive not on principle, but out of instinctive charity and in acknowledgement of the past pervasiveness of the psychosis of revolution. A reasonable man's position, the work implies, is to have been caught up emotionally in the enthusiasm of 1848, but then to have realised its excessiveness, to dislike and be pleased to thwart the vindictiveness of some in authority now, but basically to approve the restoration of authority.

The play's central political concern seems to be reconciliation, in particular the question of how to reintegrate what Kern calls the 'Wühler', who were the committed revolutionaries (HKA 27/I: 47). In its sentimental plot, too, the text thematises conciliation and forgiveness: the adulterous, then contrite 'junge Frau' is given by her severe but still-loving husband an opportunity for atonement and pardon which she will apparently take (HKA 27/I: 80–3). An allegoric connection between this and the play's politics is to be presumed. Admittedly, the work's final political gesture is a retreat: a government decree arrives proclaiming amnesty for fugitive revolutionaries only on condition that they emigrate immediately to Australia, and Anton is implausibly indicated to be very happy with such an arrangement (HKA 27/I: 82). One concludes that this is the least intolerant outcome that Nestroy felt the restored censorship would permit him to depict. But the play's political stance overall appears to be an advocacy, from a mildly anti-revolutionary position, of magnanimity and social reharmonisation. It may be asked whether this, too, is conditioned by censorship; but Nestroy was under no obligation to write about such topical matters at all.

The play has further ways of suggesting that the revolution was a phase of now-outgrown immaturity. In particular, a line of political metaphor runs through it, jokingly transferring terminology of the revolutionary period to the private sphere and trivialising its original content: 'Das wird noch a schöne Verfassung werd'n in dem Haus, –'; 'Ich [bin] ja frey, freyer als a verbothne Zeitung'; 'Durch Lügen sind sie [wife and lover] miteinander verknüpft . . . Somit erwachst mir das schöne vormärzliche Recht, geheime Polizey zu etablieren in meinem häuslichen Staat –' (HKA 27/I: 33, 49, 44). Yet, at the same time, it contains some satirical ingredients germane to the revolutionary spirit: a pastiche of judicial-bureaucratic behaviour and language in Anton's chief pursuer, Amtmann Spitz (HKA 27/I: 63–5); and a satire of aristocratic snobbery at a mixed social gathering 'im gräflichen Schlosse': 'Es wimmelt ja hir von besitzender Bourgoisie [sic]!'; 'So geht's, wenn man Leute einladet, deren Stand keinen Respect einflößen kann'; 'Das Land der Pöbelhaftigkeit wünsche ich stets Tausend Meilen von mir' (HKA 27/I: 50, 58, 56). The counter to this last attitude is social mixing. 'Warum soll auf dem Lande sich nicht Hoch und Nieder mengen?', the mildly enlightened Baron Wetterhahn remarks (HKA 27/I: 57). In fact, the play is critical of social discrimination at various levels – among parvenus as well as the nobility of birth (HKA 27/I: 27). Nestroy's play manages to combine a comparative political conservatism with social liberality, the two being reconciled by a basic mood and message of political and social (and emotional) conciliation.

There are indeed signs of a spirit of affirmation in these two post-revolutionary dramas by Nestroy (a spirit which is, arguably, pursued and reinforced by the highly successful sentimental Volksstück *Kampl*, which followed). There are the symptoms of a kind of comparative social contentment on the author's part which is some way from the destructive perceptions offered in such plays as *Lumpazivagabundus* and *Die Familien Zwirn, Knieriem und Leim*, at the beginning of Nestroy's career. Certainly Nestroy evolves, and in a direction which is more or less conservative. However, the main impression which his plays' social and political content leaves, when examined with due care, is its variability and indefiniteness. His stance shifts, as we have seen, from play to play, largely without system, affected, it is to be presumed, by contingencies of subject matter and by other, more external factors – the successes and failures of his competitors, the momentary demands of his theatrical employer, shifts in the censorship, political and social events – the specific impact of which is not easily gauged. But above all, his stance within individual plays is often very far from unified, with what one can call diverse critical impulses pulling in different ways successively, or at the same time. Given the way in which – and the purposes for which – his comedies were produced, this should not be unexpected. The elusive, apparently unresolved nature of his personal political opinions also makes it unsurprising – although dealing with it is difficult for a literary criticism which expects premeditated themes and messages. Nestroy's thematically unselfconscious literature nevertheless demands approaches which heed such ambivalence and do not gloss over it tendentiously. His plays may be frustrating in their 'polysemic' character, or lack of thematic single-mindedness, but this is also part of what makes them interesting, offering as they do a different interpretive experience from that provided by more conventional, thematically purposeful, canonically ambitious literature. In addition, the ambivalence is in its way a source of value. With *Der Talisman*, for instance, it is the lack of ideological fixity of the play which makes possible the kind of imaginative suggestiveness, the plurality of resonances around the central figures, which distinguishes the work. The text is enhanced by the fact that its author does not need to avoid contradicting himself. And something similar could be claimed of many of the other plays which have been examined here. Finally, it can be said that attention to such ambiguities is not just the only way to grasp the intricacies of Nestroy's work and outlook, but is also a source of general insight into the complex realities of people's social and political attitudes at the time. The unresolved contradictions in Nestroy's plays illuminate the nuances and tensions of real social and political thinking in and after the Vormärz, as we observe how pro- and anti-revolutionary impulses, monarchic and egalitarian sentiment, social conservatism and plebeian radicalism, and scepticism and social outrage could coexist in the same mind. These are the real-life anomalies which more formal political analysts would have sought to eliminate as they wrote, but which these plays by Nestroy leave triumphantly and authentically intact.

Notes

1. Letter of 2 April 1852, in Johann Nestroy, *Briefe*, ed. Walter Obermaier, Vienna, 1977, p. 97. This volume is an unnumbered component of Nestroy, *Sämtliche Werke. Historisch-kritische Ausgabe*, eds Jürgen Hein and Johann Hüttner, Vienna, 1977ff. (referred to subsequently in this chapter as 'HKA').
2. See, for example, Franz Mautner, 'Geld, Nestroy und Nestroy-Interpretation', in *Theater und Gesellschaft. Das Volksstück im 19. und 20. Jahrhundert*, ed. Jürgen Hein, Düsseldorf, 1973, p. 116; Bruno Hannemann, *Johann Nestroy. Nihilistisches Welttheater und verflixter Kerl. Zum Ende der Wiener Volkskomödie*, Bonn, 1977, p. 44; Bernhard Greiner, *Die Komödie: eine theatralische Sendung. Grundlagen und Interpretationen*, Tübingen, 1992, p. 302.
3. For example, Erich May, *Wiener Volkskomödie und Vormärz*, Berlin, 1975, pp. 87–98.
4. See May, *Wiener Volkskomödie*, p. 97.
5. See Wolfgang Rothe, *Deutsche Revolutionsdramatik seit Goethe*, Darmstadt, 1989, p. 82; Günter Berghaus, 'Rebellion, Reservation, Resignation: Nestroy und die Wiener Gesellschaft 1830–1860', in *Viennese Popular Theatre: A Symposium*, eds W.E. Yates and John McKenzie, Exeter, 1985, pp. 109–22 (p. 112); Erich May, *Wiener Volkskomödie*, pp. 91ff., 181–6, 225.
6. See Colin Walker, 'Nestroy's *Judith und Holofernes* and Antisemitism in Vienna', *Oxford German Studies* 12 (1981), 85–110 (104).
7. Johann Nestroy, *Gesammelte Werke. Ausgabe in sechs Bänden*, ed. Otto Rommel, Vienna, 1948–49, 2: 311 (edition referred to henceforth as 'GW'). This edition is used for plays which have not yet appeared in HKA.
8. See May, *Wiener Volkskomödie*, pp. 90–2.
9. See May, *Wiener Volkskomödie*, pp. 94f.
10. It is essentially how Friedrich Theodor Vischer, a fierce critic of Nestroy, characterised the latter's audience when he reflected on his experience of it in both 1840 and 1860 – socially wide-ranging and perniciously inclusive: 'Von unseren [North German] Theatern – und wir verstehen doch wohl auch einen Spaß – würde solche Gemeinheit mit Fußtritten gejagt, hier wurde gerade bei den widerlichsten Stellen am meisten geklatscht, und es sitzt vor diesen Vorstadtbühnen zwar nicht das Publikum des Burgtheaters, aber doch wahrlich auch nicht lauter Pöbel'. Friedrich Theodor Vischer, 'Eine Reise' (1861), in Vischer, *Kritische Gänge*, ed. Robert Vischer, 2nd edn, Munich, n.d., 1: 351.
11. Friedrich Kaiser, *Unter fünfzehn Theater-Direktoren. Bunte Bilder aus der Wiener Bühnenwelt*, Vienna, 1870, p. 17; quoted from Erich May, *Wiener Volkskomödie*, p. 90.
12. One critic who emphasises such a view of Nestroy – the playwright's supposed opposition to the 'tödlicher Druck des deutschen Idealismus'(*not* Nestroy's

phrase) – is Rio Preisner. See Preisner, 'Der konservative Nestroy: Aspekte der zukünftigen Forschung', *Maske und Kothurn* 18 (1972), 23–37 (25f.).

13. *Der Sammler*, 20 April 1833; quoted from HKA 5: 356.
14. Karl Ludwig Costenoble, *Aus dem Burgtheater. 1818–1837. Tagebuchblätter*, eds Karl Glossy and Jakob Zeidler, Vienna, 1889, p. 154; quoted from HKA 5: 355.
15. Costenoble, *Aus dem Burgtheater*, p. 335f.; quoted from W.E Yates, *Nestroy and the Critics*, Columbia, S.C., 1994, p. 5. See also Jürgen Hein, *Johann Nestroy: 'Der Talisman'. Erläuterungen und Dokumente*, Stuttgart, 1980, p. 59.
16. Karl Gutzkow, *Wiener Eindrücke* (1845), in Gutzkow, *Ausgewählte Werke in zwölf Bänden*, ed. Heinrich Hubert Houben, Leipzig, n.d., 9: 231f.
17. Berthold Auerbach, *Tagebuch aus Wien. Von Latour bis auf Windischgrätz*, Breslau, 1849, p. 19.
18. Vischer, *Kritische Gänge*, 1: 351f.
19. Eduard Bauernfeld, 'Aus Alt- und Neu-Wien', in Bauernfeld, *Erinnerungen aus Alt-Wien*, ed. Josef Bindtner, Vienna, 1923, pp. 56f.
20. Bauernfeld, *Erinnerungen*, pp. 52f.
21. Cf. Yates, *Nestroy and the Critics*, pp. 12–15.
22. See Colin Walker, 'Nestroy and the Redemptorists', in *Bristol Austrian Studies*, ed. Brian Keith-Smith, Bristol, 1990, pp. 73–115 (pp. 77–82).
23. It is interesting to find Gutzkow in 1845 attacking the Austrian regime for regularly censoring criticism of Nestroy's 'Entartung' and 'Verwilderung' by Viennese commentators (such as Saphir – see following paragraph and note). See Gutzkow, *Ausgewählte Werke*, 9: 232.
24. See Erich May, *Wiener Volkskomödie*, esp. pp. 42–63, 82–95; W.E. Yates, *Nestroy and the Critics*, p. 7.
25. May, *Wiener Volkskomödie*, pp. 53, 60.
26. Letter of late 1848 or early 1849, in Nestroy, *Briefe* (HKA), p. 82f.
27. Letters of 30 July 1858, 12 July 1859, 16 July 1859, 18 December 1860, 2–8 May 1861, in Nestroy, *Briefe* (HKA), pp. 180, 185, 187, 201, 216–18.
28. See, for example, Rio Preisner, *Johann Nepomuk Nestroy. Schöpfer der tragischen Posse*, Munich, 1968, p. 79.
29. See letter of 17 January 1836 and commentary, in Nestroy, *Briefe* (HKA), pp. 35–7.
30. Eva Reichmann, *Konservative Inhalte in den Theaterstücken Johann Nestroys*, Würzburg, 1995, pp. 20, 24.
31. Preisner, *Schöpfer der tragischen Posse*, p. 132, and 'Der konservative Nestroy', p. 27.
32. Horst Denkler, *Restauration und Revolution. Politische Tendenzen im deutschen Drama zwischen Wiener Kongreß und Märzrevolution*, Munich, 1973, p. 179.
33. Günter Berghaus, 'Rebellion, Reservation, Resignation', pp. 110–13, 117–19. See also Berghaus, *J.N. Nestroys Revolutionspossen im Rahmen des Gesamtwerks. Ein Beitrag zur Bestimmung von Nestroys Weltanschauung auf dem Hintergrund der österreichischen Sozialgeschichte des Vormärz*, Diss., Free University of Berlin, 1977, for example, pp. 225–32.
34. May, *Wiener Volkskomödie*, pp. 53f., 60, 63f., 214–16, 227.
35. Quoted from HKA 26/I, p. 196.
36. See May, *Wiener Volkskomödie*, p. 172.
37. Quoted from Jürgen Hein, *Johann Nestroy: 'Der Talisman'. Erläuterungen und Dokumente*, p. 73.
38. See Horst Denkler, *Restauration und Revolution*, p. 189; Günter Berghaus,

'Rebellion, Reservation, Resignation', pp. 114f.; Wolfgang Rothe, *Deutsche Revolutionsdramatik*, p. 82.

39. Julius Seidlitz, *Die Poesie und die Poeten in Österreich im Jahre 1836*, Grimma, 1837, pp. 182–4; quoted from HKA 5: 379.

40. One is intrigued, for example, as to whether Heine's description in Book 3 of *Die Romantische Schule* (published in late May 1833, a month and a half after *Lumpazi* was first performed) of a typical trio of Handwerksburschen, who correspond very closely to Nestroy's 'Kleeblatt', might be prompted by the play. In Heine's text, the Handwerksburschen and other 'Vagabunden' are specifically the bearers of the folk culture in which lie the seeds of final revolution. See Heinrich Heine, *Sämtliche Schriften*, ed. Klaus Briegleb, Munich, 1969–76, 3: 454, and cf. 3: 860.

41. Bruno Hannemann, *Nihilistisches Welttheater*, p. 41.

42. Cf. Peter Cersowsky, *Johann Nestroy oder Nix als philosophische Mussenzen: Eine Einführung*, Munich, 1992, pp. 53f. (and *Faust I*, 'Studierzimmer': 'Ich bin der Geist, der stets verneint!'; Goethe, *Werke. Hamburger Ausgabe*, ed. Erich Trunz, 12th edn, Munich, 1994, 3: 47).

43. This is expressed at more length, if a little crudely, by Peter Haida, 'Johann Nestroy: *Der böse Geist Lumpazivagabundus*. "Die Welt steht auf kein' Fall mehr lang"', in *Interpretationen. Dramen des 19. Jahrhunderts*, ed. Theo Elm, Stuttgart, 1997, pp. 96–119 (see p. 103f.).

44. In one way the tableau defuses criticism of the work's immorality; but when read as irony, as ultimately it must be, it ends the play on an affirmation of *Liederlichkeit*.

45. See Bruno Hannemann, *Nihilistisches Welttheater*, p. 34.

46. Cf. Heine's 'Cholera-Bericht' from Paris in Article 6 of *Französische Zustände*, in Heine, *Sämtliche Schriften*, 3: 168–80 (and see above, chapter 1).

47. Heine, *Sämtliche Schriften*, 2: 538–43; and see Michael Perraudin, 'Heine et l'Angleterre ou le médiateur en défaut', *Romantisme. Revue du dix-neuvième siècle* 101 (1998): *Heine le médiateur*, 41–9 (45f.).

48. Bruno Hannemann, *Nihilistisches Welttheater*; Rio Preisner, *Tragische Posse*; Siegfried Diehl, *Zauberei und Satire im Frühwerk Nestroys*, Bad Homburg, 1969, e.g. p.170. A more recent contribution inspired by this same aspect of Nestroy is Louise Adey Huish, 'Breaking the Bounds: Fantasy and Farce in Nestroy's Comedy', in *Theatre and Performance in Austria. From Mozart to Jelinek*, eds Ritchie Robertson and Edward Timms, Edinburgh, 1993, pp. 27–38. This asserts, not entirely persuasively, that Nestroy's plays escape the deterministic not in their content, but in their form (p. 37).

49. Cf. Jürgen Hein, 'Johann Nestroy: *Der Talisman*', in *Interpretationen. Dramen des 19. Jahrhunderts*, ed. Theo Elm, Stuttgart, 1997, pp. 203–33 (p. 217).

50. Cf. also HKA 17/I: 13: "Apetit ist das zarte Band welches mich mit [der Menschheit] verkettet welches mich alle Tag 3–4 mahl mahnt, daß ich mich der Gesellschaft nicht entreissen darf".

51. For example, Erich May, *Wiener Volkskomödie*, pp. 144–65, esp. pp. 159f., 164.

52. See Yates, *Nestroy and the Critics*, pp. 5–11, esp. p. 9.

53. Siegfried Brill, *Die Komödie der Sprache. Untersuchungen zum Werk Johann Nestroys*, Nuremberg, 1967, pp. 140–77. The grouping of these plays goes back to Otto Rommel's classification.

54. Wolfgang Rothe, in quest for a single meaning for the play, speaks immoderately of its 'secret Jacobinism'. Rothe, *Deutsche Revolutionsdramatik*, pp. 81–3, esp. p. 82.

55. Nestroy's contemporary Grillparzer spoke once, in 1844, of 'die [Frage], welche mich in der ganzen Politik am meisten interessierte – . . . die Zensur!' See Franz Grillparzer, *Sämtliche Werke. Historisch-kritische Gesamtausgabe*, eds August Sauer and Reinhold Backmann, Vienna, 1909–48, Abteilung I, vol. 13, p. 406.

56. See e.g. HKA 26/I: 194.

57. Cf. John McKenzie, '"Aufgeklärt Occonnelisch, wird Irrland rebellisch". Political Songs in Nestroy's *Freiheit in Krähwinkel'*, in *Connections. Essays in Honour of Eda Sagarra on the Occasion of her 60th Birthday*, eds Peter Skrine, Rosemary Wallbank-Turner and Jonathan West, Stuttgart, 1993, pp. 169–78 (p. 176f.).

58. See Rio Preisner, *Tragische Posse*, p. 127.

59. See, for example, Preisner, *Tragische Posse*, pp. 131–3; W.E. Yates, *Nestroy. Satire and Parody in Viennese Popular Comedy*, Cambridge, 1972, p. 157.

60. John McKenzie claims that all this is merely Nestroy 'buying off' the censor by 'including a certain amount of apparently reactionary material'; McKenzie, 'Nestroy's Political Plays', in *Viennese Popular Theatre: A Symposium*, pp. 123–38 (p. 134). I do not find this quite convincing as regards *Lady und Schneider*.

61. Also socially interesting and novel is the moment in *Lady und Schneider* when Heugeign physically intervenes to prevent violence from two angry and aggressive aristocrats against another character: HKA 26/II: 35.

62. See HKA 27/I: 145–7; also Franz Mautner, in Johann Nestroy, *Komödien. Ausgabe in sechs Bänden*, ed. Mautner, Frankfurt/M., 1979, 6: 6.

5

The Popular Nationalism of Heine's *Deutschland. Ein Wintermärchen*

There was always a strong national component in Heine's thought. His standpoint on matters of nation was and remained, in outline, that reached by Herder at the end of the Enlightenment, two generations before, namely a belief in the significance and value of national difference combined with a general refusal of xenophobia and a cosmopolitan attachment to the Rights of Man. For Heine, moreover, this was more than merely a formal position. In the late 1820s he spoke memorably (in a phrase quoted earlier) of the supplanting of nation in the modern world – 'Es giebt in Europa keine Nationen mehr, sondern nur Parteien'[1] – and of 'der große Schmerz über den Verlust der National-Besonderheiten die in der Allgemeinheit neuerer Kultur verloren gehen, ein Schmerz, der jetzt in den Herzen aller Völker zuckt' (B 2: 236). Whatever the accuracy of such pronouncements as a judgement on the tendencies of nineteenth century history, the second of these at any rate signals in Heine himself an emotional attachment to ideas of national identity which our view of him should not neglect. His own writings are both enhanced and disfigured by the national focus. The clichés of national character which abound in his works – the cold and egotistic English, parsimonious Scots, stupid Irish, heedless French, passionate Italians, avaricious Jews and others[2] – may owe something, as has been argued,[3] to the wilfully caricatural nature of Heine's satirical approach, as well as to the specific polemical requirements of the particular texts in which they occur. But there is, none the less, an element of crassness about them which is displeasing and undignified. Yet, on the other hand, it is evident that it was his instinct to give credence to notions of national difference which made him capable, as other prominent early socialist thinkers among his contemporaries were not, of anticipating to some degree the nationalist catastrophes of subsequent epochs – of discerning, in particular, that the anti-French sentiment and the anti-semitism in contemporary German nationalism were not merely a passing, soon-to-be-dispelled false consciousness, but a force of great power and importance.[4]

Connected with all this is the distinctive national ingredient which is present, too, in Heine's thinking on revolution. As we saw in chapter one, he argues in his analytical prose of the 1830s, notably in *Die Romantische Schule* and *Zur Geschichte der Religion und Philosophie in Deutschland*, that European society is progressing towards a final revolution which will bring with it full emancipation, not just political freedom but also an emancipation of consciousness – an abolition of the dichotomy of body and spirit, a freedom of the senses, a rehabilitation of the flesh. This has been a long process: since the beginning of the Christian era, the western world has been dominated by a principle of repressive spiritualism, which, however, has been gradually breaking down over the last half-millennium – with the Renaissance, the Reformation, the Enlightenment – in a process of development that the German philosophical tradition has increasingly led. At the same time, so the argument runs, the emancipated, anti-spiritual, sensual impulse has never been wholly suppressed, but has subsisted latently and largely unconsciously in the culture of the common people, in their songs and stories, myths and festivals. Above all it has survived in German folk culture, in which the pre-Christian, pagan-pantheistic element has been least successfully crushed. In this sense, Heine's *Elementargeister* of 1836–37, the catalogue of German folk myth intended on the surface to convince the Bundestag, which had just proscribed him, of his political innocuousness,[5] is a covert document of revolution. But the most forceful statement of Heine's prediction of a culminating revolution rooted in German national/popular culture is the curiously un-Utopian, unenthusiastic ending of *Zur Geschichte der Religion und Philosophie in Deutschland*, dating from 1834:

> Durch diese Doktrinen [der deutschen Philosophie] haben sich revolutionäre Kräfte entwickelt, die nur des Tages harren, wo sie hervorbrechen und die Welt mit Entsetzen und Bewunderung erfüllen können . . . Die dämonischen Kräfte des altgermanischen Pantheismus [werden] beschwör[t], und . . . jene Kampflust erwacht, die wir bei den

alten Deutschen finden . . . Wenn einst der zähmende Talisman, das Kreuz, zerbricht, dann rasselt wieder empor die Wildheit der alten Kämpfer, die unsinnige Berserkerwut, wovon die nordischen Dichter so viel singen und sagen. Jener Talisman ist morsch, und kommen wird der Tag, wo er kläglich zusammenbricht. Die alten, steinernen Götter erheben sich dann aus dem verschollenen Schutt, . . . und Thor mit dem Riesenhammer springt endlich empor und zerschlägt die gotischen Dome . . . Lächelt nicht über [mich] Phantasten, der im Reiche der Erscheinungen dieselbe Revolution erwartet, die im Gebiete des Geistes stattgefunden. Der Gedanke geht der Tat voraus, wie der Blitz dem Donner. Der deutsche Donner ist freilich auch ein Deutscher und ist nicht sehr gelenkig, und kommt etwas langsam herangerollt; aber kommen wird er, und wenn ihr es einst krachen hört, wie es noch niemals in der Weltgeschichte gekracht hat, so wißt: der deutsche Donner hat endlich sein Ziel erreicht . . . Es wird ein Stück aufgeführt werden in Deutschland, wogegen die französische Revolution nur wie eine harmlose Idylle erscheinen möchte.

Wie auf den Stufen eines Amphitheaters werden die Völker sich um Deutschland herumgruppieren, um die großen Kampfspiele zu betrachten. Ich rate Euch, Ihr Franzosen, verhaltet Euch alsdann sehr stille, und bei Leibe! Hütet Euch, zu applaudieren . . . Wenn wir früherhin, in unserem servil verdrossenen Zustande, Euch manchmal überwältigen konnten, so vermöchten wir es noch weit eher im Übermute des Freiheitsrausches . . . Ich meine es gut mit Euch, und deshalb sage ich Euch die bittere Wahrheit. Ihr habt von dem befreiten Deutschland mehr zu befürchten, als von der ganzen heiligen Allianz mitsamt allen Kroaten und Kosaken . . . (B 3: 638–40).

These rather ominous conclusions to a text that had clearly been conceived as Utopian are a significant signal and confirmation of a number of aspects of Heine's outlook: his belief in national cultural identity (and in a sense too in German cultural pre-eminence); his perception of the latent power of Germany and the potential for destructive Franco-German conflict emerging from German national sentiment; and his final ambivalence not just towards the possibility of communist revolution, but even to the more comprehensively liberating form of revolution which was supposed to be the outcome of his own teleology of emancipation. At the same time, this noteworthy passage is the nearest Heine comes to a formal statement of the basis for his main literary text associating revolution and Germanness, the poem *Deutschland. Ein Wintermärchen*, which he wrote and published a decade later in early 1844.

Deutschland. Ein Wintermärchen is not, of course, simply an attempt at poetic reformulation of the end of the treatise *Zur*

Geschichte der Religion und Philosophie, for it is also the product of the specific and personal circumstances in which it was written. The world had changed since 1834, to some degree in directions that Heine had anticipated. Not only had social revolution in Europe come to seem a good deal more imminent, but so too had national war between Germany and France. *Zur Geschichte der Religion und Philosophie* had been composed in the aftermath of the 1830 July Revolution and the Hambach Festival of 1832, when German liberal sentiment had been at its most cosmopolitan.[6] But the Rhine Crisis of 1840 – when the French regime, for internal political reasons of its own, demanded a frontier realignment – led to an upsurge of aggressive Francophobic nationalism of the kind which had characterised the era around 1813.[7] The public imagination (and, in a way, Heine's imagination, too) filled with the ideology and iconography of German nationhood.

In this context, Heine's own position became problematical. His public identity as a cosmopolitan mediator, which he had cultivated through the 1830s, had become significantly less palatable, especially given other aspects of his status – as a Jew in Parisian exile. He faced, in a sense, a market problem. The German public – which was really the only public available to him, as his decade of very modest sales in France had demonstrated[8] – was in danger of becoming alienated. Criticisms (of the kind mentioned in the *Vorwort* to *Deutschland. Ein Wintermärchen*) that were aimed against him in the growing daily press for his deficient patriotism did indeed represent a threat.[9] There was a need for him to establish his national credentials and re-root himself in Germany; and that is what his trip to and through Germany in the late autumn and early winter of 1843, and the resultant poem *Deutschland. Ein Wintermärchen* with its self-justificatory preface, sought intricately to do. It may be, indeed, that the issue was more than just one of expediency and that Heine was himself not unaffected by the new patriotic mood. His own voluntary participation, in early 1842, in the campaign to complete Cologne Cathedral might suggest this[10] (even if, by the time the *Wintermärchen* was finished, two years later, his attitude to the campaign had changed to scorn and hostility). In any event, the early 1840s had brought a new focus on patriotism and national commitment to the public mood in Germany, and the project and text of *Deutschland. Ein Wintermärchen* were Heine's response to it.[11]

For the journey to Hamburg which Heine made the basis of his poem there were also other, more personal reasons, which are all reflected in one way or another in the text. The wish to negotiate face-to-face with Campe, his publisher, about future contracts was an important one.[12] So, too, was the desire to see his 72-year-old mother after years of absence. Another was probably his concern to enhance relations with his wealthy and ailing Uncle Salomon, in whose will the poet hoped to figure prominently. Yet another was Heine's increasing sense of his own mortality. He was already afflicted by symptoms of the illness which was soon to consign him to his 'mattress grave': periodic blindness, partial facial paralysis and other problems. It is fairly clear from his letters of the time that he did not expect to live very much longer.[13] In this context, the journey was intended to enable him both to secure his wife's financial future after his death, and to see his homeland and family again while he was still able.

His composition of the poem, too, had motives beyond the thematic ones. It may have been an act of authorial self-defence, but in another respect it was a calculated exploitation of a market opportunity. As a partial consequence of the quickening of German political life to which the Rhine Crisis gave rise, a fashion developed in the early 1840s for political (and not only national-political) verse. The aesthetic inadequacies of the 'Tendenzdichter' – Freiligrath, Hoffmann von Fallersleben, Herwegh and others – were a frequent object of Heine's derision at the time. But, as his publisher Campe said, drawing attention to the extremely heavy sales of Hoffmann von Fallersleben's *Unpolitische Lieder*, which Campe had published in 1840–41, Heine would do well to try to exploit the fashion himself.[14] *Deutschland. Ein Wintermärchen* was the realisation of this suggestion, and its high sales and good royalties indicate that the calculation succeeded.[15]

Thus *Deutschland. Ein Wintermärchen* has a multiplicity of motivating factors. The central thematic purpose of the work, however, remains Heine's devising of a response to contemporary nationalism, or his dovetailing of national and revolutionary lines of thought. One of his letters talks of the work as 'antinazional';[16] but this is only true in the obvious sense of its antagonism towards the 'Pharisäer der Nationalität' (B 4: 573). The *Vorwort*, perhaps uncharacteristically for Heine's often rather sophistical prefaces, sets the premises comparatively accurately: the poet *is* a German patriot – 'Ich liebe das Vaterland eben so sehr, wie Ihr' (B 4: 574) – but it is a patriotism which does not find fulfilment in xenophobia. Instead: 'Macht . . . die schwarz-rot-goldne Fahne . . . zur Standarte des freien Menschtums, und ich will mein bestes Herzblut für sie hingeben' (B 4: 574). His patriotic fulfilment will be achieved, 'wenn wir das vollenden, was die Franzosen begonnen haben, wenn wir diese überflügeln in der Tat, wie wir es schon getan im Gedanken, wenn wir uns bis zu den letzten Folgerungen desselben emporschwingen, . . . wenn wir den Gott, der auf Erden im Menschen wohnt, aus seiner Erniedrigung retten, wenn wir die Erlöser Gottes werden, wenn wir das arme, glückenterbte Volk und den verhöhnten Genius und die geschändete Schönheit wieder in ihre Würde einsetzen . . . – . . . ganz Frankreich wird uns alsdann zufallen, ganz Europa, die ganze Welt – die ganze Welt wird deutsch werden! Von dieser Sendung und Universalherrschaft Deutschlands träume ich oft, wenn ich unter Eichen wandle. Das ist *mein* Patriotismus' (B 4: 574f.). This (slightly troubling) outburst of patriotic-revolutionary fervour (declaimed 'im Übermute des Freiheitsrausches' – to borrow a phrase from the end of *Zur Geschichte der Religion und Philosophie*; B 3: 640) is entirely concomitant with Heine's Hegelian/Saint-Simonist philosophy of liberation of the 1830s (the emancipation – evolving out of the German philosophical tradition – which is an emancipation of consciousness as well as from physical suffering and political oppression, and at the end of which man becomes god), but now with the national element emphasised and glorified as it was not previously. And it also reflects accurately the purpose of the poem *Deutschland. Ein Wintermärchen* itself, which was to juxtapose the authoritarian, repressive nationalism current in Germany with the emancipatory impulse latent in German culture.

A further aspect of Heine's patriotic hymn in his *Vorwort* is important: 'Von dieser Sendung und Universalherrschaft Deutschlands träume ich oft, wenn ich unter Eichen wandle' (B 4: 575). The phrase is a classic gesture of Heine's, faintly relativising an immoderate display of passion.[17] But it also points positively to aspects and messages of the poem itself: to the importance of *Begeisterung* for the accomplishment of revolution in Heine's view,[18] to the paradigmatic function of Heine the poet's revolutionary subjectivity ('In der Brust der Schriftsteller eines Volkes liegt schon das Abbild von dessen Zukunft', he had written a decade earlier; B 3: 467), and – most immediately – to the subjective principle according to which the poem is constructed. A technique that Heine had previously used, in earlier 'pictures of travel', was the presentation or exploration of states of consciousness in his narratorial persona which somehow represented the collective mind. Notably, the narrator of *Die Harzreise* experiences in himself and incarnates the dissonant impulses in the contemporary German soul – the poet as the subjective voice of the *Zeitgeist*. And *Deutschland. Ein Wintermärchen* continues this principle. The whole poem becomes in effect a 'walk under oak trees'.

The poem begins – slightly abruptly – right at the border ('Im traurigen Monat November wars,/Die Tage wurden trüber,/Der Wind riß von den Bäumen das Laub,/Da reist ich nach Deutschland hinüber./Und als ich an die Grenze kam . . .'; B 4: 577). Heine chose to omit a draft first canto which traced the journey back to Paris and to feelings of homesickness for Germany that he experienced there ('Ade, Paris, du teure Stadt,/Wir müssen heute scheiden . . ./Das deutsche Herz in meiner Brust/Ist plötzlich krank geworden', etc.; B 4: 1021). With this left out, the poem becomes exclusively the voice of the new – newly Germanised – consciousness which takes possession of the poet once he reaches German territory ('. . . Da fächelte mich schon deutsche Luft,/Da fühlt ich ihren Einfluß –'; B 4: 583). In fact, the implication is that the ways of writing and seeing which the poem entails are only achievable on German soil.[19]

There is a large variety of ways in which the poem's Germanness expresses itself – or in which it expressed itself for Heine. The episodic and subjective/thought-associative ('keck persönlich'[20]) character of the work's organisation is conceived by the author as Romantic: although it was its companion-piece, *Atta Troll*, which he termed 'das letzte freie Waldlied der Romantik' (B 4: 570), the imaginative processes which justified that label ('. . . Nur der eignen Lust gehorchend,/Galoppierend oder fliegend,/Tummelt sich im Fabelreiche/Mein geliebter Pegasus . . ./Trage mich, wohin du willst!'; B 4: 501f.) are also those of *Deutschland. Ein Wintermärchen*. Here, too, 'hat [der] Waldhornruf geklungen' (B 4: 606). And Romantic for Heine in this sense is German ('. . . Trage mich durch stille Täler,/Wo die Eichen ernsthaft ragen . . .'; B 4: 502). It can be added that the symbolic nature of Romantic art as defined in Heine's *Die Romantische Schule* of 1833 – as not contenting itself with phenomena for their own sake, but seeking and discerning levels of allegoric meaning to which phenomena allude (B 3: 367) – corresponds very much to the technique of the poem, with its satirical ransacking of objects and images of contemporary Germany (Pickelhaube, River Rhine, Cologne Cathedral and others). His 'politisch romantisch' poem, as he called it,[21] turns such resources of the German imagination upon and against Germany itself.

The poem's element of authorial self-reference also reinforces its

Romantic Germanness. The idea of the poet's nostalgic *Heimkehr* alludes purposely to Heine's own earlier, less cosmopolitan phase of Romantic lyricism, and specifically to his cycle in *Buch der Lieder* entitled *Die Heimkehr*, with its Romantic German townscapes and landscapes. *Die Heimkehr* itself had been a homecoming to Hamburg, with a core group of poems full of Romantic reminiscences[22] narrating that return ('So wandl ich wieder den alten Weg,/Die wohlbekannten Gassen;/Ich komme von meiner Liebsten Haus,/Das steht so leer und verlassen', etc.; B 1: 117). The revisiting of Hamburg in *Deutschland. Ein Wintermärchen* is designed to link again with this. Moreover, the Hamburg sub-cycle in *Die Heimkehr* had contained a key poem of Heine's earlier, late-Romantic identity, the *Doppelgänger* lyric 'Still ist die Nacht, es ruhen die Gassen' (B 1: 118) – in which the figure particularly associated with the Romantic author E.T.A. Hoffmann was adapted by Heine for the articulation of his own end-of-Romanticism dissonance. The Doppelgänger's reappearance in the Cologne episode of *Deutschland. Ein Wintermärchen* to express the dissonance of the political Heine is an unmistakable gesture of reconnection.[23]

Formally, the *Wintermärchen* is assertively German. Its verse form – four-line strophes of alternating tetrameter and trimeter lines with stressed endings to the former and unstressed to the latter, with an *abcb* rhyme scheme and a freely mixed iambic and anapaestic rhythm – is Germanic-balladesque. There is a range of views among commentators as to the form's exact connotations: that it is the 'Hildebrandston', echoing the Old High German epic fragment the *Hildebrandslied*, is one proposal; that it is a form of 'Nibelungenstrophe' is another; another still is that it employs the 'Vagantenstrophe', the verse form associated with a genus of folk-song concerning the deeds of rebels and brigands.[24] The *Vagantenlied* 'Der arme Schwartenhals' (from Arnim's and Brentano's collection *Des Knaben Wunderhorn*), of which Heine in *Die Romantische Schule* said: 'Dieser arme Schwartenhals ist der deutscheste Charakter den ich kenne' (B 3: 451), indeed has essentially this form, though with a much smaller anapaestic element in its rhythm than the *Wintermärchen* has. Heine's poem has also been linked formally with Bürger's seminal *Schauerballade*, *Lenore*;[25] but Bürger's text is almost exclusively iambic.[26] I am a little doubtful that the connections Heine intended are really quite as specific as this. I have indicated elsewhere how, in the early 1820s, he was consciously evolving a balladesque verse form developing and diverging from a number of prominent models of heroic ballads, which suddenly begins to figure frequently in his poetic production (in the *Romanzen* section of his *Gedichte* of 1822). Notably, this is the form of his political poem 'Die Grenadiere',[27] which is formally identical to *Deutschland. Ein Wintermärchen* except for the latter's lack of rhyme between the first and third lines of each strophe. In particular, it shares the fluent and conversational iambic/anapaestic mixing which was a distinctive skill of Heine as a versifier, unmatched by any of his contemporaries.[28] The *Wintermärchen* is formally another allusion to Heine's individual poetic past, and at the same time his own personalised invocation of his Germanic folk-ballad heritage. Here, as in other aspects of the *Wintermärchen*, a claim is discernible that Heine the poet has a truer access to such cultural roots than do his literary contemporaries and competitors.[29]

The folk-ballad aspect of the *Wintermärchen* is not only a matter of verse forms, but extends also to syntax and vocabulary, with the type of mixture of the colloquial and the archaic which was standardly the diction of early nineteenth-century folk-song imitation. The poem falls easily and naturally – 'mit großer Leichtigkeit . . .'[30] – into this idiom: 'Da rieb der Kaiser sich die Händ,/Schien sonderbar sich zu freuen'; 'Und als ich zu meiner Frau Mutter kam,/Erschrak sie fast vor Freude'; 'So sprach ich, da hört ich im Wasser tief/Gar seltsam grämliche Töne'; 'Das sind die Wölfe, die heulen so wild,/Mit ausgehungerten Stimmen', etc. (B 4: 587, 603, 611, 621). Often there are moments of folk-song archaism which are close to parody: 'In meiner Brust, ich glaube sogar,/Die Augen begunnen zu tropfen'; 'Nicht übel gefiel mir das neue Kostüm/Der Reuter, das muß ich loben'; 'Und als ich an die Rheinbrück kam,/Wohl an die Hafenschanze'; 'Es ward mir unleidlich, ich drehte mich um/Und sprach: Jetzt steh mir Rede' (B 4: 577, 582, 587, 590). However, in contrast to *Atta Troll*, with its Hispanic trochee verse form and perpetually mock-bombastic tone, the manner of the *Wintermärchen* is essentially not self-parodying, but is meant seriously. Above all, the poem is simply full of folksong reminiscences. The beginnings of the earlier cantos in particular offer such echoes: 'Ade, Paris, du teure Stadt,/Wir müssen heute scheiden' (to recall the *Wunderhorn* song 'Abschied von Bremen'); 'Und als ich an die Grenze kam'; 'Zu Cöllen kam ich spät Abends an'; 'Und als ich an die Rheinbrück kam'; 'Von Cöllen war ich drei Viertel auf Acht . . .'; 'Von Harburg fuhr ich in einer Stund'; 'Minden ist eine feste Burg,/Hat gute Wehr und Waffen!' (after Luther) (B 4: 577, 583, 587, 598, 617, 621, 1021). The text was conceived, so Heine's correspondence indicates, as 'ein Cyklus von 20 Gedichten . . . versifizirte Reisebilder'[31] – thus, presumably, as a sequence of cameos each with a folk-song or folk-song-like beginning. In addition, thematically crucial episodes frequently have a folk-song basis. Thus the 'neues Lied, . . . besseres Lied' of Canto 1 – 'Und wachsen uns Flügel nach dem Tod,/So wollen wir Euch besuchen/Dort oben, und wir, wir essen mit Euch/Die seligsten Torten und Kuchen' (B 4: 578) – recalls *Schlaraffenland Wunschlieder*, of the kind that generated Heine's earlier poem 'Mir träumt': ich bin der liebe Gott' ('. . . Und Kuchen ess ich und Konfekt . . .'; B 1: 139, *Heimkehr* 66[32]). The mother-son exchange about food in Canto 20 – '. . . Verschlucke ich den süßen Saft,/Und ich lasse die Schalen liegen' (B 4: 623) – is, with its refrain repetitions, a 'Zwiegespräch im Volksliedstil' (to quote Ernst Elster[33]), inter alia like the 'Edward, Edward' ballad of which the young Heine was very fond.[34] And the revolutionary revenge song of Ottilie in Canto 14, 'Sonne, du klagende Flamme', is, or is explicitly said to be, a 'Volksgesang' told to the poet at his nurse's knee (B 4: 606f.). In some sense (to be further investigated below), *Deutschland. Ein Wintermärchen* itself is clearly intended to be a German folk-song.

Another important generic identity of the text is that of epic. Heine's correspondence signals it to be (like *Atta Troll*) a mock epic – 'humoristisches Reise-Epos'[35] – so a bathetic play on the discrepancy between ancient tales of heroes and an anti-heroic modernity. However, we know from elsewhere in Heine's works that he took the idea of epic quite seriously. The end of *Die Nordsee* III is particularly preoccupied – after Herder – with the notion of great epic poems as the documents in which ancient peoples expressed their own deepest character: the Mahabharata, Iliad and Odyssey, Edda, Song of Roland, Nibelungenlied, and others (B 2: 238f.). The poet also speaks there of how the story of Bonaparte's and his army's defeat in the Russian Campaign, as recounted in Ségur's *Histoire de Napoléon et la grande armée pendant l'année 1812* (Paris, 1824), constitutes a modern equivalent ('ein Lied, . . . das . . . , in seinem Tone und Stoffe, den epischen Dichtungen aller Zeiten gleicht und gleich steht'; B 2: 238). Its difference, appropriate to a more democratic and collectivistic age, is its collective hero: 'Ja, dieses ist ein wahres Epos, Frankreichs Heldenjugend ist der schöne Heros, der früh dahinsinkt, wie wir solches Leid schon sahen in dem Tode Baldurs, Siegfrieds, Rolands und Achilles' (B 2: 239). In the companion-piece to *Die Nordsee* III, *Ideen. Das Buch Le Grand*, there are signs with the figure of the Tambour Le Grand that Heine intended that his text should itself possess such modern folk-epic resonances. And it is reasonable to think that the 'Reise-Epos' *Deutschland. Ein Wintermärchen* is meant to repeat this principle, though with a more specifically German focus than in the 1820s – a German folksong (for the epics are pre-eminently folk-songs: Ségur's work was a 'französisches Volkslied'; B 2: 238) conveying the essence of contemporary Germany. Its (mock-)epic hero is formally the poet himself, Odysseus-like on his journey homeward to Hamburg-Ithaca via a series of mythic locations and encounters. But its hero is also the German people, to whose cultural memory the poet has unique access.

The basic conceit of the poem, as was suggested above, is the notion that the poet's German imagination is rekindled as he crosses the border on to German territory, or into German air. This perception even found its way into Heine's correspondence of the time: 'Hab auch auf meiner Reise mancherley Verse gemacht, die mir mit größerer Leichtigkeit gelingen, wenn ich deutsche Luft athme'.[36] His Romantic poetic soul is re-stimulated. Echoes of his old songs and his old poetic inspirations appear, as we have seen. The capacity of his Romantic self to speak to Nature – as in *Die Harzreise*[37] – is regained (when he addresses the wolves in the Teutoburger Wald in Canto 12, or the River Rhine in Canto 5). And he begins to dream. As the poem itself tells us, the Germans are pre-eminent in the realm of dreams: 'Franzosen und Russen gehört das Land,/Das Meer gehört den Briten,/Wir aber besitzen im Luftreich des Traums/Die Herrschaft unbestritten' (B 4: 592).[38] The penchant for dream was also, of course, a characteristic of the poet's youthful persona – with his *Traumbilder* poems and with the dreams with which his Romantic consciousness was opened in *Die Harzreise*.[39] Accordingly, the multiplicity of dreams in *Deutschland. Ein Wintermärchen* is intended as a symptom of the reopening of his German soul.

Much of the specific content of his dreams, and the content of the work as a whole, is German saga. Poet and poem evoke Germany above all through its myths and legends. The narrated journey, we noted, follows a contrived route (only partially corresponding to Heine's real itineraries) through legendary places – Charlemagne's capital Aachen, the Rhine, Cologne with its cathedral, the Teutoburger Wald, site of the Hermannsschlacht – on the way to Hamburg. Barbarossa's mythically indispensable Kyffhäuserberg, located far away in Thuringia, is invoked through dream alone. And there are other such legendary allusions: Blue-beard and Ottilie, the goosemaid princess with her horse Falada (in Canto 14), and the interesting processional scene at the end of the text (to be discussed below). The poet emphasises the deep-root-edness of these stories, or at any rate some of them, in his own heart, 'mein abergläubisches Herz' (B 4: 610), told to him as they supposedly were in childhood by his 'Amme' from the Münsterland, who 'wußte, in großer Menge,/... Märchen und Volksgesänge' ('Wie pochte mein Herz, wenn die alte Frau/Von der Königstochter erzählte . . .'; 'Mit stockendem Atem horchte ich hin,/Wenn die Alte ernster und leiser/Zu sprechen begann und vom Rotbart sprach . . .'; B 4: 607f.).

The contemporary situation to which the *Wintermärchen*'s mythical content is a reaction is the intensive utilisation of such *Kulturgut* by bourgeois nationalism, the 'Pharisäer der Nationalität' (B 4: 573), in unholy alliance with Romantic reactionaries in the established governments, for their own xenophobic and illiberal agenda. Patently the text elaborately ridicules such usurpation: the crass Hermannsschlacht myth, the fetishisation of the River Rhine (with Becker's 'Rheinlied'), the bigotries behind the *Dombau* pro-ject, the use of the Barbarossa story as an imperialistic model for German unity. This is not to say – contrary to the suggestions of some commentators on Heine's approach to myth – either that, in 1844, he had grown newly disillusioned with myth as a positive force, or that his awareness of its pernicious potential as a tool of aggressive nationalism was new.[40] Rather, the situation of the early 1840s refocused his mind on notions that he had long held.

Always, for Heine, mythical thinking – an analogical, imagin-ative, enthusiastic, poetic, irrational thinking in images and stories rather than concepts – was a path to powerful understandings not accessible through reason. Hence his unconventional stated prefer-ence for the 'mythicist' Plato over the anti-mythological Aristotle.[41] Such thinking was also closely allied with the alogical understand-ing which was extolled in *Die Nordsee* III and *Das Buch Le Grand* as an ability of the Great Men of History, specifically Napoleon ('einen Verstand . . . , der . . . nicht wie der unsrige diskursiv, son-der intuitiv . . . , vom synthetisch Allgemeinen, der Anschauung eines Ganzen als eines solchen, zum Besonderen geht . . . Was wir durch langsames analytisches Nachdenken und lange Schlußfolgen erkennen, das hatte jener Geist im selben Momente angeschaut und tief begriffen'; B 2: 234f.); which, in *Die Nordsee* III and *Die Harzreise*, was also presented as characterising the consciousness of the common people ('tiefes Anschauungsleben'; B 2: 119); and which was hinted equivocally in all these texts to be an attribute of the poet himself with his creative imagination (see also above, chapter one). It is such consciousness, indeed, that generates bodies of myth: 'Nur durch solch tiefes Anschauungsleben . . . entstand die deutsche Märchenfabel' (B 2: 119). Myth-formation is not, for Heine, a mystic process: there is in the end a kind of materialism in his view. The mythic epic poems of ancient peoples – the Indians, the Greeks – 'sind ihre Geschichte' (B 6/1: 613), even if we have not yet 'die Gesetze entdeck[t], nach welchen [sie] das Geschehene ins phantastisch Poetische umwandeln' (B 6/1: 613f.). And myth-formation still takes place: the literature of the revolutionary and Napoleonic era in France, the 'Memoiren von Staatsleuten, Soldaten und edlen Frauen, wie sie in Frankreich täglich erscheinen, bilden einen Sagenkreis' (with the figure of Bonaparte at its centre); '. . . Die Ségursche Geschichte des Rußlandzuges ist ein Lied, ein französisches Volkslied, das zu diesem Sagenkreise gehört', etc. (B 2: 238). Moreover, the making of myths is identity- and community-forming, but it is not invariably good. What Heine discerned in German nationalism – at least from the very early 1820s – was a mythogenic process which was pernicious and dangerous because it was so powerful. Such danger is in a sense the inspiration of *Deutschland. Ein Wintermärchen*, in which very old symbols and legends of Germanness – such as Barbarossa – are seen coexisting in nationalist mythology with new or comparatively new ones (the Hermannsschlacht, the Rhine, the Kölner Dombau, the Pickelhaube), and being exploited indiscriminately.

If myths can still be made, Heine as poet and tribune may also have an active mythopoeic role, not only rediscovering or revaluing them but also creating them. In *Deutschland. Ein Wintermärchen*, some ancient stories – specifically those said to have been told to the poet in infancy by his nursemaid from the Münsterland – are plumbed by him for their emancipatory and revolutionary content: the story of the *Gänsemagd*-princess and her faithful horse Falada (from a fairytale in the Grimms' collection) and the Bluebeard/*Ulrich und Ännchen* song of Ottilie (apparently adapted by Heine from a folk-song volume in his possession)[42] become, as tales of injustice and retribution, allegories of revolution; Barbarossa is, or can be, a messianic myth of political redemption and retribution.[43] The implication is that this is the latent content of these stories, expressions of the German people's deep but unconscious aspirations, and the poet's role is to bring such meanings to consciousness. But the *Wintermärchen* does a good deal more with its mythology. A parallel was drawn above in passing between the poet-exile's return to Hamburg and Odysseus's journey to Ithaca. In fact, the text purposely offers several such links. The poet in the fortress of Minden is Odysseus in the Cyclops's cave: 'Ach! meine Seele ward betrübt,/Wie des Odysseus Seele,/Als er gehört, daß Polyphem/Den Felsblock schob vor die Höhle'; '... Ich heiße Niemand, bin Augenarzt/Und steche den Star den Riesen' (B 4: 618). The poet's longing for Germany specifically echoes that of Odysseus for Ithaca: 'Ich sehnte mich nach dem blauen Rauch,/Der aufsteigt aus deutschen Schornsteinen'; 'Aber Odysseus/Sehnt' sich, auch nur den Rauch von Ithakas heimischen Hügeln/Steigen zu sehn und dann zu sterben!'[44] Elsewhere, Campe is the poet's 'Mentor' (Odysseus's guide), Hamburg is Troy, the Hamburg prostitutes are Helens, and so on.(B 4: 625, 630, 635). In addition, the poet's glimpse into Hammonia's chamber pot is probably intended to echo Virgil's Aeneas consulting the Delphic oracle.[45] And various (titanic or quasi-titanic) classical parallels are built into the text: the poet is Prometheus, with the Prussian eagle eating his liver, or he is the giant Antaeus, rejuvenated by touching German soil (and perhaps he is even – by suggestive analogy – Daedalus and Sisyphus) (B 4: 579, 605, 619, 642). Such connections are more than just an erudite game (although they are that, too). They represent a strategy of mythological syncretism, a mingling of mythical systems designed, in a sense, to relativise German national myth, or to intimate a new mythology of supranational character.[46] The Christian-messianic allusions in the poem are also part of this: the poet's Odysseus-like longing for Hamburg-Ithaca is immediately followed by an imaging of the journey as the progress to Golgotha: 'Ich sehnte mich nach den Plätzen sogar,/Nach jenen Leidensstationen,/Wo ich geschleppt das Jugendkreuz/Und meine Dornenkronen' (B 4: 634). The Sisyphus reference adjoins an address to Christ on a roadside crucifix: 'Mit Wehmut erfüllt mich jedesmal/Dein Anblick, mein armer Vetter,/Der du die Welt erlösen gewollt,/Du Narr, du Menscheitsretter!' (B 4: 605) – which, in turn, connects with the German-messianic myth of Barbarossa in the three cantos that follow. In the poet's Cologne dream in Canto 7, Old Testament myth – specifically, the Passover story from Exodus (chap. 12, v. 13ff.) – is also added to the mixture, as being yet another expression of revolutionary-emancipatory aspiration (B 4: 593).[47] And the catalogue could continue.[48]

Finally, there is modern myth, too. There are the little contributions made to a new mythology of liberation by recent German authors: '. . . Und weicht Ihr nicht willig, so brauch ich Gewalt/Und laß Euch mit Kolben lausen!' (B 4: 595).[49] But above all there is Napoleon, the most recent messiah and always the central figure in Heine's modern pantheon. As is well known, Heine's attitude to the historical Napoleon was equivocal and could be quite censorious: 'War wirklich die Zeit des Kaiserreichs in Frankreich so schön und beglückend . . .? Ich glaube nicht. Die Äcker lagen brach und die Menschen wurden zur Schlachtbank geführt' (B 3: 309, *Über die französische Bühne*). But he saw Bonaparte as having great mythic/symbolic importance, 'als ein durch Unglück gesühnter und durch Tod gereinigter Repräsentant der Revolution, als ein Sinnbild der siegenden Volksgewalt' (B 3: 162, *Französische Zustände*); 'seine ungeheure Geschichte wird endlich ein Mythos' (B 2: 374). Accordingly, very many of the representations of Napoleon in Heine's own texts are in a specifically, consciously mythicising tone: the sections on Napoleon in Düsseldorf in *Ideen. Das Buch Le Grand*, Napoleon as messiah and god; the poet on the field of Marengo in *Reise von München nach Genua* (B 2: 273–6, 372–82); and others. The poet himself aims to contribute to the building of the myth. Moreover, a syncretistic element is in play here, too – for example, with Napoleon-Christ-God in *Das Buch Le Grand*. In fact, Heine's very first depiction of Napoleon, the ballad *Die Grenadiere* of around 1820, operates in such a way, for it seems to germanise Napoleon, idolising him in Germanic balladesque style, in a poem full of resonances of the German folk heritage (its songs, its language, its legends). It tells of a Napoleonic Second Coming. Perhaps, indeed, Napoleon in *Die Grenadiere* is intended somehow to blend with, or, as it were, to cosmopolitanise, the stories of Second Comings that are present in the German popular imagination, which means particularly Barbarossa.[50] In *Deutschland. Ein Wintermärchen* Napoleon reappears, as the poet tells of witnessing his funeral in 1840 in Paris: 'Der Kaiser ist auferstanden seitdem,/Doch die englischen Würmer haben/Aus ihm einen stillen Mann gemacht,/Und er ließ sich wieder begraben . . ./Den Elysäischen Feldern entlang,/Durch des Triumphes Bogen,/Wohl durch den Nebel, wohl über den Schnee/Kam langsam der Zug gezogen' (B 4: 597). Very striking is the seemingly incongruous folk-song reminiscence in the penultimate line ('Wohl durch den Nebel . . .', noted by Hans Kaufmann[51]), repeating the dualism of *Die Grenadiere*. In the context of the *Wintermärchen* as a whole, one realises that Napoleon is to be seen as another mythic incarnation, like Barbarossa,[52] of the people's desire for a Second Coming and emancipatory redemption; and the poet's suggestive combining of the two myths – modern and ancient, cosmopolitan and German – is part of the mythopoeic programme which the poem represents. To reinforce a point made earlier, it really is not convincing to suggest (as do Markus Winkler and, more obliquely, Jürgen Brummack) that *Deutschland. Ein Wintermärchen* expresses resignation on Heine's part about the emancipatory potential of German myth and of a modern mythologising based upon it.[53]

It is a little hard to know how literally Heine believed in the idea of a revolutionary Second Coming. One of the punchlines of the *Wintermärchen* is the anti-messianic conclusion to Canto 16, addressed to Barbarossa: 'Geh, leg dich schlafen, wir werden uns/Auch ohne dich erlösen' ('. . . Bedenk ich die Sache ganz genau,/So brauchen wir gar keinen Kaiser') (B 4: 615f.). On the other hand, Heine's immoderate enthusiasm in the 1850s at the rise of Napoleon III (B 6/1: 509f.), and his excitement in the 1840s when he met Lassalle (B 5: 99f., 767), suggest he wished to believe. At least he believed in the necessity of a latest and last Great Man of History ('der rettende König der Welt', as the famous passage on messianism – Barbarossa and other figures – in *Ludwig Börne. Eine Denkschrift* calls him; B 4: 121). The *Wintermärchen* certainly has an insistent line of messianic reference, with Barbarossa, Bonaparte, Jesus Christ and the Christ-like poet himself – and the idea 'des neuen Gotts,/Des großen Unbekannten', which the poet of the text bears in his head ('Im Kopfe trage ich Bijouterien,/Der Zukunft Krondiamenten,/Die Tempelkleinodien des neuen Gotts . . .'; B 4: 580) and which therefore (since the poem bespeaks the poet's mind) has presumably itself engendered the several mythic incarnations in the work. Nevertheless, the messianic element is not the most important aspect of the revolutionary creed that the text contains. The poet's 'Krondiamanten . . . der Zukunft' are the vision of the Utopian future condition of man and society which Heine had been mapping out since the early 1820s (with the drama *Almansor* and with *Die Harzreise*), which were confirmed and reinforced for him by his discovery of Saint-Simonism, and which essentially he maintained, after the discrediting of the Saint-Simonists and amidst the emergence of numerous competing socialisms in the 1830s and 1840s, at least until his own physical collapse in 1848. The 'earthly messiah' is only the agent of such a future. Its dimensions are signalled repeatedly in the *Wintermärchen* and its preface: a 'Himmelreich . . . auf Erden', inhabited by a 'neues Geschlecht . . . mit freien Gedanken, mit freier Lust', thus in which 'das arme, glückenterbte Volk' has been redeemed 'aus seiner Erniedrigung', freed both from physical deprivation and from the 'Skelette des Aberglaubens' which have kept it in spiritual bondage (B 4: 575, 578, 595, 642). In this world of 'Rosen und Myrten, Schönheit und Lust,/Und Zuckererbsen nicht minder' (B 4: 578), the objects of gratification will be freely available, and man in his new, harmonious and unrepressed state – free of Nazarene guilts, at one with his body, the surrounding world of nature and the divine – will be able to enjoy them. This is, so to speak, the 'Sommernachttraum' dreamed by the poet in his Winter's Tale. It has to be said that it is an imprecisely delineated Utopia, more poetic vision than concretely envisaged social reality. But Heine's adherence to it was enduring.

As was noted earlier, Heine's proposition is that such a Utopia is latent in the soul of the common people, particularly those of Germany. This means not only that the hope of it is there – the hope of revolutionary justice and liberation contained in the old songs and legends of the people – but also its seed. The German people is predisposed to such a liberation of the senses. Moreover, so is the poet, who seems in so many respects to share the people's deep impulses (again: 'In der Brust der Schriftsteller eines Volkes liegt schon das Abbild von dessen Zukunft'; B 3: 467). Apart from anything else, the *Wintermärchen* is a journal of sensual rediscovery. The poet intoxicates himself on Rhine wine, punch and rum, especially the first of these (and by this means, too – as well as through dream – puts himself in the visionary state that reveals to him Germany's past and future, enables him to commune with the figures of German myth, and so on; B 4: 583f., 599, 629, 640[54]). He also eats. Like the impulse to dream, an urge to eat (and drink) assails him when he reaches Germany: 'Da fächelte mich schon deutsche Luft,/Da fühlt ich ihren Einfluß –/Auf meinen Appetit. Ich aß/Dort Eierkuchen mit Schinken,/Und da er sehr gesalzen war,/Mußt ich auch Rheinwein trinken' (B 4: 583). The text's repeated invocations and eulogies of German feeding – meals in Cologne, at the inn in Hagen, at his mother's house in Hamburg, and 'im Keller von Lorenz' with Campe, together with further imagery of food which the poet introduces at various stages (B 4: 583, 598f., 622f., 625, 629, etc.) – signal the essential sensualism which he and the German people share. His only bad meal on the journey, one observes, is in the Prussian fortress of Minden ('. . . Das Essen wollt mir nicht schmecken'; B 4: 618). Also noteworthy are the parodies of patriotic and other spurious idealism in a language of food: of Arndt's *Vaterlandslied* ('Der Gott, der Eisen wachsen ließ') in a mock-prayer ('Ich danke dem Schöpfer in der Höh,/. . . Der auch Zitronen wachsen ließ,/Die Austern zu betauen': B 4: 629), and of Schillerian bombast with 'Sei mir gegrüßt, mein Sauerkraut' ('. . . Jedwedem fühlenden Herzen bleibt/Das Vaterland ewig teuer –/Ich liebe auch recht braun geschmort/Die Bücklinge und Eier'; B 4: 598).[55] Not such pomposity, but his own sensualism – so it is implied – represents the real Germany and its values.

The other form of sensuality which makes up the alternative German value system that the poem is offering is sexual, part of the critique of the moralism and sexual hypocrisy of the wealthy class which was an ingredient in Heine's writing from such early poems as 'Sie saßen und tranken am Teetisch' (B 1: 95f., *Intermezzo* 50) through to *Die Göttin Diana* and *Der Doktor Faust. Ein Tanzpoem.* The Wild Hunt in *Atta Troll*, of course, pointed among other things to an erotic, sensually unrepressed aspect of the German *Volksseele*. And the defiant sexuality of the final cantos of *Deutschland. Ein Wintermärchen* – in which the intoxicated poet obeys his libido and goes in search of prostitutes ('Der Rheinwein stimmt mich immer weich/Und löst jedwedes Zerwürfnis/In meiner Brust, entzündet darin/Der Menschenliebe Bedürfnis'; B 4: 629), and later reminisces about previous experiences with them ('"Du suchst die schönen Seelen vielleicht,/Die dir so oft begegent/Und mit dir geschwärmt die Nacht hindurch,/In dieser schönen Gegend"'; B 4: 630) – has an equivalent purpose. The mock-idealistic language and the episode itself are intended to offend the sensibilities of polite German readers (the 'viele Töchter gebildeter Stände an der Spree, wo nicht gar an der Alster, [die] über mein armes Gedicht die mehr oder minder gebogenen Näschen rümpfen werden'; B 4: 573), and to challenge them, by confronting them with a more 'natural', unrepressed state of being. The poem implies, in particular, that contemporary German nationalism's tedious moralism (which, for example, casts the Rhine absurdly as a fair virgin; B 4: 587) is a gross misapprehension of the real character of the people.[56]

It is true that the final scenes of the *Wintermärchen* – Lorenz's wine-cellar, the Dreckwall and Hammonia's garret – do not quite constitute a sensual Utopia. As Jürgen Brummack has pointed out, the Hamburg episodes of the poem altogether contain a good deal of reference to mortality and decay.[57] In particular, most of the prostitutes whom the poet previously knew are now dead. Hammonia too, given her age and in other respects, hardly represents ideal sensuality. In many ways one is reminded of the focus on sensuality and prostitution in Büchner's post-Saint-Simonist drama of a decade previously, *Dantons Tod*, in which a sensualistic ideal was juxtaposed with a social reality of deprivation and fatal sexual disease. This was the antinomy represented above all by the subtle figure of Marion, in whom an ideal and a reality of eroticism were in contradiction, but without one finally abolishing the other. So it is, too, in *Deutschland. Ein Wintermärchen*, in which the Hamburg scenes temper or refine the poem's sensualist ideal of 'Rosen und Myrten, Schönheit und Lust' (B 4: 578), but are not intended to annihilate it.

The Hamburg ending and the meaning it imposes on the work as a whole have been a significant point of dispute in commentaries on the poem. Hans Kaufmann's memorable Marxist analysis of 1958 is relatively neglectful of the Hamburg cantos. Hammonia is said to represent a discredited 'spießbürgerliche Erscheinungsform des alten, vorrevolutionären Deutschlands' – to be swept aside in the revolutionary future that Heine is predicting. The contents of her commode represent 'die Zukunft Altdeutschlands'. Generally, the Hamburg chapters are said to be concerned with the peripheral 'Privatinteresse' of the poet.[58] Jürgen Brummack's significant discussion of the text in 1979 shares and extends Kaufmann's view of Hammonia as the voice of the philistine bourgeoisie, but makes her thematically central. Essentially he finds in the anti-ideality of the Hamburg episodes and the reflections on the poet's personal problems a (part-parodistic) relativisation of the text's Utopian start. He suggests that the work shows an incipient pessimism, born of a new feeling that the poet's self-image as 'Ritter der Idee' is not fully reconcilable with his real self and the real world. On balance, the *Wintermärchen* maintains its Utopianism, but (so it is implied) the shift of mood towards that of the mattress grave is now discernible.[59]

Brummack's quite subtle position has been exceeded by a number of other critics in recent decades who find the *Wintermärchen* to be a basically negative work. Stefan Würffel, for instance, ridicules Kaufmann's notion that (according to Heine's poem) 'in [Germanias] Zukunft sich die jahrhundertealten Freiheitsträume realisieren', for supposedly ignoring the reality of 'die Heinesche Diktion. . . , die, was immer sie sagt, . . . aufhebt'. Ross Atkinson asserts firmly that the work is 'no political manifesto or *Kampfschrift*', but rather a tissue of self-cancelling ironies. We also have Klaus Briegleb, who has recently analysed it as an expression of proto-*nachmärzlich* resignation and apolitical aestheticisation; and Gerhard Höhn, who summarises the organisation of the work as an 'optimistische Prophezeiung am Anfang und . . . pessimistische Zukunftsvision am Schluß'.[60]

These are, it seems to me, excessive judgements. Brummack's notion that the text contains gestures of personal weakness, designed to complicate and in some measure destabilise the stance of authority and power with which the poem begins (and concludes), is reasonable – though such a proceeding is not an innovation in Heine's works: an opposition or alternation of power and prostration is much more strongly characteristic of such early texts of his as *Ideen. Das Buch Le Grand* and *Buch der Lieder*. Heine's frequently-used device of subjectively coloured narration – a narration (travelogue or otherwise) which registers mood shifts on the part of the poet – indeed almost imposes such variations. Among the variations that can be read into the *Wintermärchen* is certainly the anticipation of a range of different possible political futures. Brummack's thesis is that Hammonia expresses an expectation of 'praktische äußere Freiheit' – in other words, the bourgeois mercantile freedom of the new capitalist Germany (and that this is the principal novelty which struck Heine on his return in 1843).[61] However, it can also be said that an expectation of Prussian imperial hegemony is quite strong (and certainly *more* evident) in the work.

At any rate, it is true that the text, and Heine's mode of writing in general, permit, so to speak, a plurality of outcomes. However, that does not mean that the *Wintermärchen* is as a whole relativistic. The conclusion of the Hammonia episode, with the poet's dream fantasy of marriage to her and castration by the censor's scissors, does blur matters, though the notion that she represents a distinct and significant ideological position is not wholly convincing. One suspects that part of Heine's dissatisfaction at the work's 'nothdürftig[er] . . . Schluß' may have related to this passage and its indeterminate character.[62] The text's final statement, however, in Canto 27, is an emphatic reaffirmation of the beginning of the work: 'Es wächst heran ein neues Geschlecht,/Ganz ohne Schminke und Sünden,/Mit freien Gedanken, mit freier Lust –/Dem werde ich Alles verkünden./Schon knospet die Jugend, welche versteht/Des Dichters Stolz und Güte', etc. (B 4: 642).

Moreeover, it is noteworthy that even the preceding episode, the dreamed-of marriage to Hammonia, entails yet another return to the world of German folk legend with which the text has been so preoccupied. Canto 27 calls it an imitation of Aristophanes's *The Birds*, which it may indeed be (Heine's invocation of a prototypal political-satirical *Volksschriftsteller*); but it is also, and in a way more importantly, another of the poet's orgiastic Wild Hunts, like the 'Traum der Sommernacht' (B 4: 501) of the Eve of St. John, the midsummer solstice, in *Atta Troll* (B 4: 537–48), Walpurgisnacht in *Die Harzreise* (B 2: 140), and the Bacchanal of the 'herbstliche Tagesgleiche' in *Die Götter im Exil* (B 6/1: 403). Presumably the 'Wundernacht' (B 4: 641) on which Heine's 'Winter-Märchen' ends is the midwinter solstice, a final affirmation of the folk Germanness which has held the poet-narrator – and Heine the author – in thrall throughout the epic. With its systematic focus on the potential for emancipation in the German folk soul (the German people's mythical memory and its capacity for sensual enjoyments, all of which the poet himself, 'deutscheste Bestie' that he is,[63] instinctively shares and can uniquely articulate), the *Wintermärchen* is really a remarkably forceful and thoroughgoing assertion of Heine's emancipatory ideology, and certainly not in any substantial sense a document of pessimism and resignation.

Notes

1. Letter of 11 November 1828, in Heine, *Säkularausgabe. Werke, Briefwechsel, Lebenszeugnisse*, eds Nationale Forschungs- und Gedenkstätten der klassischen deutschen Literatur (Weimar) and Centre National de la Recherche Scientifique (Paris), Berlin and Paris, 1970ff., 20: 351 (edition referred to subsequently in this chapter as 'HSA'). Versions of the same phrase occur also in *Reise von München nach Genua* and in the paralipomena to *Die Stadt Lucca*. See Heine, *Sämtliche Schriften*, ed. Klaus Briegleb, Munich, 1969–76, 2: 376, 634; edition henceforth as 'B'. Briegleb's *Werkausgabe* is the most frequently used edition of Heine; I employ it as the basis for quotation here on account of its wide availability.
2. See, for example, B 1: 569, 2: 429, 552, 3: 136, 577, 5: 163f.
3. Siegbert Prawer, *Frankenstein's Island. England and the English in the Writings of Heinrich Heine*, Cambridge, 1986, p. 337.
4. See Michael Perraudin, 'Heine et l'Angleterre ou le médiateur en défaut', *Romantisme. Revue du dix-neuvième siècle* 101 (1998): *Heine le médiateur*, 41–9.
5. See Heine's letter of 4 February 1836, HSA 21: 138.
6. See, for example, Heine himself in *Ludwig Börne. Eine Denkschrift*, B: 4, 88–91. Cf. also Hagen Schulze, *Der Weg zum Nationalstaat. Die deutsche Nationalbewegung vom 18. Jahrhundert bis zur Reichsgründung*, Munich, 1985, pp. 76–8.

7. See Schulze, *Der Weg zum Nationalstaat*, pp. 80–4.
8. See Michael Werner, *Genius und Geldsack. Zum Problem des Schriftstellerberufs bei Heinrich Heine*, Hamburg, 1978, esp. pp. 78–81.
9. Cf. also Heinrich Laube's warnings to him in 1842 about the public rage which anti-national elements in *Atta Troll* were likely to generate. Letter by Laube of 27 November 1842, HSA 26: 49f.
10. See Heinrich Heine, *Historisch-kritische Gesamtausgabe der Werke (Düsseldorfer Ausgabe)*, ed. Manfred Windfuhr, Hamburg, 1973–97, 4: 1102f., commentary by Winfried Woesler (edition henceforth as 'DHA').
11. It was also the mood that generated Theodor Storm's and his friend Theodor Mommsen's collecting of sagas and other popular cultural material from Schleswig-Holstein in the early 1840s. See below, chapter 8.
12. See Heine's letters of 25 November and 6 December 1843 to his wife Mathilde, HSA 22: 81f., 86.
13. See inter alia Heine's letters of 12 April and 25 November 1843, 17 April 1844, and his will of 7 April 1843, HSA 22: 53f., 55, 82, 99f.
14. See Campe's letter of 27 November 1842, HSA 26: 48.
15. See, for example, Heine's letters of 5 June and 19 December 1844, HSA 22: 109, 146; also Werner, *Genius und Geldsack*, p. 67, and Werner Bellmann, *Heinrich Heine: 'Deutschland. Ein Wintermärchen'. Erläuterungen und Dokumente*, Stuttgart, 1990, pp. 115, 117.
16. Letter of 14 September 1844, HSA 22: 126.
17. It is what the end of *Die Harzreise* does, also the Marengo episode in *Reise von München nach Genua*, the end of *Die Stadt Lucca*, and other passages. See B 2: 164–6, 374ff., 526–9.
18. Cf. the notion of 'Freiheitsrausch' in *Zur Geschichte der Religion und Philosophie in Deutschland* (B 3: 640); the poet's own revolutionary 'Begeisterung' in the *Nachschrift* to *Die Stadt Lucca* (B 2: 529); Paris as 'die Stadt der Freiheit, der Begeisterung und des Martyrtums, die Heilandstadt', in *Französische Zustände* (B 3: 180); and the (enthusiastic) suggestion from the French version of *Elementargeister* that: 'Peut-être le dieu de la révolution ne peut-il remuer par la raison le peuple allemand, peut-être est-ce la tâche de la folie d'accomplir ce difficile ouvrage? Quand le sang lui montera une fois, . . . son oreille ne pourra plus entendre que la grande voix de l'homme' (B 3: 1016).
19. Cf. Heine's letter of 29 December 1843, HSA 22: 91: 'Hab auf meiner Reise mancherley Verse gemacht, die mir mit größerer Leichtigkeit gelingen, wenn ich deutsche Luft athme'. Cf. also *Die Romantische Schule*, B 3: 465: 'Nur jenseits des Rheins können solche Gespenster gedeihen; nimmermehr in Frankreich. Als ich hierher reiste, begleiteten mich meine Gespenster bis an die französische Grenze. Da nahmen sie betrübt von mir Abschied'.
20. Cf. Heine's letter of 17 April 1844, HSA 22: 100.
21. See ibid.
22. See Michael Perraudin, *Heinrich Heine: Poetry in Context. A Study of 'Buch der Lieder'*, Oxford, 1989, pp.72–80.
23. There are several other reminiscences of *Buch der Lieder* in the *Wintermärchen*: in the Cologne episode, both the bleeding wound in the poet's heart and the sudden dream awakening (B 4: 593, 595) are designed to recall motifs both of the *Traumbilder* and *Fresko-Sonette* in *Junge Leiden* (see, for example, B 1: 71), and of the cycle *Lyrisches Intermezzo*: compare the final strophe of Canto 7, B

4: 595, with that of *Intermezzo* 64, B 1: 103; and the beginning of Canto 8 (Strophes 5–6) alludes to 'Im wunderschönen Monat Mai' (B 4: 596, 1: 75).

24. See, for example, Winfried Woesler, DHA 4: 929; Hans Kaufmann, *Politisches Gedicht und klassische Dichtung. Heinrich Heine: 'Deutschland. Ein Wintermärchen'*, Berlin, 1958, p. 106; Jürgen Brummack, *Satirische Dichtung. Studien zu Friedrich Schlegel, Tieck, Jean Paul und Heine*, Munich, 1979, pp. 175–6.

25. See DHA 4: 930.

26. It could be added that this is also the one feature differentiating the *Wintermärchen* metrically from Ernst Moritz Arndt's patriotic-xenophobic 'Vaterlandslied. 1812', which Heine mockingly travesties elsewhere in his epic (Canto 23, B 4: 269).

27. See Michael Perraudin, '"Der schöne Heros, der früh dahinsinkt . . ." Poesie, Mythos und Politik in Heines "Die Grenadiere"', in *Interpretationen. Gedichte von Heinrich Heine*, ed. Bernd Kortländer, Stuttgart, 1995, pp. 32–50.

28. Also a feature of the verse of the *Wintermärchen* is occasional, random asonantic and alliterative harmonies between the final words of the first and third lines of strophes. See, for example, Canto 15, B 4: 610ff.

29. Heine also uses the metre and rhyme pattern of the *Wintermärchen* exactly for some other ancient-and-modern political ballads with German or English subject matter: *Der Tannhäuser* in *Neue Gedichte* and *Schelm von Bergen, Karl I* and *Schlachtfeld bei Hastings* in the *Historien* in *Romanzero* (B 4: 348ff., 6/1: 19ff.).

30. To adapt the phrase from Heine's letter of 29 December 1843 to Campe (see above); HSA 22: 91.

31. Letter of 20 February 1844, HSA 22: 96.

32. See Perraudin, *Poetry in Context*, pp. 143–86, esp. p. 175f.

33. Heine, *Werke*, ed. Ernst Elster, 4 vols, Leipzig, 1925, 3: 421.

34. See Perraudin, *Poetry in Context*, p. 115f., 162f.

35. Letter of 20 February 1844, HSA 22: 96. See also letter of 19 December 1844, HSA 22: 146.

36. Letter of 29 December 1843, HSA 22: 91.

37. See B 2: 113, 125f., 130, 158–60.

38. The *Englische Fragmente* make explicit an extension of this notion, namely the emancipatory capacity of such dreaming. See B 2: 536f.: 'Spottet nicht unserer Träumer, dann und wann, wie Somnambüle sprechen sie Wunderbares im Schlafe, und ihr Wort wird Saat der Freiheit'.

39. B 1: 20–37, 2: 108f., 120f., 128f., etc.

40. See notably Markus Winkler, *Mythisches Denken zwischen Romantik und Realismus. Zur Erfahrung kultureller Fremdheit im Werk Heinrich Heines*, Stuttgart, 1995, pp. 193, 201, 210f. Cf. also Jürgen Brummack, *Satirische Dichtung*, p. 196.

41. See Michael Perraudin, 'Irrationalismus und jüdisches Schicksal. Die thematischen Zusammenhänge von Heines *Ideen. Das Buch Le Grand*', in *Aufklärung und Skepsis. Internationaler Heine-Kongreß 1997 zum 200. Geburtstag*, eds Joseph Kruse, Bernd Witte and Karin Füllner, Stuttgart, 1998, pp. 279–302 (pp. 296–8).

42. Brüder Grimm, *Kinder- und Hausmärchen*, ed. Heinz Rölleke, 3 vols, Stuttgart, 1980, 2: 24–30, also 149f., *Die klare Sonne bringt's an den Tag*. See also Woesler, DHA 4: 1130f. And cf. *Des Knaben Wunderhorn. Alte deutsche Lieder*, eds Ludwig Achim von Arnim and Clemens Brentano, 3 vols, Heidelberg, 1806–8, 1: 274f. (reproduced in Clemens Brentano, *Sämtliche Werke und Briefe*,

eds Jürgen Behrens, Wolfgang Frühwald and Detlev Lüders, Stuttgart, 1975ff., vol. 6).

43. In Heine's poem 'Deutschland! (Geschrieben im Sommer 1840)' some of the imagery of these portions of the *Wintermärchen* is clearly prefigured: 'Deutschland ist noch ein kleines Kind,/Doch die Sonne ist seine Amme;/Sie säugt es nicht mit stiller Milch,/Sie säugt es mit wilder Flamme./. . ./Es ist ein täppisches Rieselein,/Reißt aus dem Boden die Eiche' etc. (B 4: 454) – the 'Amme', the sun and flame of revolution. And as the poem concludes, the 'Rieselein' becomes (like) the most famous of all German mythical heroes: 'Dem Siegfried gleicht er, dem edlen Fant,/Von dem wir singen und sagen;/Der hat, nachdem er geschmiedet sein Schwert, Den Amboß entzwei geschlagen!/Ja, du wirst einst wie Siegfried sein,/Und töten den häßlichen Drachen, /Heisa! Wie freudig vom Himmel herab/Wird deine Frau Amme lachen!'. Thus even the Nibelungen can be recast as a myth of revolution.

44. B 4: 634 and *Odyssey*, Book 1, v. 57ff. Quoted from Bellmann, *Erläuterungen*, p.57.

45. B 4: 639; see, for example, Bellmann, *Erläuterungen*, p. 60, and cf. DHA 4: 1155f. This is on the whole more plausible than the alternative suggestion, that the allusion is to Pandora's Box. See B 4: 1043.

46. The notion that important aspects of Heine's thought involve a kind of syncretism deserves further development. One critic who uses the term is Jeffrey Sammons, in 'Heinrich Heine: The Revolution as Epic and Tragedy', in *The Internalized Revolution. German Reactions to the French Revolution, 1789–1989*, eds Ehrhard Bahr and Thomas Saine, New York, 1992, pp. 173–96, see p. 175.

47. See Margaret Rose, 'The Idea of the "Sol Iustitae" in Heine's *Deutschland. Ein Wintermärchen*', *Deutsche Vierteljahresschrift*, 52 (1978), 604–18, esp. p. 611.

48. Yet another mythic suggestion is added by a letter of Heine's, of 28 October 1843, HSA 22: 70: 'mon pèlerinage . . . à Hambourg'.

49. Echoing Goethe's *Erlkönig*.

50. Recently prominently evoked in the Grimms' *Deutsche Sagen* (1816–18) and in Rückert's poem 'Barbarossa' of 1817. See Friedrich Rückert, *Werke*, ed. Richard Böhme, 6 vols in 3, Berlin n.d., 2: 47f., and Brüder Grimm, *Deutsche Sagen*, ed. Hans-Jörg Uther and Barbara Kindermann-Bieri, 3 vols, Munich, 1993, 1: 42–4.

51. Kaufmann, *Politisches Gedicht*, p. 114.

52. Cf. Wulf Wülfing, 'Luise gegen Napoleon, Napoleon gegen Barbarossa. Zu einigen Positionen Heines in einem Jahrhundert der Mythenkonkurrenzen', in *Aufklärung und Skepsis. Internationaler Heine-Kongreß 1997*, pp. 395–407.

53. Winkler, *Mythisches Denken*, pp. 193, 201, 210f. et al.; Brummack, *Satirische Dichtung*, p. 196; and see above, note 40.

54. This is a notion traceable back to the Heine of the 1820s, to the image of the Cup of Giamshid and the idea of the power of the intoxicated imagination in *Ideen. Das Buch Le Grand* and the poem *Im Hafen*. This imagery, in turn, has its roots for Heine in Goethe's *West-östlicher Divan*, of which it is a central ingredient. See Perraudin, *Poetry in Context*, pp. 119–42.

55. The *pathetisch* 'Sei mir gegrüßt' primarily invoked, I think, Schiller's famous poem *Der Spaziergang*. There are various other moments of apparent Schillerian pastiche through the poem; see DHA 4: 1150, 1155f.

56. An equivalent targeting of taboos is certainly also evident in the faecal episode of Hammonia's chamber-pot. On this aspect, see Paul Peters, 'Bildersturm auf die Germanomanie. Heines *Wintermärchen* als Poesie der Destruktion', in

Heinrich Heine, *Deutschland. Ein Wintermärchen*, eds Ursula Roth and Heidemarie Vahl, Stuttgart, 1995, pp. 201–223.

57. Brummack, *Satirische Dichtung*, p. 187.

58. Kaufmann, *Politisches Gedicht*, pp. 150, 153, 156.

59. Brummack, *Satirische Dichtung*, p. 184.

60. Stephan Würffel, *Der produktive Widerspruch. Heinrich Heines negative Dialektik*, Bern, 1986, pp. 225, 230; Ross Atkinson, 'Irony and Commitment in Heine's *Deutschland. Ein Wintermärchen*', *Germanic Review*, 50 (1975), 184–202, see pp. 184, 187, 193, 201; Klaus Briegleb, '"Das bessere Lied" – Nachmärz im Vormärz. Zu Heinrich Heines Weg der Kunst Dezember 1841–Januar 1844', in *Nachmärz. Der Ursprung der ästhetischen Moderne in einer nachrevolutionären Konstellation*, eds Thomas Koebner and Sigrid Weigel, Opladen, 1996, pp. 20–42; Gerhard Höhn, *Heine-Handbuch. Zeit, Person, Werk*, Stuttgart, 1987, p. 102.

61. Brummack, *Satirische Dichtung*, pp. 183, 194.

62. Letter of 17 April 1844, HSA 22: 100. One also has a sense that critical attempts to present Hammonia as the coherent mouthpiece of a single ideological attitude are like similar attempts with the figure of Atta Troll – whose continually shifting voices are, in fact, an essential aspect and consequence of the text's ironic (and specifically *tendenzfeindlich*) mode of discourse.

63. Letter of 7 March 1824, HSA 20: 148.

6

Revolution and Desire.
Grillparzer and Stifter's *Bunte Steine*

In January 1860, an exchange of letters took place between Adalbert Stifter and Franz Grillparzer, the only one recorded between them. Congratulating Grillparzer on what was supposed to be his seventieth birthday (it was actually his sixty-ninth), the then fifty-four-year-old Stifter proclaimed and exhorted:

> Wenn es wahr ist, was ich seit einiger Zeit zu sehen glaube, daß auch die alte österreichische Kunst, statt die höchsten Kräfte des Menschen in holder Schönheit empor zu heben, zur Unterhaltungsdirne werden will, die sich an alle untergeordneten und oft wilden Triebe wendet, nur nicht an die höchste menschliche Kraft, so müssen die, welche Großes und Gutes aus der älteren Dichtkunst gezogen haben, zusammen treten, und die hoch halten, welche jene edlere Kunst brachten.[1]

Grillparzer's reply to this, two days later, appears sympathetic, but is not in total agreement:

> . . . Den Lumpen wird der Fortschritt leicht, was soll denn aber derjenige thun, der zu seinem Unglück Überzeugungen hat? Wenn auch nicht die Wahrheit, doch die Richtigkeit unserer höchsten Gedanken und Empfindungen hängt denn doch von der Übereinstimmung des Menschengeschlechtes ab. Da kann denn doch nur ein Narr seiner so sicher sein, daß ihn der gemeinsame Lärm seiner Zeit nicht in's innere Wanken brächte.[2]

This would seem in many ways to represent a characteristic divergence of attitude between the two authors. Stifter complains about the immorality of contemporary literature, suggesting particularly that it is sexually licentious,[3] and advocates a campaign of moral renewal by those who know moral truth. Grillparzer's response is passive, resigned in tone and ambivalently relativistic: our sublimest notions are undermined if most other people do not share them, and *if* they do not share them, then one would be a fool not at least to have doubts oneself. Stifter, presumably, is such a fool. This is the Grillparzer who always acknowledged – or part of whom acknowledged – that the public's response to his works, even when hostile, had validity,[4] and that art produced without the corrective of a mass public – of an 'einem Eindruck sich hingebende Masse', which possesses '[ein] Gefühl der *Menschheit als Ganzes*'[5] – was liable to become distorted, sterile and absurd. More specifically in the context of the exchange with Stifter, Grillparzer's reply implies that modern writing which, 'statt die höchsten Kräfte der Menschen in holder Schönheit empor zu heben, . . . sich an alle untergeordneten und oft wilden Triebe wendet', might not be entirely misguided.[6]

It is certainly the case that a major difference between these two writers (who otherwise have so many resemblances) is Grillparzer's much greater disposition overtly to acknowledge the reality of desire. The little poem which Grillparzer wrote in 1819, admittedly in the more dynamic early part of his career, entitled *Kuß*, could really never have come from Stifter:

Auf die Hände küßt die Achtung,
Freundschaft auf die offne Stirn,
Auf die Wange Wohlgefallen,
Sel'ge Liebe auf den Mund;
Auf geschloßne Aug die Sehnsucht,
In die hohle Hand Verlangen,
Arm und Nacken die Begierde,
Übrall sonst die Raserei. (HKA I/10: 27)

We encounter many characters in his works, mostly male characters, though also on occasion female ones, who are in a state of desire, often destructive, sometimes liberating: Jaromir in *Die Ahnfrau*, but also his sister Berta; Rustan but also Gülnare in *Der Traum ein Leben*; Don Cäsar in *Ein Bruderzwist*, with a desire which is also hatred;[7] or Alfonso in *Die Jüdin von Toledo*, released from repression into uncomprehended sexual feeling (DKV 3: 497f., 501, 507[8]), the final consequence of which is the destruction of its object. In particular, Grillparzer's Hero and Leander play *Des Meeres und der Liebe Wellen*, completed and first performed in

April 1831, is concerned with such experience. Here we have both Leander and Hero, like Alfonso in *Die Jüdin*, released suddenly from familially induced emotional repression, Leander into an aggressive, possessive male desire (for the sake of which he swims the waters of the Hellespont), Hero into an experience of erotic self-surrender and disindividuation:

> – wie der Mensch, der müd am Sommerabend
> Vom Ufer steigt ins weiche Wellenbad,
> Und, von dem lauen Strome rings umfangen,
> In gleiche Wärme seine Glieder breitet,
> So daß er, prüfend, kaum vermag zu sagen:
> Hier fühl' ich mich und hier fühl' ich ein Fremdes –. (DKV 3: 16)[9]

Leander is also accompanied and supported in the play by his friend Naukleros, an epitome of unneurotic, energetic, assertive maleness, for whom desire again expresses itself in the anonymous, formless imagery of the waves:

> Gute Götter, wars nicht,
> Als ob die Erde aller Wesen Fülle
> Zurückgeschlungen in den reichen Schoß
> Und Mädchen draus gebildet, nichts als Mädchen?
> ....
> Im Ganzen ein begeisternd froher Anblick:
> Ein wallend Meer, mit Häuptern, weißen Schultern
> Und runden Hüften an der Wellen Statt. (DKA 3: 33)[10]

Such urges, clearly, are the 'Wellen . . . der Liebe' of the work's title.

But the play creates a significant further connection. As Naukleros and Leander make their dynamic and aggressive entry into the orderly, rigorously sexless domain of the temple of Hero and her uncle, the Chief Priest, on the day of her priestly initiation, they accompany, or rather are part of, a mass of *Volk*, impatient for gratification, uncontrollable, flood-like: 'Laßt ein das Volk und haltet Ordnung, hört ihr?'; 'Auch dort von rückwärts wächst des Volkes Drang'; 'Um uns . . . strömt dort das Volk in Haufen' (DKV 3: 25f.). 'Glück mit uns!', they cry, in response to the priests' injunction, 'Den Göttern Ehrfurcht!' (DKV 3: 28f.). The chaotic, urge-driven Volk are, it is implied, part of the same force as the desire which drives the play's hero and heroine.

Just one character in the play seems to be above such disorderly inclinations, namely the High Priest, the guardian of the temple's and Hero's purity and advocate of the supreme virtue of 'Sammlung' (moderation, self-control and suppression of ego; DKV 3: 46), which Grillparzer elsewhere extolled.[11] Yet at the end, as the Priest engineers Leander's drowning, it is apparent that he, too, acts from passions of his own: pseudo-paternal possessiveness, jealousy and rage (DKV 3: 67f.); and finally he is the play's prime tragic figure, left alone to face his own guilt (DKV 3: 94). The implication of this, which is significant for Grillparzer's future writing, is that the urges which manifestly direct the disorderly and lustful masses in one way or another beset all of us, however we may seek to build moral and cultural barriers against them. 'Laßt ein das Volk und haltet Ordnung, hört ihr?' says the Priest himself in Act One; 'Auch über Euch wacht sorglich, eben heut;/Die Lust hat ihren Tag' (DKV 3: 26).

Des Meeres und der Liebe Wellen has Grillparzer's characteristic ambivalence: acceding to passion does not liberate, yet neither does resisting or repressing it. In any event, the play's view of the lustful masses is not particularly a hostile one. In the years that follow, the attitudes he strikes vary, according to context. At the one extreme we have a poem such as *Bretterwelt*, of 1835, in which the poet as playwright exults in his sensual oneness with the mass:

> . . . Am Arme seines Nachbars im Gedränge
> Fühlt Jeder die gesteigert fremde Glut
> Und über sie kommt das Gefühl der Menge,
> In dem der Mensch verzehnfacht, schlimm wie gut,
> Der weiß, er teilt im Blicke mit sein Wissen,
> Der Fühlende im Atem sein Gefühl;
> Der Einzelne ist seinem Selbst entrissen,
> Zählt nur als Woge, schwindend im Gewühl.
> Dann aber – fort von deinem Aug die Wolke,
> Dann sprechen wir zu Dem und Jenem nicht,
> Dann sprechen zur Gesamtheit wir, zum Volke,
> Und Die sinds wert, daß man mit ihnen spricht. (HKA I/10: 158)

At the other extreme we have the famous images of horrific plebeian chaos from *Ein Bruderzwist in Habsburg*, seemingly written a little before 1848:[12]

> Ists doch als ginge wild verzehrend Feuer
> Aus dieser Rolle,[13] das die Welt entzündet
> Und jede Zukunft, bis des Himmels Quellen

Mit neuer Sündflut bändigen die Glut,
Und Pöbelherrschaft heißt die Überschwemmung. (DKV 3: 434)

Grillparzer's personal politics were a kind of fluctuating conservative scepticism,[14] hostile to the stupidities and corruption of the Habsburg regime and the ruling aristocracy,[15] but also hostile to all forms of nationalism (for example, HKA I/13: 178f., 217–19), sceptical about constitutionalism ('[Bin] kein unbedingter Freund der Konstituzionen'; HKA I/13: 182), anti-republican, anti-democratic, more sympathetic to notions of liberty than of equality (e.g. HKA I/13: 184), but above all fearful of violent disorder and social disintegration. In 1848 his initial sympathy for the revolution was tepid and hedged about by warnings; in fact, it was more relief at the revolution's apparent moderation than enthusiasm.[16] It was also very short-lived: by the second half of the year he was identified as a 'Schwarz-Gelber', composing embarrassing eulogies to Field-Marshall Radetzky, the Butcher of Milan, and impelled to flee Vienna twice.[17] The revolutionary year fixed him, more or less, in a standpoint of what might be called pessimistic legitimism.

What is again interesting about his political pronouncements, however, is the prominent role that passion ('Leidenschaft') and, more narrowly, desire play in them. Above all, as he describes with horror and distaste the popular Revolution in mid 1848 – 'gräßliche[r] Gang der Ereignisse', 'die Unbilden und das Geheul der Menge' (HKA I/13: 205f.) – there is a strong sense that events are driven by an illicit excitation and enjoyment: 'pöbelhafte Lustigkeit', 'zuströmende[r] Spaß', 'Straßenunterhaltungen', 'aufgeregt', 'genußsüchtig' (HKA I/13: 204, 207). But, significantly, such impulses are not restricted to the 'Straßenpöbel' (HKA I/13: 205). Other nations, for example, watch revolutionary events in Vienna in 1848 'mit Wollust' (HKA I/13: 204). Most strikingly, his earlier characterisation of Metternich's politics, which he held directly responsible for the Revolution,[18] presented them also as an expression of pernicious desire: 'Der eigentliche Leitstern seiner Handlungen [blieb] immer das *Gelüsten*' (HKA I/13: 166; also 174).

The text of Grillparzer's in which such perceptions come together most emphatically is his story *Der arme Spielmann*, published in mid-1847 and apparently written in stages over the preceding sixteen years, spanning the gap, one might say, between the Revolutions.[19] This tale of the naive, incompetent, socially downwardly mobile old fiddler Jakob encourages a range of intriguing

readings: as ironic autobiography (with different aspects of or perspectives on the authorial self represented in the inept fiddler and
his energetic, proficient narrator), as a discussion of artistic production and reception, as reflections on musical aesthetics, as an
affirmation or undermining of German Classicism, as a game
played with levels of narration, and others.[20] But its social side is
particularly interesting. Its initial pages, apparently composed
within a year of the July Revolution, to which Grillparzer had
reacted with a measure of approval,[21] are an extraordinary, powerful evocation of the 'Volksfest' of *Brigittenkirchtag* in Vienna. The
description emphasises the collective, anti-individual character of
the festival, the suspension of social barriers and proprieties, the
wave- and flood-like motion of the crowd (echoing the flow of the
nearby Danube), and the urge for gratification which drives it
('Aufruhr der Freude, . . . Losgebundenheit der Lust', 'der breite
Hafen der Lust', 'lustgierig', 'genußlechzend'; HKA I/13: 37–40).
The description also hints at parallels with popular revolution:
'Genommen, verloren und wiedergenommen, ist endlich der
Ausgang erkämpft'; 'Ein neu Hinzugekommener aus bewegten
Ländern [these last three words were deleted for the final version]
fände die Zeichen bedenklich' (HKA I/13: 37, 334); and conno-
tations of Bacchanalia are signalled, with the phrase 'das
saturnalische Fest' (HKA I/13: 37) and other mythic suggestions.[22]
As has been argued, this portion of Grillparzer's story in several
respects shows the influence of Goethe's depiction from 1788 of
the Roman Carnival, 'dieses moderne Saturnal'.[23] Goethe's text,
produced in the climate which immediately preceded the French
Revolution, is a reflection on lust, liberty and the breakdown of
social control, in which the author basically rejoices. His conclusion is hedonistic: that the 'Maskengesellschaft' of the Carnival
acts to remind us of 'die Wichtigkeit jedes augenblicklichen . . .
Lebensgenusses'.[24] And this is also more or less the point of view
of Grillparzer's narrator, who takes in the *Volksfest* with impres-
sionistic, as it were irrational, even intoxicated perceptions,
describes how he himself becomes part of the 'genußlechzende
Menge', the 'lustgierige Kirchweihgäste' (HKA I/13: 39f.), as they
wash across the Danube bridges, and asserts his relish for humanity in such a condition ('als ein leidenschaftlicher Liebhaber der
Menschen, vorzüglich des Volkes, . . . als ein Liebhaber der
Menschen sage ich, besonders wenn sie in Massen für einige Zeit
der einzelnen Zwecke vergessen und sich als Teile des Ganzen
fühlen, in dem denn doch zuletzt das Göttliche liegt – als einem

Solchen ist mir jedes Volksfest ein eigentliches Seelenfest, eine Wallfahrt, eine Andacht'; HKA I/13: 39).[25] This is the playwright-narrator as a pagan, worshipper of Dionysus. And the narrator is drawn to the Spielmann by related impulses: 'mein . . . anthropologische[r] Heißhunger', 'ich zitterte vor Begierde nach dem Zusammenhange' (HKA I/13: 41f.).

Jakob the Spielmann himself, however, seems in almost all respects to represent the opposite principle: struggling against the stream of the crowd ('. . . arbeitete sich mühsam durch die dem Feste zuströmende Menge in entgegengesetzter Richtung'; HKA I/13: 41); resisting the demands of a vulgar public on his music (HKA I/13: 42); and determined always to live life according to patterns of self-imposed order: 'Der Mensch . . . muß sich . . . in allen Dingen eine gewisse Ordnung festsetzen, sonst gerät er ins Wilde und Unaufhaltsame (HKA I/13: 43, cf. 42f.). In particular, he is shown resisting the moral chaos of the masses in his own little room, where a chalk line on the floor divides his pristine domain from the extreme, grimy 'Unordentlichkeit' of his room-mates, 'zwei Handwerksgesellen' (HKA I/13: 48f.). An absolute moral code directs his actions.

Jakob is not the only character in the story who is resisting the amoral world of the masses. Barbara, the stout and efficient shopkeeper's daughter whom Jakob loves and who in some way loves him, is also an adherent of physical and moral order (HKA I/13: 74f., 80) – but she is driven eventually, by the Spielmann's own incompetence for life, regretfully to relinquish him and marry the butcher who has been making advances to her (HKA I/13: 61, 76): 'Ich muß nun hinaus unter die groben Leute, wogegen ich mich so lange gesträubt habe' (HKA I/13: 75). The butcher's trade, and the physicality associated with him when he appears in the story (HKA I/13: 61, 81), correspond to a side of Barbara which she has striven against, but they appear in absolute contrast to the Spielmann's own asceticism and scrupulousness.

There is a difficulty with the Spielmann's integrity, however. He is, indeed, absolutely scrupulous, as well as trusting, self-giving and uninterested in conventional gratifications (HKA I/13: 57), an image of the kind of priestly abstention from and unfitness for life which Grillparzer liked to depict. But, as is often the case with such characters of Grillparzer's, total purity is not possible, and both in the Spielmann's relationship with Barbara, and in his music itself, there is an ingredient of desire – 'Begierde', 'Verzückung', 'Wollust', 'Genuß' (HKA I/13: 46f., 49, 59).[26] The

Spielmann is not prey to the egotistic *Leidenschaften* of rage and envy and pride which beset, despite everything, such other ascetics as the Oberpriester in *Des Meeres und der Liebe Wellen* and Rudolf in *Ein Bruderzwist*; but a version of the lustful impulse which we also see driving the Volk remains in him.

Grillparzer's story is also, it has been noted, a kind of social satire.[27] The world which surrounds the Spielmann and for which he is not fit is altogether one of amoral *Leidenschaft*. Very much after the fashion of Nestroy's key play of *Vormärz* Vienna, *Lumpazivagabundus*, Hanswurstian principles are cynically shown to be by no means the preserve of the masses, but to permeate the social structure. Not only are Barbara's plebeian father and husband greedy and dishonest, but the Spielmann's work colleagues in the *Kanzlei* are spiteful, his more successful brothers are a gambler and a liar, his father's secretary is an embezzler and his father the *Hofrat* himself, at the pinnacle of society, is 'ehrgeizig und heftig' (HKA I/13: 51), cruel and corrupt. The culture that faces the Spielmann – a heartless mercantile and bureaucratic world of speculation, deceit and manipulation – is morally unlovely. Grillparzer's feeling, at least in this text, seems again a little like Nestroy's in *Lumpazi* and elsewhere: a kind of ambivalent attraction to the pure, anonymous *Triebhaftigkeit* of the masses, but scorn for the hypocritical manifestations of such desires among the civilised.

The denouement of Grillparzer's story, probably composed in the mid 1840s, is a reprise of the imagery of the beginning, but with the flood now reality, not metaphor, as the Spielmann dies following an inundation that overwhelms the impoverished quarter in which he lives. This is presumed to be a reminiscence of the flood which struck the Leopoldstadt in 1830 (28 February-1 March),[28] one of the several natural or not-so-natural disasters which either befell or arose out of the plebeian slums at this time (flood, cholera and revolt). The Spielmann does battle against the water, in the most effective moment of action of his life, but catches cold and perishes. The significance of the episode is left ambiguous. He appears to die as a consequence of his final sally into the waters, undertaken in order to rescue a minor amount of money – perhaps a token of ultimate pointlessness – and his landlord's 'Steuerbücher' – maybe a final affirmation of social order (HKA I/13: 79f.). Possibly we are to take the ending as symbolising that he is finally joining battle against his own disorderly urges, or possibly that Grillparzer, in the alarming period which immediately preceded 1848,[29] is enjoining his passive contemporaries to a kind of moral activism against the pending chaos. All this is conceivable, but none of it is made clear. At the very least, though, it is apparent that the Dionysian relish of the story's tremendous beginning[30] has slipped from view, leaving the floods only really signalling violence and destruction.

Stifter came across *Der arme Spielmann* in mid-1847 in the proofs for the 1848 edition of the belletristic almanac *Iris*, which was also to contain one of his own stories.[31] He was exceedingly impressed by it, as the review he wrote of it very shortly afterwards for the Augsburg *Allgemeine Zeitung* shows (HKG 8/1: 28–30). In particular, he saw the modesty, restraint and moral dignity ('sittliche Würde') of the text and its protagonist as a contrast and antidote to the violent, vulgar bombast of Hebbel and his tragedies, whose prominence in contemporary Austrian cultural life he deplored (SW 17: 247–50). As is well known, Stifter's interest in the *Spielmann* was such that it became the basis for two stories he composed soon afterwards, *Der arme Wohlthäter*, of late 1847, and *Der Pförtner im Herrenhause*, probably written during the course of 1848.[32] These were the texts which he adapted and retitled in 1852, for the anthology *Bunte Steine*, as *Kalkstein* and *Turmalin*. Such acts of 'homage' were not in themselves abnormal for Stifter: several of his stories give sign of such overt borrowing, and he was not an adherent of the kind of individualistic aesthetic of originality which might have precluded it. Nevertheless, the double recourse to the *Spielmann* is striking; both stories are quite strongly dependent on the model; and the influence can be said to have been an important one, as the image of the 'Sonderling' with which Stifter's two stories experiment can be traced on through into his principal novel, *Der Nachsommer*, of a few years later.[33]

What is significant about Stifter's reception of the *Spielmann*, however, is the context in which he read it. Grillparzer's novella may not have been of recent composition, as we have said, but for its readers of the time it was a text bound up with the preliminaries to the 1848 Revolution. Even Stifter's review of August 1847 is to be seen in that connection (especially if put together with the content of the private letter he wrote shortly before, proposing the article[34]): in art such as Hebbel's, he indicates, there is a perturbing and pernicious immoderation and disorderliness of the emotions, whereas Grillparzer's restrained story induces 'am Schlusse die beruhigendste sittliche Auflösung und eine lohnende Erhebung'.[35] The wider implications of this distinction are elaborated subsequently, notably in his essay *Über Stand und Würde des Schriftstellers*, of April 1848, in which he contrasts moral authors, who strive to show 'die Menschheit . . . in ihrer sittlichen und menschlichen Blüte', with irresponsible ones, themselves of 'unsittlicher Character' and 'ohnmächtig . . . hing[egeben] an Leidenschaften', who 'rechnen auf die Begierden und Leidenschaften der Menschen' (HKG 8/1: 35, 44f.). In a letter of late 1849 this even becomes: 'Die Revolution ist . . . aus dem Frasenthume der Afterlitteratur hervorgegangen'; he is, he says, busy writing a cultural critique, *Briefe aus der Gegenwart*, in which 'die Revolution aus der Holheit unserer Sitten und Litteratur hergeleitet [wird]'.[36]

Curiously, this does not exactly mean that Stifter was unenthusiastic about 1848. The strong idealistic ingredient in his outlook, not shared by Grillparzer, meant that he welcomed March 1848 as a new dawn of humanity, one of those moments when 'wir das Ideal zur Wirklichkeit verkörpert sehen', as an apparently like-minded friend later wrote to him;[37] and, as the Revolution progressed and radicalised, he went through a significantly slower process of disillusionment than did Grillparzer. In the early months he was politically active in Vienna, and in May even gained election as a 'Wahlmann' for the Frankfurt Parliament.[38] It was only after the violent upheavals of mid May that clear disaffection began to set in: 'Ich bin ein Mann des Maßes und der Freiheit – beides ist jezt leider gefährdet'; 'die Leidenschaft . . . hastet . . . fort'.[39] The moral restraint which has characterised the Revolution hitherto is slipping, its leaders are showing 'Despotengelüsten': 'Mancher Ehrenmann ist jezt plözlich von bösen Leidenschaften und gierigen Gelüsten beherrscht – er war nehmlich nie ein Ehrenmann, sondern seine Triebe waren blos gehemmt, jezt fühlt er den Damm weg, und sie strömen aus'.[40] Here, very strikingly, we are back with exactly the imagery that gripped Grillparzer: social revolt as sexual desire, rendered in metaphors of stream and flood.

In subsequent months, moments of hope periodically resurfaced in Stifter that a civilised and moral – 'sittlich groß' – new society (constitutional monarchy) might emerge from the Revolution.[41] But by September he was essentially anticipating either a proletarian 'Hunnenzug' or 'die Knute',[42] meaning reactionary repression ('die rothe Republik . . . oder . . . eine Militärdictatur'[43]). When the latter came, he was reconciled (and was not in Vienna to bear the brunt of it).

What his letters and essays of 1849 indicate is a revision of attitude. The Revolution is seen as having been a time when 'Sitte Heiligkeit Kunst Göttliches nichts mehr ist, und jeder Schlamm und jede Thierheit, weil jezt Freiheit ist, ein Recht zu haben wähnt, hervor zu brechen'.[44] The aims of March 1848, to create 'freie Staatsbürger' who are rational, moral, not prey to *Leidenschaft*, inwardly as well as outwardly free, must be achieved by action from above: 'Wenn der Staat ihre Erziehung und Menschwerdung in erleuchtete Hände nimmt, kann allein die Vernunft, d.i. Freiheit, gegründet werden, sonst ewig nie'; 'das einzige Mittel: "Bildung!"'[45] Such optimism for yet another new dawn is an interesting reflection of the Austrian situation in the aftermath of 1848: liberal Austrians, having witnessed both more extreme forms of social disorder and the bloody nationalist uprisings which 1848 gave rise to around the Empire, seem generally to have been less dispirited by the Restoration of 1849 than were their North German counterparts. Moreover, the Restoration was accompanied initially by significant concessions to the liberal mood;[46] and for relatively uncompromised 'moderates' such as Stifter, new possibilities of influence and power appeared to open up. Stifter was recruited to apply his ideas on moral education (which were publicly known through his journalism) as the Inspector in charge of Primary Schools in Oberösterreich, a post which he occupied for many years, with declining enthusiasm. As he embarked on it, though, it was with high expectations of contributing to the moral *Läuterung* through education which society now needed. And he expected simultaneously to do this through his art: 'Die aufgeregten Affecte [werden] wieder in ein Bett zurückkehren', 'Die Menschen . . . werden . . . sich bald von dem trüben und unreinen Strudel abwenden, und wieder die stille einfache . . . heilige und sittliche Göttin [Kunst] anbeten'[47] – one notes the inevitable flood imagery. His conception of his own art moderated in line with this, becoming more – even more – a matter of public responsibility. As a 'Staatsbeamter' who was 'der Öffentlichkeit verfallen',[48] his writing was now firmly an aspect of his role and position as educator.

That, more or less, and allowing for the beginnings of fresh demoralisation, was the position he had reached by 1852, as he assembled his 'Festgeschenk für die Jugend', *Bunte Steine*, a '[Bei]trag . . . zum . . . anbrechenden Morgenroth Östreichs'.[49] It is reflected, at least formally, by the anthology itself. Above all, its famous *Vorrede* is, as one critic has said,[50] an anti-revolutionary manifesto, with its 'sanftes Gesetz' of moderation, self-control and moral order ('. . . Gerechtigkeit Einfachheit Bezwingung seiner selbst Verstandesgemäßheit Wirksamkeit in seinem Kreise Bewunderung des Schönen . . .'; HKG 2/2: 12), its censure of violent emotions (HKG 2/2: 12), its claim that in nature too not the violent spasms but the even, gradual processes are truly 'großartig', because 'welterhaltend' (HKG 2/2: 10), and its suggestion that there is a steady progress of history towards rationality and virtue, but which regresses dangerously in phases when the passions take over ('Genuß und das Sinnliche, . . . Haß . . . und Neid. . . , . . . Unsitte und . . . Laster, . . . üppige . . . Schwärmerei'; HKG 2/2: 15f.). In general ways it can be seen, too, how his alterations of previously written stories for the collection reflect this view, as overt manifestations of violent emotion (including all signs of ill will on the part of the characters) are suppressed, representations of the functioning of nature in its 'gelassene Unschuld'[51] are greatly extended, and reconciliatory endings are (mostly) reinforced.[52] In detail, however, the picture is not at all as simple as this: often the texts have internal complications or intricate geneses which tend in other directions, and individual stories and the anthology as a whole are capable of contradicting each other. This becomes particularly evident as one traces the line of development which emerged from the influential encounter with Grillparzer's *Armer Spielmann*.

Stifter's first *Spielmann*-related story, *Der arme Wohlthäter*, and its adaptation *Kalkstein*, share a wide and obvious range of features with Grillparzer's text: a peculiar yet saintly hero of extreme moral and personal fastidiousness whom this disposition has made somehow incompetent for practical life (this is less well sustained in Stifter than in Grillparzer); signs of the hero's unbalanced and oppressive upbringing (though in Stifter's version all traces of external malevolence towards him are removed); his infatuation with an 'ordinary' girl, whom he perceives from a vantage point in his own imprisoning house; a narrator (meeting, seeking out and eliciting the history of the hero) who is interested and sympathetic, but temperamentally and culturally very different from the hero; and the hero's eventual discovery of a purposeful and active role for himself supporting a community in extremis.[53] Also, in connection with this last item, Stifter's story echoes Grillparzer's in focusing centrally on a tremendous flood, preceded in this case by violent storm. It is curious to note the emphasis placed on these elements in Stifter's story, given his claim in the *Vorrede* to *Bunte Steine* that moments of natural upheaval and catastrophe lack greatness – that they are merely 'einzeln' and 'einseitig', secondary to the grand, calm processes which are fundamental to nature, the expressions of nature's own 'sanftes Gesetz' (HKG 2/2: 10).

As one critic in particular has demonstrated, there is a dimension of neurosis to the asceticism and extreme cleanliness of the *Landpfarrer*, Stifter's hero, and the story signals this to have adolescent sexual roots.[54] One notes with interest that Stifter has apparently perceived the sexual ingredient in the Spielmann's behaviour. *Der arme Wohlthäter*, in particular, makes the sexual connection patent, as the Pfarrer tells of watching his beloved, the washerwoman's daughter, from the bushes with 'begierig' eyes (HKG 2/1: 107). In *Kalkstein*, of 1852, such explicitness is removed: the description of the relationship becomes less overtly erotic.[55] But its symbolic reflections are retained: the peach he presents to her, and the gleaming white *Wäsche*, at once sensuous and pristine, which he cannot relinquish in later life. The detail of his discomfort in the presence of his tenant's attractive daughter is also kept (HKG 2/1: 97; 2/2: 98). And at significant points these reflections are actually reinforced.[56] Stifter in 1852 wishes to make his hero's experience of desire more discreet, but not to excise it.

Part of the symbolic reflection of these desires, it is evident, is the natural upheavals the story contains, the storm and the flood, the presentation of both of which is considerably lengthened for *Kalkstein*. The fierce 'Gewitter' which both men listen to, but the exact functioning of which the Pfarrer understands while the narrator does not, is the object in *Kalkstein* of an extraordinary extended description which it would not be unreasonable to call orgasmic (HKG 2/2: 77f.). On this as on other occasions, one wonders whether Stifter realised the full force of his evocation.[57] The Pfarrer also understands (as the narrator does not) how the flood functions. He is able to guide the poor children of the locality away from a dangerous depth in the flooded terrain, as they wade in the waters, by himself standing up to his waist in water in the muddy hole ('. . . denn das Wasser bei Überschwemmungen sei trüb, und lasse die Tiefe und Ungleichheit des Bodens unter sich nicht bemerken'; HKG 2/2: 92). Finally, it emerges at the story's end that his life's endeavour, completed upon his death, has been to build a new schoolhouse which will spare the local children the dangers of fording the river in its regular periods of flood.

This symbolism is in the first instance psycho-sexual. The Pfarrer knows – he still knows, and struggles with – the depths and storms of desire, and is able thereby to help innocent youth negotiate its perils. But clearly it is to be taken socially, too, above all in the context of Grillparzer's text about the flood of the amoral masses, on which Stifter's story is modelled, and of Stifter's own writings in the revolutionary period (echoing Grillparzer's) about *Begierde* – 'böse . . . Leidenschaften und gierige . . . Gelüste', 'trübe[r] und unreine[r] Strudel', 'Schlamm und . . . Thierheit' etc., etc.[58] – as the core of the impulse which makes revolution.

One further aspect of *Der arme Wohlthäter* and *Kalkstein* is of interest in this connection and in relation to the *Spielmann*, namely the way Grillparzer's element of social satire is transmitted by Stifter. As was noted above, the Pfarrer's family and familial milieu differ utterly from the Spielmann's in their complete lack of malevolence towards him. His brother is supportive and unselfish, his teacher caring, his father thoughtful and well intentioned, the workers are fond of him, his girlfriend does not bully him, and even her mother only rebukes him once. In Stifter's stories at this period, almost everyone is *nice*. Moreover, both his father and her mother seem to be engaged in productive, effective and reputable economic activity, he with his tannery business, she with her expanding *Wäscherei*. The text draws attention to the dynastic character of the father's business, which has expanded over three generations from the work of a single travelling journeyman to a substantial factory with international connections (HKG 2/2: 99–101). The laundry is also a growing enterprise, with invest- ments and increasing numbers of employees (HKG 2/2: 112f.). The picture seems sunny, yet somehow all is not well. Not only does the tannery collapse after the Pfarrer's brother takes over (no-one is at *fault*, the narrative emphasises; HKG 2/2: 116f.), but the Pfarrer's own disturbed development is in some unspecific way a product of this environment (one is reminded a little of the Buddenbrooks). The house communicates the situation symboli- cally, the child being sequestered in the garden wing of a great mansion, then in the garden itself, cut off from the flow of ordinary life by a high wall, seeing life outside, including the girl, through 'Eisengitter' (HKG 2/2: 112), and with his life always supervised and controlled. These elements were greatly reinforced for *Kalkstein*. The meanings are by no means entirely clear; but the implication is, indeed, of a kind of *Unbehagen*, a society somehow excluding, or excluding itself from, necessary domains of being.

Stifter's second *Spielmann* story, *Der Pförtner im Herrenhause* (later *Turmalin*), seems to have been written, as we said, during 1848 itself, almost certainly in late spring and early summer.[59] Grillparzer's prominent framing narrative and intrusive narrator have gone, and the inept and saintly hero with his interesting family history has gone too. On the other hand, the sites of the story – the homes of the hero – are much closer to those of the *Spielmann*, namely a *Bürgerhaus* in the Viennese *Innere Stadt* and a *Vorstadt* slum (this is the only one of the *Bunte Steine* with other than a rural setting). What the first version of the story presents is a tale of bourgeois adultery which leads to the insanity of the cuckold – but apparently not so much on account of the grief of betrayal, as because of the shame he, in his 'tiefe Liebe und . . . Reinheit des Gemüthes' (HKG 2/1: 133), feels towards his wife for the 'außerordentliche[r] Wuth' (HKG 2/1: 116) with which he first reacted to her confession of her deed. An outbreak of *Leidenschaft* in an otherwise *reines Gemüt* produces psychic disturbance. Thus deranged, he disappears with his child, to reappear years later living in an ancient, decaying house in the *Alservorstadt*, the house itself being clearly an image of its occupant's psychosis. His daughter, whom he keeps locked in their basement, from which only the feet of passers-by can be glimpsed, is herself psychologically and physically impaired.

Paraphrased like this, it is perhaps not surprising that Stifter thought such a plot needed to be adapted or obscured. In any case, when he changed it in 1852, he added in particular an affirmative ending (the girl is cured of both her *Wasserkopf* and her mental retardation thanks to fresh air and good food), and also greatly augmented the presentation of the hero at the beginning. Here the hero, the 'Rentherr', is placed with his wife in a psychically symbolic house, with locks, *Gitter*, passageways and bizarrely decorated rooms, including, in the wife's chamber, a peculiar angelic crib for their baby, suggesting unhealthy protectiveness and denial of childish nature (HKG 2/2: 138f.). Stifter has thus added to his story a powerful implication of bourgeois repression and derangement, even prior to the catastrophic adultery.

The most interesting aspect of the story, however – in both its versions – is the domain the author depicts in contrast to the hero's deranged house or houses. His reappearance is narrated by a female friend of the principal storyteller: she and her family occupy 'eine sehr angenehme freundliche Vorstadtwohnung', with a pleasant garden, views in one direction 'über [den Garten] hinweg auf die erste Anhöhe, die sich außerhalb der großen Stadt erhebt', and in the other upon 'die breite heitere Vorstadtgasse, in welcher . . . ein bewegtes, wenn auch nicht gar zu betäubendes Leben herrschte' (HKG 2/1: 118). 'Namentlich war es uns wegen der

Kinder angenehm, die damals gerade im Heranblühen waren. Sie durften in den Garten gehen; . . . wir . . . hatten . . . auch nicht weit in das Freie; und da in den Vorstädten der Raum nicht so gespart wird, so waren die Gemächer und die ganze Umgebung sehr luftig und gesund' (HKG 2/1: 118f.). Not only psychologically but also socially this is a picture of good health, in absolute antithesis to the ruin in which the hero lives and dies: decrepit, grimy, black, with barred windows, and with 'unterirdische Wohnungen' of a kind 'welche jetzt schon immer mehr und mehr zu verschwinden beginnt' (HKG 2/1: 121) – tokens, thus, of a dying social world.

The inner narrator also tells at one point of a walk with her husband from the theatre in the Innere Stadt back across the *Glacis* (the ring of parkland, formerly moat, just outside the city wall) into their Vorstadt: 'Wir traten aus dem finstern Stadtthore, der heitere Grasplatz und die vielen Bäume empfingen uns, das holde dämmerige, hier erst recht sichtbare Licht umgab uns, und mancher einzelne Wanderer und manches Paar begegnete uns noch', etc. (HKG 2/1: 120). In the *Turmalin* version of the story, this picture of Vorstadt openness, freedom and clean living is in some ways actually reinforced ('die luftige und freie Wohnung'; the 'freie erhellte Schönheit' of the Glacis; HKG 2/2: 149, 151), although the distinction *between* Glacis and Vorstadt seems to become stronger, and the 'Stadtthor', the gate to the domain of wealth and power, ceases to be 'finster'. But it is hard not to see these passages of Stifter's text as essentially a product of the spring optimism of 1848, when the Vorstädte could briefly appear as a place of freedom, clarity and healthy, unrepressed life. He would have been unlikely to write it a year earlier; and he could not have written it a few months later, in the face of 'Hunnenzüge' of proletarians, filled with their 'Leidenschaften und . . . Gelüste' (SW 17: 285f., 304), emerging out of these same suburbs.

One or two other small changes are made to the text for *Turmalin* which seem characteristic. The demolition of the ancient house seems to become very slightly a source of regret, where previously it was apparently welcomed (HKG 2/1: 134; 2/2: 179). The Vorstadt populace in the inner narrator's account becomes at one point a vulgar and brutish crowd ('Personen aus den niederen Ständen, welche . . . eine Art dumpfer Theilnahme, die dieser Gattung eigen ist, herbei geführt hatte'; HKG 2/2: 169). There are hints in the narrator otherwise of newly categorical, even repressive tendencies (HKG 2/1: 133; 2/2: 177). Suggestions of extreme orderliness on her part are introduced (HKG 2/1: 126; 2/2: 161).

And her singular deference to and anxiety at her husband's authority appear to be strengthened (HKG 2/1: 122, 124, 130; 2/2: 155, 158f., 168). Not only is the bourgeois (Innere-Stadt-) neurosis of the Rentherr and his wife reinforced, but a hint of such neurosis seems to creep into the inner narrator herself, in spite of the liberating Vorstadt environment the author originally gave her.

One story only in the *Bunte Steine* is unproblematically the product of the time of the book's compilation, namely the amazing *Kazensilber*, which was written for the collection in 1852.[60] It has no direct relation to the Grillparzer story which moulded *Kalkstein* and *Turmalin*; but in several respects it crystallises the issues developed by those two stories. Here we have, in the wealthy Upper Austrian farming family, their 'stattlicher Hof' overlooked by the great northern mountains, people of surpassing niceness – humane, generous, thoughtful and fond, as well as rational, efficient and productive. It is very easy to see their world as an idyll; but it is not one. A distinction one critic draws generally with Stifter, though not specifically in connection with this particular text, is between guilt and something called 'Seinsverfehlung': characters who are not actively culpable, yet whose lives are somehow flawed.[61] Whether or not such a distinction is legitimate, some such subtle flawedness, a kind of faint cultural defectiveness, is what applies to the adults in *Kazensilber*,[62] and it manifests itself particularly in their contact with the 'braunes Mädchen', the anonymous and mysterious *Volksmädchen* who becomes friends with their three children and is part-adopted by the family, but eventually disappears again without trace up into the forests.

In the first place, the family's life is faintly denatured. Their farming entails the erection of innumerable physical barriers and protections against the raw nature which symbolically looms over them (glass-houses, windbreaks, guard-rails, walls, fences and dams; HKG 2/2: 243f., 247). Every winter, when nature is at its most raw, parents and children escape to the 'Hauptstadt' (HKG 2/2: 245, 283f.). Even when they are in the country, the emphasis is on the civilised character of their lives – with the forced or preserved fruits and other denatured foods they eat (HKG 2/2: 287f., 291), and their elaborate and protective clothing (purchased by mail order!) (HKG 2/2: 246, 284f.). The parents seek to control, domesticate and prettify nature, to render it orderly and clean. They try to do this both to their farmstead and to the *braunes Mädchen* (HKG 2/2: 278, 280, 307, 309). The braunes Mädchen herself, by contrast, is dirty (HKG 2/2: 282). It is interesting to observe Stifter so clearly suggesting limits to values of order and 'Reinheit' (though in other stories of the collection, too, such a sense in the end insinuates itself).

Part of their problem – that of the parents and of the grand-mother who lives with them – is materialism. They wish to reward with cash those who give them disinterested help (HKG 2/2: 272). Their little son is almost killed when the farm burns down because his mother is distracted by concern for a 'Kästchen', implicitly a jewel box, and the grandmother by fear of looting (HKG 2/2: 296f., 302). The children themselves find it hard to express love other than through material giving (HKG 2/2: 295; cf. 287). The city to which the family flees each year is a materialistic place of glamorous shops and fine goods (HKG 2/2: 284). The grandmother tells the children that the streams in the hills can be sifted to yield gold (whereas in fact what they contain is the beautiful and valueless stone called Kazensilber; HKG 2/2: 256f.). The *Märchen* she tells are of natural spirits exploited; one in particular ends strikingly with a banal sequence of great enrichments (HKG 2/2: 256). Their materialism is also utilitarianism: as they prepare to reward the braunes Mädchen for saving their children, it is with a view 'ihm sein Leben vielleicht nüzlicher machen [zu] können' (and on the proviso, 'so lange es [das Mädchen] sich nicht schädlich erweist') (HKG 2/2: 274). And their view of nature is the same.

Their basically alienated outlook, the story clearly indicates, is ultimately inadequate to nature's realities, as they twice fail to comprehend the onset of natural catastrophes – a devastating hail-storm followed by flood, and then the fire that consumes their farm – and in each case would have lost children if the braunes Mädchen had not intervened (HKG 2/2: 260–5, 296–306). It is even she who guides them safely through the flood waters which follow the hailstorm (HKG 2/2: 267). The children themselves, mean-while, are not yet quite so hidebound as their elders. They have an impulse to seek a wilder, freer, less controlled domain (cf. HKG 2/2: 251f., 313), up and up into the wild woods and their meetings there with the braunes Mädchen, a childhood freedom a little like that granted to the inner narrator's children in the Vorstadt in *Tur-malin*.

The violent forces of nature which the adults in *Kazensilber* can-not deal with are to be understood in various ways, like the flood in *Kalkstein*. They are literal nature: Stifter was indeed interested in how modern man came to terms with the natural world. They are ontological images: it cannot be wrong to see them, like the ice-waste in *Bergkristall*, as symbols of the basic existential exposedness of man, from which culture seeks to shield him. By analogy with *Kalkstein*, they are psychological, too: behind and within these people's controlled and controlling lives, despite everything, lies *Leidenschaft* – not the Landpfarrer's sexual desire, perhaps, but greed and pride and a kind of lust for power. In Stifter's Viennese sketch *Ein Gang durch die Katakomben*, of ten years earlier, a work whose imagery of the abyss lurking beneath a modern world of wealth and enjoyment has many resonances, there is a notable short passage which elucidates what the culture and values of the adults of *Kazensilber* signify: '*Unser* Zeitgeist [geht] auf das sogenannte Praktische. . . , worunter sie meistens nur das Materiell-nützliche, oft sogar nur das Sinnlich-wollüstige verstehen' (SW 15: 49). Their utilitarian practicality is in the end sensualistic, a form of pernicious desire.

Finally – again thinking back to *Kalkstein* and beyond, to its model *Der arme Spielmann* – there is a social symbolism in the fierce nature which besets and perturbs the farm and its occupants.[63] And this is not merely on the basis that storm and flood and fire were standard images of revolution for the conservative mind in and after the *Vormärz*. The braunes Mädchen in *Kazensilber* is not just a figure from folktale and folk-song, although she is that too (the 'Sture Mure' of the grandmother's Märchen; HKG 2/2: 248); she is also social reality. The adults of the family find it hard initially to register her existence: on various occasions, even after she has saved the children, she is strikingly overlooked and ignored (HKG 2/2: 270, 308). Once they have part-domesticated her, however, and she then disappears again, the father of the family sets out to find her. When he does this, it entails a climb up from his tidy farmstead into the wilder and wilder reaches of the northern mountains, 'gegen Mitternacht . . . empor' (HKG 2/2: 244, 252): 'auf den Berg . . . hinter der Grenze seiner Besizthümer', 'an dem Steingehege aufwärts', across the 'Haide', through the 'Moore' until 'er kam . . . zu den hohen Wäldern' (HKG 2/2: 292). At the same time it is a social journey. A whole, unsuspected substructure of the rural proletariat opens up: the 'arme Häusler', making 'Fässer und Bottiche', the 'Steinbrecher', the 'Haideleute', the peat cutters in the 'Moorhütten', the 'Holzhauer', the 'Pechbrenner', the 'Waldhüttler'. It is an extraordinary catalogue, a social descent into the catacombs. And at the end he fails to find her, 'der Vater kehrte wieder nach Hause' (HKG 2/2: 292).

This story, like the others, is thematically elusive. But what it seems to say is that modern bourgeois society, with its urge for possession and control which is itself, deep down, irrational *Leidenschaft*, 'das Sinnlich-wollüstige', neglects and disregards domains both of the self and of society in which a kind of freedom potential may exist. Once the braunes Mädchen has gone, her 'Erscheinung sank wie andere immer tiefer in das Reich der Vergangenheit zurük' (HKG 2/2: 315). Only the son, Sigismund, still suffers: '[Es] war, als husche der Schatten des braunen Mädchens an ihm vorüber, er fühlte ein tiefes Weh im Herzen' (HKG 2/2: 315) – Sigismund, whom the text elsewhere calls 'muthig heiter und frei. . . ; . . . wenn seine Rede tönte, flogen ihm die Herzen zu' (HKG 2/2: 313). It is hinted that there is a kind of physical affection between the two of them (HKG 2/2: 304, 312), different in nature from what connects the other characters. It is also notable that an important element of the control which the parents seek to impose on the braunes Mädchen and which she perceives, in the end, as alien and destructive, namely covering her body, restricting her movement, making her decent (also *feminising* her), is a repression of her sensuality and an inculcation of shame.

Finally and briefly, the social and sexual patterns of *Kazensilber* are corroborated – essentially they are prefigured – by one further story of the *Bunte Steine, Die Pechbrenner/Granit* (of 1847–48 and 1852 respectively). The child-narrator of this story is taken by his grandfather, partly literally and partly imaginatively (through the tale the grandfather recounts to him), on a journey similar to that which *Kazensilber* presented. It is initiated by Andreas the pitch-seller's invasion of the child's pristine domestic order (HKG 2.2: 31), an intrusion akin in many respects to that represented by the braunes Mädchen. It leads, also equivalently, through the grandfather's demonstration to him during their long walk of the economic and social structure of the rural poor, beyond and away from the world of the prosperous farmers:

> Siehst du, diese Rauchsäulen kommen alle von den Menschen, die in dem Walde ihre Geschäfte treiben. Da sind zuerst die Holzknechte, die an Stellen die Bäume des Waldes umsägen, daß nichts übrig ist als Strünke und Strauchwerk . . . Dann sind die Kohlenbrenner . . . Dann sind die Heusucher . . . Dann sind die Sammler . . . Endlich sind die Pechbrenner . . . Wo ein ganz dünnes Rauchfädlein aufsteigt, mag es auch ein Jäger sein . . . Alle diese Leute haben keine bleibende Stätte in dem Walde; denn sie gehen bald hierhin, bald dorthin. (HKG 2/2: 34f.)

It culminates in the plague tale of the Pechbrenner (HKG 2/2: 36–58). This does not assert that the plague *comes* from the poor: the pitch-burner family in the story is trying to escape the contagion. None the less, in a suggestive and approximate way an analogy is implied: the blackness of the pitch, the plague as black death, prevalent contemporary associations of cholera and revolution, and the latter's threat to social and moral order. We are back with the imagery of Gotthelf's revolutionary allegory *Die schwarze Spinne*, by which Stifter may very well have been influenced.[64] In contrast to *Die schwarze Spinne*, however, Stifter's story suggests a kind of homeopathy:[65] his hero is drawn beyond his own social domain and in some measure enlightened by the experience. And it is significant, again, that an aspect of this enlightenment is an introduction to moderate desire. The grandfather describes to him his recollection of his wife, the child's grandmother, as a young girl in imagery which is mutedly erotic (as well as pious: the combination seems clearly to be intended; HKG 2/2: 40). Moreover, the narrator's own subsequent and peculiarly enduring memory of the Pechbrenner story is likewise desirous: 'Die ganze Geschichte des Großvaters weiß ich, ja durch lange Jahre, wenn man von schönen Mädchen redete, fielen mir immer die feinen Haare des Waldmädchens ein' (HKG 2/2: 60). Both these elements, strikingly, were added to the text in 1852, when it became *Granit*, having been absent from *Die Pechbrenner*, the earlier version (cf. HKG 2/1: 23f., 54f.).

The implication – of this story as of *Kazensilber* – is actually an affirmation of a modicum of desire, a desire which is natural, immediate, unsublimated (and unexcessive), as being a requirement for psychological and social good health. This is not what Stifter's Vorrede to *Bunte Steine* says; and it is far from what is implied in the letter to Grillparzer in 1860. It is discernible, though, in one way or another in several of the stories in the anthology – and appears actually to be strengthened in his writing of 1852, as he reflected on social conclusions to be drawn from recent revolutionary turmoil. One judges that it is what at least part of the Stifter of the early *Nachmärz* believed, a subtle modification in his understanding of both social and – immediately linked with this – psycho-sexual realities and necessities.

Notes

1. Adalbert Stifter, *Sämmtliche Werke*, eds August Sauer, Gustav Wilhelm and others, Prague, Reichenberg, Graz, 1904–60, 19: 218f. (edition henceforth in notes and text of this chapter as 'SW'); letter of 15 January 1860. My thoughts for this discussion developed out of conversations on Grillparzer and Stifter with Angus Forsyth, postgraduate student at Birmingham, who has also made helpful comments on the draft of the chapter.

2. Franz Grillparzer, *Sämtliche Werke. Historisch-kritische Gesamtausgabe*, eds August Sauer and Reinhold Backmann, Vienna, 1909–48, Abteilung III, vol. 4, p. 20 (edition subsequently in this chapter as 'HKA'); letter of 17 January 1860.

3. It seems likely that Stifter was thinking, at least in part, of Nestroy and his *Volkstheater*. Cf. Stifter's late essay 'Über Beziehung des Theaters zum Volke', in Adalbert Stifter, *Werke und Briefe. Historisch-kritische Gesamtausgabe*, eds Alfred Doppler and Wolfgang Frühwald, Stuttgart, 1978ff., 8/1: 118–24, esp. 123 (edition henceforth as 'HKG').

4. See his famous *Tagebuch* entry of 20 April 1831 on the performance failure of *Des Meeres und der Liebe Wellen*: 'Am 5 dieses Monats Hero und Leander aufgeführt; *nicht* gefallen'; HKA II/9: 25. See also his aphorism, dated 1821, 'Wenn auch das Publikum nicht der oberste Richter in Kunstsachen ist, so ist es die Jury, die, ohne die Gesetze zu kennen, mit schlichtem Sinn den Fall betrachtet und im allgemeinen sein: Schuldig oder Nichtschuldig ausspricht'; HKA II/7: 361.

5. *Bruchstück aus einem Literaturblatt vom Jahre 1900* (ca. 1835), HKA I/13: 112–14, see 113.

6. Three decades earlier, in 1830, he had observed, 'Die sogenannte moralische Ansicht ist der gröste Feind der wahren Kunst, da einer der Hauptvorzüge dieser letztern gerade darin besteht, daß man durch ihr Medium auch jene Seiten der menschlichen Natur genießen kann, welche das Moralgesetz mit Recht aus dem wirklichen Leben entfernt hält'; HKA II/8: 369. And elsewhere: 'Zu behaupten. . . , daß der eine Teil der menschlichen Natur das Recht habe an die Stelle des Ganzen einzutreten ist lächerlich. Der Trieb, die Neigung, das Instinktmäßige sind ebenso göttlich als die Vernunft' (ca. 1851); HKA I/14: 139f. See also Ian Roe, '*Der arme Spielmann* and the Role of Compromise in Grillparzer's Work', in *Grillparzer's 'Der arme Spielmann'. New Directions in Criticism*, ed. Clifford Bernd, Columbia, S.C., 1988, pp. 133–44, esp. 137, 142.

7. Franz Grillparzer, *Werke in sechs Bänden*, ed. Helmut Bachmaier, Frankfurt/M., 1986ff., 2: 22, 39f., 47, 63f.; 3: 129–31; 376f., 446–50 (edition henceforth as 'DKV').

8. 'Ist sie nicht schön?. . ./Und wie das wogt und wallt und glüht und prangt . . .'; DKV 3: 507.

9. Hero in fact says this – unknowing – before the experience actually happens to her.

10. This is followed by a further two dozen lines in similar mood.

11. Cf. Grillparzer's poem *An die Sammlung* of 1833; HKA I/11: 104f. See also Bachmaier, commentary, in DKV 2: 631f.

12. See DKV 3: 752.

13. 'Diese Rolle' is the bill of (their) rights proposed by the burghers of Prague.

14. *Pace* Bruce Thompson, 'Grillparzer, Revolution and 1848', in *Essays on Grillparzer*, ed. Bruce Thompson and Mark Ward, Hull, 1978, pp. 81–91, esp. 83f., 90.

15. See his prose satires, HKA I/13: 143–8.
16. See, for example, his poem *Mein Vaterland* of late March 1848, HKA I/10: 227f.
17. See HKA I/10: 230f., I/13: 211–14 (and 411); also Thompson, 'Grillparzer, Revolution and 1848', pp. 86–8.
18. See his poem *Vorzeichen*, HKA I/10: 224–6.
19. See Helmut Bachmaier, *Franz Grillparzer: 'Der arme Spielmann'. Erläuterungen und Dokumente*, Stuttgart, 1986, pp. 93–7, and HKA I/13: 309–14, commentary by Reinhold Backmann.
20. For most of these, see *Grillparzer's 'Der arme Spielmann'. New Directions in Criticism*, ed. Bernd.
21. See Hans Höller, 'Porträt des Herrschers als Seher, Künstler und als alter Mann. Grillparzers *Ein Bruderzwist in Habsburg*', in *Franz Grillparzer*, ed. Helmut Bachmaier, Frankfurt/M., 1991, pp. 321–42, esp. 322; also HKA II/9: 3f.
22. These are expounded – somewhat excessively – by Bachmaier, *Grillparzer: 'Der arme Spielmann'. Erläuterungen und Dokumente*, pp. 97–104.
23. Goethe, *Werke. Hamburger Ausgabe*, ed. Erich Trunz, 12th edn, Munich, 1994, 11: 484– 515, esp. 514. See Reinhold Backmann, HKA I/13: 333–8, commentary; Helmut Bachmaier, *Grillparzer: 'Der arme Spielmann'. Erläuterungen und Dokumente*, pp. 6–18; Naomi Ritter, 'Poet and Carnival: Goethe, Grillparzer, Baudelaire', in *Grillparzer's 'Der arme Spielmann'. New Directions in Criticism*, pp. 337–51, esp. 337f.
24. Goethe, *Werke*, 11: 515.
25. There have been influential attempts in recent criticism of Grillparzer's story to view his narrator as personally deeply flawed, a snob and a hypocrite who is the target of the author's thoroughgoing censure. In this view, what the narrator says about the Volksfest is inferior writing, pretentious and trite. See in particular John Ellis, 'The Narrator and his Values in *Der arme Spielmann*', in *Grillparzer's 'Der arme Spielmann'. New Directions in Criticism*, pp. 27–44, esp. 34–41. This is misguided and misleading. It is true that the narrator of *Der arme Spielmann* is not simply Grillparzer, because the Spielmann is Grillparzer, too. But he is at least part of him, the author's public persona (he is, after all, identified in the text as a successful dramatist; HKA I/13: 39) and even his inner self in certain moods. Grillparzer's narrator is a whimsical, partial authorial self-portrait, containing moments of implied self-criticism. But his is not a comprehensively defective voice, the object of unmitigated authorial irony, as is the case, notably, with Kleist. And the proposition that the tour de force about the Volksfest at the beginning of the story is intended by Grillparzer to be read as bad writing is absurd.
26. The one account of the story which reveals this aspect successfully is that by William Reeve, 'Proportion and Disproportion in *Das arme Spielmann*', in *Grillparzer's 'Der arme Spielmann'. New Directions in Criticism*, pp. 93–110, esp. 101, 104–9.
27. See Wolfgang Paulsen's (generally unhelpful) article, 'Der gute Bürger Jakob. Zur Satire in Grillparzers *Der arme Spielmann*', *Colloquia germanica* 2 (1968), 272–98.
28. See Bachmaier, *Grillparzer: 'Der arme Spielmann'. Erläuterungen und Dokumente*, pp. 84–8, and Backmann, HKA I/13: 324f., commentary.
29. Cf. the poem *Vorzeichen* of (apparently) January 1848; HKA I/10: 224–6 (also referred to above).
30. See above, note 25.

31. See Stifter, SW 17: 246–55, esp. 250–2, letter of 21 August 1847 to Aurelius Buddeus; also HKG 2/3: 367–9, commentary by Walter Hettche.
32. See HKG 2/3: 367, 411f. Aspects of the relationship are discussed at a certain length by Kurt Vancsa, 'Grillparzers *Der arme Spielmann* und Stifters *Der arme Wohltäter*', in *Festschrift für Eduard Castle zum 80. Geburtstag*, Vienna, 1955, pp. 99–107, and Mark Ward, 'The Truth of Tales: Grillparzer's *Der arme Spielmann* and Stifter's *Der arme Wohltäter*', in *From Vormärz to Fin de Siècle. Essays in Nineteenth Century Austrian Literature*, ed. Mark Ward, Blairgowrie, 1986, pp. 15–39. The latter essay focuses largely on questions of narratorial ambiguity in the two texts.
33. Although such earlier stories as *Wirkungen eines weißen Mantels* (subsequently *Bergmilch*) and *Brigitta* also in various ways prefigure Risach in *Der Nachsommer*, a particular combination of bizarrerie and usefulness seems to link Risach with the heroes of *Kalkstein* and *Turmalin*, and to lead back from there to the *Spielmann*.
34. Letter of 21 August 1847 to Buddeus, SW 17: 246–55 (see above).
35. HKG 8/1: 29. Cf. also letter of July 1847 to Gustav Heckenast, SW 17: 240f.
36. 13 October 1849, to Heckenast, SW 18: 15. In another letter of 1849, meanwhile, he speaks of how Grillparzer would be an ideal choice as minister of education! Letter of 6 March 1849 to Heckenast, SW 17: 323f.
37. Letter to Stifter by Betty Paoli, 18 October 1848, SW 23: 58.
38. See Stifter's letter of 11 May 1848 to Betty Paoli, SW 22: 199, and article mentioning Stifter in *Constitutionelle Donau-Zeitung*, 1 May 1848, SW 17: 437f.
39. Letter of 25 May 1848 to Heckenast, SW 17: 284.
40. Ibid., SW 17: 285f.
41. For example, letter of 30 July 1848 to Joseph Türck, SW 17: 295–7; cf. also letter of 8 September 1848 to Heckenast, SW 17: 304.
42. Letter of 8 September 1848 to Heckenast, SW 17: 304.
43. This phrase is from a letter *to* Stifter by Betty Paoli, 18 October 1848, SW 23: 57.
44. Letter of 6 March 1849 to Heckenast, SW 17: 322.
45. Ibid. Cf. also Stifter's 'Wiener Stimmungsbild' for the *Augsburger Allgemeine Zeitung* (no. 10) of 10 January 1849, SW 16: 42–5.
46. See Stifter's article *Die octroirte Verfassung*, in the *Linzer Zeitung* (no. 57) of 10 March 1849, SW 16: 56–62. Notable, too, is the liberal language used by the luminaries of the old regime even after the fall of the Revolution. See Radetzky, writing on 20 May 1849 in praise of the 'Institut der Bürgerwehr' ('ein schöner und großer Gedanke') as a guarantor of private property, the freedom of the person and the rule of law; in Grillparzer, HKA I/13: 415. Similarly, the letter by the Statthalter of Oberösterreich to Graf Stadion, Minister of the Interior, proposing Stifter for an educational inspectorship, talks of 'die Regulierung des Erziehungs- und Unterrichtswesens, aus dem der künftige freie Staatsbürger hervorgehen soll'; letter of 22 March 1849, in *Adalbert Stifters Leben und Werk in Briefen und Dokumenten*, ed. Kurt Gerhard Fischer, Frankfurt/M., 1962, p. 222.
47. Letter of 13 October 1849 to Heckenast, SW 18: 14.
48. Article mentioning Stifter in *Allgemeine Zeitung*, 30 December 1849, *Stifters Leben und Werk in Briefen und Dokumenten*, p. 235.
49. Letter of 6 December 1850 to Heckenast, SW 18: 55.
50. Ursula Naumann, *Adalbert Stifter*, Stuttgart, 1979, p. 36. See also Paul Requadt, 'Stifters *Bunte Steine* als Zeugnis der Revolution und als zyklisches Kunstwerk',

in *Adalbert Stifter. Studien und Interpretationen. Gedenkschrift zum 100. Todestage*, ed. Lothar Stiehm, Heidelberg, 1968, pp. 139–68. Requadt's is a very good account of Stifter's politics around 1848, but has much less of significance to say on the stories of *Bunte Steine* and their political implications.

51. The phrase is from the preamble to his earlier story *Abdias*, of 1843; HKG 1/5: 237.

52. Cf. J.W. Smeed, 'The First Versions of the Stories Later Appearing in Stifter's *Bunte Steine*', *German Life and Letters* 12 (1958/59), 259–63; HKG 2/2, 2/3, commentary; John Whiton, 'Symbols of Social Renewal in Stifter's *Bergkristall*', *Germanic Review* 47 (1972), 259–80, esp. 279f.; John Reddick, 'Tiger und Tugend in Stifters *Kalkstein*: eine Polemik', *Zeitschrift für deutsche Philologie* 95 (1976), 235–55, esp. 238f., 248f., 251f.

53. I do not find the claim of Walter Hettche and (before him) Kurt Vancsa, that *Der arme Wohlthäter* was already largely conceived when Stifter encountered *Der arme Spielmann*, textually at all convincing. See HKG 2/3: 367.

54. See Reddick, 'Tiger und Tugend in Stifters *Kalkstein*', pp. 243–50.

55. Compare HKG 2/1: 106f. with 2/2: 113–16; see also Reddick, ibid, and Martin and Erika Swales, *Adalbert Stifter. A Critical Study*, Cambridge, 1984, p. 211.

56. See Reddick, ibid., pp. 248, 252. One notes, for example, the strengthening of the motif of the Landpfarrer's strawberry-eating from the earlier to the later version, HKG 2/1: 78 and 2/2: 78.

57. An even more immodest passage is the description of the tumescent balloon in *Der Condor*; HKG 1/4: 23f.

58. SW 17: 285f., 322, 18: 14.

59. See HKG 2/3: 411f., commentary.

60. See HKG 2/4: 171, commentary. The spelling 'Kazensilber' follows that used in HKG.

61. Paul Requadt, 'Stifters *Bunte Steine* als Zeugnis der Revolution', p. 157.

62. An emphatic – slightly over-emphatic – statement of such a view is provided by Eve Mason in her book *Stifter: 'Bunte Steine'*, London, 1986, pp. 71–6. See also Mason, 'Stifters *Bunte Steine*: Versuch einer Bestandsaufnahme', in *Adalbert Stifter heute. Londoner Symposium 1983*, ed. Johann Lachinger, Alexander Still-mark and Martin Swales, Linz, 1985, pp. 75–85, esp. 77f. That this is not a universal understanding of the text is indicated by Christoph Begemann's recent and well-received *Die Welt der Zeichen. Stifter-Lektüren*, Stuttgart, 1995, pp. 302–9 – which seems not to perceive that the behaviour of the adults in *Kazensilber* is problematical. Martin and Erika Swales talk subtly of a 'dual perspective' – also 'central friction' – which this text (in common with others by Stifter) presents: a 'register of assent' that permits a positive estimation of the characters and their qualities, and at the same time 'a diametrically opposed perspective' of scepticism and censure. See Swales, *Adalbert Stifter*, pp. 184f., 188.

63. 'Um das Haus liegen . . . in nähern und fernern Kreisen Hügel, die mit Feldern und Wiesen bedekt sind, manches Bauerhaus . . . zeigen, und auf dem Gipfel jedes Mal den Wald tragen, der wie nach einem verabredeten Geseze alle Gipfel jenes hügligen Landes besezt. Zwischen den Hügeln, die oft, ohne daß man es ahnt, in steile Schluchten abfallen, gehen Bäche ja zuweilen Giesbäche, über welche Stege und in abgelegenen Theilen gar nur Baumstämme führen . . . Das ganze Land geht gegen Mitternacht immer mehr empor, bis die größeren düsteren breitgedehnten Wälder kommen . . .' (HKG 2/2: 244).

64. On *Die schwarze Spinne*, see chapter 3, above. A good comparative and contrastive discussion of the two stories is: Pierre Cimaz, 'Unheil und Ordnung in Stifters Erzählung *Die Pechbrenner*, im Vergleich mit Gotthelfs *Schwarzer Spinne*', *Etudes germaniques* 40 (1985), 374–86.

65. We did note such a principle operating, if somewhat differently, in Gotthelf's *Die Wassernot im Emmental*. See chapter 3.

7

Mörike's *Mozart auf der Reise nach Prag*, the French Revolution and the Revolution of 1848

One of the interests of the novella *Mozart auf der Reise nach Prag*, which Mörike first published in 1855, is its sheer functional variety. It is cryptic autobiography, transposed and wilfully hyperbolic, but undeniably cast in its author's self-image. It is biography, too, a psychological study intended to be essentially faithful to the character of its subject (if not entirely true to the events of his life). It is a piece of historical evocation, as it were after Walter Scott, rendering in careful detail and for their own sake the objects and behaviour of a past world. It is a discussion on the nature of artistic inspiration and creation. And it is also – though opinions differ as to precisely in what way – an exercise in generic transposition, an attempt or attempts at reproduction of one art form as another, specifically music as poetry; a term the text itself uses, slightly confusingly, is 'gemalte Symphonie'.[1] To this catalogue, however, a further element should be added, one which is less evident than the others, but is a important undercurrent in the text even so; for, in its muted way, the work is also a political reflection, offering judgments on the political constellation of the not-so-very-distant epoch in which it is set which also directly impinge on the author's own era.

Mozart auf der Reise nach Prag is sited 'in den Angeln einer historischen Weltwende' (to quote Werner Zemp, one of the few critics who refer at all convincingly to this aspect of the work[2]). Its action occurs in the autumn of 1787, so on the very brink of the French Revolution and in the dying moments of the aristocratic cultural and political hegemony of the *ancien régime* – at the end of a 'beinahe vergötterte[s] Zeitalter. . . , worin wir heutzutage freilich des wahrhaft Preisenswerten wenig finden können, und das schon eine unheilvolle Zukunft in sich trug, deren welterschütternder Eintritt dem Zeitpunkt unserer harmlosen Erzählung bereits nicht ferne mehr lag' (SW 1055). The Schinzbergs, into whose garden Mozart strays and whose orange-tree heirloom he damages early in the story, present an image of that world at its best – generous, cultured, gracious, refined – while at the same time they also exemplify some of its weaknesses. Mozart, composing *Don Giovanni*, intrudes into this society, to the consternation and excitement of the Schinzbergs, and his plucking and cutting of an orange from their tree (the tree itself being interpretable, as the text itself tells us with not uncharacteristic frankness, 'als lebendes Symbol der feingeistigen Reize eines beinahe vergötterten Zeitalters . . .'; SW 1055) parallels and symbolizes the irruption that the Revolution brought of destructive, chaotic forces into the prevailing aristocratic tranquillity.[3]

The irruption that Mozart represents is both social and artistic. Mörike, having read Niemtschek's and Oulibicheff's biographies[4] and other material around his topic, was certainly aware of his subject's problematical social position, dependent on whimsical and unreliable aristocratic patronage, yet injecting a marked anti-aristocratic element into his work and life (for example, with the critique of aristocratic behaviour in *The Marriage of Figaro* and *Don Giovanni* itself; or with the advocacy of a bourgeois ideal in *The Magic Flute*, and the personal masonic commitments which underlay this). Mörike's readers, in the highly class-conscious environment of mid nineteenth century Germany, are likely to have known and understood it, too. And, in any event, the uncomfortable class situation of Mozart the character (nicely signalled in the novella by the 'nachlassiger . . . Zopf' he wears; SW 1025), and its resonances in his encounter with the Schinzbergs, will have been evident in the 1850s in a way in which, now, they are not.

More immediately apparent, however, is the artistic upheaval which Mozart brings. For what Mozart produces and represents, the novella indicates, is a revolution in music. Already in earlier work, his adherence to the graceful, playful, trivial patterns of the Rococo has become only a matter of form, merely the starting point for a far more profound musical utterance. The concerto he plays before the assembled company is described as:

eines jener glänzenden Stücke, worin die reine Schönheit sich . . . in den Dienst der Eleganz begibt, so aber, daß sie, gleichsam nur verhüllt in diese mehr willkürlich spielenden Formen und hinter eine Menge blendender Lichter versteckt, doch in jeder Bewegung ihren eigensten Adel verrät und ein herrliches Pathos verschwenderisch ausgießt (SW 1044).

But with *Don Giovanni* even this degree of conventional restraint is left behind, to produce a music which reaches into the depths, revealing and releasing new forces in the human psyche – intense and chaotic, creative and destructive. This is the music described towards the end of the novella, in apocalyptic phrases, as Mozart plays the opera's climax:

'Ich griff einen Akkord und fühlte, ich hatte an der rechten Pforte angeklopft, dahinter schon die ganze Legion von Schrecken beieinan-derliege, die im Finale loszulassen sind' . . . Jener furchtbare Choral 'Dein Lachen endet vor der Morgenröte!' erklang durch die Totenstille des Zimmers. Wie von entlegenen Sternenkreisen fallen die Töne aus silbernen Posaunen, eiskalt, Mark und Seele durchschneidend, herunter durch die blaue Nacht . . . 'Jetzt gab es für mich begreiflicherweise kein Aufhören mehr. Wenn erst das Eis einmal an *einer* Uferstelle bricht, gleich kracht der ganze See und klingt bis an den entferntesten Winkel hinunter'. (SW 1075f.)

One critic has observed how the 'Schlußchoral' description is noticeably violent, with its tearing, cutting and breaking.[5] But we may add that what it focuses on particularly is a range of images of natural chaos and destruction: with this music, not only the cracking of the ice across a lake is evoked, but also the 'Schauspiel einer unbändigen Naturkraft', or the 'Brand eines herrlichen Schiffes' (SW 1076f.). Here we have images which – not-withstanding their metonymic attachment in the last two instances to the Don Juan character himself – are powerfully reminiscent of those that the literature of half a century before had offered specifically to characterize the French Revolution. Notably one thinks of Goethe's *Hermann und Dorothea*, its 'schreckliche[r] Brand', 'Gewitter', 'Menschen . . . hingerissen vom Strome', 'schwanken[der] Boden', 'Chaos und Nacht'[6] – but also of *Unter-haltungen deutscher Ausgewanderten*, *Novelle*, *Die natürliche Tochter*, Schiller's *Das Lied von der Glocke*, Brentano's *Godwi* and others. And they are images which, as we have seen in previous chapters, had become almost commonplace in writing since then to denote that and subsequent social revolutions.[7] With the climax of *Don Giovanni* in Mörike's text, the author is telling us, what we have is the French Revolution's musical counterpart.

As Benno von Wiese noted, 'diesem Mozart ist die Gesellschaft nicht mehr gewachsen'.[8] The Schinzbergs and their friends are kindly, gracious and cultured, even if the Graf himself is 'etwas laut' (SW 1043);[9] but their cultural life, epitomized by Max's poem and its jokey ending (SW 1057),[10] seldom rises above Rococo triviality, and Mozart's final concert exceeds the appreciative capacities of most of them: 'Genau genommen waren, dem Geist, der Einsicht, dem Geschmacke nach, Eugenie und ihr Verlobter die einzigen Zuhörer, wie der Meister sie sich wünschen mußte, und jene war es sicher ungleich mehr als dieser' (SW 1074). As a whole, they as an audience have 'einen von unserem Verhältnis unendlich verschiedenen Stand', and – apart from the privilege they enjoy of witnessing the composer himself perform –

bei weitem nicht den günstigen [Stand] wie wir, da eine reine und vollkommene Auffassung eigentlich niemand möglich war, auch in mehr als *einem* Betracht selbst dann nicht möglich gewesen sein würde, wenn das Ganze ungekürzt hätte mitgeteilt werden können. (SW 1073)

The newness and incompleteness of what they hear inhibit their appreciation, but so, too, does the fact of who they are. The audience of the post-Revolutionary, bourgeois, Romantic and post-Romantic age is infinitely better equipped to grasp this music.

What is so interesting about Mörike's conception is the way it links art and politics. The advent of Mozart's music is not merely a metaphor for the explosion of the French Revolution upon European society – and nor, on the other hand, is the Revolution just a metaphor for his musical innovation, as at least one critic seems to suggest.[11] Rather, they are integrally related phenomena: European Romantic art (for that is what Mörike is describing in Mozart, an art which opens up new dimensions and depths of inner experience, irrational and mysterious) and the bourgeois revolution, unleashing new *social* forces upon the world, are developments in tandem. This is a socio-cultural (not merely intellectual-historical) conception of startling acuity and modernity, with no literary precedents of which I am aware.[12]

There is one further intriguing aspect of Mörike's reflection. The text emphasizes as a facet of Mozart his naturalness. This is shown not only by his affinity with a natural world free of human artifice (his joy at the Bohemian pine forest, 'nicht etwa nur so una finzione di poeti'; SW 1026), but also, in particular, by his capacity for deep empathy with the *Volk* (seen in his encounters with characters in an inn in the Viennese *Vorstädte*; SW 1066–9). Moreover, it is indicated to be not contrary to, but somehow a function of, his creativity. However, as he composes *Don Giovanni*, despoiling the symbol of aristocratic culture in the castle garden, it is a character from the Volk who breaks in upon his reverie. This is the gardener, whom Mozart, as he talks later of the meeting, describes in a series of strangely intense and menaced images, jocular in tone though they seem: 'Nemesis', '. . . des entsetzlichen Mannes', 'ein Ausbruch des Vesuvio', 'die Katastrophe', 'der Satan', 'ein Gesicht wie aus Erz – . . . dem grausamen römischen Kaiser Tiberius ähnlich' (SW 1052).[13] One notes here especially the associations of natural disaster. As a character in the story, the gardener is seen mainly in the position of a downtrodden feudal servant: uncertain and fearful as to how he should treat the intruder, his social superior, then kept waiting, ignored or brusquely dismissed by his masters, and finally reproached sharply for his negligence (SW 1040f). But as he appears before Mozart in the garden, the image is less passive and submissive: 'groß', 'breitschulterig', 'ein Gesicht wie aus Erz' (SW 1038, 1052). It is, rather, that of the grim-featured, menacing 'Proletarier' who figures so frequently in literature (not to mention in journalism) of Mörike's time.[14] In the former, too, but especially in the latter aspect of his appearance in the story, the gardener hints at a further social dimension to the text: namely, the suggestion that, in the social as well as imaginative depths which Mozart's revolutionary creativity opens up, there may also lie a nemesis which is not only personal-psychological but also sociopolitical, the nemesis of his class. In relation to Mörike, this is quite a surprising conception. Clearly it does not lie on the surface of the text, and one suspects it is not even entirely on the surface of Mörike's own consciousness, although it is, as we know, by no means unfamiliar in literature of the time. It is, for instance, not at all far from the analysis of the French Revolution itself which, as we saw in chapter two, Büchner's *Dantons Tod* contains; the social picture Grillparzer's play *Ein Bruderzwist in Habsburg* offers in semi-parabolic form[15] is closer still; and it undoubtedly has affinities with the social pronouncements in the texts by Gotthelf and Eichendorff examined earlier. But there are further indicators which can be adduced to suggest that such a meaning is indeed present on some level of Mörike's text, and why.

Mörike's own political attitudes and commitments are interesting. If a good deal of Mörike criticism is to be believed, he had next to none: the received image of him suggests complete apoliticality. But this is by no means accurate.[16] It is true that Mörike was never really politically active: he voted when given the chance, but he never stood for political office or involved himself otherwise in political organisations or manifestations. But political conviction and commitment need not entail political action, and in reality we can find in Mörike, notably in the decade or so preceding the publication of *Mozart* in 1855, evidence of powerful political enthusiasms and concerns.

Where such concerns emerge most forcefully of all is in the preliminaries to, and the course and aftermath of, the Revolution of 1848. This is as one might expect. 1848 was (with the arguable exception of the *Reichsgründung* of 1871) the most important political occurrence in Germany during Mörike's adult life, and his letters confirm it was his own major political experience, too. 'Das Jahr 1848', he says in December 1850, '[hat] meinen Blick begieriger, anhaltender als jemals in die Welt gerichtet'[17] – implying, too, that this was a permanent development. At the height of the events themselves they are the recurring subject of his correspondence. Letter after letter tells of his avid reading of the newspapers; in the May of 1848 he tells a correspondent that he 'kann neben den täglichen Zeitungen kaum mehr ein Buch in die Hand nehmen, das keine politische Verwandtschaft hat';[18] and even in October 1850, long after the onset of the Reaction, the newspaper is his 'Nachtlektüre', its political contents his 'tägliches Gespräch'.[19]

His response to the events of the bourgeois revolution is intensely enthusiastic. In the Swiss *Sonderbundkrieg* of November 1847, harbinger of the revolution proper, he rejoices in the victory of the liberal constitutionalists of the Swiss Confederation against the conservative secessionist *Sonderbund*.[20] The 'Sturm der Weltbegebenheiten'[21] in February and March 1848 – Louis Philippe's fall in France, then the apparent triumph of liberal constitutionalism in Germany, the limiting of monarchic power in the states, and the signs of progress towards national unification – is all a marvellous and uplifting spectacle: 'Wer hat sich in diesen paar Wochen nicht größer als sein ganzes Leben lang empfunden!'[22] As the year progresses, he continues to watch the 'große Zeitläufte', the 'hohe Bewegung der heutigen Tage',[23] with excitement and optimism. He participates in the elections for the

Frankfurt National Assembly in April (though his preferred candidate is defeated), follows the proceedings in Frankfurt closely (he expresses particular admiration for the assembly president, Heinnch von Gagern), enthuses about the advance by a German army through Schleswig-Holstein into Danish Jutland in May and rails against Austrian obstructionism towards unificatory developments.[24] In the autumn, as the Reaction gains ground, he shares the prevailing depression among German liberals, yet still hopes for a final positive outcome ('. . . die herbe Geburt unserer Freiheit . . . Wir werden doch noch Freude dran erleben!').[25] And in 1849 and 1850, as the revolution is defeated and absolutist power restored in most of Germany, he talks of 'die gegenwärtigen schlechten Zeiten', of how 'traurig' and 'betrübt' the political situation is, laments the failure of 'die deutsche Sache' and speaks of a general betrayal of political hopes ('grausam . . . von gewissen Seiten um [die] schönsten Hoffnungen betrogen').[26]

Inactive though he himself was – several of his letters apologise for this inactivity on grounds of ill-health[27] – Mörike may be said to have existed in a lively political environment during the revolutionary period. He was closely associated with – visited by and in correspondence with – several of the most prominent liberal political figures of 1848 in southwest Germany. These were individuals who were long-standing friends of his: Friedrich Theodor Vischer, David Friedrich Strauß, Ludwig Uhland, Karl Mayer – of whom all but Mayer became elected parliamentarians, either in Frankfurt or at the Württemberg assembly in Stuttgart. The indications are that Mörike's own views were a little to the right of most of theirs. Vischer and Uhland belonged to the 'Linkes Zentrum' or bourgeois left ('Württemberger Hof') at Frankfurt,[28] Mayer's allegiances seem to have been equivalent, and so, at any rate early in the revolution, were those of Strauß. Mörike himself cast his vote in the Frankfurt election of April 1848 in Mergentheim against Robert Mohl, who joined the Linkes Zentrum, and for Friedrich Bassermann, who eventually joined the moderate 'Rechten' (the 'Casino' group);[29] and Gagern, whom Mörike praised highly in July, represented the same position.[30] But on the other hand, Mörike was able in his letter praising Gagern to speak with interest and no acrimony of the radical Robert Blum (whom imperial forces executed in Vienna a few months later), and he was generally sympathetic and enthusiastic towards his slightly more radical friends' political involvements and utterances.[31] Altogether, we may say, Mörike's politics – liberal-constitutionalist-nationalist – are securely in the middle of the normal spectrum of German bourgeois political attitudes of the time.

A couple of important concomitants of this standpoint should be remarked on. First, Mörike's position vis-à-vis monarchic-aristocratic authority was always a little problematical. Not, in a way, unlike the real Mozart, he was for a long while dependent on or desirous of princely favour – for the grant and continuation of his pension (the responsibility of the King of Württemberg), for sinecures or bursaries of which he had (vain) hopes, at various stages, from the Kings of Prussia, Württemberg and probably also Bavaria, and for various gifts, such as money and jewellery, which he actually received for his work.[32] His letters on these matters are predictably ingratiating. Indeed, he may well have felt real gratitude for the favours he did receive, since it is hard to accept largesse wholly cynically. But in his private letters, and not only in the revolutionary years, a sharp note of dislike of monarchy and 'Hochadel' also periodically appears. In 1843 he quotes approvingly David Friedrich Strauß's attack on the important, politically symbolic project of the *Kölner Dombau*, 'welcher auch ihm . . . von seiten der Fürsten als reiner Hokuspokus . . . erscheint'.[33] In 1847 (admittedly after his failed attempts to curry favour at the Prussian court) he treats his friend Hartlaub to a long, angry, scurrilous joke about Frederick William IV's well-known procreative difficulties,[34] reminiscent of poems of Heine's on similar subjects.[35] In March 1848 he attacks the 'Benehmen der Fürsten bis auf die letzte Zeit', particularly the 'dummer Hochmut des preußischen Königs', and is pleased 'daß ihnen nicht einmal der Schein einiger Sympathie für das siegreiche Volk und seinen Willen übrig blieb'.[36] The remark of 1849, quoted above, about how Germany's 'schönste Hoffnungen' have been betrayed 'von gewissen Seiten' points in the same direction.[37] Most interesting of all, in a letter to Hartlaub in 1850, well after the revolution's defeat, he ridicules a mutual acquaintance's nostalgia for a now past age of provincial aristocratic culture, and then adds:

> Du hast gewiß den starken Zorn- und Jammerschrei des alten Amdt aus der Deutschen Zeitung auch gelesen: 'Wer mag den Deutschen widerstehn, wenn sie wollen zuammengehn!' Er sagt nur, was ein jeder weiß und fühlt, und doch meint man, es müßte alle Welt aufrütteln und das ganze verruchte Schachbrett der Fürsten vom Tisch herabwerfen.[38]

What this implies is that Mörike will not object if the united Germany he desires is a (constitutional) monarchy, but he is not actually committed to the monarchic principle. And that final phrase is unequivocal in its hostility.

Of course, the March Revolution was not only a manifestation and (temporary) triumph of liberal constitutionalism over absolutism, although certainly that was what the liberal politicians who were Mörike's friends, the newspapers he read, and he himself, wanted it to be. Other social forces were also at work, forces which were the consequence, not of the denial of political power to the middle classes that was the bourgeois revolution's motivation, but of the widespread deprivation afflicting the lower classes in early-industrial Germany; which articulated much more radical political demands and quite different economic ones; and which were manifested in far more extreme and disorderly forms of political action. Mörike, like most of his class, was largely unsympathetic to the element of popular revolt – urban rioting, rural uprisings – which also marked the revolutionary year in Germany (and it was particularly strong in the Southwest). Like the rest of his class, again, he was frightened by it, even if he had some understanding of its causes. Already in early March 1848 Mergentheim, where he was living (some 80 km north-east of Stuttgart), was threatened by a 'böse Wetterwolke', a 'wilder Haufe von ungefahr 800 Köpfen aus dem Badischen'.[39] This was a band of impoverished peasants and rural handicraftsmen who had already burned down the Prinz von Hohenlohe-Bartenstein's castle and destroyed his 'Domänenkanzlei' in Niederstetten, where the 'Lager- und Saalbücher' (records of land dues and other charges) were kept, attacked their Jewish creditors and caused these and the local aristocratic landowners to flee to the bigger towns.[40] The burghers of Mergentheim were being formed into a militia to defend the town. The newspapers of the time tell of similar events from elsewhere in the region. Thus, the *Allgemeine Zeitung* of 12 March notes:

Auch aus anderen Orten des Württembergischen Unterlandes sowie aus dem Badischen werden die beklagenswerthesten Szenen berichtet, in denen vor allem der Haß gegen die Edelleute sich ausspricht, in deren Zins- und Schuldbuch sie stehen.[41]

And Mörike reports:

Es sei, so meinen einige, zu fürchten, daß die heimlich Unzufriedenen der benachbarten Dörfer, ja der hiesigen Bevölkerung selbst sich den auswärtigen Rotten anschließen möchten, sobald sie hoffen könnten, die kleine Macht der guten Bürger im Nachteil zu sehn, dann der Wut in Plünderung und Mißhandlung der sogenannten Vornehmen und der Begüterten kein Ziel sein würde. Diese Sorge scheint bis jetzt unter den höheren Ständen nicht herrschend zu sein . . . Ein redlicher und gescheiter Mann, ein Handwerker. . . , mit dem ich gestern lang vertraulich sprach, gab mir indes ganz unzweideutig zu verstehn, daß Stadt und Umgegend weit Schlimmeres verberge, als 'die Herren' sich einbilden könnten.[42]

This was as near as the 'proletarian' revolution came to Mörike, but eight or nine kilometres (the nearest place this letter mentions) clearly felt close, and on various occasions subsequently a note of distaste and/or anxiety is perceptible as he reacts to events which have or might have similar implications. He is unenthusiastic about the disorder surrounding elections: before the April election for Frankfurt he avoids the 'Völkerversammlung' which many of his fellow citizens attend in nearby Niederstetten, and he deplores the aggressive treatment accorded in Mergentheim to supporters of the less favoured candidate.[43] And when, in the following year, Uhland, now banished from Frankfurt and on his way to the *Rumpfparlament* in Stuttgart, passes through Mergentheim with various other *Abgeordnete* (and pays a call on Mörike), Mörike watches the resulting popular demonstration and celebration from a safe distance, without favour:

Nach 10 Uhr ging der Lärm des Volkes auf den Straßen an; ein Tisch mit Lichtern für die Musiker ward vor dem Gasthof aufgestellt und der gewöhnliche Spektakel mit Vivats und dergl. aufgeführt. Ich konnte nicht davor schlafen, stand vom Bett auf und sah mit Gretchen bis nach 12 Uhr durch das letzte Fenster des runden Zimmers dem Getreib der Menschenmenge zu.[44]

The implication is discernible that Uhland's politics (Left Centre at Frankfurt, then one of the more moderate members of the very radical *Rumpfparlament*) come too close in their popularism to stimulating social disorder.

Mörike's attitudes to the various organised, politically led revolts during the revolutionary period are equivalent. When Uhland, on his visit in 1849, 'beklagte den badischen Aufstand' (of May 1849),[45] Mörike's agreement is evident, but with a suggestion of 'I told you so'. Similarly, a year before, when revolutionary forces under the general leadership of Friedrich Hecker and including a 'legion' recruited by the poet Georg Herwegh had appeared in the Southwest, Mörike talked with alarm and without enthusiasm of how 'in allem Ernste . . . ich jetzt mehr als jemals glaube, wir haben einen Bürgerkrieg in Deutschland zu gewarten'.[46] After the defeat of these forces and the ignominious flight of Herwegh, he speaks of the latter with a scorn and dislike clearly mixed with relief.[47] The only exception might be Mörike's interesting reaction to the Viennese 'October Revolution', of early October 1848, when power in Vienna passed, amidst much bloodshed, from a bourgeois ministry of dubious liberal credentials to what was in effect a Jacobin republic of workers and students:

> Ich las mit warmem Kopf soeben die Nachricht von der neuen Wiener Revolution in der Zeitung. Die Wirkung dieser Auftritte kann möglicherweise für Deutschland eine gute sein, sofern Oestreich Ursache hat, sich desto ernstlicher an unsere Sache anzuschließen.[48]

Even here, however, Mörike welcomes not the revolutionary 'Auftritte' themselves, but the prospect they suggest of compelling a less imperially-minded ministry, one more sympathetic to the constitutional nationalism of Frankfurt; and, in any case, he was writing when reports of the Viennese events had only just begun arriving in southwest Germany,[49] before the new regime's character was known. Here again, it is Mörike's 'moderate', liberal-nationalist, bourgeois-constitutionalist sympathies which underlie his response.[50]

It seems inescapable that the momentous political events of 1848/49, to which Mörike reacted with such an intensity of emotion (joy and enthusiasm, alarm and, eventually, despair), had their impact on the demonstrably political *Mozart auf der Reise nach Prag*, a work which Mörike appears to have begun writing at most three years or so after the revolution's end and which he had in mind before the revolution started.[51] The only question is, what exactly is the nature of the relationship?[52]

To begin with, there are clearly affinities between the social view which the Mörike of the revolutionary period held and that suggested by the novella. His letters indicate firm awareness that the revolution is more than an antagonism of ideas, but is also a conflict of classes, a bourgeoisie emancipating itself from aristocratic dominance, but itself under threat from the mass poor. Moreover, there is nothing remarkable in Mörike's possessing such an awareness: the newspapers which he read so avidly articulate it continually. And the same three-class system – aristocrat-bourgeois-Volk – with hints, delicate but present, of antagonisms or discrepancies between them, is what the Mozart-novella also depicts. The general social picture the text contains, in short, is one impressed forcibly on its author's mind by his experience of the conflicts of the revolutionary year.

However, there is a further, more specific connection, which concerns the locus of a significant part of Mörike's story. The 1848 revolution in Germany had certain principal sites. Stadelmann suggests the March Days themselves to have had three points of focus, the 'Dreieck Nordbaden [i.e. adjoining Mörike's own home], Wien und Berlin'.[53] But as the year progressed, while Frankfurt became the centre and focus of political argument, Vienna was the place where the most exciting revolutionary events occurred, where the revolution was seen at its most radical and where its antagonisms were most marked and violent. This is reflected clearly in contemporary newspapers, which report in tremendous detail the stages of revolutionary development in the city: in mid-March the overthrow of Metternich, the concession of constitutional government, the creation of an armed National Guard, and rioting and the destruction of factories by the poor in the Vorstädte; then the 'May Revolution', when promulgation of insufficiently liberal constitutional measures was followed by mass protests (first mainly by bourgeois militia and students, but subsequently augmented by large numbers of 'Arbeiter' marching into the city), the fall and replacement of a relatively conservative ministry and the Emperor's flight from Vienna; then August and the 'Praterschlacht', when rebellious workers, again trying to march on the inner city, were met and defeated, amid bloodshed, by the militia; then the revolution of early October, when a government suspected of collaboration with reactionary forces was toppled, confused and bloody street battles took place, in which the poor for the first time gained firearms, and eventually government by a radical Committee of Public Safety was instituted; and, finally, in late October, the siege and recapture of the city by the imperial armies under Fürst Windischgrätz.[54]

As the reports for the *Schwäbischer Merkur* of Stuttgart and the *Allgemeine Zeitung* of Augsburg, two of the newspapers Mörike evidently saw frequently, show,[55] what was distinctive about the revolution in Vienna – then the only real *Großstadt* in the German states – was the strength and immediacy of the proletarian menace for the middle-class revolutionaries. Already in the March Days the victorious burghers in the inner city, rejoicing in Metternich's overthrow and the accession to their constitutional demands, looked over their shoulders in alarm at the 'tobende[r] Pöbel' in the

Vorstädte, fearing 'Anarchie und besonders die Macht des losen Haufens'.[56] One of the first acts of the new, armed National Guard (and one reason for its creation) was to stand guard at the locked gates of the inner city, shoulder to shoulder with regular troops and equipped with ordnance, 'um das Volk aus den Proletariervorstädten abzuhalten in die Stadt zu kommen'.[57] In Berlin in March 1848, by contrast, though there was actually much *more* bloodshed than in Vienna, such antagonism was largely absent. At each subsequent stage of the revolutionary year, the liberal commentators in Vienna strike the same note. In May, first 'die Stadtthore [werden] gesperrt . . . um den Andrang der Arbeiter aus den Vorstädten zu verhindern'.[58] Later, a 'Masse von mehr als 20,000 Proletariern' is said to be waiting at the *Burgtor* to attack the city, a 'wüstes, zerlumptes Raubgesindel'; then the gates are opened, 'tausende von Arbeitern strömen in die Stadt', inducing fears of 'die nackte Revolution', a 'Zustand . . . der gränzenlosesten Anarchie', a 'ganzliche Auflösung alles Bestehenden und allgemeine Plünderung aller Besitzenden'.[59] The 'Praterschlacht' in August gives rise in the inner city to a 'panischer Schreck' and the cry 'Die Arbeiter dringen zu den Thoren herein!'[60] And afterwards one writer, who ascertains: 'So haben wir . . . einen Arbeiteraufstand erlebt', registers significantly that this is the price now being paid for the way 'das hungernde . . . Proletariat von unsern leichtsinnigen und gewissenlosen Stimmführern [im] Mai zu ihren Bundesgenossen herbeigerufen [wurde]'.[61] Finally, in the Viennese October, which saw the nearest Germany came to a triumph of proletarian power, the commentators first express the old alarm ('In Wien [steht] das Proletariat in vollen Waffen', 'aus einem solchen Kampfe kann nur Anarchie hervorgehen'), then alternate between complaint at the 'Pöbel-herrschaft' ('Terrorismus') in the city and sympathy with the resistance shown against the invading armies of the Reaction.[62]

These class antagonisms and anxieties also expressed themselves, as the reports quoted above indicate, in Vienna's distinctive social geography. Compared with very many modern metropolises, in which the areas fashionable among the ruling elite may shift considerably from epoch to epoch, Vienna grew up and has remained largely fixed in a pattern of social as well as geographical concentricity, with the 'Innere Stadt' within the old city ramparts (now replaced by the 'Ring') the home of aristocracy and subsequently also the higher bourgeoisie, while the Vorstädte outside the ramparts ('Basteien'), but within the 'Linienwall' or outer fortifications of the city (the present-day 'Gürtel') developed in the 18th and early 19th centuries to house first the city's artisans and servants and then the growing working class and petite bourgeoisie of the industrial age. Obviously the social constitution of areas of the city changed over time – notably, as it grew in the *Gründerzeit* and thereafter, the 'Arbeiterviertel' were pushed outwards – but the essential concentric pattern persisted. And it is peculiarly apparent in 1848, when the *Basteien* become concretely a bastion for the bourgeoisie against the chaos of the masses which 'tobt in den Vorstädten'.

It is a factor in the literature of Vienna, too. The social interchange across the line of the (by then nonexistent) wall is of recurring interest in Schnitzler's writing at the turn of the century.[63] It figures periodically, too, in plays by Nestroy *(Eine Wohnung ist zu vermieten, Das Mädl aus der Vorstadt)* and in works by his folktheatrical heirs (for example, Horváth's *Geschichten aus dem Wiener Wald)*. It also appears, of course – differently, but especially interestingly – in Grillparzer's story *Der arme Spielmann,* published late in 1847. As we saw in chapter six, this work, powerfully recollecting past revolutionary events and anticipating pending ones, describes the movements of the massed Volk on *Brigittenkirchtag* in Vienna at once as a chaotic force of nature ('der Strom des Volkes, . . . sich ergießend in Alles deckender Überschwemmung') and a battling army ('An den Toren der Stadt wächst der Drang. Genommen, verloren und wiedergenommen . . .').[64] Here the movement is, in fact, peaceful, and it is also strictly a flowing outwards from, rather than into, the city. But it is nevertheless intended to convey (as the rest of Grillparzer's novella conveys), both realistically and symbolically, fearful anticipation of the social chaos and destruction of orderly values which mass proletarianisation promises. And in imagery and mood, as well as in setting, it is very close to what is found in the liberal newspaper reports of revolutionary events in Vienna in 1848.

Mörike himself cannot have been unfamiliar with much of this. It is quite likely he read Grillparzer's novella not very long after its appearance (in one of the most prominent of contemporary annual anthologies of fiction[65]), and, if so, he must have had a fore- or afterknowledge of its correspondences in the real events of 1848. At least one critic has suggested that, with the references in the Mozart-novella to Mozart's fondness for the *Prater* and particularly for the 'Volksfest [am] Brigitten-Kirchtag', Mörike in fact 'pays a veiled tribute' to the *Spielmann*.[66] Mörike was also clearly quite well informed about Vienna's geography, including its social geography, although he never visited the city. In part, this familiarity may have come from studying town plans and travelogues,[67] in addition to the biographies of Mozart which he read. But it must also have come in large measure from the innumerable reports from Vienna, going into endless detail about the places of the city and their significance, which he consumed during the course of 1848.

Mörike's knowledge is apparent at various junctures in the story, but above all in one particular passage. This is the extended 'Sommerspaziergang' which Mozart is described as taking one afternoon, from his apartment, out into the Vorstädte, where he has his encounter with a number of characters from the Volk, and then once more back home. This walk is described in precise detail. From his home in the 'Stadt', the inner city, he wanders, 'nachdenklich lässig', past the arsenal, 'über den sogenannten Hof' and past a church, and on as far as the 'Schottentor', the northwest gate. There he climbs the rampart, where a sentry stands guard over the big guns protecting the city, and contemplates the view across the 'Glacis' (the open land which was previously the city moat) to the Vorstädte and beyond. Then he wanders on, presumably through the gate, and out along the 'Währingergasse' into the 'Alservorstadt'. Here, obeying 'ein kaum bewußter Trieb, sich unter anspruchslosen, natürlichen Menschen in etwas zu vergessen', which has also evidently brought him out of the city in the first place, he is drawn into an inn-cum-ropemaker's shop and his encounter with the people there. Afterwards, he sets off home, hurrying; but when he reaches the Glacis, instead of passing through the Schottentor into the inner city, he slackens his pace, turns right and progresses slowly round the city outside the wall, entering finally in the south through the 'Kärntnertor' (SW 1065–9). This journey, expressive most evidently of that urge for naturalness and freedom from constraint (social, artistic and psychological) which characterises Mozart throughout the novella, is essentially similar to what Grillparzer's novella shows: the flow outwards from the order, discipline and 'Enge' of the inner city into the chaotic, formless world of the Vorstädte (though Mörike's picture, with Mozart returning *reluctantly* within the walls, is ultimately a less negative one). In fact, Mozart's walk in Mörike's story – past the symbols of authority and social control in the *Innere Stadt*, out beyond the ramparts into the disorderly domain of the Volk, then unwillingly back inside the constraining walls –

is a socially symbolic journey, its principle and its details (Zeughaus, Schottentor, Währingergasse, Alservorstadt, etc.: all familiar sites of 1848) suggested to the author by his experience of the 1848 Revolution and his knowledge of its extreme manifestations in the German *Großstadt* Vienna.[68]

I should not wish to claim (as one might be tempted to) that these facets of Mörike's text are some esoteric 'true meaning' to the work, artfully concealed by the author beneath unimportant surface themes in order to delude censors or reactionary patrons. On the whole, it seems to me that, notwithstanding what has been shown here, the author's principal concerns as he wrote the work were not political, but artistic and psychological. However, Mörike's creative process, the kind of 'künstlerisch geistesabwesend' ('nachdenklich lässig') receptiveness to stimulus and 'Eingebung' which he describes in Mozart himself, allows and encourages admission of such additional dimensions into his text. The French Revolutionary reflection discussed early in this chapter is, I think, substantially planned and conscious. The scheme suggested – Mozart's romantic-revolutionary music and the social revolution of 1789 as interlinked phenomena – is too sophisticated and is signalled in too much detail for this not to be so. The symbol of the orange tree, with its elaborate history and then Mozart's abuse of it, the date at which the text is set and the narratorial comments on that dating, the well-known socio-historical implications of Mozart's own work and career, the depiction of the Schinzbergs' cultural life and Mozart's artistic irruption upon it: such a complex of elements indicates considerable organisation. The connections with 1848 and revolutionary Vienna, which are not so coherent and systematic, appear accordingly less reflected and premeditated. Yet, equally, it seems unlikely that they were merely subliminal, no more than a reflex of which the author had no awareness. When, just a couple of years after the tremendous events of 1848 with their particular Viennese focus, Mörike wrote of Mozart's Vienna and Mozart's socially revolutionary position, he may not exactly have planned his work as a historical parable thematising 1848; but if not, then, as he composed it, the connections will none the less have thrust themselves upon him. He must have had at least a residual sense of what it was in his own attitudes and experience that made him lend his Mozart-novella the political-historical dimension it has, and of the ways such causes were, as we have seen, working themselves out in the details of his text.

Notes

1. Eduard Mörike, *Sämtliche Werke*, ed. Herbert Göpfert, 5th edn, Munich, 1976, p. 1050 (edition subsequently in this chapter as 'SW'). See, for example, Hans Hering, 'Mörikes Mozartdichtung', *Zeitschrift für deutsche Bildung* 10 (1934), 360–6; Franz Mautner, 'Mörikes Mozart auf der Reise nach Prag', *Publications of the Modern Languages Association of America* 60 (1945), 199–220 (210f., 216); Ralph Farrell, *Mörike: 'Mozart auf der Reise nach Prag'*, London, 1960, pp. 27–48. The present chapter is a revised version of an essay which appeared first in *Monatshefte* 81 (i) (1989), 45–61, and subsequently, in German, in *Forum Vormärz Forschung. Jahrbuch* 3 (1997): *1848 und der deutsche Vormärz*, 237–57. It is published here with thanks to the University of Wisconsin Press.
2. Werner Zemp, *Mörike. Elemente und Anfänge*, Frauenfeld, 1939, p. 46.
3. Besides Zemp, further critics who offer brief but credible reflections on this issue are Benno von Wiese, *Eduard Mörike*, Tubingen, 1950, p. 280f., and S. Prawer, 'The Threatened Idyll. Mörike's *Mozart auf der Reise nach Prag*', *Modern Languages* 44 (1963), 101–7 (see p. 104f.). These three variously share my sense that Mörike and his music in the novella are themselves harbingers of pending historical developments. By contrast, several other critics present them rather as merely typical of the late Rococo, not pointing beyond it, 'an end, not a beginning' – thus Maurice Benn, 'Comments of an *Advocatus Diaboli* on Mörike's *Mozart auf der Reise nach Prag*', *German Life and Letters* 25 (1971/72), 368–76 (see p. 372). Similarly Walter Heinsius, 'Mörike und die Romantik', *Deutsche Vierteljahresschrift* 3 (1925), 194–230 (see p. 227); Helga Slessarev, *Eduard Mörike*, New York, 1970, p. 120.
4. Prague, 1798, and Stuttgart, 1847, respectively (the latter from the Russian).
5. Prawer, 'The Threatened Idyll', p. 105.
6. Goethe, *Werke. Hamburger Ausgabe*, ed. Erich Trunz, 12th edn, Munich, 1994, 2: 444, 449f., 462, 498–50.
7. Found repeatedly, as we have observed, in later Eichendorff (*Das Schloß Dürande, Die Entführung, Der Adel und die Revolution*), Grillparzer (*Der arme Spielmann, Ein Bruderzwist in Habsburg*), Gotthelf, Heine, Stifter and others. See also the third section of this chapter, below. Cf., in addition, Hans-Wolf Jäger, *Politische Metaphorik im Jakobinismus und im Vormärz*. Stuttgart, 1971, esp. p. 31f.
8. Von Wiese, *Eduard Mörike*, p. 287.
9. See also SW 1041f.
10. Cf. also SW 1042.
11. Von Wiese, *Eduard Mörike*, p. 292.
12. There *are* significant literary precedents for some elements of Mörike's text, but they do not concern this aspect. Notably, the fourth of E.T.A. Hoffmann's *Kreisleriana* seems to be the model for Mörike's rendering of Romantic music in literary prose. See Hoffmann, *Sämtliche Werke*, ed. Walter Müller-Seidel, Munich, 1960–65, 1: 41–9, esp. 42–5.
13. Also 'Unhold', SW 1040.
14. See, for example, Heine's 'Die schlesischen Weber', or Canto 10 of *Atta Troll*, Nestroy's *Freiheit in Krahwinkel* (Act 3), poems by Freiligrath such as 'Von unten auf', etc., and chapters 1 and 3, above. As noted in my introduction, the concept 'proletarian' in this context is difficult, having been subsequently appropriated by Marx, who gave it the restricted meaning of the wage-slaves of

capital which it commonly has nowadays. In the very widespread usage of the 1840s, however, it was broader, denoting the deprived and dispossessed underclass in general. When the term is employed in the present discussion, it echoes this usage.

15. Especially Act 3, as the burghers of Prague are warned of the social chaos and ultimate 'Pöbelherrschaft' which their demands for political emancipation will engender. Grillparzer, *Sämtliche Werke. Historisch-kritische Gesamtausgabe*, eds August Sauer and Reinhold Backmann, Vienna, 1909–48, Abteilung I, vol. 6, pp. 260–6.

16. Few critics have much to say on Mörike's political concerns. Rudolf Krauß's brief article, 'Eduard Mörike und die Politik', *Euphorion* 1 (1894), 129–36, is a series of quotations from the poet's correspondence with little commentary. Hans-Egon Holthusen's biography *Eduard Mörike*, Hamburg, 1971, has a short, vague chapter on 'Mörike und die politischen Köpfe' (pp. 72–83). Most interestingly, the end of a little-known essay by the economic historian Jürgen Kuczynski, 'Der "Zauber der Beschränkung" und das "holde Bescheiden" Eduard Mörikes', in Kuczynski, *Gestalten und Werke*, Berlin, 1969, pp. 163–83, offers what is also a series of epistolary quotations, but with a well-informed commentary (see especially pp. 177–82). Finally, Helmut Koopmann has pointed in recent times to revolutionary allusions in an early ballad by Mörike. See Helmut Koopmann, 'Weltenbrand hinterm Berg. Eduard Mörike, *Der Feuerreiter*'; in: Koopmann. *Freiheitssonne und Revolutionsgewitter. Reflexe der Französischen Revolution im literarischen Deutschland zwischen 1789 und 1840*, Tübingen, 1989, pp. 123–42. *Mozart auf der Reise nach Prag* is admittedly not mentioned here, and a more conservative view of revolution is ascribed to Mörike in Koopmann's account than that which will emerge in the present discussion.

17. Letter of 31 December 1850, in Mörike, *Unveroffentlichte Briefe*, ed. Friedrich Seebaß, Stuttgart, 1941 (henceforth in this chapter as 'SUB'), p. 210.

18. 30 May 1848, in *Eduard Mörikes Briefe*, eds Karl Fischer and Rudolf Krauß, 2 vols, Berlin, 1904 (henceforth 'FK'), 2: 171.

19. 18 October 1850, in *'Frauenlieb' und Treu. 250 Briefe Eduard Mörikes an Wilhelm Hartlaub*, ed. Gotthilf Renz, Leipzig, 1938 (henceforth 'R'), p. 324.

20. 1 December 1847, R 294f.; 27 December 1847, SUB 184.

21. 24 March 1848, R 299.

22. Ibid.

23. 26 April, 30 June 1848, SUB 191, 195.

24. Respectively 26 April 1848, SUB 187ff., and Mörike, *Briefe*, ed. Friedrich Seebaß, Tübingen, 1952 (henceforth 'SB'), p. 651f.; 14 July 1848, R 302 (cf. also 24 July 1848, R 305); 5 May 1848, R 301.

25. 20 November 1848, R 310; 6 November 1848, SB 666.

26. Respectively 17 February 1849, SUB 198; 26 June 1849, 12 June 1850, SUB 201, 208; 26 June 1849, SUB 201; 30 August 1849, FK 2: 186.

27. 24 March 1848, R 299, 30 August 1849, FK 2: 185, 8 February 1851, SB 683: '. . . wo ich Tag für Tag aufgelegt war, alles das Meinige frohlockend in die Schanze zu schlagen'.

28. Cf. Frank Eyck, *The Frankfurt Parliament 1848–1849*, London, 1968, pp. 110, 386.

29. 26 April, 30 June 1848, SUB 190f., 195 (see also 418). Cf. Eyck, *The Frankfurt Parliament*, pp. 193, 180. Bassermann gained election to the Frankfurt Parliament later.

30. 14 July 1848, R 302 (also cited above). Cf. Eyck, *The Frankfurt Parliament*, p. 190f., and *Die Revolution von 1848. Eine Dokumentation*, ed. Walter Grab, Munich, 1980, pp. 130–6.
31. 5 May 1848, SB 655, 26 April 1848, SUB 188.
32. Respectively 3 June 1843, SB 581–4, 23 April 1847, 23 April 1851, SUB 174f., 210f.; 19 April 1845, SB 594–6, and 19 April 1844, FK 2: 81, 1 May 1851, SB 688, 15 December 1855, FK 2: 260; 31 December 1846, R 275f., 2 January 1847, 18 January 1848, SUB 165f., 184.
33. 20 March 1843, SB 572f.
34. 27 March 1847, SB 627f.
35. For example, 'Der Wechselbalg' (1844).
36. 24 March 1848, SB 650.
37. 30 August 1849, FK 2: 186.
38. August 1850, R 317f.
39. 10 March 1848, SB 648, also FK 2: 166.
40. See *Allgemeine Zeitung* (Augsburg), ed. Gustav Kolb (henceforth 'AZ'), 10 March 1848 (no. 70), p. 1110.
41. AZ, 12 March 1848 (no. 72), p. 1138. Cf. *Schwäbischer Merkur* (Stuttgart), ed. Elben (henceforth 'SM'), 11 March, 12 March 1848 (nos 70, 71), pp. 301, 314.
42. 10 March 1848, SB 648, also FK 2: 166f. (longer version of letter).
43. 26 April 1848, SB 651f.
44. 11 June 1849, R 313, also FK 2: 184.
45. Ibid.; and cf. Rudolf Stadelmann, *Soziale und politische Geschichte der Revolution von 1848*, Munich, 1948, pp. 181–4.
46. 26 April 1848, SB 653, also SUB 191. See also Wolfram Siemann, *The German Revolution of 1848–49*, transl. Christiane Banerji, London, 1998 (originally *Die deutsche Revolution von 1848/49*, Frankfurt/M., 1985), pp. 68–71.
47. 5 May 1848, R 302, also FK 2: 170, and 17 May 1848, FK 2: 170. Cf. AZ, 1 May 1848 (no. 122), p. 1940f., 5 May 1848 (no. 126), p. 2003. Note that this renowned liberal newspaper's attitude to the rising is just as hostile as Mörike's. Cf. also Stadelmann, *Soziale und politische Geschichte*, pp. 85–7.
48. 13 October 1848, FK 2: 180. Cf. Wolfgang Häusler, *Von der Massenarmut zur Arbeiterbewegung. Demokratie und soziale Frage in der Wiener Revolution von 1848*, Vienna, 1979, p. 376ff., and Stadelmann, *Soziale und politische Geschichte*, pp. 140–5.
49. In the *Schwäbischer Merkur* first on 12 October 1848 (no. 270), pp. 1571–4.
50. Again, the correspondents of the liberal *Allgemeine Zeitung* strike a similar attitude.
51. See letter of 24 December 1852, SUB 230, and Hartlaub, letter to Mörike, 8 June 1847, in Gerhard Storz, *Eduard Mörike*, Stuttgart, 1967, p. 380.
52. Just a few critics acknowledge that the novella might somehow relate to the political realities of the era when it was written. S. Prawer, 'The Threatened Idyll', p. 105, proposes vaguely a 'cautious parallel . . . with Mörike's feeling about his own provincial world in a Germany that was rapidly being transformed by the railways and the *Zollverein*'. Horst Steinmetz, *Eduard Mörikes Erzählungen*, Stuttgart, 1969, p. 130, talks promisingly but a little obscurely of how the process of centring the story on a 'fiktive Gesellschaft', which Mörike used consistently in his earlier fiction, is here showing 'deutliche Zeichen einer Auflösung', and that this 'könnte mit den gesellschaftlichen Entwicklungen der Zeit zusammenhängen, in denen das Jahr 1848 eine erhebliche Rolle spielt'.

Gerhart von Graevenitz, 'Don Juan oder die Liebe zur Hausmusik. Wagner-Kritik in Eduard Mörikes Erzählung *Mozart auf der Reise nach Prag*', *Neophilologus* 65 (1981), 247–62, comes closest to my approach in his remarks linking the French Revolution in the novella with 1848: 'Man kann es in symbolischen Jahreszahlen ausdrücken: durch Mozarts *Don Giovanni* ist die Epoche von 1789 angesprochen. 1848 ist der Schatten über der Entstehungszeit von Mörikes Novelle' (p. 248). However, von Graevenitz's focus (as his title indicates) is different from my own, the detailed parallels I am concerned with are not elicited there, and, in the idealisation he discerns in Mörike's depiction of the Schinzbergs' society (p. 254), his discussion takes a directly contrary line.

53. Stadelmann, *Soziale und politische Geschichte*, p. 65.

54. See Häusler, *Massenarmut*, p. 137ff.

55. The *Schwäbischer Merkur* was Mörike's principal newspaper, which he received daily by post (one day after publication). However, his letters indicate (and it would anyhow be likely) that he read others regularly, and the only one his correspondence names in the late 1840s is the *Allgemeine Zeitung*, the leading liberal paper of southern Germany. The *Allgemeine Zeitung* is incidentally also the source of much material for the *Merkur*, which frequently reproduces whole articles from it.

56. AZ, 19 March 1848 (no. 79), 'Außerordentliche Beilage', pp. ii-iii.

57. SM, 19 March 1848 (no. 78), p. 368.

58. AZ, 20 May 1848 (no. 141), p. 2245. Cf. SM, 21 May 1848 (no. 141), p. 751.

59. SM, 23 May 1848 (no. 143), p. 763.

60. SM, 30 August 1848 (no. 233), p. 1332.

61. Ibid.

62. Respectively SM, 12 October 1848 (no. 270), p. 1572; AZ, 11 October 1848 (no. 285), p. 4492; AZ, 7 November 1848 (no. 312), p. 4917; AZ, 21 October 1848 (no. 295), p. 4648, SM, 11 November 1848 (no. 296), p. 1715; SM, 25 October 1848 (no. 281), p. 1643.

63. Analysed particularly in Rolf-Peter Janz and Klaus Laermann, *Arthur Schnitzler: Zur Diagnose des Wiener Bürgertums im Fin de Siècle*, Stuttgart, 1977.

64. Grillparzer, *Sämtliche Werke. Historisch-kritische Gesamtausgabe*, I/13: 37.

65. *Iris. Deutscher Almanach für 1848*, ed. Gustav Heckenast, Pest, 1847, in which, as we saw, Stifter also published.

66. SW 1029. G. Wallis Field, 'Silver and Oranges: Notes on Mörike's Mozart-Novelle', *Seminar* 14 (1978), 243–54, see p. 246. Cf. also Maurice Benn, in Mörike, '*Mozart auf der Reise nach Prag*', ed. Benn, London, 1970, p. 66. It is also likely that Mörike knew Stifter's stories responding to *Der arme Spielmann*, and that he was affected by them (see below, final note).

67. Cf. Karl Pörnbacher, *Eduard Mörike: 'Mozart auf der Reise nach Prag'. Erläuterungen und Dokumente*, Stuttgart, 1976, p. 57.

68. One can speculate also on this episode's possible relationship to Stifter's story *Der Pförtner im Herrenhause/Turmalin*. As we saw in the previous chapter, this, too, describes a walk by two of its characters, in more or less the same Viennese location, with an underlying social symbolism.

8

Heimatlos. Theodor Storm, the *Volk* and the Aftermath of 1848

The best-known of Theodor Storm's early writings, his novella *Immensee*, was written and first published in 1849, and was strikingly successful, with almost an edition a year in the decade following its first appearance (and over thirty in the years up to Storm's death).[1] It has been suggested by more than one commentator that this work of resignation, passivity and crucial missed chances is the author's quasi-allegorical expression of the mood of the German bourgeoisie in the aftermath of 1848.[2] Certainly it is true that, if such was indeed the prevailing mood, the text suits it very well; and perhaps this was a cause of its popularity (even if the much greater contemporary success of Gustav Freytag's energetic and positive *Soll und Haben* suggests the bourgeoisie to have been capable of other moods, too[3]). However, *Immensee* cannot really be seen as the expression of its author's own participation in a new *Zeitgeist*. Storm had written in a very similar fashion before the 1848 Revolution and its failure. His first published story, *Marthe und ihre Uhr* of 1847, shows a central figure whose persona clearly prefigures in significant respects that of Reinhard, the non-hero of *Immensee*, a woman whose conditioned instincts of repressive self-denial and disposition to attach herself emotionally and imaginatively to inanimate objects, particularly ones evoking her childhood, are symptom and cause of an unfulfilled and lonely life, blighted by the inability to seize the present. One could read into her object fetishes an interesting contemporary critique of Biedermeier culture; but in any event, if a historical judgement on the mind of the age is intended – in either of these stories – then the onset and collapse of the revolution have made no difference. Related reflections are to be found in Storm's poems of the 1840s, too. A text such as 'Wer je gelebt in Liebesarmen,/Der kann im Leben nie verarmen' (LL 1: 33f.), written in 1844, clearly contains both the recipe for fulfilment which the stories' protagonists miss and the warning of the danger to which they succumb. Finally (not that this proves anything), Storm continues to repeat such patterns for decades to come, with characters who miss the chances for emotional fulfilment due to their own ineffectualities, neuroses, delusions, manias and urges. This was, inter alia, how Storm viewed himself – as 'ein Mensch, der nicht die Ruhe hat, die Göttin Gelegenheit bei ihrem goldblonden Schopf zu fassen; solche Leute wie wir greifen zu früh zu, und wenn sie dann wirklich vorüberkommt, so haben wir schon die Hände voll; aber was wir ergriffen, es ist uns selten das Rechte'.[4] 'Nun – man muß zufrieden sein', he adds unconvincingly.

Thus 1848 was not really a caesura in Storm's consciousness. However, the revolution did bring about important – and largely negative – developments in his own life. Storm spent the revolutionary years in his home town of Husum, in Schleswig. From there he witnessed the uprising of March 1848, the Danish military occupation which followed, the defeat of the Danes by a (largely) Prussian army in April and the establishment of a 'provisorische Regierung' for Schleswig-Holstein in Rendsburg, elections, meetings and community reforms;[5] then the Prussian abandonment of the Duchies in the autumn of 1848 and dissolution of the Provisional Government, recommencement of the uprising without Prussia in 1849, warfare until the final Danish defeat of Schleswig-Holstein forces at Idstedt in July 1850, and the complete Danicisation of Schleswig thereafter.[6] Though he claimed not to have been politically active or especially committed,[7] Storm did write a handful of liberal-nationalistic articles for a newspaper which was financed by the Provisional Government[8] (and co-edited by his friend Theodor Mommsen); and as the Schleswig-Holstein conflict came to a climax in 1850 he found himself increasingly patriotically distressed and enraged.[9] On the other hand, it is interesting that, in the midst of 'diese heillosen Tage' and a political situation 'der allgemeinen Calamität',[10] his personal – familial – life, as reflected in his letters, seems uncharacteristically happy. His marriage had apparently begun to work, the embarrassing and enduring adultery on his part which had blighted its early stages ceased in 1848, and he was generally enjoying his first experience of fatherhood[11] (with his son Hans, born that year). Politically, as he says, his 'Heimath' may have become 'ganz wie [die] Fremde',[12] but his own home had an element of idyll – to be seen, for example, in his luscious description of preparations for and family celebration of Christmas in 1851.[13]

After the final Danish victory, however, matters changed. By late 1852, Storm's situation as a lawyer with nationalistic, anti-Danish sympathies had become intolerable in Schleswig, and in 1852 he and his family moved to Potsdam, to what was initially an unpaid post in the Prussian judiciary. This self-exile – first in Potsdam, later in Prussian Heiligenstadt – was the beginning of a long period of professional uncertainty, poverty, and nostalgia for Schleswig-Holstein, which came to an end only with the Prusso-Danish war and his return to a then Prussian-ruled Husum in 1864. When Storm looked to Husum from Potsdam and Heiligenstadt in the years of absence, his exile seemed like the destruction of an idyll, or a banishment from Paradise, where the Paradise was Heimat. In his letters from the 'fremdes Land' that Prussia was,[14] he was filled with longing for the childishly recollected sights and tastes and smells of Husum, and with a sense of it as a place of family and community belonging and wholeness ('– wo wir in einer Athmosphäre von Familientradition leben', and where most other families are integrally linked with his own[15]). Particularly Christmas, a festival with which he was somewhat obsessed, was the time for such nostalgia, and for creating in exile a temporary – familial and *heimatlich* – idyll: 'So sind wir denn eifrig beschäftigt, uns in das zo ziemlich graue Leben für einen Abend ein kleines Paradies hineinzubauen'.[16]

For Storm, 1848 itself was also primarily concerned with Heimat. For him as a Schleswig-Holsteiner and unwilling Danish subject, the Revolution was far more a matter of national identity and national emancipation than of class politics and constitutional freedoms (in the way it was for most of Storm's literary contemporaries from less marginal regions). The anti-aristocratism that became insistent in his writings after the takeover of Schleswig-Holstein and subsequent unification of Germany by Bismarck's Prussia (notably his historical 'Chroniknovellen' of the 1870s) did find expression in the 1840s and 1850s, too,[17] but it was not an issue for him in the Revolution. The rights or otherwise of a discrete class of proletarians can barely be said to have concerned him either, if one excepts a minor expression of unease in one of his newspaper reports at the potential threat to 'Ordnung und Sicherheit' of a public election by direct and universal (male) suffrage, in which large numbers of labourers participated.[18] By way of comparison, his later friend Mörike in socially not dissimilar Swabia was strongly preoccupied throughout the revolutionary period, as we saw in chapter seven, both by constitutional politics from Frankfurt and by the threat to life and property of a *Volk* stimulated into rebellion. For Storm at this time, and indeed for most of his career as a writer, 'Volk' was, by and large, not a concept of class but of national belonging, able to include all classes except, normally, the aristocracy – and the latter only excluded themselves by their self-chosen supra-national character: 'Es gibt eine Sorte im deutschen Volk,/Die wollen zum Volk nicht gehören,/Sie sind auch nur die Tropfen Gift,/Die uns im Blute gären'.[19] The only question, indeed, is to what extent Storm's 'Volk' is that of Germany or of Schleswig-Holstein: the answer is that it is inconsistent, and sometimes unclear, but frequently enough it is the latter. Volk and Heimat are, for Storm, closely allied.

This spirit is articulated in a number of his writings of the time. It figures in some questionable poems such as the one entitled 'Ostern', of 1848, which ends with a Schleswig seaside landscape:

Hier stand ich oft, wenn in Novembernacht
Aufgor das Meer zu gischtbestäubten Hügeln,
Wenn in den Lüften war der Sturm erwacht,
Die Deiche peitschend mit den Geierflügeln.

– and with the Danes warded off like the sea itself by Schleswig's human defences:

Und jauchzend ließ ich an der festen Wehr
Den Wellenschlag die grimmen Zähne reiben;
Denn machtlos, zischend schoß zurück das Meer –
Das Land ist unser, unser soll es bleiben! (L 1: 56f.)

The most remarkable expression, however, is the novella *Ein grünes Blatt*, of late 1850, probably written at a stage when the impending defeat of the Schleswig-Holstein cause had become clear.[20] This work's bourgeois hero, a Schleswig-Holsteinian freedom fighter, is shown, while on leave from the front, passing through an intensely evoked local landscape:

Um ihn her war alles Getier lebendig, was auf der Heide die Junischwüle auszubrüten pflegt; das rannte zu seinen Füßen und arbeitete sich durch's Gestäude, das blendete und schwärmte ihm vor den Augen und begleitete ihn auf Schritt und Tritt. Die Heide blühte, die Luft war durchwürzt von Wohlgerüchen;

then past archaeological vestiges of ancient Schleswig –

> In seiner Nähe, zur Seite des Steiges, lag ein niedriger Hügel, voll Brombeerranken und wilder Rosenbüsche, ein Grabmal unbekannten Volkes, wie hier viele sind. Er stieg hinauf und übersah auch von diesem höheren Standpunkte noch einmal die unermeßliche Fläche.

– to his destination, 'eine einsame Kate . . . am Saume des Waldes' (LL 1: 334f.). Then, inside this example of simple vernacular architecture he shares simple vernacular food with the cottage's occupants, an ancient and pure-minded member of the rural Volk and his blonde, pig-tailed granddaughter, 'kindlich fast, doch kräftigen Baues' (LL 1: 335, 340f.). Finally, with the hero apparently in a state of mild erotic desire, she accompanies him through more vibrant Schleswigian nature towards the nearby town, so that he can return to his regiment. At their parting, she asks why he must go to war. '"Es ist für diese Erde", sagte er, "für Dich, für diesen Wald – – – damit hier nichts Fremdes wandle, kein Laut Dir hier begegnet, den Du nicht verstehst . . . – unverfälschte, süße, wunderbare Luft der Heimat!"' (LL 1: 347). The story ends with a faintly obscure poem about the girl, supposedly written by the hero in his diary:

> Und webte auch auf jenen Matten
> Noch jene Mondesmärchenpracht,
> Und ständ' sie noch im Blätterschatten
> Inmitten jener Sommernacht,
> Und fänd' ich selber wie im Traume
> Den Weg zurück durch Moor und Feld –
> Sie schritte doch vom Waldessaume
> Niemals hinunter in die Welt. (LL 1: 347f.)

What Storm said subsequently, when called upon by puzzled associates to explain the poem and, in particular, its last couplet, suggests that the girl and her world were somehow to be seen and conserved as idyll, not to be taken, so to speak, into 'den körperlichen und dauernden *Besitz*', but to exist as an ideal inspiration for real political action.[21] All this was evidently not entirely clear in Storm's own mind (and it must be said that he wrote better stories). But the combination of an idyllicisation of Heimat and a hint of the idyll's unreality is significant and suggestive.

Several years before *Ein grünes Blatt,* as one of his very first literary enterprises, Storm had become involved with likeminded friends in a project to collect and disseminate texts of Schleswig-Holstein folk culture – verses and sayings, fairytales, sagas and myths. This activity, under the acknowledged influence of the Grimms and other Romantic *Volkskundler,* was part of a wave of such provincial collecting which occurred around 1840. It is to be seen in the specific political context of that time, the Rhine Crisis and the upsurge not only of national sentiment but also of conscious national myth-making that followed it. The mythopoeic contortions of Heine's *Deutschland. Ein Wintermärchen* are equally the result of this climate.[22] Storm's own undertaking was explicitly termed, in the open letter of 1843 which his collaborator Theodor Mommsen wrote and he signed, a 'zeitgemäßes Unternehmen' for 'patriotisch Gesinnte' which would generate 'eine vaterländische Sagensammlung'.[23] Also noteworthy is the approach to their material that Storm, in conjunction with Mommsen, adopted: the oral or written texts that he acquired were subjected where appropriate to a rigorous 'Purifikation', required to ensure the original sagas' 'Unverletzlichkeit als Emanation des ganzen Volks- und Heimathgeistes'.[24] They must be restored to ideal form, and above all must not be turned into novellas,[25] with the connotations these are implied to have of impure modernity and rootlessness.

This material was published in various places in the mid 1840s, notably in an apparently enthusiastically received volume of *Sagen, Märchen und Lieder aus Schleswig, Holstein und Lauenburg* of 1845, edited by Karl Müllenhoff. By this time, however, Storm had backed out of the project. He had practical reasons for doing so (as he pursued his law career). But one can envisage alternative grounds for disaffection, given the signs which exist in other respects of a breakdown in his folk ideal. The fact is that Storm's realist eye would not allow him to idealise the Volk for long. In his novellas we find many portrayals of the real common people as flawed and problematic, both individually and collectively. From at least the story *Veronica,* in 1861,[26] through *Auf der Universität* (1862), *Draußen im Heidedorf* (1872), *Renate* (1877), *Im Brauer-Hause* (1879) and *Ein Doppelgänger* (1886) to *Der Schimmelreiter* of 1888, we see popular communities, both rural and urban, which are repositories of bigotry and stupidity. It was noted above how the ending of *Ein grünes Blatt* amounted to an admission that the folk Heimat in the story was unreal. And there is already a tendency perceptible in Storm from the late 1840s, at least, to present the elements of folk culture which had been idealised by previous generations and by many of his contemporaries as a kind of 'schöner Schein'. *Immensee* is significant in this regard. For its hero, Reinhard, folk-songs 'sind Urtöne, . . . sie schlafen in Waldes-gründen; . . . Sie werden gar nicht gemacht; sie wachsen, sie fallen aus der Luft, sie fliegen über Land wie Mariengarn, hierhin und dorthin, und werden an tausend Stellen zugleich gesungen' (LL 1: 320f.). As a child and young man he is preoccupied with them, col-lecting them for scrutiny like the flowers which he also picks and presses in books (LL 1: 324); in old age he lives surrounded by 'Repositorien und Bücherschränken', to contain the collected objects of the 'Studien, an denen er einst die Kraft seiner Jugend geübt hatte' (LL 1: 296, 328). The implication is that his Romanti-cising ethnographic and botanical fixation represents a kind of sur-rogate activity, and a delusory evasion of immediate engagement with life. The folk-song collector – certainly a self-parody by Storm – is now not so much a patriotic hero as an emotional inadequate.

Reinhard, too, is preoccupied from an early stage with *Märchen*, which are the basis of his childhood fantasy life, and at a crucial stage of maturation, when unneurotic adult love for the girl Elisabeth might have developed on the basis of an undistorted apprehension of her nature and identity, he can only see her as a fairytale heroine, that is, mythically ('Der Kuckuck lacht von ferne,/Es geht mir durch den Sinn:/Sie hat die goldnen Augen/Der Waldeskönigin') – to be written down at home 'in seinen alten Pergamentband' (LL 1: 304). In the same sense the term 'Märchen' is frequently used in Storm's poetry at the time, as signifying an ideality which is certainly unreal and may in the end be perni-cious nonsense: 'blaue Märchen', 'blaue Märchenwunder', 'Märchenwelt', 'Wundermärchenschloß' etc. (LL 1: 22, 40, 53, 56).[27] It is, moreover, directly analogous with the way in which myth itself and myth-making appear in the middle-period and later Storm: diabolic and daemonic imagery in the narrative of the novella *Renate*, which turns out to be a projection of the narrator's conditioned religious bigotry (LL 1: 527–32, 544ff., 562f., 575, 584); or the daemonised, eroticised gods in the mind of the narrator-hero of *Von jenseit des Meeres*, which contaminate – temporarily – his perception of the heroine (LL 1: 671–4). In such usage, myth, like folktale, has become not a revelation of deep truths, but a false con-sciousness.

In Storm's poetry, the majority of it written between the mid 1840s and the mid 1850s, one can observe concomitantly the symptoms of a kind of collapse of the *Volkstümlich*, as it collides with and is discredited by a real world of temporality, social conflict, *Triebhaftigkeit* and other facets of unideal truth. It is a process somewhat reminiscent of the one that was taking place thirty years before in the early poetry of Heine – who for Storm was the best of modern lyric poets. There are signs of a relative metrical shift, away from the *Volkston* and eventually towards iambic pentameters as a form suited to the representation of the bitterest realities of life (with such poems as 'Hyazinthen', 'Lucie' and 'Einer Toten'; LL 1: 23, 30f.). There are interesting signs too of a realistic scepticism at the idyllic imagery of the folk idiom in poetry. Verses such as the stark couplet, 'Graues Geflügel huschet/Neben dem Wasser her', in the poem 'Meeresstrand' (LL 1: 14), are a consciously de-idealising gesture. The poem 'Die Stadt' makes the point explicitly:

Am grauen Strand, am grauen Meer
Und seitab liegt die Stadt;
Der Nebel drückt die Dächer schwer,
Und durch die Stille braust das Meer
Eintönig um die Stadt.

Es rauscht kein Wald, es schlägt im Mai
Kein Vogel ohn Unterlaß;
Die Wandergans mit hartem Schrei
Nur fliegt in Herbstesnacht vorbei,
Am Strande weht das Gras . . . (LL 1: 14)

– as the couplet 'Es rauscht kein Wald . . .' denies and rejects the clichés of conventional, harmonious poetic landscape. There is altogether a sense that the essential content of folk- song is ideal. Storm wrote very few dialect poems, but those he did write, such as 'An Klaus Groth' and 'Gode Nacht' (LL 1: 37f., 92), stand out among the general negativity of his verse as positive affirmations of simple values of piety and trust, which a realistic awareness would not allow ('Noch eenmål låt uns spräken:/Goden Åbend, gode Nacht!/De Månd schient op de Däken,/Uns' Herrgott hölt de Wacht'; LL 1: 38).

Similar are Storm's *Fiedellieder* of 1843 and *Die neuen Fiedellieder* of 1871, poems in a naive *Volkston* and sung by a joyful 'Spielmann' character quite free of unsatisfied yearnings, fear of death, religious scepticism, tormented desire and all the other facets of Storm's normality. These poems are also interesting in their manifest relatedness to Eichendorff – apparently unintentional in the early cycle, and conscious in the later one (which is in fact a sort of retelling in verse of part of *Aus dem Leben eines Taugenichts*). Storm remarked subsequently how 'Die Fiedellieder konnte ich, wenn überhaupt, so nur in dem alten Ton fortsetzen, der aus meiner Studentenzeit stammt, wo ich noch unselbständig unter Eichendorffs Einfluß stand'.[28] It is true that many of Storm's earliest lyrics are embarrassingly Eichendorffian. The following, for instance, is actually by Storm:

> Vom Himmel in die tiefsten Klüfte
> Ein milder Stern herniederlacht;
> Vom Tannenwalde steigen Düfte
> Und hauchen durch die Winterlüfte,
> Und kerzenhelle wird die Nacht.[29]

– from a poem, incidentally, which is about Christmas.[30] *Die neuen Fiedellieder*, though, signal not only that Storm's early attachment to Eichendorff was a phase of youthful unoriginality, but also that it represented a now relativised idyllicism, which the Romantic Eichendorff, like folk-song proper, represented. Moreover, the phrase 'Es rauscht kein Wald' in 'Die Stadt', of 1851, points – if the rejection it expresses is aimed at any specific Romantic pseudo-folk poet – to Eichendorff. The poem that ended *Ein grünes Blatt*, too, with its implicit idyllic unreality, had an Eichendorffian beginning: 'Und webte auch auf jenen Matten/Noch kein Mondesmärchenpracht . . .' (LL 1: 347).[31] Finally, such a view was even what Storm projected into Eichendorff the man, when he met him in Berlin in 1854: 'In seinen *stillen blauen* Augen liegt noch die ganze Romantik seiner wunderbaren poetischen Welt'.[32] It is a world – a 'heile Welt' – which Storm considered he had outgrown, or the basic fictionality of which he felt he had come to recognise.

The implication of Storm's mature writing (and, indeed, ultimately, even if he did not know it at the time, of his early writing, too) is that the real world is 'un-heil': in the real world man is, as it were, estranged and in the widest sense *heimatlos*. There is a range of interlinking Heimaten – paradises – to which the human being might aspire, and from which he or she might be banished. Locality is obviously one, the place to the physical features of which, natural and man-made, one is by birth and upbringing attached. Community is another, as is family, and also marital love. The individual is estranged by egotistic impulses, manias and delusions, also by ageing, boredom, illness, and even hard work; in the earlier writings the root of his alienation is, above all, the power of uncontrolled sexual desire. This is what numerous of Storm's powerful poems of the late 1840s and early 1850s signal, poems of intense and problematic sensuality such as 'Die Stunde schlug' (originally entitled 'Frevel'):

Die Stunde schlug, und deine Hand
Liegt zitternd in der meinen,
An meine Lippen streiften schon
Mit scheuem Druck die deinen.

Es zuckten aus dem vollen Kelch
Elektrisch schon die Funken;
O fasse Mut, und fliehe nicht,
Bevor wir ganz getrunken!

Die Lippen, die mich so berührt,
Sind nicht mehr deine eignen;
Sie können doch, so lang' du lebst,
Die meinen nicht verleugnen.

Die Lippen, die sich so berührt,
Sind rettungslos gefangen;
Spät oder früh, sie müssen doch
Sich tödlich heimverlangen. (L 1: 21f.)

Or we may take a poem such as 'Die Kleine':

Und plaudernd hing sie mir am Arm;
Sie halberschlossen nur dem Leben,
Ich zwar nicht alt, doch aber dort,
Wo uns verläßt die Jugend eben.

Wir wandelten hinauf, hinab
Im dämmergrünen Gang der Linden;
Sie sah mich froh und leuchtend an,
Sie wußte nicht, es könne zünden.

Ihr ahnte keine Möglichkeit,
Kein Wort von so verwegnen Dingen,
Wodurch es selbst die tiefste Kluft
Verlockend wird zu überspringen. (LL 1: 33)

Here, the manner of the poem is, and the initial scene appears, idyllic, but what emerges as the text progresses is a reality of faintly paedophile male desire. Elsewhere, the sexuality may seem to be more positively presented (and in non-poetic contexts Storm was indeed disposed on occasion to affirm the value of marital sexuality):

Im Sessel du, und ich zu deinen Füßen,
Das Haupt zu dir gewendet, saßen wir;
Und sanfter fühlten wir die Stunden fließen,
Und stiller ward es zwischen mir und dir;
Bis unsre Augen in einander sanken
Und wir berauscht der Seele Atem tranken. ('Dämmerstunde'; LL 1: 24)

Yet even here we are in a concrete, socially identifiable real world, and the lovers' final erotic communication is preceded by silence.

This is a kind of lyrical realism. Other poems take it in the direction of other life-experiences, texts with such explicit titles as 'Wohl fühl ich, wie das Leben rinnt', 'Die Zeit ist hin', 'Spruch des Alters', 'Ein Sterbender', 'Beginn des Endes', 'Waisenkind' and 'Verirrt' (LL 1: 22f., 25, 79–82, 86, 89f.). But, again, the sense is of a reality in which the individual is essentially, unidyllically alone and without refuge.

The same sense of life occupies Storm's stories, too: an estrangement which is partly the human condition, but which is also partly the consequence of culpable failings. Reinhard in *Immensee* is an exile, from love and homeland, because of his inability to perceive his beloved as she is, undistorted, and to grasp the opportunity for happiness she offers. In turn, so the initial version of the text confirms, this is somehow related to the problematic sexual impulses and experiences of his adolescence.[33] The hero of *Aquis submersus*, of 1875, ends up similarly bereft, having destroyed his chance of marital and familial joy by the force of his lust, but also by impulses of rage, violence and pride to which he is liable. The deadly sins figure significantly in Storm's later works. In *Hans und Heinz Kirch*, rage and avarice destroy family harmony and lead to filial exile; in *Renate*, a potential idyll of fulfilled love is broken up by the social and individual impulses which constitute religious bigotry. The list could continue.

In the very early (and rather bad) story *Celeste. Eine Phantasie*, of around 1840, the consequence of the hero-narrator's uncontrolled, feral (specifically, 'hyena-like') sexual desire, significantly, is actually allegorised as exile on a desert island, far from home: 'Denn jenseit des dunkeln, unermeßlichen Meeres lag unsre Heimat, unsre freundliche Heimat; aber die treulosen Wellen hatten die schwankende Brücke zerschellt und führten die Trümmer weit und weiter hinweg in verschwimmende Ferne, wo sie unsern Augen entschwanden, wie die süßgehegten Hoffnungen unsrer Seele' (LL 4,265). In many other stories, other idylls are depicted from which the hero is symbolically excluded because of the disfiguring mania that grips him: beautiful enclosed gardens, forest retreats or happy, sunlit houses, in such works as *Drüben am Markt* (1861), *Im Nachbarhause links* (1875), *Eekenhof* (1879), *Die Söhne des Senators* (1879–80), *Ein Fest auf Haderslevhuus* (1885), *Zur Chronik von Grieshuus* (1883–4), and others.

However, the situation can become more complicated. Idyllicism can itself be a form of mania. That is the implication of Reinhard's distorted casting of Elisabeth as a 'Waldeskönigin' in *Immensee*. In *Waldwinkel* (1874), the hero seeks to create for himself, in a bizarrely walled house in the forest, an island of love, out of society; but it is based on false and disturbed expectations of his own and his chosen partner's dispositions. The hero of *Drüben am Markt* creates an idyllic boudoir in his little house for the beloved whom he dare not approach and with whom he is inescapably incompatible. In *Im Saal* (1848), one of Storm's minority of stories with a positive ending, the young man who wishes to demolish and rebuild his family ballroom as a nostalgic reminiscence of the time of his grandmother's youth is rebuked by her for what is implied to be unhealthy imaginative excess ('Du bist ein Phantast!'; LL 1: 294). There are other such examples. Moreover, not only are the heroes' self-generated idylls in *Waldwinkel*, *Drüben am Markt*, *Marthe und ihre Uhr* and so on basically deranged places, but even the paradises Storm himself generates at the level of his own narrative – such as the childhood episodes many of his stories contain as counterpoints to the depressive adulthood that follows – turn out to have thoroughly unidyllic complications, for they are in fact realistic worlds in which character psychology and relationships are already formed. The distance between male and female which comes with puberty and sexual awareness may be absent, but patterns such as aggression, submission, rebellion, conformity, fancifulness and banality, are often seen to be well established. So it is in *Aquis submersus*, *Von jenseit des Meeres*, *Auf der Universität*, *Auf dem Staatshof* and many, many other stories.

In the same vein: it was noted above how, in Storm's mind, the idyllic was or came to be associated with the *Volkstümlich*. But his own folkish writings frequently turn out to contain beneath their surface of simplicity and ideality, as it were willy nilly, the same kind of messages about human flaws as his consciously 'modern' texts. It is striking, for example, how the sagas that he contributed to his and his colleagues' project of the early 1840s again and again concern character failings, psychological derangements and moral transgressions, especially in family contexts.[34] Moreover, something rather similar also applies to Storm's own 'Märchen'.

Storm wrote two small groups of so-called 'Märchen', *Der kleine Häwelmann* and *Hinzelmeier* in 1849 and 1850, and *Die Regentrude*, *Bulemanns Haus* and *Der Spiegel des Cyprianus* in 1863–64. Their composition must be seen as an imaginative reaching-out to Heimat: the groups clearly coincide with the two historical moments in his lifetime at which the freedom and integrity of Schleswig-Holstein were most strongly in question. Storm's apparent puzzlement in 1863, that 'ich jetzt, wo ich wie niemals durch unsere schleswig-holst. Verhältnisse politisch aufgeregt bin, durch unabweisbaren Drang zur Märchendichtung getrieben [werde]',[35] seems rather unobservant. However, with the exception of *Die Regentrude*, which does actually concern a return to paradise, the 'Märchen' themselves are tremendously unidyllic. *Bulemanns Haus* is a ferocious story of avarice and misanthropy, which the protagonist directs particularly towards his own family. *Der Spiegel des Cyprianus*, partly based itself on Schleswig-Holstein saga,[36] tells of parenthood and step-parenthood, virtue and villainy, murder and retribution. To Storm's annoyance, it was censored by its publisher for its insufficiently harmonious picture of the family.[37] *Hinzelmeier*, of 1850, is a characteristically Stormian fable, but in allegoric form, of an individual choosing obsessively to pursue the 'Stein der Weisen' instead of seizing life and love when offered – but all against the peculiar background of the hero's parents, who are secretly able to rejuvenate themselves infinitely, so they remain forever the same while their son grows older and older and finally dies. This is on some level an oedipal fable, the unideal antithesis of the family idylls that the real Storm with his Christmases sought to create.

Finally – and, in a way, best – there is *Der kleine Häwelmann*, another in the great tradition of savage nineteenth century German children's literature (*Rapunzel*, *Struwwelpeter*, *Max und Moritz* et al.). *Häwelmann* – which was the nickname Storm used for his own one-year-old first-born, Hans – gives every sign of having been intended by its author as a humorous celebration of infancy. But in the end it is a terrible tale of hubris, nihilistic exposure and, in effect, oedipal conflict and retribution – as the demanding baby, bellowing 'Mehr, mehr!', leaves its exhausted mother behind and takes off in its cot, up the wall, out of the house, through town and forest and into the heavens, before being seized by the red rising sun and cast into the sea ('Ja und dann? Weißt du nicht mehr? Wenn ich und du nicht gekommen wären und den kleinen Häwelmann in unser Boot genommen hätten, so hätte er doch leicht ertrinken können!'; LL 4: 24). Signalled in these stories, one might say, is a deeper reality of family life, including of that of Storm himself, than even his contemporaneous domestic letters acknowledge.

Storm spent just twelve of his seventy years in literal – geographical – exile, or what he perceived as such, in the aftermath of the 1848 Revolution. But his literature as a whole is a literature of exile. It concerns man's banishment and estrangement, by dint of the individualistic psychological impulses which direct and overwhelm him, and the unmistakable temporality and final irrelevance of his existence, a banishment from the idyllic Heimaten of joy and wholeness which he longs for and seeks. At each stage of his works, even where these idylls – of homeland, harmonious community, happy family and marital love – seem credible, a pessimistic sense of their unreality and unattainability, and of the predominance of a bitterer truth, ultimately asserts itself. As he once said, 'Mir fehlt auch in dieser Beziehung die Heimat'.[38]

Notes

1. See Storm, *Sämtliche Werke*, eds Karl Ernst Laage and Dieter Lohmeier, 4 vols, Frankfurt/M., 1987, 1: 1020f. References preceded by 'LL' in the text and notes of the present chapter relate to this edition.
2. See, for example, Peter Goldammer, *Theodor Storm. Eine Einführung in Leben und Werk*, Leipzig, 1980, p. 60; Winfried Freund, *Theodor Storm*, Stuttgart, 1987, p. 45f.
3. Cf. Roy Cowan, 'The History of a Neglected Masterpiece: *Der arme Spielmann*', in *Grillparzer's 'Der arme Spielmann'. New Directions in Criticism*, ed. Clifford Bernd, Columbia, S.C., 1988, pp. 9–26 (pp. 14 and 21).
4. Letter by Storm to A. Nieß, 8 January 1881, quoted from David Jackson, *Theodor Storm. The Life and Works of a Democratic Humanitarian*, Oxford, 1992, p. 152.
5. See Storm, newspaper reports of 1848, in LL 4: 311–25, esp. 318f.
6. In early 1851 the Danes occupied Schleswig and the Austrians Holstein, a situation which was ratified by the Londoner Protokoll of 18 May 1852.
7. See letters by Storm to Laura Setzer and Hartmut Brinkmann, 14 October 1850 and 6 April 1851, in *Theodor Storm – Hartmut und Laura Brinkmann. Briefwechsel*, ed. August Stahl, Berlin, 1986, pp. 25 and 31.
8. See LL 1: 793.
9. See letters by Storm of 6 April and 7 May 1851, *Storm – Brinkmanns. Briefwechsel*, pp. 28, 31 and 38.

10. Letter by Storm, Weihnachtssonntag 1851, *Storm – Brinkmanns. Briefwechsel,* p. 51f.

11. See, for example, letters by Storm, 28 March and 8 July 1852, *Storm – Brinkmanns. Briefwechsel,* pp. 59 and 67.

12. Letter by Storm of 6 April 1851, *Storm – Brinkmanns. Briefwechsel,* p. 31.

13. Letter by Storm of Weihnachtssonntag 1851, *Storm – Brinkmanns. Briefwechsel,* p. 48.

14. Letter by Storm to his parents, 9 June 1854, in *Briefe in die Heimat aus den Jahren 1854–1864,* ed. Gertrud Storm, Berlin, 1907, p. 46.

15. Letter by Storm to his parents, 17–19 December 1854, *Briefe in die Heimat,* p. 50f.

16. Letter by Storm to his parents, 13–20 December 1856, *Briefe in die Heimat,* p. 74.

17. For example, at the end of *Im Saal* (LL 1: 293); with the Junker student in *Immensee* (LL 1: 305); or with Anne Lene's predatory aristocratic suitor in *Auf dem Staatshof* (LL 1: 409f.).

18. LL 4: 318.

19. 'Es gibt eine Sorte', poem of 1864, LL 1: 85.

20. See LL 1: 1049.

21. See LL 1: 1045.

22. See above, chapter 5.

23. Quoted from Theodor Storm, *Anekdoten, Sagen, Sprichwörter und Reime aus Schleswig-Holstein,* ed. Gerd Eversberg, Heide, 1994, p.92.

24. See Storm, *Anekdoten,* p. 96f.; there, inter alia, letter by Storm to Mommsen, 13 February 1843.

25. See Storm, *Anekdoten,* p. 96.

26. Set admittedly in Catholic central Germany.

27. This can be contrasted with the very early poem 'Märchen' of 1843, banally Romantic in its presentation of the 'Land der Märchen' as a sublime world, which is denied to the philistine but accessible to the poet (LL 1: 103).

28. Letter by Storm to Ludwig Pietsch, quoted by Peter Goldammer in Storm, *Sämtliche Werke,* ed. Goldammer, 4 vols, Leipzig, 1986, 1: 722.

29. Ibid., 1: 111. Cf. LL 1: 12 and 765.

30. See also LL 1: 52, 'Herbst', str. 4.

31. Cf. also 'O süßes Nichtstun' of 1851, in which a moment of self-conscious and now-uncharacteristic harmony is associated with an Eichendorffian manner (LL 1: 33); and similarly 'Ein Grab schon weiset manche Stelle', also of 1851 (LL 1: 26).

32. Letter by Storm to Hans Speckter, 24 February 1854, in Storm, *Briefe,* ed. Peter Goldammer, 2 vols, Berlin, 1972, 1: 229. See also Michael Perraudin, 'Theodor Storm's Eichendorff', *German Life and Letters* 42 (1989), 281–95, esp. 283. As that article shows, there is more to Storm's reception of Eichendorff than this relatively routine understanding. In particular, in novellas of the 1860s and 1870s Eichendorff's conjunction of mythical imagery and sexual themes is productively adapted by Storm.

33. See LL 1: 1027–30; also E. Allen McCormick, *Theodor Storm's Novellen. A Study in Literary Technique,* Chapel Hill, 1964, chap. 1, pp. 1–37, 'The Two *Immensee*'s'.

34. See, for example, Storm, *Anekdoten, Sagen,* pp. 7–13, 15f., 19ff., 25f.; Nos. 2, 3, 5, 7, 8, 11, 13, 16.

35. Letter by Storm to his parents, 29 December 1863, in Storm, *Briefe in die Heimat*, p. 211.
36. See Storm, *Sämtliche Werke*, ed. Goldammer, 1: 770.
37. See ibid., 1: 771.
38. Letter by Storm to his parents, 26 June 1855, in *Briefe in die Heimat*, p. 61.

Conclusion

These chapters have in the end presented, even if inexplicitly, a kind of narrative. It is one which begins with the relatively muted and idealistic representation of the Volk in the 1820s, in some respects a throwback to the earliest days of the folk revival during the eighteenth century. It progresses through the July Revolution of 1830 and the great shock to political consciousness in Germany which that brought – displayed in literary texts for which the Volk had suddenly become, for good or ill, a momentous political force that promised revolution. It shows the strengthening of these perceptions in the years up to 1848, as social conditions deteriorated and social conflicts became aggravated; but at the same time it also records the intensified focus on the Volk as a national entity in the Germany of the newly xenophobic 1840s. Finally, it registers in various ways the aftermath of the 1848 Revolution, the *Nachmärz*: here we see not merely (and even not always) a condition of bourgeois political disillusionment, we see also the signs of a change in the image of the Volk, which actually tends to become less threatening and daemonic, more human and individual. As I suggested in my introduction, the outcome of 1848 brought, for all its political disappointments, a degree of release from the agitated, even disturbed kind of preoccupation with the Volk which characterised the Vormärz.[1] Clearly this is not an absolute development: there are texts of the 1850s whose way of seeing really does not register such a shift. But in a general way it is the new world into which German society was moving, a world for which the common people were no longer a formless mass, but a section of society with personal needs and motivations and interests; this is, one might say, social progress, part of the process which led factually to the advances in working-class political organisation and economic empowerment of the ensuing decades. At the same time, we also witness, or seem to witness, signs of a shift in the reception of the folk revival accompanying this development. If the Hungry Forties saw no noticeable diminution – indeed, rather, they saw an increase – in interest in folk-literary manifestations, such a diminution did occur in the 1850s. Storm's effective reduction of his own earlier passion for folk material to the status of a misplaced idyllicism must be regarded as symptomatic of such change.

What seems particularly significant in the case of Storm is his presentation of the deepest realities of human psychology as antithetical to what is represented by the Volk. One of the most striking aspects of writing of the 1830s and 1840s (with prefigurations already in literature from the time of the French revolution onwards) was the analogy implied between social and psychic disorder, the sense – powerfully felt by writers such as Eichendorff, Grillparzer and others – that the chaos of the masses and the chaos of individual mind and instinct mirrored each other, and that the problem of the one was somehow the problem of the other. It is clear that the preoccupation with the psycho-sexual did not drift out of German writing after 1848 or 1850. Storm himself, an epitome of the guilt-ridden high Victoriana of German literature, illustrates that well enough. But its intimate connection with the theme of the Volk does seem to lessen substantially as compared with the position in the Vormärz. In those decades, as we have seen, social disorder and revolt was a matter of such concern – whether manifested as anxiety or excitement – that it could be perceived and rendered in literature as something akin to a corporeal experience.

It is true that not all of our authors can be said to write of the Volk directly as a sort of bodily intrusion. That is a judgement which applies more evidently to conservative writers such as Eichendorff and Gotthelf than to radicals such as Heine and Büchner. On the other hand, for almost all of them we find the Volk representing or posing questions of the most fundamental kind concerning human nature and morality in relation to the physical self. For the sensualist Heine as for Büchner, for Nestroy-Hanswurst or for Grillparzer, the Volk is the focus not just for social and political perturbations of various kinds, but also for an investigation of the ethics of established society, all of them in one way or another associating with an examination of the masses the issue of a recognition of the physical reality of man, and of the need for a revision of moral and intellectual understanding to reflect that reality. And even in the work of the most ethically conservative writers, such as Eichendorff, Gotthelf and Stifter, there is an implicit recognition that these are dimensions which must be acknowledged and addressed. The Volk is indeed, as I suggested at the outset of this book, a focal preoccupation of the epoch: for it is a meeting point not only of its social experiences, historical knowledge, and aesthetic practice and inheritance, but also of its most urgent reflections on the physical and moral nature of man. It would not be unreasonable to call it the issue of the age.

Notes

1. Cf. Louis Chevalier, *Classes laborieuses et Classes dangereuses à Paris, pendant la première moitié du 19e siècle*, Paris, 1978 (original edn., 1958), p. 613, which registers (and quotes Tocqueville in support of) a similar change after 1848 in France.

Bibliography

This bibliography lists works which have been referred to specifically in the text or notes above. Other works that were consulted are not included.

Adelung, Johann Christoph. *Versuch eines vollständigen grammatisch-kritischen Wörterbuches Der Hochdeutschen Mundart*, 5 vols, Leipzig, 1774–86.

Adey Huish, Louise. 'Breaking the Bounds: Fantasy and Farce in Nestroy's Comedy', in *Theatre and Performance in Austria. From Mozart to Jelinek*, eds Ritchie Robertson and Edward Timms, Edinburgh, 1993, pp. 27–38.

Allgemeine Zeitung, ed. Gustav Kolb, Augsburg, 1848.

Arnim, Bettina von. *Dies Buch gehört dem König*, Berlin, 1843.

Arnim, Ludwig Achim von, and Brentano, Clemens, eds. *Des Knaben Wunderhorn. Alte deutsche Lieder*, 3 vols, Heidelberg, 1806–8, 1: 479; reproduced with original page numbers in Clemens Brentano, *Sämtliche Werke und Briefe*, eds Jürgen Behrens, Wolfgang Frühwald and Detlev Lüders, Stuttgart, 1975ff., vols 6–9.

Atkinson, Ross. 'Irony and Commitment in Heine's *Deutschland. Ein Wintermärchen*', *Germanic Review*, 50 (1975), 184–202.

Auerbach, Berthold. *Tagebuch aus Wien. Von Latour bis auf Windischgrätz*, Breslau, 1849.

Baader, Franz von. *Sämmtliche Werke*, ed. Franz Hoffmann, Leipzig, 1851–60, Part 1, vol. 6 (*Gesammelte Schriften zur Societätsphilosophie, 2. Band*), inter alia pp. 55–72: 'Über die Revolutionirung des positiven Rechtsbestandes' (1831); pp. 73–108: 'Über den Evolutionismus and Revolutionismus oder die posit. und negat. Evolution des Lebens überhaupt und des socialen Lebens insbesondere' (1834); pp. 125–44: 'Über das dermalige Missverhältniss der Vermögenslosen oder Proletairs zu den Vermögen besitzenden Classen der Societät in Betreff ihres Auskommens sowohl in materieller als intellectueller Hinsicht aus dem Standpuncte des Rechts betrachtet' (1835).

Bachmaier, Helmut. *Franz Grillparzer: 'Der arme Spielmann'. Erläuterungen und Dokumente*, Stuttgart, 1986.

Bahr, Ehrhard, and Saine, Thomas. *The Internalized Revolution. German Reactions to the French Revolution, 1789–1989*, New York, 1992.

Bauernfeld, Eduard. *Erinnerungen aus Alt-Wien*, ed. Josef Bindtner, Vienna, 1923.

Begemann, Christoph. *Die Welt der Zeichen. Stifter-Lektüren*, Stuttgart, 1995.

Beisbart, Ortwin. 'Kinder- und Jugendliteratur', in *Hansers Sozialgeschichte der deutschen Literatur vom 16. Jahrhundert bis zur Gegenwart*, vol. 5, *Zwischen*

Restauration und Revolution 1815–1848, eds. Gert Sautermeister and Ulrich Schmidt, Munich, 1998, pp. 339–65.

Bellmann, Werner. *Heinrich Heine: 'Deutschland. Ein Wintermärchen'. Erläuterungen und Dokumente*, Stuttgart, 1990.

Benn, Maurice. 'Comments of an *Advocatus Diaboli* on Mörike's *Mozart auf der Reise nach Prag'*, *German Life and Letters* 25 (1971/72), 368–76.

Berghaus, Günter. *J.N. Nestroys Revolutionspossen im Rahmen des Gesamtwerks. Ein Beitrag zur Bestimmung von Nestroys Weltanschauung auf dem Hintergrund der österreichischen Sozialgeschichte des Vormärz*, Diss., Free University of Berlin, 1977.

———. 'Rebellion, Reservation, Resignation: Nestroy und die Wiener Gesellschaft 1830–1860', in *Viennese Popular Theatre: A Symposium*, eds W.E. Yates and John McKenzie, Exeter, 1985, pp. 109–22.

Bernd, Clifford, ed. *Grillparzer's 'Der arme Spielmann'. New Directions in Criticism*, Columbia, S.C., 1988.

Bernstein, Basil. 'Social Class, Language and Socialization', in *Language and Social Context*, ed. Pier Paolo Giglioli, Harmondsworth, 1972, pp. 157–78.

Bitzius, Albert, see Gotthelf, Jeremias.

Böll, Heinrich. *Wo warst du, Adam?* Cologne, 1951.

Böning, Holger. 'Volkserzählungen und Dorfgeschichten', in *Hansers Sozialgeschichte der deutschen Literatur vom 16. Jahrhundert bis zur Gegenwart*, vol. 5, *Zwischen Restauration und Revolution 1815–1848*, eds. Gert Sautermeister and Ulrich Schmidt, Munich, 1998, pp. 281–312.

Bormann, Alexander von. 'Philister und Taugenichts. Zur Tragweite des romantischen Antikapitalismus', *Aurora. Jahrbuch der Eichendorff-Gesellschaft*, 30/31 (1970/71), 94–112.

Bornscheuer, Lothar. *Georg Büchner: 'Woyzeck'. Erläuterungen und Dokumente*, Stuttgart, 1972.

———, ed. *Revolutionsbilder – 1789 in der Literatur*, Frankfurt/M., 1992.

Böschenstein, Renate. 'Mythos und Allegorie: Zur Eigenart von Gotthelfs Schreiben', in *Erzählkunst und Volkserziehung. Das literarische Werk des Jeremias Gotthelf. Mit einer Gotthelf-Bibliographie*, eds Walter Pape, Hellmut Thomke and Silvia Serena Tschopp, Tübingen, 1999, pp. 151–70.

Boyle, Nicholas. *Goethe: The Poet and the Age. Vol. 2. Revolution and Renunciation 1790–1803*, Oxford, 2000.

Brentano, Clemens. *Sämtliche Werke und Briefe*, eds Jürgen Behrens, Wolfgang Frühwald and Detlev Lüders, Stuttgart, 1975ff.

Briegleb, Klaus. *Opfer Heine? Versuche über Schriftzüge der Revolution*, Frankfurt/M., 1986.

———. '"Das bessere Lied" – Nachmärz im Vormärz. Zu Heinrich Heines Weg der Kunst Dezember 1841–Januar 1844', in *Nachmärz. Der Ursprung der ästhetischen Moderne in einer nachrevolutionären Konstellation*, eds Thomas Koebner and Sigrid Weigel, Opladen, 1996, pp. 20–42.

Brill, Siegfried. *Die Komödie der Sprache. Untersuchungen zum Werk Johann Nestroys*, Nuremberg, 1967.

Brummack, Jürgen. *Satirische Dichtung. Studien zu Friedrich Schlegel, Tieck, Jean Paul und Heine*, Munich, 1979.

Büchner, Georg. *Sämtliche Werke und Briefe*, ed. Fritz Bergemann, Leipzig, 1922.

———. *Werke und Briefe. Münchner Ausgabe*, eds Karl Pörnbacher, Gerhard Schaub, Hans-Joachim Simm and Edda Ziegler, Munich, 1988.

Bunyan, Anita. '"Volksliteratur" und nationale Identität. Zu kritischen Schriften Bertold Auerbachs', in *Deutschland und der europäische Zeitgeist. Kosmopolitische Dimensionen in der Literatur des Vormärz*, ed. Martina Lauster, Bielefeld, 1994, pp. 63–89.

Bürger, Gottfried August. *Sämtliche Werke*, eds Günter and Hiltrud Häntzschel, Munich, 1987.

Cersowsky, Peter. *Johann Nestroy oder Nix als philosophische Mussenzen: Eine Einführung*, Munich, 1992.

Chevalier, Louis. *Classes laborieuses et Classes dangereuses à Paris, pendant la première moitié du 19e siècle*, Paris, 1978; original edn, 1958.

Cimaz, Pierre. 'Unheil und Ordnung in Stifters Erzählung *Die Pechbrenner*, im Vergleich mit Gotthelfs *Schwarzer Spinne*', *Études Germaniques* 40 (1985), 374–86.

Conze, Werner. 'Vom "Pöbel" zum "Proletariat". Sozialgeschichtliche Voraussetzungen für den Sozialismus in Deutschland', *Vierteljahrsschrift für Sozial- und Wirtschaftsgeschichte*, 41 (1954), 333–64.

Costenoble, Karl Ludwig. *Aus dem Burgtheater. 1818–1837. Tagebuchblätter*, eds Karl Glossy and Jakob Zeidler, Vienna, 1889.

Cowan, Roy. 'The History of a Neglected Masterpiece: *Der arme Spielmann*', in *Grillparzer's 'Der arme Spielmann'. New Directions in Criticism*, ed. Clifford Bernd, Columbia, S.C., 1988, pp. 9–26.

Dedner, Burghard. 'Politisches Theater und karnevalistische Revolution. Zu einem Metaphernkomplex bei Heinrich Heine', in *Signaturen – Heinrich Heine und das neunzehnte Jahrhundert*, ed. Rolf Hosfeld, Berlin, 1986, pp. 131–61.

Denkler, Horst. *Restauration und Revolution. Politische Tendenzen im deutschen Drama zwischen Wiener Kongreß und Märzrevolution*, Munich, 1973.

Diehl, Siegfried. *Zauberei und Satire im Frühwerk Nestroys*, Bad Homburg, 1969.

Eichendorff, Joseph von. *Werke in sechs Bänden*, eds Wolfgang Frühwald, Brigitte Schillbach and Hartwig Schultz, Frankfurt/M., 1985–93.

Ellis, John. *One Fairy Story too Many. The Brothers Grimm and Their Tales*, Chicago, 1983.

———. 'The Narrator and his Values in *Der arme Spielmann*', in *Grillparzer's 'Der arme Spielmann'. New Directions in Criticism*, ed. Clifford Bernd, Columbia, S.C., 1988, pp. 27–44.

Erk, Ludwig, and Böhme, Franz. *Deutscher Liederhort*, 3 vols, Leipzig, 1893.

Espagne, Michel. 'Heine als Gesellschaftskritiker in Bezug auf Karl Marx', in *Rose und Kartoffel. Ein Heinrich Heine-Symposium*, ed. Antoon van den Braembussche, Amsterdam, 1988, pp. 55–68.

Eyck, Frank. *The Frankfurt Parliament 1848–1849*, London, 1968.

Fairley, Barker. *Heinrich Heine. An Interpretation*, Oxford, 1954.

Farrell, Ralph. *Mörike: 'Mozart auf der Reise nach Prag'*, London, 1960.

Fehr, Karl. *Jeremias Gotthelf (Albert Bitzius)*, Stuttgart, 1985.

Field, G. Wallis. 'Silver and Oranges: Notes on Mörike's Mozart-*Novelle*', *Seminar* 14 (1978), 243–54.

Fink, Gonthier-Louis. 'Volkslied und Verseinlage in den Dramen Büchners', *Deutsche Vierteljahresschrift* 35 (1961), 558–93.

Fischer, Kurt Gerhard, ed. *Adalbert Stifters Leben und Werk in Briefen und Dokumenten*, Frankfurt/M., 1962.

Freitag, Egon. *Goethes Alltags-Entdeckungen. 'Das Volk interessiert mich unendlich'*, Leipzig, 1994.

Freund, Winfried. *Theodor Storm*, Stuttgart, 1987.

Frühproletarische Literatur. Die Flugschriften der deutschen Handwerksgesellen-vereine in Paris 1832–1839, ed. Hans-Joachim Ruckhaberle, Kronberg, 1977.

Frühwald, Wolfgang. 'Der Regierungsrat Joseph von Eichendorff. Zum Verhältnis von Beruf und Schriftstellerexistenz im Preußen der Restaurationszeit, mit *Thesen zur sozialhistorischen und wissenssoziologischen Perspektive einer Untersuchung von Leben und Werk Joseph von Eichendorffs*', *Internationales Archiv für Sozialgeschichte der deutschen Literatur* 4 (1979), 37–67.

Fulda, Daniel. 'Geburt der Geschichte aus dem Gedächtnis der Familie: Gotthelfs historische Erzählungen im Kontext vormärzlicher Geschichtsdarstellung', in *Erzählkunst und Volkserziehung. Das literarische Werk des Jeremias Gotthelf. Mit einer Gotthelf-Bibliographie*, eds Walter Pape, Hellmut Thomke and Silvia Serena Tschopp, Tübingen, 1999, pp. 83–110.

Geerdts, Hans-Jürgen. 'Georg Büchners Volksauffassung', *Weimarer Beiträge* 9 (1963), 642–9.

Glück, Alfons. 'Der *Woyzeck*. Tragödie eines Paupers', in *Georg Büchner: 1813–1837. Revolutionär, Dichter, Wissenschaftler*, Basel, 1987, pp. 325–32.

Goethe, Johann Wolfgang von. *Werke. Hamburger Ausgabe*, ed. Erich Trunz, 12th edition, Munich, 1994.

Goldammer, Peter. *Theodor Storm. Eine Einführung in Leben und Werk*, Leipzig, 1980.

Gotthelf, Jeremias. *Sämtliche Werke in 24 Bänden*, plus 18 *Ergänzungsbände*, eds Rudolf Hunziker, Hans Bloesch, Kurt Guggisberg and Werner Juker, Munich and Bern, later Erlenbach-Zurich, 1911–1977.

Grab, Walter, ed. *Die Revolution von 1848. Eine Dokumentation*, Munich, 1980.

———. *Heinrich Heine als politischer Dichter*, Heidelberg, 1982.

Graevenitz, Gerhart von. 'Don Juan oder die Liebe zur Hausmusik. Wagner-Kritik in Eduard Mörikes Erzählung *Mozart auf der Reise nach Prag*', *Neophilologus* 65 (1981), 247–62.

Greiner, Bernhard. *Die Komödie: eine theatralische Sendung. Grundlagen und Interpretationen*, Tübingen, 1992.

Grillparzer, Franz. *Sämtliche Werke. Historisch-kritische Gesamtausgabe*, eds August Sauer and Reinhold Backmann, Vienna, 1909–48.

———. *Werke in sechs Bänden*, ed. Helmut Bachmaier, Frankfurt/M., 1986ff.

Grimm, Jacob and Wilhelm. *Deutsches Wörterbuch*, ed. Moritz Heyne, 16 vols, Leipzig, 1885–1954.

———. *Kinder- und Hausmärchen*, ed. Heinz Rölleke, 3 vols, Stuttgart, 1980.

———. *Deutsche Sagen*, ed. Hans-Jörg Uther and Barbara Kindermann-Bieri, 3 vols, Munich, 1993.

Grimm, Reinhold. 'Coeur und Carreau. Über die Liebe bei Georg Büchner', in *Georg Büchner, I/II: Text und Kritik, Sonderband*, ed. Heinz Ludwig Arnold, Munich, 1979, pp. 299–326.

Guthrie, John. *Lenz and Büchner: Studies in Dramatic Form*, Frankfurt/M., 1984.

Gutzkow, Karl. *Ausgewählte Werke in zwölf Bänden*, ed. Heinrich Hubert Houben, Leipzig, n.d.

Haida, Peter. 'Johann Nestroy: *Der böse Geist Lumpazivagabundus*. "Die Welt steht auf kein' Fall mehr lang"', in *Interpretationen. Dramen des 19. Jahrhunderts*, ed. Theo Elm, Stuttgart, 1997, pp. 96–119.

Hamerow, Theodore. *Restoration, Revolution, Reaction. Economics and Politics in Germany, 1815–1871*, Princeton, 1958.

Hannemann, Bruno. *Johann Nestroy. Nihilistisches Welttheater und verflixter Kerl. Zum Ende der Wiener Volkskomödie*, Bonn, 1977.

Hardenberg, Friedrich von, see Novalis.

Hardtwig, Wolfgang. *Vormärz. Der monarchische Staat und das Bürgertum*, Munich, 1985.

Hauff, Wilhelm. *Werke*, ed. Max Drescher, 6 vols, Berlin, n.d.

Häusler, Wolfgang. *Von der Massenarmut zur Arbeiterbewegung. Demokratie und soziale Frage in der Wiener Revolution von 1848*, Vienna, 1979.

Hein, Jürgen. *Johann Nestroy: 'Der Talisman'. Erläuterungen und Dokumente*, Stuttgart, 1980.

——. 'Johann Nestroy: *Der Talisman*', in *Interpretationen. Dramen des 19. Jahrhunderts*, ed. Theo Elm, Stuttgart, 1997, pp. 203–233.

Heine, Heinrich. *Werke*, ed. Ernst Elster, 4 vols, Leipzig, 1925.

——. *Sämtliche Schriften*, ed. Klaus Briegleb, 6 vols, München, 1969–76.

——. *Säkularausgabe. Werke, Briefwechsel, Lebenszeugnisse*, eds Nationale Forschungs- und Gedenkstätten der klassischen deutschen Literatur (Weimar) and Centre National de la Recherche Scientifique (Paris), Berlin and Paris, 1970ff.

——. *Historisch-kritische Gesamtausgabe der Werke (Düsseldorfer Ausgabe)*, ed. Manfred Windfuhr, Hamburg, 1973–97.

Heinsius, Walter. 'Mörike und die Romantik', *Deutsche Vierteljahresschrift* 3 (1925), 194–230.

Herder, Johann Gottfried. *Sämmtliche Werke*, ed. Bernhard Suphan, 33 vols, Berlin, 1877–99.

Hering, Hans. 'Mörikes Mozartdichtung', *Zeitschrift für deutsche Bildung* 10 (1934), 360–6.

Hill, David. 'Bürger and "das schwankende Wort *Volk*"', in *The Challenge of German Culture. Essays Presented to Wilfried van der Will*, eds Michael Butler and Robert Evans, London, 2000, pp. 25–36.

Hilton, Julian. *Georg Büchner*, London, 1982.

Hinck, Walter. 'Georg Büchner', in *Deutsche Dichter des neunzehnten Jahrhunderts*, ed. Benno von Wiese, Berlin, 1969, pp. 200–22.

Hinderer, Walter. *Büchner-Kommentar*, Munich, 1977.

Hoffmann, E.T.A. *Sämtliche Werke*, ed. Walter Müller-Seidel, Munich, 1960–65.

Höhn, Gerhard. *Heine-Handbuch. Zeit, Person, Werk*, Stuttgart, 1987.

Hölderlin, Friedrich. *Sämtliche Werke und Briefe*, ed. Jochen Schmidt, 3 vols, Frankfurt/M., 1992–94.

Holl, Hanns Peter. *Gotthelf im Zeitgeflecht. Bauernleben, industrielle Revolution und Liberalismus in seinen Romanen*, Tübingen, 1985.

Höller, Hans. 'Porträt des Herrschers als Seher, Künstler und als alter Mann. Grillparzers *Ein Bruderzwist in Habsburg*', in *Franz Grillparzer*, ed. Helmut Bachmaier, Frankfurt/M., 1991, pp. 321–42.

Holthusen, Hans-Egon. *Eduard Mörike*, Hamburg, 1971.

Iris. Deutscher Almanach für 1848, ed. Gustav Heckenast, Pest, 1847.

Jackson, David. *Theodor Storm. The Life and Works of a Democratic Humanitarian*, Oxford, 1992.

Jäger, Hans-Wolf. *Politische Metaphorik im Jakobinismus und im Vormärz*, Stuttgart, 1971.

Jansen, Josef. *Georg Büchner: 'Dantons Tod'. Erläuterungen und Dokumente*, Stuttgart, 1969.

Janz, Rolf-Peter, and Laermann, Klaus. *Arthur Schnitzler: Zur Diagnose des Wiener Bürgertums im Fin de Siècle*, Stuttgart, 1977.

Kaiser, Friedrich. *Unter fünfzehn Theater-Direktoren. Bunte Bilder aus der Wiener Bühnenwelt*, Vienna, 1870.

Kals, Hans. *Die soziale Frage in der Romantik*, Cologne, 1974.

Kaufmann, Hans. *Politisches Gedicht und klassische Dichtung. Heinrich Heine: 'Deutschland. Ein Wintermärchen'*, Berlin, 1958.

Keller, Gottfried. *Keller über Gotthelf*, eds Franz Carigelli and Heinz Weder, Bern, 1969.

Kleist, Heinrich von. *Sämtliche Werke und Briefe in vier Bänden*, eds Ilse-Marie Barth, Klaus Müller-Salget, Stefan Ormanns and Hinrich Seeba, Frankfurt/M., 1987–97.

Klotz, Volker. *Geschlossene und offene Form im Drama*, Munich, 1960.

Kocka, Jürgen, *Lohnarbeit und Klassenbildung. Arbeiter und Arbeiterbewegung in Deutschland 1800–1875*, Berlin and Bonn, 1983.

———. *Arbeitsverhältnisse und Arbeiterexistenzen. Grundlagen der Klassenbildung im 19. Jahrhundert*, Bonn, 1990.

Köhnke, Klaus. '"Der Mensch in der Welt": Untersuchungen zu Eichendorffs Versepen', *Aurora. Jahrbuch der Eichendorff-Gesellschaft*, 37 (1977), 7–20.

Koopmann, Helmut. 'Eichendorff, *Das Schloß Dürande* und die Revolution', *Zeitschrift für deutsche Philologie*, 89 (1970), 180–207.

———. 'Heines politische Metaphorik', in *Heinrich Heine. Dimensionen seines Wirkens*, ed. Raymond Immerwahr, Bonn, 1979, pp. 68–83.

———. 'Das Nachbeben der Revolution. Heinrich von Kleist: Das Erdbeben in Chili', in Koopmann, *Freiheitssonne und Revolutionsgewitter. Reflexe der Französischen Revolution im literarischen Deutschland zwischen 1789 und 1840*, Tübingen, 1989, pp. 93–122.

———. 'Weltenbrand hinterm Berg. Eduard Mörike, *Der Feuerreiter*'; in: Koopmann. *Freiheitssonne und Revolutionsgewitter. Reflexe der Französischen Revolution im literarischen Deutschland zwischen 1789 und 1840*, Tübingen, 1989, pp. 123–42.

Krapp, Helmut. *Der Dialog bei Georg Büchner*, Darmstadt, 1958.

Krauß, Rudolf. 'Eduard Mörike und die Politik', *Euphorion* 1 (1894), 129–36.

Kreutzer, Leo. *Heine und der Kommunismus*, Göttingen, 1970.

Krüger, Peter. 'Eichendorffs politisches Denken', *Aurora. Jahrbuch der Eichendorff-Gesellschaft*, 28 (1968), 7–32, and 29 (1969), 50–69.

Kuczyinski, Jürgen. *Die Geschichte der Lage der Arbeiter in Deutschland von 1789 bis in die Gegenwart*, vol. 1/1, *1789 bis 1870*, Berlin, 1954.

———. 'Der "Zauber der Beschränkung" und das "holde Bescheiden" Eduard Mörikes', in Kuczynski, *Gestalten und Werke*, Berlin, 1969, pp. 163–83.

Kulenkampff, Jens. 'Geschichtsphilosophie vor und nach der Französischen Revolution: Kant und Hegel', in *Revolutionsbilder – 1789 in der Literatur*, ed. Lothar Bornscheuer, Frankfurt/M., 1992, pp. 1–22.

Labov, William. 'The Logic of Nonstandard English', in *Language and Social Context*, ed. Pier Paolo Giglioli, Harmondsworth, 1972, pp. 179–215.

Lefebvre, Jean Pierre. 'Marx und Heine', in *Heinrich Heine. Streitbarer Humanist und volksverbundener Dichter. Internationale wissenschaftliche Konferenz, Weimar 1972*, ed. Karl-Wolfgang Becker, Weimar, 1973, pp. 41–61.

Lehmann, Werner. *Textkritische Noten. Prolegomena zur Hamburger Büchner-Ausgabe*, Hamburg, 1967.

Lindemann, Klaus. *Eichendorffs 'Schloß Dürande'. Zur konservativen Rezeption der Französischen Revolution*, Paderborn, 1980.

——. *Johannes Gotthelf: 'Die schwarze Spinne'. Zur biedermeierlichen Deutung von Geschichte und Gesellschaft zwischen den Revolutionen*, Paderborn, 1983.

Lukács, Georg. 'Heine und die ideologische Vorbereitung der 48er Revolution', in *Text und Kritik* 18/19: *Heinrich Heine*, ed. Heinz Ludwig Arnold, 1st edn, 2nd impression, Munich, 1971, pp. 31–47.

McCormick, E. Allen. *Theodor Storm's Novellen. A Study in Literary Technique*, Chapel Hill, 1964.

McKenzie, John. 'Nestroy's Political Plays', in *Viennese Popular Theatre: A Symposium*, eds W.E. Yates and John McKenzie, Exeter, 1985, pp. 123–38.

——. '"Aufgeklärt Occonnelisch, wird Irrland rebellisch". Political Songs in Nestroy's *Freiheit in Krähwinkel*', in *Connections. Essays in Honour of Eda Sagarra on the Occasion of her 60th Birthday*, eds Peter Skrine, Rosemary Wallbank-Turner and Jonathan West, Stuttgart, 1993, pp. 169–78.

Martens, Wolfgang. 'Zum Menschenbild Georg Büchners. *Woyzeck* und die Marionszene in *Dantons Tod*', *Wirkendes Wort* 8 (1957/58), 13–20.

——. 'Über Georg Büchners *Woyzeck*', *Jahrbuch des Wiener Goethe-Vereins* 84/85 (1980/81), 145–56.

Mason, Eve. 'Stifters *Bunte Steine*: Versuch einer Bestandsaufnahme', in *Adalbert Stifter heute. Londoner Symposium 1983*, ed. Johann Lachinger, Alexander Stillmark and Martin Swales, Linz, 1985, pp. 75–85.

——. *Stifter: 'Bunte Steine'*, London, 1986.

Mautner, Franz. 'Mörikes *Mozart auf der Reise nach Prag*', *Publications of the Modern Languages Association of America* 60 (1945), 199–220.

——. 'Wortgewebe, Sinngefüge und "Idee" in Büchners *Woyzeck*', *Deutsche Vierteljahresschrift* 35 (1961), 521–57.

——. 'Geld, Nestroy und Nestroy-Interpretation', in *Theater und Gesellschaft. Das Volksstück im 19. und 20. Jahrhundert*, ed. Jürgen Hein, Düsseldorf, 1973.

May, Erich. *Wiener Volkskomödie und Vormärz*, Berlin, 1975.

Mayer, Thomas Michael. 'Büchner und Weidig – Frühkommunismus und revolutionäre Demokratie', in *Georg Büchner, I/II: Text und Kritik, Sonderband*, ed. Heinz Ludwig Arnold, Munich, 1979, pp. 16–298.

——. 'Büchner-Chronik', in *Georg Büchner, I/II: Text und Kritik, Sonderband*, ed. Heinz Ludwig Arnold, Munich, 1979, pp. 357–425.

——. 'Zu einigen neuen Lesungen und zur Frage des "Dialekts" in den *Woyzeck*-Handschriften', *Georg-Büchner-Jahrbuch* 7 (1988/89), 172–218.

Mende, Dirk. *Untersuchungen zu den Volksliedeinlagen in den Dramen Georg Büchners*, Diss., Stuttgart, 1972.

Mende, Fritz. 'Heine und die Folgen der Julirevolution', in Mende, *Heinrich Heine. Studien zu seinem Leben und Werk*, Berlin, 1983.

——. 'Heine und die "Volkwerdung der Freiheit"', in Mende, *Heinrich Heine. Studien zu seinem Leben und Werk*, Berlin, 1983.

Mörike, Eduard. *Eduard Mörikes Briefe*, eds Karl Fischer and Rudolf Krauß, 2 vols, Berlin, 1904.

——. *'Frauenlieb' und Treu'. 250 Briefe Eduard Mörikes an Wilhelm Hartlaub*, ed. Gotthilf Renz, Leipzig, 1938.

——. *Unveröffentlichte Briefe*, ed. Friedrich Seebaß, Stuttgart, 1941.

——. *Briefe*, ed. Friedrich Seebaß, Tübingen, 1952.

——. *Mozart auf der Reise nach Prag*, ed. Maurice Benn, London, 1970.

————. *Sämtliche Werke,* ed. Herbert Göpfert, 5th edn, Munich, 1976.

Müller, Wilhelm. *Werke. Tagebücher. Briefe,* ed. Maria Verena Leistner, 5 vols plus *Registerband,* Berlin, 1994.

Musäus, Johann Karl August. *Märchen und Sagen,* ed. Angela Müller, Cologne, 1997.

Naumann, Ursula. *Adalbert Stifter,* Stuttgart, 1979.

Nestroy, Johann. *Gesammelte Werke. Ausgabe in sechs Bänden,* ed. Otto Rommel, Vienna, 1948–49.

————. *Sämtliche Werke. Historisch-kritische Ausgabe,* eds Jürgen Hein and Johann Hüttner, Vienna, 1977ff.

————. *Briefe,* ed. Walter Obermaier, Vienna, 1977; unnumbered volume of Nestroy, *Sämtliche Werke. Historisch-kritische Ausgabe,* Vienna, 1977ff.

————. *Komödien. Ausgabe in sechs Bänden,* ed. Franz Mautner, Frankfurt/M., 1979.

Nipperdey, Thomas. *Deutsche Geschichte 1800–1866. Bürgerwelt und starker Staat,* Munich, 1983; in English as *Germany from Napoleon to Bismarck, 1800–1866,* transl. Daniel Nolan, Dublin, 1996.

Novalis. *Schriften. Die Werke Friedrich von Hardenbergs,* eds Paul Kluckhohn and Richard Samuel, Stuttgart, 1960.

Opitz, Alfred. '"Adler" und "Ratte": schriftstellerisches Selbstverständnis und politisches Bewußtsein in der Tiermetaphorik Heines', *Heine-Jahrbuch* 20 (1981), 22–54.

Parker, Charles. 'The Actuality of Working-Class Speech', in *Workers and Writers. Proceedings of the Conference on Present-Day Working-Class Literature in Britain and West Germany, held in Birmingham, October 1975,* ed. Wilfried van der Will, Birmingham, 1976, pp. 98–105.

Paulsen, Wolfgang. 'Der gute Bürger Jakob. Zur Satire in Grillparzers *Der arme Spielmann',* *Colloquia germanica* 2 (1968), 272–98.

Perraudin, Michael. *Heinrich Heine: Poetry in Context. A Study of 'Buch der Lieder',* Oxford, 1989.

————. 'Theodor Storm's Eichendorff', *German Life and Letters* 42 (1989), 281–95.

————. '*Mozart auf der Reise nach Prag,* the French Revolution, and 1848', *Monatshefte* 81 (i) (1989), 45–61; subsequently, in German, in *Forum Vormärz Forschung. Jahrbuch* 3 (1997): *1848 und der deutsche Vormärz,* 237–57.

————. 'Towards a New Cultural Life: Büchner and the "Volk"', *Modern Language Review* 86 (1991), 627–44.

————. 'Babekan's "Brille", and the Rejuvenation of Congo Hoango. A Reinterpretation of Kleist's Story of the Haitian Revolution', *Oxford German Studies,* 20/21 (1991–92), 85–103.

————. '"Der schöne Heros, der früh dahinsinkt . . ." Poesie, Mythos und Politik in Heines "Die Grenadiere"', in *Interpretationen. Gedichte von Heinrich Heine,* ed. Bernd Kortländer, Stuttgart, 1995, pp. 32–50.

————. 'Wilhelm Müller und seine Zeitgenossen. Zum Charakter nachromantischer Poesie', in *Kunst kann die Zeit nicht formen: Dokumentation der 1. internationalen wissenschaftlichen Konferenz aus Anlaß des 200. Geburtstages von Wilhelm Müller (1794–1827),* eds Ute Bredemeyer and Christiane Lange, Berlin, 1996, pp. 312–27.

————. 'Irrationalismus und jüdisches Schicksal. Die thematischen Zusammenhänge von Heines *Ideen. Das Buch Le Grand',* in *Aufklärung und Skepsis.*

Internationaler Heine-Kongreß 1997 zum 200. Geburtstag, eds Joseph Kruse, Bernd Witte and Karin Füllner, Stuttgart, 1998, pp. 279–302.

———. 'Heine und das revolutionäre Volk. Eine Frage der Identität', in *Vormärzliteratur in europäischer Perspektive II. Politische Revolution – Industrielle Revolution – Ästhetische Revolution*, eds Martina Lauster and Günter Oesterle, Bielefeld, 1998, pp. 41–55.

———. 'Heine et l'Angleterre ou le médiateur en défaut', *Romantisme. Revue du dix-neuvième siècle* 101 (1998): *Heine le médiateur*, 41–9.

———. 'Heinrich Heines Welt der Literatur. Realistisches und Antirealistisches in seinem Werk', *Vormärzliteratur in europäischer Perspektive III. Zwischen Daguerreotyp und Idee*, ed. Martina Lauster, Bielefeld, 2000, pp. 15–29.

Peters, Paul. 'Bildersturm auf die Germanomanie. Heines *Wintermärchen* als Poesie der Destruktion', in Heinrich Heine, *Deutschland. Ein Wintermärchen*, eds Ursula Roth and Heidemarie Vahl, Stuttgart, 1995, pp. 201–223.

Plaul, Hainer, and Schmidt, Ulrich. 'Die populären Lesestoffe', in *Hansers Sozialgeschichte der deutschen Literatur vom 16. Jahrhundert bis zur Gegenwart*, vol. 5, *Zwischen Restauration und Revolution 1815–1848*, eds. Gert Sautermeister and Ulrich Schmidt, Munich, 1998, pp. 313–38.

Pörnbacher, Karl. *Eduard Mörike: 'Mozart auf der Reise nach Prag'. Erläuterungen und Dokumente*, Stuttgart, 1976.

Prawer, Siegbert. 'The Threatened Idyll. Mörike's *Mozart auf der Reise nach Prag*', *Modern Languages* 44 (1963), 101–7.

———. *Frankenstein's Island. England and the English in the Writings of Heinrich Heine*, Cambridge, 1986.

Preisner, Rio. *Johann Nepomuk Nestroy. Schöpfer der tragischen Posse*, Munich, 1968.

———. 'Der konservative Nestroy: Aspekte der zukünftigen Forschung', *Maske und Kothurn* 18 (1972), 23–37.

Propp, Vladimir. *Morphology of the Folktale*, Bloomington, Indiana, 1958.

Reddick, John. 'Tiger und Tugend in Stifters *Kalkstein*: eine Polemik', *Zeitschrift für deutsche Philologie* 95 (1976), 235–55.

———. 'Mosaic and Flux: Georg Büchner and the Marion Episode in *Dantons Tod*', *Oxford German Studies* 11 (1980), 40–67.

———. *Georg Büchner. The Shattered Whole*, Oxford, 1994.

Reeve, William. 'Proportion and Disproportion in *Das arme Spielmann*', in *Grillparzer's 'Der arme Spielmann'. New Directions in Criticism*, ed. Clifford Bernd, Columbia, S.C., 1988, pp. 93–110.

Reichmann, Eva. *Konservative Inhalte in den Theaterstücken Johann Nestroys*, Würzburg, 1995.

Requadt, Paul. 'Stifters *Bunte Steine* als Zeugnis der Revolution und als zyklisches Kunstwerk', in *Adalbert Stifter. Studien und Interpretationen. Gedenkschrift zum 100. Todestage*, ed. Lothar Stiehm, Heidelberg, 1968, pp. 139–68.

Ries, Franz Xaver. *Zeitkritik bei Joseph von Eichendorff*, Berlin, 1997.

Ritter, Naomi. 'Poet and Carnival: Goethe, Grillparzer, Baudelaire', in *Grillparzer's 'Der arme Spielmann'. New Directions in Criticism*, ed. Clifford Bernd, Columbia, S.C., 1988, pp. 337–51.

Roe, Ian. 'Der arme Spielmann and the Role of Compromise in Grillparzer's Work', in *Grillparzer's 'Der arme Spielmann'. New Directions in Criticism*, ed. Clifford Bernd, Columbia, S.C., 1988, pp. 133–44.

Rose, Margaret. 'The Idea of the "Sol Iustitae" in Heine's *Deutschland. Ein Wintermärchen*', *Deutsche Vierteljahresschrift*, 52 (1978), 604–18.

Rothe, Wolfgang. *Deutsche Revolutionsdramatik seit Goethe*, Darmstadt, 1989.

Rückert, Friedrich. *Werke*, ed. Richard Böhme, 6 vols in 3, Berlin n.d.

Rudé, George. *The Crowd in the French Revolution*, Oxford, 1959.

Sagarra, Eda. *A Social History of Germany 1648–1914*, London, 1977.

Sammons, Jeffrey. 'Heinrich Heine: The Revolution as Epic and Tragedy', in *The Internalized Revolution. German Reactions to the French Revolution, 1789–1989*, eds Ehrhard Bahr and Thomas Saine, New York, 1992, pp. 173–96.

Sautermeister, Gert, and Schmidt, Ulrich, eds. *Hansers Sozialgeschichte der deutschen Literatur vom 16. Jahrhundert bis zur Gegenwart*, vol. 5, *Zwischen Restauration und Revolution 1815–1848*, Munich, 1998.

Schieder, Wolfgang. *Anfänge der deutschen Arbeiterbewegung. Die Auslandsvereine im Jahrzehnt nach der Julirevolution von 1830*, Stuttgart, 1963.

Schiller, Friedrich. *Werke. Nationalausgabe*, eds Julius Petersen, Lieselotte Blumenthal and Benno von Wiese, Weimar, 1943ff.

Schlegel, Friedrich. *Schriften zur Literatur*, ed. Wolfdietrich Rasch, Munich, 1970.

Schulze, Hagen. *Der Weg zum Nationalstaat. Die deutsche Nationalbewegung vom 18. Jahrhundert bis zur Reichsgründung*, Munich, 1985.

Schwäbischer Merkur, ed. Elben, Stuttgart, 1848.

Secci, Lia. 'Die Dionysische Sprache des Tanzes im Werk Heines', in *Zu Heinrich Heine*, eds Luciano Zagari and Paolo Chiarini, Stuttgart, 1981, pp. 89–101.

Seeger, Ludwig. 'Schweizerische Belletristik. *Bilder und Sagen aus der Schweiz*, von Jeremias Gotthelf', in *Einundzwanzig Bogen aus der Schweiz*, ed. Georg Herwegh, Zurich, 1843; reprinted, ed. Ingrid Pepperle, Leipzig, 1989, pp. 453–5.

Seidlitz, Julius. *Die Poesie und die Poeten in Österreich im Jahre 1836*, Grimma, 1837.

Sengle, Friedrich. *Biedermeierzeit. Deutsche Literatur im Spannungsfeld zwischen Restauration und Revolution 1815–1848*, 3 vols, Stuttgart, 1971–80.

Shakespeare, William. *Complete Works*, ed. W.J. Craig, Oxford, 1971.

Siemann, Wolfram. *The German Revolution of 1848–49*, transl. Christiane Banerji, London, 1998; originally *Die deutsche Revolution von 1848/49*, Frankfurt/M., 1985.

Slessarev, Helga. *Eduard Mörike*, New York, 1970.

Smeed, J.W. 'The First Versions of the Stories Later Appearing in Stifter's *Bunte Steine*', *German Life and Letters* 12 (1958/59), 259–63.

Stadelmann, Rudolf. *Soziale und politische Geschichte der Revolution von 1848*, Munich, 1948.

Steinmetz, Horst. *Eduard Mörikes Erzählungen*, Stuttgart, 1969.

Sternberger, Dolf. *Heinrich Heine und die Abschaffung der Sünde*, Hamburg, 1972.

Stifter, Adalbert. *Sämmtliche Werke*, eds August Sauer, Gustav Wilhelm and others, Prague, Reichenberg, Graz, 1904–60.

———. *Werke und Briefe. Historisch-kritische Gesamtausgabe*, eds Alfred Doppler and Wolfgang Frühwald, Stuttgart, 1978ff.

Stöber, August. *Elsässisches Volksbüchlein*, Strasbourg, 1842.

Storm, Theodor. *Briefe in die Heimat aus den Jahren 1854–1864*, ed. Gertrud Storm, Berlin, 1907.

———. *Briefe*, ed. Peter Goldammer, 2 vols, Berlin, 1972.

———. *Sämtliche Werke*, ed. Peter Goldammer, 4 vols, Leipzig, 1986.

————. *Theodor Storm – Hartmut und Laura Brinkmann. Briefwechsel*, ed. August Stahl, Berlin, 1986.

————. *Sämtliche Werke*, eds Karl Ernst Laage and Dieter Lohmeier, 4 vols, Frankfurt/M., 1987.

————. *Anekdoten, Sagen, Sprichwörter und Reime aus Schleswig-Holstein*, ed. Gerd Eversberg, Heide, 1994.

Storz, Gerhard. *Eduard Mörike*, Stuttgart, 1967.

Swales, Martin and Erika. *Adalbert Stifter. A Critical Study*, Cambridge, 1984.

Thomke, Hellmut. 'Gotthelfs "Konservativismus" im europäischen Kontext', in *Erzählkunst und Volkserziehung. Das literarische Werk des Jeremias Gotthelf. Mit einer Gotthelf-Bibliographie*, eds Walter Pape, Hellmut Thomke and Silvia Serena Tschopp, Tübingen, 1999, pp. 227–41.

Thompson, Bruce. 'Grillparzer, Revolution and 1848', in *Essays on Grillparzer*, ed. Bruce Thompson and Mark Ward, Hull, 1978, pp. 81–91.

Thompson, E.P. *The Making of the English Working Class*, Harmondsworth, 1968.

Ullman, Bo. *Die sozialkritische Thematik im Werk Georg Büchners*, Stockholm, 1972.

Vancsa, Kurt. 'Grillparzers *Der arme Spielmann* und Stifters *Der arme Wohltäter*', in *Festschrift für Eduard Castle zum 80. Geburtstag*, Vienna, 1955, pp. 99–107.

Vietta, Silvio. 'Sprachkritik bei Büchner', *Georg-Büchner-Jahrbuch* 2 (1982), 144–56.

Vischer, Friedrich Theodor. *Kritische Gänge*, ed. Robert Vischer, 2nd edn, Munich, n.d.

Walker, Colin. 'Nestroy's *Judith und Holofernes* and Antisemitism in Vienna', *Oxford German Studies* 12 (1981), 85–110.

————. 'Nestroy and the Redemptorists', in *Bristol Austrian Studies*, ed. Brian Keith-Smith, Bristol, 1990, pp. 73–115.

Ward, Mark. 'The Truth of Tales: Grillparzer's *Der arme Spielmann* and Stifter's *Der arme Wohltäter*', in *From Vormärz to Fin de Siècle. Essays in Nineteenth Century Austrian Literature*, ed. Mark Ward, Blairgowrie, 1986, pp. 15–39.

Wehler, Hans-Ulrich. *Deutsche Gesellschaftgeschichte*, vol. 2, *Von der Reformära bis zur industriellen und politischen 'Deutschen Doppelrevolution' 1815–1848/49*, 2nd edn, Munich, 1989.

Werner, Michael. *Genius und Geldsack. Zum Problem des Schriftstellerberufs bei Heinrich Heine*, Hamburg, 1978.

Whiton, John. 'Symbols of Social Renewal in Stifter's *Bergkristall*', *Germanic Review* 47 (1972), 259–80.

Wiese, Benno von. *Eduard Mörike*, Tubingen, 1950.

————. *Signaturen. Zu Heinrich Heine und seinem Werk*, Berlin, 1976: chap. 3, 'Das tanzende Universum'; chap. 4, 'Zum Problem der politischen Dichtung Heinrich Heines'.

Winkler, Hans. *Georg Büchners 'Woyzeck'*, Diss., Greifswald, 1925.

Winkler, Markus. *Mythisches Denken zwischen Romantik und Realismus. Zur Erfahrung kultureller Fremdheit im Werk Heinrich Heines*, Stuttgart, 1995.

Wülfing, Wulf. 'Luise gegen Napoleon, Napoleon gegen Barbarossa. Zu einigen Positionen Heines in einem Jahrhundert der Mythenkonkurrenzen', in *Aufklärung und Skepsis. Internationaler Heine-Kongreß 1997 zum 200. Geburtstag*, eds Joseph Kruse, Bernd Witte and Karin Füllner, Stuttgart, 1998, pp. 395–407.

Würffel, Stephan. *Der produktive Widerspruch. Heinrich Heines negative Dialektik*, Bern, 1986.

Yates, W.E. *Nestroy. Satire and Parody in Viennese Popular Comedy*, Cambridge, 1972.

————. *Nestroy and the Critics*, Columbia, S.C., 1994.

Zemp, Werner. *Mörike. Elemente und Anfänge*, Frauenfeld, 1939.

Index

Index of Persons and Primary Works

237